CARTOON CAPERS

The History of Canadian Animators

by
Karen Mazurkewich

McArthur & Company

Toronto

McArthur & Company
322 King Street West, Suite 402
Toronto, Ontario
M5V 1J2

Design & Typography by Bill Stewart, Big Bang Design

Cover illustration by Cordell Barker

Printed in Canada by Transcontinental Printing

CANADIAN CATALOGUING IN PUBLICATION DATA

Mazurkewich, Karen 1963 -

    Cartoon capers : the history of Canadian animators

    ISBN 1-55278-093-7

1. Animators — Canada. 2. Animation (Cinematography) — Canada.
I. Title

NC1766.C3M39 1999   741.5'8'0971   C99-931742-3

For Martin

Contents

Introduction

Let there be light. And celluloid. And paint.
Across North America, the darkness receded.
Animation was reborn.

Not since the Golden era of the 1940s has animation had such a broad appeal and touched so many people. Liberated from their Saturday morning ghetto, cartoons have returned to the theatres and invaded the Internet. Animation has also transformed prime-time television with retro graphics and vulgar gags: burps, farts and other nasties are now daily fare.

But beyond the shock value is an enduring appeal. Today's two-dimensional characters deliver social commentary wrapped in a self-deprecating package that disarms even the most disenfranchised youth.

While the popular aesthetic indulges adolescent sensibilities, animation's renaissance is not simply about the survival of the grossest. It is also about quality drawing and rendering. By emphasizing craftsmanship, animation's reformers have attracted new fans, and won greater respect for the art form.

Canadians are playing a decisive role in this resurgence. Insiders joke that Canucks are the gypsy kings of the animation world. In fact, Canadians are flexing their graphic muscle in every major international studio. Many of the world's favourite villains and side-kick stars are forged by Canadians. So are many of the New Age 3-D creatures that populate the big screen.

High profile directors such as John Kricfalusi (*Ren & Stimpy*), Danny Antonucci (*Ed, Edd n Eddy*), and Richard Williams (*Who Framed Roger Rabbit*) have fought hard to reinstate full-blown stretch-and-squash animation with fantastic gags. While they man the front lines, an army of animators is pulling the strings behind the scenes.

These contemporary stars are the cultural descendants of a northern dynasty that long ago perfected the art of parody and parable. Their Canadian roots can be traced back to the Montreal cartoonist, Raoul Barré, who moved to New York and animated the *Animated Grouch Chasers* series in 1914. Since that first defection south of the border, Canadian artists have both infiltrated foreign studios and built an industry at home.

The National Film Board's animation unit, headed by Norman McLaren, inspired the homegrown proliferation. The NFB's original mandate was to operate as the government's mouthpiece during World War II. Yet McLaren and his compatriots transcended the didactic messages commissioned by the Department of Defence, and produced artistic films laced with humour. NFB animated shorts not only promoted the sale of war bonds, but managed to lighten the mood of a nation preoccupied with war and death. The NFB's tradition of impertinent, satirical, in-your-face shorts filtered into the mainstream. Its original mandate was propaganda, but its legacy is art and innovation.

Master drawers at the NFB inspired two generations of animators. Many who learned experimental techniques at the feet of McLaren soon left their own imprint on the international scene. George Dunning (*Yellow Submarine*), Gerald Potterton (*Heavy Metal*), Richard Williams (*Arabian Knight*), and Michael Mills (*History of the World in Three Minutes Flat*), established their own studios and trained an army of animators who have circumvented the globe and infiltrated Walt Disney Studio, Pixar and DreamWorks SKG.

Satellite studios in Vancouver and Winnipeg gave rise to new styles. Operating in geographical isolation, regional animators spawned a new sub-species of toon. The Vancouver fetish for rubbery creatures with a proclivity for gross behaviour, and the Winnipeg prediliction for spastic flair, have had a lasting impact on the international scene. This regional creativity has been lionized, copied and commercialized.

The emergence of film schools such as Sheridan College, and the Emily Carr Institute of Art and Design, bolstered the local community. Companies such as Hanna-Barbera and Filmation once ruled the TV world. Now, indigenous studios such as Nelvana, Cinar and Cine-Groupe — with their direct pipeline to domestic talent — are comfortably situated in the top echelons of cartooning. Once slaves to service production, these companies went on to build libraries and develop proprietary characters.

Cartoonists are attracted to animation because they can create and control entire kingdoms. From the safety of their drawing boards, they seek world domination. What began as a little adventure by Canadian artists into the 2-D animated realm has turned into a wild 3-D caper.

This digital takeover has been orchestrated by mild-mannered geeks of the Far North. These visionaries redesigned primitive software to perform hyperrealistic feats that have changed the feature film world forever. Early work at the National Research Council in Ottawa and the University of Waterloo was harnessed by computer hackers who have designed the world's best 3-D software programs. In ways that were unforeseen a half-century ago, models and puppets have been replaced by computer-generated images.

The graphic canvas has been stretched to infinity and beyond. Extinct beasts are being brought back to life and flesh-and-bone superheroes reanimated from the pages of comic books. Canadians did not invent animation, but they have engineered a polite takeover. In this parallel universe, so too shall the meek geeks inherit the earth.

Acknowledgements

I first became interested in writing a book on Canadian animation when I researched a feature story about our local pop culture heroes and discovered that virtually no literature existed on the subject. How could Canadians enjoy such an international reputation in the field, without anyone writing a definitive survey of our accomplishments?

When Richard Williams came to lecture at the Ontario College of Art in the early nineties, I resolved that he would be my very first interview. But Williams would have nothing to do with me. The publicist's invitation was quickly revoked; Williams would not speak if a journalist was camped in the audience. I had fallen flat on my face before even starting. I sat on the idea for a couple more years.

But the seed had been planted, and in 1994 I resumed the quest. Fortunately, most of my subsequent interview requests met with more favourable responses. Over the years, and between projects, I've criss-crossed Canada, travelled to the United States and England in search of animators and their hidden stashes of drawings and cels. I'd like to thank all the animators who opened their homes, basement storage areas and even diaries to me. Some have literally taken artwork down from their walls so it can be in this book.

Graphics played a key role in this project, and the challenge of presenting them in a coherent and intelligent manner fell upon Bill Stewart. Animation is the art of drawings that move, and Bill has brought this book to animated life with his elegant layout.

Any fan of Canadian animation will instantly recognize Cordell Barker's unmistakable graphic style on the front cover. I'm honoured that he agreed to illustrate the book jacket.

There are two major contributors I'd like to acknowledge. Marcel Jean researched and wrote a large portion of Chapter 5, which focuses on French Canadian production at the NFB. For her part, Mary Maddever selected and wrote about the top six commercials in Canada in the past two decades.

I've also received a lot of help researching this book. Jane Devine, Katherine Kasirer and Andrea Haman contributed valuable research, and Sheila Kunst laboured long and hard to produce a comprehensive index. Historian Gene Walz was also generous with this time and information, and I've liberally poached from his research for my first chapter on the early animators such as Charlie Thorson.

I owe a debt of gratitude to Marc Glassman, who brought my first magazine article to the attention of publisher Kim McArthur. Both have remained strong supporters of the project. I would also like to acknowledge the support of the Ontario Arts Council.

And finally, to my husband, Martin Regg Cohn, whose journalist insights, editing suggestions and personal support helped me transform a mountain of documents into prose: All my love.

Karen Mazurkewich
August, 1999

chapter 1

Snow White and
the Great White North

O nce upon a time, in a far away land — a place of snow and ice — there lived a middle-aged man named Charlie. A photoengraver for the Eaton's mail-order catalogue, Charlie drew cartoons in his spare time for the local newspaper. Most days he ate at a greasy spoon named the Wevel Cafe. At odd hours, he would slide into a back booth, order a sandwich and coffee, and watch the pretty waitress carry plates of food to hungry customers. He always carried a sketch pad, and from his corner seat he amused himself by drawing caricatures of the restaurant's patrons.

Charlie became infatuated with the cafe's dark-haired hostess, soon proposing marriage. But Charlie's hopes for a third trip to the altar were dashed. The artist would only possess the fair waitress on paper.

Eventually Charlie made his way to the warmer climes of California to work for an entrepreneur named Walt Disney. In 1934, the Walt Disney Studio was a small animation house producing theatrical shorts. Its founder had big dreams — to animate a feature-length fantasy film based on the Grimm Brothers' fairy tale, *Snow White*. As a character designer, Charlie was part of a team assigned to find a face for Walt Disney's fabled princess. The image of the waitress from the wintry flat lands of his hometown found its way from Charlie's memory to the drawing board at Disney, and onto the silver screen.

There is much truth to this prairie tale. Winnipeg-born Charlie Thorson did in fact work in Disney's story department between 1935 and 1937, and contributed preliminary model sheets for Snow White. While legendary animator Grim Natwick rightfully takes most credit for the character, Thorson contributed to Snow White's design, according to historian Gene Walz. Many of the earlier conceptual drawings submitted to Disney caricatured Hollywood starlets. Thorson submitted an infantilized version of Snow White. Based on a Byronic fantasy, Thorson's princess lacked the sexual coyness of Betty Boop, the only humanized female cartoon in use at the time.[1] Thorson's more innocent approach helped Disney realize his ultimate child-woman heroine.

Charles Thorson designed some of Disney's cute characters including Elmer the Elephant (below).

Verifying the precise extent of Thorson's input at Disney is like finding a needle in a haystack. Disney actively discouraged employees from signing model sheets, and Thorson never received a film credit. By sifting through correspondence, the remnants of a portfolio, and some signed storyboards still in the Walt Disney Archives, Walz found evidence of Thorson's impact on Disney.

Thorson moved back and forth between the feature unit and the comic shorts unit that made the *Silly Symphonies*. He quickly learned Disney's house style and refined it, easily drafting cherubic infants and anthropomorphized animals. The Disney blueprint included dumbbell body proportions, pear-like limbs, oversized cylindrical heads, and expressive eyes that reflected both wonderment and vulnerability. He had effectively mastered the art of cute. [2]

Thorson was the original Canadian designer of Disney sidekick characters. Many contemporary Canadian animators such as Nik Ranieri, Duncan Majoribanks and Mike Surrey are masters of the comic support cast. But Thorson was the first. Working alongside key designer Albert Hurter, Thorson established poses and redrafted pencil sketches for Snow White's Seven Dwarfs. The animals he designed for *Little Hiawatha* resurfaced as secondary forest creatures in *Snow White and the Seven Dwarfs*, and they influenced Disney contemporary Walt Kelly, who went on to produce the popular newspaper comic strip *Pogo*. Even Tex Avery cribbed Thorson's dog design in *Toby Tortoise* for his popular Droopy Dog cartoons.

Soon after his arrival at Disney, Thorson was handed the task of designing and storyboarding a short film featuring Elmer the Elephant, a cute pachyderm who is teased about his big floppy ears and trunk. Elmer's self-esteem is restored after he heroically uses his trunk to douse the blaze in Tillie Tiger's home. Elmer was typical of Thorson's touch.

Perhaps Thorson's greatest legacy to animation is his post-Disney work at MGM and Warner Bros. Thorson left Disney in 1937 and moved to MGM, where he worked on adapting the *Captain and the Kids* comic strip, and *Old Smokey*, directed by Bill Hanna. In a letter to his brother, he boasted of "offers from every studio in Hollywood," and wrote: "My reputation has reached every cartoon studio engaged in the business."[3] Perennially in debt to his younger sibling, Thorson may have been trying to buy time on his promissory note by extolling his job prospects. Whatever the motive for plugging himself,

Thorson was, in fact, attracting attention. The trade journal *Variety* duly
noted his move to Schlesinger
Studios (soon to be renamed
Warner Bros.) in July 1938.

Thorson's name was
invoked in the controversial
debate concerning the inventor
of Bugs Bunny. Over the years
there has been much ink spilled
over the authorship of the
Warner Bros. hero. In response to
allegations that he was falsely taking credit for Bugs Bunny, Thorson
wrote Edward Selzer, president of
Warner Bros. Cartoon Division: "I definitely [sic] did create the original pictures of "Bug's Bunny" and these pictures
were made solely by myself and without the assistance or
direction of anyone else. The same applies to "Sniffles," and
every other cartoon character I claim to have originated. At
the same time, I do not claim and I never have claimed the full
credit for the popularity of "Bugs Bunny," "Sniffles" or any
other character whose pictures I have created. And I have on
every occasion that I have been questioned regarding "Bugs
Bunny" clearly stated that it was the funny voice, the funny
story situations he was placed in, and the funny animation —
all of these qualities combined made "Bugs Bunny" popular.
And I have also added that since I made his original pictures,
he has changed somewhat — his figure has been streamlined
and his expression exaggerated by the animator."[4]

Thorson joined Schlesinger's at a pivotal time. Its bankable animation stars — Porky Pig and Daffy Duck — entertained audiences, but their popularity did not yet match that
of Mickey Mouse or Betty Boop. The studio hired Thorson as
chief character designer to tweak existing toons and develop
new ones. Thorson was by then no spring chicken. He was 48,
nearly double the age of the medium's new blood, animation
supervisors Chuck Jones and Ben "Bugs" Hardaway. His relative obscurity may have been due to his heavy drinking, and
his inability to stay in one studio for long. But he soon made
his mark.

When the studio made a sequel to *Porky's Duck Hunt*
(1937), director Joseph Benson "Bugs" Hardaway dressed the
duck character in a rabbit suit and called it, *Porky's Hare Hunt*.
Audiences in New York responded warmly to the short, but it
was clear a redesign was needed. Thorson undertook the task.
He knocked off a model sheet with sketches for a buck-

*Was Winnipeg waitress
Kristin Solvadottir
the inspiration
for Snow White?*

toothed bunny rabbit. Since the model sheet was drawn at the request of Hardaway, Thorson labeled his creation "Bugs' Bunny." The name stuck.

Thorson's "Bugs" was used in *Hare-um Scare-um* (1939) and in two Chuck Jones shorts — *Presto Change-O* (1939), and *Elmer's Candid Camera* (1940). Thorson's Disneyesque rabbit with its pear-shaped body, protruding rump, and gloved hands was later streamlined. The rounded Disney design was stretched out and the rabbit's expressions exaggerated, first by designer Bob Givens and later by animator Robert McKimson.[5] The revisions included adding a tip to the cottonball tail, shortening the neck, extending the legs, almost erasing the nose and broadening the cheeks. And of course, director Tex Avery breathed life into the rabbit by transforming Bugs into a wise-cracking, confident smart-aleck who always gets the last word.

Thorson moved to Fleischer Studios after a year at Warner's and worked on the twenty-minute special, *Raggedy Ann and Raggedy Andy* (1941). But by the late forties, he had drifted back to Canada. He was broke, out of work, and sick. Back in Winnipeg, he almost certainly stopped in to spin a yarn at the old Wevel Cafe. His romanticized version of the Snow White character was passed on through letters to Kristin Solvadottir, the young waitress he once adored. Solvadottir, in turn, told her daughter that she was Snow White.[6] As with Bugs Bunny, many people had helped to shape Snow White; but a picture taken of the waitress at age 22 bears a remarkable likeness to Disney's first heroine.

While at Schlesinger Studios, Thorson, a master of the cute bunny, knocked off a model sheet with sketches for a buck-toothed rabbit. The moniker he scribbled on the bottom was "Bugs' Bunny." The name stuck.

There was little commercial work in Canada in the late forties. The Winnipeg production house, Phillips-Gutkin-Associates, was operating and Thorson was briefly employed by them. He dreamed that his children's book, *Keeko*, would become a big hit and be spun off into a series that would make him rich. It didn't. In the end, while his characters continued to gain popularity, a painful muscular condition cut short his career in animation and illustration.

Charlie Thorson was not the only animator to get his start in Winnipeg. He wasn't even the first. Canadian animation was born in a tarpaper shack in Winnipeg's North End in 1910. In their draughty, makeshift studio, Jean Arsin and Charles Lambly toughed out the prairie winters and produced 35-mm paper-animated films. All of their works have been lost. The oldest surviving piece of animation is a 1919 morality tale called *The*

Man Who Woke Up. Produced for the Federated Budget Board of Winnipeg, the film by J.A. Norling and William Ganson Rose features a Scrooge-like character who wakes up from a terrible dream a changed man and a supporter of charities. Lambly made a cutout 25-minute film called *Romulus and Remus* (1926), commissioned by the Archdiocese of Montreal, according to his assistant, Francis J.S. Holmes. The film has been lost.

In Toronto, Walter Swaffield, Harold Peberdy and Bert Cob were producing frame-by-frame films before 1920. None of their films survived. Blaine Irish, former cameraman for Pathé News in Chicago, produced several animated cartoons in 1922 featuring a cat called Tom who possessed "a tail whose powers cannot be matched by wood or pen."[7] Irish and his art director, Percy Joselin, superimposed animation over photographic backgrounds and attempted several silhouette cartoons. The series was popular enough for Filmcraft Industries to sign a deal with the *Toronto Daily Star* to advertise the shows. Irish's series were widely seen in Canada, but he was unable to pick up a foreign distributor. Irish died suddenly at the age of 32 in October, 1923, before he was able to crack the US market and make a further contribution to Canadian cinema.

In 1927, Bryant Fryer of Galt, Ontario, successfully pitched a proposal to make silhouette puppet films for the distribution firm Cranfield and Clarke, which later produced Canada's first feature film flop, *Carry on Sergeant*. Fryer studied illustration and etching at the Arts Students League in New York and envisioned his solo works to be an "extension of the ancient art of the Chinese shadow play."[8]

Colonel W.F. Clarke convinced Filmart, a film titling company, to underwrite the production of Fryer's animated shorts, *Shadowlaughs*. With his assistant, Geoffrey Keighley, Fryer crafted an animated short using layered black paper cutouts on a sloping glass surface. *Follow the Swallow* is a prehistoric tale of a bird that is chased by a Neanderthal man and his dinosaur.

Bryant Fryer's silent short One Bad Knight *is one of the first animated films ever produced in Canada.*

The pacing in Fryer's first *Shadowlaughs* short is sloppy, but he got it right the second time around with *One Bad Knight*. Billed as a "medieval romance," *One Bad Knight* stars an aging hero who regales his grandson with tales of his energetic courtship of the boy's grandmother. The tale starts in the Hot Dog, a notorious "Knight Club," where a lithe dancer is entertaining the crowd. Sir Ronald falls for the nimble beauty on stage, but she is spirited away by Rancid Randolf, the bad guy. With the help of a dragon and his loyal horse, the brave knight Sir Ronald rescues the lady. The supposedly imperiled heroine has always been in complete control of the situation, but rewards her persistent suitor by marrying him.

Produced in just two months, Fryer's first films were never released theatrically. With Cranfield and Clarke's company teetering on bankruptcy, Filmart could not foresee any return on its investment. Fryer's small operation was shut down. It would take six years before Fryer could find another backer.

Toronto distillery tycoon Albert Gooderham made it possible for Fryer to produce a new series of cutout films in 1933. With a fresh cash infusion, Fryer made further adjustments to the technology. He eliminated the flickering effect of his earlier works by replacing his hand-crank camera with a motorized model. *Sailors of the Guard, Bye Baby Bunting*, and *Jack the Giant Killer* were produced back-to-back that same year. The films are technically competent, the animation smooth, and the stories lively. But lack of distribution avenues derailed Fryer once again. His dream of starting a Canadian animation studio was squashed by an American film lobby.[9]

In 1933, Canadian theatre ownership was dominated by Famous Players Canadian Corporation, an offshoot of Paramount Pictures, the company that released Fleischer cartoons. Famous Players did not welcome Canadian competition, and promptly dispatched a Fleischer representative to offer Fryer and his assistant jobs in the United States. Fryer declined. The job offer may have been an attempt to divert Fryer from building a rival studio in Canada.[10] After completing a package of fine shorts, Fryer found himself completely shut out of the market. Not one distributor could be tempted to pick up an option. Fryer's brave attempt to forge an indigenous industry was thwarted. He eventually succumbed to US pressure and accepted an offer to work in California.

Fryer returned to Canada to join the Royal Canadian Air Force during World War II. Despite his vast experience, he was never invited to join the National Film Board of Canada. He never made another animated film.

French-Canadian artist Raoul Barré developed new techniques that revolutionized the American animated film.

Until 1939, animation production in Canada was rare. The talent, however, was not. Like Fryer, most artists drifted across the border to find jobs in New York and Los Angeles, where animation was becoming a popular entertainment medium.

One of the earliest and most distinguished pioneers of animation was Quebec-born Raoul Barré, who moved from Montreal to New York in 1903 to work as an illustrator. Trained at the Ecole des Beaux-Arts and the Academie Julian in Paris, Barré returned to his birthplace and formed part of the nucleus of the impressionist school in Montreal and Toronto. Comic strips came to Quebec in 1902, when the daily newspaper *La Presse* published a series of Barré's illustrations entitled *Pour un diner de Noël*. *La Patrie* published his strips, *Les Contes du Père Rhault* (1906), and *A l'hotel du Père Noël* (1913); in the late twenties he founded the magazine *Le Taureau* with his son-in-law and aspiring politician Gaspard Fauteux. This French-Canadian visionary will be remembered for

Montreal's La Presse *newspaper published a series of Barré's illustrations entitled* Pour un diner de Noël.

his major contributions to animation. According to historian André Martin, "He was at the very source of 20th century consciousness, caught between traditional forms of expression and new means of reproduction."[11] Not only did Barré innovate several techniques, his surreal gags defined the genre in its formative years. Abandoning the decorative drawing style popularized by turn-of-the-century magazines, Barré chose to simplify his graphics for greater comedic impact. Martin believes Barré's shorts were the forerunners of the "riotous burlesque" characterizing the work of Walter Lantz, Bob Clampett and Tex Avery.

As a young commercial artist in New York, Barré became fascinated with the moving pictures of McCay and Bray, and made advertising films with partner William C. Nolan in 1912. Two years later, the pair opened one of the first animation

Mutt and Jeff, a cartoon based on the popular syndicated comic strip by Captain Bud Fisher, was animated in Barré's New York studio.

studios, hired Gregory LaCava and Frank Moser, and produced *Animated Grouch Chaser* series. Barré improved McCay and Bray's rudimentary registration techniques by creating the peg system, which ensured smoothness of movement. The studio also instituted the "slash system," which reduced drawing time by slashing or separating appendages or characters that moved from stationary objects. Thus an animator could move an arm or leg without redrawing the torso, or move one character while one next to it remained motionless. These innovations proved to be "a decisive trigger in the industrial organization of American animated film."[12]

Barré's most lucrative project was *Mutt and Jeff,* based on the popular syndicated comic strip by Captain Bud Fisher. The rights to the strip had been acquired by cartoonist Charles Bowers, who moved into Barré's studio after attempting to produce a couple of shorts on his own. Unfortunately, the battles with his new partner left Barré exhausted and disillusioned. He went into semi-retirement between 1919 to 1926, and only returned to Pat Sullivan's studio to animate ten Felix the Cat shorts, including the classics: *Felix Hunts the Hunter, Felix in Germ-mania, Felix Trumps the Ace* and *Pedigreedy.*

Barré returned to Montreal for his last animation endeavour. Under the auspices of the Educational Art and Film Company of Montreal, Barré hired students to work on a production entitled *Le Roi microbus 1er.* It was a project Barré hoped would evolve into a co-production with France, but he died in 1930 before it was completed.

Barré returned from self-imposed exile to animate ten Felix the Cat shorts.

Today's generation of Canadian expatriates jokingly blame their animation antics on the cold expanse of our Great White North. Attributing Canadian innovation to bitterly cold temperatures and blizzards is romantic nonsense. What some Canadians do possess is a remarkable ability to imitate and parody American art. There are advantages to being an outsider. Barré, Thorson and others exploited it, as their Canadian successors continued to do so successfully in the decades to come.

chapter 2

Pass the Ammunition: Animation and the War Effort

established in peacetime, the National Film Board of Canada (NFB) was really a product of the war. Had Hitler not marched into Poland on September 1, 1939, the NFB would probably have remained an advisory board, and founder John Grierson would never have gained the clout to create the legendary film unit. Invited to Canada in 1938 to serve as a government media advisor, Grierson subsequently became interim commissioner of the newly established National Film Board of Canada. The outbreak of war gave him the leverage to take over the government's bureaucratic newsreel service and transform the NFB into a full-fledged production studio. The metamorphosis took two years. Grierson eventually absorbed the Canadian Motion Picture Bureau and added 55 people to the initial staff of two. Their mission: to provide cultural ammunition for the war effort.

John Grierson was a self-described "prophet" brought over from Britain to liberate Canadians from their national apathy. His spiritual crusade, as defined by Prime Minister William Lyon Mackenzie King, was to palpitate the country's patriotic heart, and engender unity through films.

In theory, Grierson was the father of Canadian cinema; in practice, he was a complex man with divided loyalties — to Canada, to Britain and to American commercial interests. While Grierson fulfilled the NFB mandate to "interpret Canada to Canadians and to the world," he also used the agency as a platform for British propaganda, and on occasion engaged the services of US studios.

Grierson was on retainer with the British government's Imperial Relations Trust — considered an arm of British intelligence — long after accepting the appointment as Canadian film commissioner. In addition, he maintained strong ties with American multinationals, and supported the monopolistic practices of the Motion Picture Association of America (MPAA). Although his political agenda was rather schizophrenic, Grierson remained single-minded about his role as communicator: "I look on cinema as a pulpit, and use it as a propagandist."[13] This conviction bridged any ideological schisms.

During World War II animation recruits like Jim MacKay learned the ropes by crafting titles for newsreels.

As founder of the British documentary movement of the thirties, Grierson favoured actuality footage, but he also considered animation a powerful dissemination tool. He even encouraged experimental forms of animation at the Government Post Office (GPO) Film Unit and the EMP Film Unit — the two British studios he headed between 1928 and 1936.

Grierson called upon his faithful cinematic followers in Britain to help lead the documentary cavalry, but it took almost two years for him to hire the creative resources for an animation department. Instead, Grierson commissioned Walt Disney Studio to produce four films, at 3 minutes each, for the war effort at a total cost of US$20,000.

Grierson's decision to work with Disney was predicated in part on the age-old marketing practices of recognition factor and speed of delivery. Disney proved to be a savvy service house during the war. It retained the right to recycle its characters and shorts, and after a five-year period, regained all distribution rights to the NFB films. After several delays, due to the Disney strike and a shortage of perchlorethylene (film cleaning fluid), the shorts featuring Donald Duck, the Three Little Pigs, and the Seven Dwarfs, were delivered and released to the Canadian public between December 1941 and June 1942.

Stop That Tank!, produced in co-operation with the Department of National Defence, stars Hitler himself leading a tank charge into an ambush of Canadians sporting MK-1 anti-tank rifles. Hitler gets bumped into hell, where he has a temper tantrum in front of the devil. Un-impressed, the devil trans-lates the fuehrer's garbling: "Adolph says it's not fair ... the fuehrer says against your anti-tank rifles we simply can't win." This early animated film for the NFB portrays Hitler as a babbling lunatic.

Hitler materializes again as a hungry wolf in *The Thrifty Pig*, a take-off on Disney's *Three Little Pigs*. The moral substitute for brick houses in this pic-ture is war savings certificates. The big bad wolf sporting a swastika armband is unable to blow up the last edifice constructed of war bond bullion. In case the message isn't evident in that symbolism, the film concludes with the transformation of a war bond cer-tificate into bullets and guns that shoot down German planes.

A third commissioned short fea-tures Donald Duck battling his alter ego to purchase the bonds. In a fourth installment, Disney's seven wise dwarfs march in the fore-ground of Canada's Parliament buildings as they heigh-ho, heigh-ho their way from the mines to the bank, ready to trade in their loot for Five For Four bonds. Seen today, the image is jarring: America's cultural icons invading Canada's capital. At least one Canadian critic saw the films as early proof that Grierson was "actively working for the benefit of the Hollywood majors."[14]

Despite Grierson's clear support for the US movie indus-try, Disney's advance on Canadian soil was short-lived. Grierson's goal was always to build a self-sufficient studio — if not a commercial production centre, at least a non-theatrical one. At the same time as he enlisted Disney's support, Grierson was recruiting experimental filmmaker Norman McLaren. Over the next four years, the NFB's staff ballooned to 787; production soared to 40 films a year, none of them fea-turing Disney's anthropomorphized animals.

Phil Ragan was the one American who maintained ties with the NFB throughout the war. Hired in 1940 to produce a

Phil Ragan produced 35 films for the NFB during World War II. Empty Rooms Mean Idle Machines *(above)* suggests that Canadians rent their spare rooms to workers joining new plants.

film that explained the need to curb inflation, the Philadelphia-based diagram expert produced 36 films for the NFB during the war. His popular *Plugger* series featured a cartoon family who learn about the importance of Victory loans, government price controls, renting out rooms to new plant employees and electricity conservation.

The war years were a chaotic period in the history of Canadian cinema. Grierson recruited top documentary directors and photographers such as Stuart Legg, Don Foster, Stanley Hawes, Raymond Spottiswoode, Don Fraser, and Julian Roffman. Few cameramen were dispatched to the field; most of the work was done in the editing suite using "borrowed" footage. The Canadian employees were greenhorns. "There was so little experience in filmmaking at the NFB that if a new director or cameraman saw something move on screen he thought he had beaten D.W. Griffith at his own game," wrote Roffman in a letter to Marjorie McKay.[15]

Dollar Dance, *a playful missive created by Norman McLaren made Disney's wartime works seem heavyhanded.*

Scottish animator Norman McLaren played a key role in Grierson's master plan. Grierson had discovered McLaren at the Glasgow School of Art in Scotland, and hired him to work at the General Post Office's Film Unit in Britain. Now Grierson wanted to bring him to the NFB to establish an animation unit.

McLaren was not enamoured of the idea of leaving his new home in New York to make hard-core propaganda for the Canadian government. Control was paramount for an agency producing propaganda during a war, and McLaren was understandably wary. He had already fallen victim to censorship at the GPO in London, and wasn't looking for a repeat experience. Grierson reassured him that the kinds of experiments he was doing under Guggenheim grants would be permissible at the new studio. It was a significant promise. McLaren took Grierson at his word, and in 1941 packed his bags and moved to Ottawa.

McLaren never sought control over content, but there could be no compromise over style. As long as the message was somewhere in the film — even if it was in the last 10 seconds — McLaren was free to choose any graphic style he desired. In return, McLaren produced artistic gems with didactic messages. Grierson kept his word and never meddled. It was a creative symbiosis.

The oars of propaganda only skimmed the political waters in McLaren's films. Even Disney's World War II works were heavy-handed compared to McLaren's lighthearted approach. He effortlessly bridged entertainment and wartime missives with playful images that danced to lively tunes. *Mail Early for Christmas* (1941), a film made by drawing directly on 35-mm film with India ink, was a friendly reminder to Canadians to mail their letters early so the beleaguered Post Office would not get bogged down during the holidays. *Hen Hop* (1942), McLaren's second film for the NFB, is an innovative scratch-on-film that soft-peddles the sale of war bonds. In *Dollar Dance* (1943), McLaren animates a toe-tapping, square-dancing dollar sign to remind audiences to fight inflation (*Five For Four*).

The only grim film McLaren produced during the height of the war was *Keep Your Mouth Shut* (1944), a scary short intended to discourage gossip. McLaren and George Dunning intercut short documentary sequences with animation of a three-dimensional white skull on a black background to represent a lurking evil presence. The skull introduces himself as the guy who overhears what you say and passes it on to the enemy. "I seem to recognize some of you," it states pointedly. Subliminal swastikas flicker in the eye sockets, and the words "Attention," and "Keep Your Mouth Shut," constantly flash on and off. The film ends with an admonition: "loose lips sink ships."

Grierson believed that the "cartoon and the trick approach are by far the most valuable way of putting over public messages."[16] He was sensitive to the fact that his first man of visual ruse, Norman McLaren, was not the model public relations man. But with the verve of a true iconoclast, Grierson officiated at this unlikely marriage between art and propaganda: "It takes a long, long imaginative policy of national public relations to see the social justification for McLaren and experimental films of that kind." Yet he clearly felt the shotgun wedding was worth the effort. "The justification is easy because it means that Canada can hold up her face in the art world abroad. And a distinguished face."[17]

Grierson's investment in the animation experiment was confined to hiring McLaren and backing his vision. The rest was left to McLaren himself. McLaren did not have an ambitious agenda. Initially, he sought assistance only when needed.

Experimental artist Norman McLaren was not enamoured of the idea of leaving his new home in New York to make hardcore propaganda for the Canadian government.

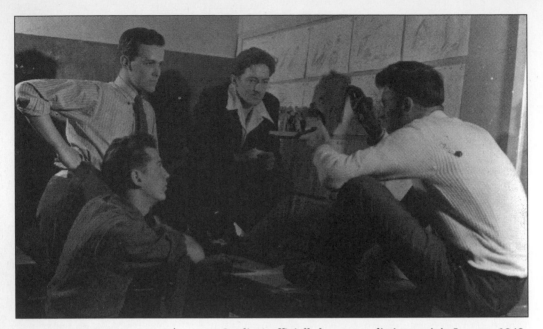

Norman McLaren discusses perspective with new NFB animation recruits René Jodoin, George Dunning and Jim MacKay.

Studio A officially became a distinct unit in January 1943. McLaren's first real recruit for the new studio was Jim MacKay, a graduate of the Ontario College of Art, whose only real experience was drawing diagrams for the Workers' Educational Association's filmstrips.

A tour of Canada's top art schools and word-of-mouth led to the recruitment of George Dunning, René Jodoin, Jean-Paul Ladouceur, Laurence Hyde, Arthur Price and Grant Munro. Evelyn Lambart, another graduate from the Ontario College of Art, was promoted from the titles department, and for years was one of the few women to work within the studio.

McLaren always reviewed portfolios supplied by instructors before meeting potential candidates. Grant Munro almost skipped his rendezvous with the "chap" from the National Film Board. He had a hot date with an out-of-town girlfriend that day and a job interview was not a priority. Not wanting to disappoint his favourite Ontario College of Art instructor Frank Carmichael (of the famous Group of Seven), Munro made it to the meeting. McLaren explained that the man who did titles for the Film Board — they were all hand produced at the time — was having serious eye problems and the NFB needed somebody immediately. "So I — God, why Norman didn't walk out of the building — I said, 'Well, you've come to the wrong person. I hate lettering,'" Munro recalls. "Well, anybody else would have just said 'Fuck you.' But Norman said: 'Well, you don't have to letter in white paint on black card, you know. If you speak to the director of the film, you could discuss maybe doing the titles in pipe cleaner or Plasticine.' I paused for a moment and asked: 'Or salt?' 'Or salt,' McLaren replied. And I said, 'Great! I'll take the job!' And wouldn't you know it. My first title was a documentary called *Salt From the Earth* directed by Gudrun Parker. So I went down to the Ottawa market and bought a piece of cow salt and carved Roman letters into it."[18]

McLaren initiated his enlisted men in diagrams and lettering. They ranged from mundane assignments such as titling *Pass the Ammunition* to inventive approaches to map making. One involved peeling and sectioning a grapefruit to illustrate how cartographers try to maintain perspectives when they flatten the globe. The unit's primary task was to complete tasks ordered by the documentary gang marshaling the *World in Action* and *Canada Carries On* series. Occasionally, the young animation crew was handed short film subjects with sensible themes related to agricultural output and wartime rationing.

Laurence Hyde, an expert at wood block prints, animated two practical films for farmers during wartime: *Murder in the Milk Can* (1944) and *More Pigs* (1944). A superb graphic artist, Hyde's work was beautiful but static, and he soon moved into the educational (filmstrip) division of the board.

McLaren encouraged simplicity and spontaneity by training his new recruits on a machine that allowed them to draw directly on film stock. After practising on McLaren's contraption, Jim MacKay produced the austerity film *Stitch and Save* (1943), urging Canadian housewives to reuse clothing. George Dunning's debut, *Grim Pastures* (1944), reminds farmers to supply fodder to their cattle. Using elegant sweeping curves to capture the grace of a running stallion, and solid geometric shapes to depict a hearty cow, Dunning proved he had embraced McLaren's minimalist teachings.

The unit's most popular shorts were a series of animated songs intended to boost morale on the home front and abroad. By 1944, Canadians were suffering from war fatigue. Grierson felt some "leavening" should be added to the mix of footage from the front lines of Europe and factories, so he commissioned a

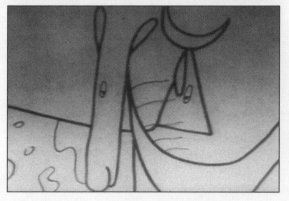

George Dunning's geometric animation from Grim Pastures.

I've Got a Sixpence, one of the films in the Let's All Sing Together *series.*

Simple paper cutouts of horses used in Arthur Price's animated rendition of Old MacDonald Has a Farm.

Grant Munro's puppet protagonist featured in the film, Oh, My Darling Clementine, *was so homely Canadian viewers logged complaints with NFB projectionists working in the regions.*

series of sing-along films. Grierson hoped the musical experience would connect Canadians sitting side-by-side in a darkened room in some church basement. He was also personally fascinated with the fact that many European folk songs, which had died out in their native countries, were still being sung in Canada.

As a result, he instituted *Chants populaires/Let's All Sing Together,* a series based on popular ditties. Everyone in the studio was encouraged to craft a film using a recording of their choice. Early series' shorts, such as René Jodoin's *Alouette,* simply depicted a stylized icon that bounced across the lyrics. As the series progressed, the animators were given more creative latitude. McLaren himself chose a more illustrative style with *C'est l'aviron* (1945), an ode to Quebec's landscape, and *Là-haut sur les montagnes.* Arthur Price, a theatrical designer for army events, made *Old MacDonald Has a Farm, Oh Susannah* and *Shortenin' Bread* (1945), by moving simple paper cutouts across static backgrounds.

MacKay and Munro's contributions telegraphed artistic promise with their striking white cutouts set against black backdrops. Unlike paper puppeteer Bryant Fryer, who strove to make realistic figurines, Munro's early design style was clownish. The comedic choice was appropriate given the limited articulation of their early puppets. For example, the circus performer of *The Man on the Flying Trapeze* (1945) undertakes a series of high-flying tricks — an activity that involves maximum mobility in major joints and does not require subtle acting.

But not all reports were kind. Munro received one nasty response for his interpretation of a homely woman in *Oh, My Darling Clementine* (1945). An NFB projectionist registered several complaints in his report from the prairie region, including this one from local critic, A.L. Stinson: "The sooner you get rid of that lavatory laureate, Grant Munro, the better." [19]

Clementine was indeed an ugly duckling complete with gangly limbs and duck-like feet. Of course, that depiction made the song all the funnier; but the black humour was apparently lost on some.

By far the most innovative cutout artist in the mid-forties was George Dunning. Even as a student, Dunning's flair for design was evident. Before being snapped up by the NFB, Dunning had set up his own little illustration studio in Toronto. Dunning was McLaren's second recruit, but he became his premiere protégé, and went on to produce such award-winning films as *The Flying Man* and *Yellow Submarine* (1968)

George Dunning used metal cutouts to make Cadet Rouselle. *The film was part of the NFB's* Chants populaires *series.*

outside the NFB. Whereas MacKay preferred cutouts with replaceable parts, Dunning favoured jointed paper marionettes. *Three Blind Mice* (1945), a film Dunning choreographed and animated with Robert Verrall and Grant Munro, stars a paper trio of rodents that tumble, stumble and injure themselves in sync with the macabre children's song. With crisp precision, Dunning uses his puppets to teach industry employees about safety rules.

These early films, with their strong lines and sparse detail, became a template for other studio animators. MacKay, Munro, Ladouceur and others eventually adopted a similar stylistic approach. The most derivative is MacKay's *Ten Little Farmers* (1949), another workers' safety film, which stars a line-up of accident prone farmers.

The economic restrictions imposed during the war meant everything had to be very bold and stylized. The animators relied on strong musical tracks to augment the awkward linear shapes and stiff appendages of their paper and metal dolls.

Staff composer Louis Applebaum scored many of the early films including *Grim Pastures*, *Three Blind Mice*, and

The early sing-along films served as a leavening agent to lift the spirits of Canadians during the war.

ONCE I WAS HAPPY BUT NOW I'M FORLORN,

LIKE AN OLD COAT THAT IS TATTERED AND TORN,

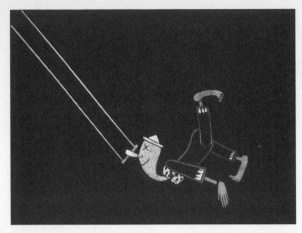

The Man on the Flying Trapeze is an early example of the striking paper cutout films produced by the first NFB animators.

Ten Little Farmers. The Four Gentlemen Quartet lent their voices to many soundtracks during this period.

The repetitive choreography of the paper cutouts, combined with the recurring choruses of popular songs, were conducive to the kind of interactivity Grierson wanted to generate in the church basements and union halls.

The NFB animators tapped into the familiar and friendly musical memories and adapted them visually. They were robust films that encouraged audiences to sing along and stamp their feet. The spirit of these "chansons d' illustrateurs" lives on at the NFB. In recent years, filmmakers like Chris Hinton, John Weldon and Cordell Barker have adapted and animated Canadian songs such as "Blackfly," "Log Driver's Waltz," and "The Cat Came Back."

During the forties, Norman McLaren spent much of his time solving technical and artistic problems encountered by his new animators. His sacrifices, at times, were great. When Munro was struggling to calibrate the speed of a slide lantern in his film *The Man on the Flying Trapeze*, McLaren stayed behind one evening to assist. All night long, McLaren sat beside the camera stand, watching and guiding. Munro didn't know it at the time, but McLaren was suffering from appendicitis. While obviously in pain, McLaren held off going to the hospital until Munro completed his experiment.

The unit's esprit de corps was legendary. Despite poor ventilation and insulation, the crew worked through heat waves, cold snaps and even dust storms that formed when a strong breeze blew through the dilapidated John Street offices in Ottawa. The equipment was dangerous, and the arc lighting terrible. When the animators cranked up humidity levels to preserve their cel paint, it literally rained inside the building. Having created an artificial rainstorm, the animators responded in a predictably loony way: they donned bathing suits and pith helmets.

War fatigue evolved into a post-war hang-over. In the summer of 1945, Grierson and top documentary director Stuart Legg left the NFB. It was up to the new government film commissioner, Ross McLean, to reorient the agency from propaganda to public service. Eager to work exclusively on his own films, McLaren handed over the departmental reins to MacKay. Sapped of energy, McLaren felt his duty was done. It was time for him to return to the pure pursuit of art.

Three young recruits in the summer of 1945 would have a long-term impact on the post-war studio — Colin Low, Robert Verrall and Wolf Koenig. They pushed the unit away from experimental graphics, and encouraged traditional techniques such as cel animation.

Stanley Takes a Trip counsels parents and kids about nutrition. The film marks the NFB's transition from war propaganda to educational media.

Colin Low was hired as George Dunning's assistant. Low was equal parts inventor and artist. His life has been spent pushing the envelope of technology. He reinvented the documentary film form, made realistic models of 3-D space that caught the attention of American director Stanley Kubrick, and was a leading figure in the creation of Imax technology. For 12 years, he ran the animation department. His arrival ushered in a new era in Canadian cel animation.

Robert Verrall was a 17-year-old Toronto high school student when he saw an animation exhibition assembled by Jim MacKay and George Dunning. One film, *C'est l'aviron*, knocked Verrall off his feet. He was hooked. Hired as a summer student by McLaren in May 1945, Verrall assisted Dunning and Munro on *Three Blind Mice* (1945).

Programmed as part of the *Let's All Sing Together* series, *Three Blind Mice* proved a perfect escape for filmmakers who wanted to flex their creative muscles. The sing-along films also served as a buffer immediately after the war when the NFB made the transition from propaganda to educational fare. As producer Guy Glover so aptly put it, "our biggest subject, or biggest kind of unifying ... phenomenon had disappeared."[20] The challenge was how to make peace exciting.

The studio slowly redirected its energy into public service films on dental hygiene and diet. Unlike the whimsical *Let's All Sing Along* series, the films of the early fifties were extremely pragmatic. In *Stanley Takes a Trip* (1950), MacKay introduces the basic food groups in a direct and homey way. The subject matter may have been dry, but MacKay's filmic approach in *Teeth Are to Keep* (1949) was fresh enough to elicit

fan mail from one of the most innovative American studios: United Productions of America (UPA). Canadian-born Stephen Bosustow, a partner of UPA, wrote: "We believe it is one of the freshest, best pictures of its kind that we have ever had the pleasure of seeing."[21] Written by Canadian poet P.K. Page, the film stood the test of time; it remained in circulation for more than 40 years.

During the NFB's start-up phase, the material of choice was paper because it was cheap and did not require much instruction — merely an artistic sensibility and imagination. In the years that followed the war, colour began to seep into the films. The most visually lush film in the forties was *Family Tree* (1949), a colourful cutout film directed by Dunning and Lambart. *Family Tree* was the first film to celebrate Canadian pluralism by chronicling the waves of settlement in the country's history. It had a richer palette than other NFB films, featuring turquoise skies and velvet green forests.

Cel animation was practically non-existent during the war because the cellulose nitrate used to produce acetate was needed for explosives. Dunning took one stab at simple cel animation with *Auprès de ma blonde*, and MacKay produced two cel shorts, *Good-Bye Mr. Gyp* (1943), and *Bid It Up Sucker* (1943). Immediately after the war, most animators trained in paper cutout animation balked at cel production. But the victory of graphic animation over cel cartoons was short-lived. Cel enthusiasts gained ground in the mid-fifties. Although a handful of cel films were produced in the early forties, their style was so crude that NFB archivists often refer to the colour film *Teamwork – Past and Present* (1952) as the NFB's first real cel film.

The studio flirted briefly with 3-D puppet animation. Arthur Price, an enlisted soldier constructing sets for the army's theatrical productions, joined the NFB and produced the studio's first puppet film, *Come to the Fair* (1949), with Grant Munro. It was a primitive exercise featuring clumsily stuffed puppets and poor lighting. Strings adhered to props and unnatural shadows destroyed the illusion. Price did not stay at the NFB, and left to pursue a career in printmaking and sculpture. Further development of puppet animation fell on the shoulders of Ladouceur and Munro who continued to explore the genre, along with Alma Duncan, Wolf Koenig, Gerald Budner and Evelyn Lambart.

Carving her props and heads from balsa wood, Duncan produced the eight-minute short puppet film *Folksong Fantasy* while under contract at the NFB between 1949-51. The film is based on three folk tales about a sparrow who slays a robin, the taming of a shrew (not Shakespeare's version), and a song about riddles.

Bid It Up Sucker, *one of the first limited cel films produced at the NFB.*

Jean-Paul Ladouceur, Wolf Koenig and Evelyn Lambart collaborated on a series of films based on the folk songs sung by Allan Mills. The most dramatic of the three films produced is *Barbara Allen* (1953), the tragic tale of a young lover who loses his will to live after the death of his lady love. Two roses grow at their graves and the entwining thorny stems symbolize their eternal love. The dramatic lighting and pliable puppets are a vast improvement over *Come to the Fair* and Ladouceur and Koenig's early effort *Sur le pont d'Avignon* (1951), a puppet pantomime based on an old French folk song describing the elegant citizenry dancing on a bridge in Avignon.

Unfortunately, puppet animation died out at the NFB after Munro directed the immensely popular traffic safety film

One Little Indian (1954). Despite its apparent appeal, and low production costs, puppet animation at the NFB did not take off as it did in the East Bloc countries. Animator Colin Low postulates that Munro and others may have abandoned the genre after McLaren privately critiqued their artistic merit. Visiting animator Bretislav Pojar, and most recently Brian Duchscherer, later revived the tradition at the NFB.

"All together, it was a bit of a hodgepodge of experiments. When you worked through one set of materials, you moved to another approach out of boredom," says Low, who found the sedentary nature of animation exhausting, and soon tired of "the flat, decorative styles."

Tight budgets meant Low could not plunge whole-heartedly into 3-D animation. Instead he focused on special effects. After a one-year leave, Low redirected his energy into a large-scale science film, *Challenge: The War Against Cancer* (1950). This film cast the mold for future science documentaries. Sober and intelligent, the documentary treats scientists as space explorers on a quest to investigate the complex universe that is cancer. Low and Evelyn Lambart spent a year drawing the molecular world. Low contributed to the science-fiction genre by applying his animation talent to uncovering the secrets of the Cosmos with later films such as *Universe* (1955).

※ ※ ※ ※ ※

The National Film Board was the voice of Canada during World War II. Its newsreels and films were distributed to overseas units, army brigades stationed in Canada, unions, theatrical venues and rural film circuits. By June 1945, the NFB had produced 335 films. Out of this body of work, 35 came from the animation unit, which also contributed to countless maps, diagrams and titles for other films.

Yet having taken on the Nazis, the agency would eventually have to contend with an incipient evil that threatened its very existence — a McCarthyite purge. Grierson's name was smeared, filmmakers were fired or resigned, and low morale plagued the NFB in the late forties and early fifties, following revelations that a one-time secretary of Grierson's, Freda Linton, was implicated in a Soviet spy scandal called the Gouzenko affair.

Igor Gouzenko, a cipher clerk from the Soviet embassy in Ottawa, defected with documents concerning a Soviet spy ring in Canada. Because of Linton's apparent involvement, Grierson was summoned to testify before a royal commission in the spring of 1946. Although never indicted on charges, the commission suggested that Grierson was a Communist sympathizer. By casting aspersions on the political integrity of its founder, critics tarred the whole institution with a red brush.[22]

By 1948, MPs in Ottawa were attacking the NFB for mismanagement. Critics accused the institution of wasting taxpayer's money, competing unfairly with the private sector, and sheltering Communists. The latter charge prompted the minister responsible for the Board, Robert Winters, to bring in management consultants. The RCMP was already running security checks on all employees. On November 19, 1949, the *Financial Post* reported that for security reasons, the Department of National Defence no longer used the NFB for classified work. The future of government support was at stake.

At least 10 people lost their jobs in the 1949-50 inquisition. Film Commissioner Ross McLean learned that he was to be replaced by Arthur Irwin, former publisher of *Maclean's* magazine. Irwin's job was to clean house and "restore confidence in the Film Board," he said.[23]

Irwin was asked to expel at least 33 people. Instead, he offered three scapegoats who were considered "security risks." Two of the alleged Communists were employed by Studio A. One of them was animator/scriptwriter Allan Ackman, a collaborator on the first colour cel animated film produced at the NFB. Greta Eckmann, a promising young animator, was told not to reapply when her contract expired, because her husband had joined the Communist party. McLaren, a one-time Communist Party

Allan Ackman (standing at storyboard) was one of three filmmakers fired from the NFB for his communist beliefs.

member, was spared. It was later rumored that Mackenzie King had shielded McLaren from RCMP investigations. And Irwin had no intention of losing his star filmmaker — the only NFB artist who made it onto his extensive Christmas card list.

Ackman and Ekman's removal came as an enormous surprise to staffers such as Robert Verrall, who considered the administration to be an enlightened one "that welcomed free spirits and, in fact, was staffed by people who were, for the most part, openly left-wing."[24] Impressed with Ekman's ability to work in exquisite miniature, and a fan of her short *Twirligig*, McLaren tried to intercede on her behalf. He failed. Several of his associates believe that McLaren's Oscar-winning film *Neighbours* was partly inspired by the callous dismissal of some of his staff.

Those working inside the walls of the NFB considered the Communist threat an innocuous one. Marjorie McKay, one of Grierson's assistants, remembers being invited to a Communist cell meeting in 1946 or 1947. It didn't strike her as nefarious: "They knitted; it was pathetic," she reported in her writings.[25] Allan Ackman was a proselytizer of Marx, Engels and Lenin, and could be a crashing bore on the subject, but everyone in the unit liked him and considered him harmless. Even Irwin did not take the red menace too seriously. But outside its hallowed halls, the NFB had gained a terrible reputation as an eccentric operation employing a bohemian element that kept strange hours, wore odd clothes, and threw wild parties.[26]

Irwin surmised that conservative politicians found the influx of creative types into the nation's capital rather disconcerting. "Ottawa was a pretty provincial capital in those days," said Irwin.[27] The tensions of the period provided "a wonderful opportunity for the people who believed in conspiracy and saw a conspiracy under every raspberry bush, and those who are inclined to be critical of people who have reformist ideas or leftist ideas or Communist ideas or something that is different from what they support," he said.

Irwin did stabilize the NFB during his three-year tenure as film commissioner from 1949 to 1952. The government's fears were allayed, but the early enthusiasm was gone. Ackman and Ekman's careers were badly affected. They were never able to get access to the RCMP files and there was no appeal mechanism. It is unclear how many good artists were discouraged from even applying to the NFB for work.

The whole place fell into a depression. MacKay and Dunning moved to Toronto to open up a commercial studio. Shortly afterwards, the animation studio was reabsorbed into Studio B under executive director Tom Daly. Colin Low was named chief of the animation division. An era had ended.

The NFB survived wartime chaos and the maelstrom of bad publicity, but its mandate and priorities had shifted.

chapter 3

Propaganda Message

Governments spend fortunes during wartime on morale-building stuff, because they know instinctively that that's what people need — they need the courage to go ahead and face the uncertainties in the world. But they forget that courage is just as necessary in peace time.

— Wolf Koenig

n the United States, animation as entertainment was the creed after World War II. Most American studios stopped cranking out sponsored films in order to concentrate on theatrical shorts. In Canada, the propagandistic nature of the NFB's early films was never eliminated, merely sublimated. Sponsored films became the bread-and-butter of the National Film Board's animation wing for the next 25 years.

The highly motivated animators elevated the sponsored film from work horse to art house. There was never a subject too dull. Even a film clip warning fishermen about fish rot found its way onto the international festival circuit. The sponsorship era brought a third wave of animators into the studio. The NFB conducted a cross-pollination experiment — mixing and matching filmmakers from around the world. Meanwhile, Norman McLaren and an elite group of artists continued to bend the rules of conventional filmmaking and set new standards in the field.

The studio's wartime foundation shifted when Jim MacKay resigned in 1949. Animation was annexed to the documentary unit under executive producer Tom Daly, but it was given its own modest budget. Twenty-five-year-old Colin Low was named the new unit head. It was a decision by acclamation because most of the senior staff had left. Daly simply walked into the studio and asked whom they wanted to head it: "Colin," everyone shouted.

Low was a popular choice with the young NFB staffers. He was a perfectionist who fought the bureaucracy for new equipment and in return demanded polished products from his filmmakers. Most of all, Low was ambitious — he wanted to compete with the big boys of animation south of the border. He went on an information-gathering trip to the United States, visited five studios, and evaluated their production phases. He placed particular emphasis on the Walt Disney and UPA studios.

Low was also a favourite of veteran executive producer Tom Daly, and became the unspoken leader of the pack of maverick filmmakers that included Bob Verrall, Wolf Koenig and

Colin Low, named new studio head in 1949, is one part artist and one part inventor.

Roman Kroitor. During the fifties and early sixties, they were the poster boys of the NFB, given enviable freedom and support, and allowed to explore different mediums and styles. Kroitor worked primarily as a documentary director, but he frequently contributed storyboard ideas to the animation unit or experimented on new equipment with Low.

Wolf Koenig was hired in 1948 as an editing assistant. He would start his day at 5 a.m. and work until 9 p.m. splicing films. He spent the rest of his days cruising the halls looking for odd jobs and absorbing all the technical knowledge he could. A lot of time was spent hanging around the animation department. "I was a pest, a nuisance," says Koenig.[28] "They had to hire me to get rid of me." Low offered Koenig a position after two film projects were unceremoniously dumped into his lap.

Allan Ackman had just scripted two films –*The Age of the Beaver,* a film about the fur trade, and *Team Work – Past and Present,* an elaborate film about the trade union movement — when he was swept up by the McCarthyite wave and pushed out the door. The latter film was slated to be the first big cel production, and Low was caught off-guard by the scope of the project.

Cel animation was a sophisticated art form in the United States, but in Canada the first group to try it used British paints that didn't properly adhere to acetate. Instead, the team, comprising Low, Verrall and Koenig, experimented with different concoctions. Low tried mixing egg with tempera paint and baking it onto the cels. Finally someone let him in on the "secret." Low learned that Grumbacher cel paint stuck to acetate and was now on the market. They also discovered that adding gelate to India ink eliminated paint chipping. The paint omelet problem was solved.

Teamwork – Past and Present (1951), a film that traces the proletariat/owner relationship throughout history, was a competent if not especially artistic first crack at full cel animation. Ironically, the film itself was a lesson in labour management. The whole crew learned the techniques from scratch, and production was arduous. At first, it took an entire week for six artists to ink and paint 150 cels. Even these were dirty and full of mistakes. It took two months before the team could get production levels to 1,000 cels per week. The esti-

Teamwork – Past and Present *(top and bottom) was the first coloured cel film to be produced at the NFB. It was started by Allan Ackman, a polemist fired from the NFB in 1951 for his Communist views. Colin Low and a team of six artists finished the film.*

mated budget doubled. But there were more headaches. The paper backgrounds buckled and the cels caused refraction shadows, so repainting was necessary. In addition, the NFB's cramped and dusty studio space on John Street caused paint abrasions, and the two animation drawing boards bought from the United States were insufficient.[29]

Don Mulholland, head of English Production, ridiculed Colin Low's complaints about the abject working conditions. He forwarded Low's report to Film Commissioner Arthur Irwin with an appended note: "I thought you might be interested in reading the attached which is not a Dickensian description of an 18th century torture chamber, as it may first appear, but only a delineation of the working conditions in our Art Department. Strikes me, Colin Low may be wasting his talent in the Animation Department. Maybe we should have him scripting sob stories."[30]

Despite enormous technical problems with their first film, Colin Low, Wolf Koenig and Robert Verrall attempted a second cel film entitled The Romance of Transportation *(top and bottom). The Academy of Motion Pictures pitted* The Romance of Transportation *against* Neighbours *in 1953.*

It was an inauspicious start, but the new troika swiftly moved on. Their second kick at the cel can, *The Romance of Transportation in Canada*, earned them an Academy Award nomination in 1953. *The Romance of Transportation* was a watershed film for the NFB. It was the first "cartoony" film produced entirely on cel — no paper backgrounds. Koenig turned out to be a natural cartoonist, and ended up animating most of the film, while Low and Verrall concentrated on background design and direction. Koenig's bulbous-nosed, buggy-eyed characters became a blueprint for a new generation of Canadian animators. Koenig made effective use of key positions and scrimped on the in-betweens, just like the UPA innovators.

Cartoon gags for the straight-laced public sector threw the government's emissary for a loop. Robert Winters, minister in charge of the NFB, sat through a sneak preview of the film in silence. When the lights came on, he turned in anger to film commissioner Arthur Irwin and demanded to know who had authorized the film. "I did," replied Irwin, "and what's more, I predict right now that the film will win international awards."[31] Its reception in the United States and Canada prompted Irwin's successor, Grant McLean, to assert that the animation department should produce more such films.

Cel animation had long been considered too expensive and too commercial for Canada's film studio. *The Romance of Transportation* shattered that perception. It was a history lesson suitable for the classroom, but riveting enough for a mass audience. It played six months in New York's Loews Theater.

The commercial success of *The Romance of Transportation* was not universally applauded within NFB ranks. McLean's suggestion to shift more resources into cel production created a philosophical rift between the first generation of NFB animators who advocated economical techniques such as paper cutouts, and the post-war hires who wanted to experiment with the more expensive cel process.

Evelyn Lambart was part of the camp that hated cel animation. In her opinion, cel animation was simply an assemblyline process and all the characters looked the same — cute. "Colin managed to sell them on doing [cel animation] and that's when they began having people who just did cel and didn't have to have any brains," says Lambart. "[Norman and I] didn't want anything to do with it. That was Colin's business. He felt we should do it to compete with the US. But we could never compete with them, not with the kind of money [US studios] had."[32]

In the opposite corner stood Koenig, who still believes that cel animation is the only technique that permits full facial expression and fluidity of movement. He rejects Lambart's sweatshop analogy: "The NFB only employed a handful of inkers and painters, and they were all flexible — they were able to do other work in the department."

The Academy of Motion Picture Arts and Sciences unwittingly pitted these two camps against each other when it nominated both *The Romance of Transportation*, and Norman McLaren's *Neighbours* for the Academy Awards held in 1953.* McLaren won the prestigious prize, but not the war. A decade later, cel animation ruled the roost at the NFB. The transition took years. There was no coup in 1953, partly because the architects of this new revolution eventually got sidetracked making documentaries. Low and Koenig crossed genres and made vanguard cinéma-vérité films including *Corral, City of Gold, Lonely Boy* and *Circle of the Sun*.

Low, however, hired young filmmakers with experience in cel animation who would carry the baton. Gerald Potterton was the first in a wave of talented European animators who would enhance the Film Board's reputation. As a young animator at the London animation house Halas and Batchelor, Potterton worked as an assistant and in-betweener on the feature film *Animal Farm*. But the London smog was depressing and Potterton decided to escape to the wilds of Canada. He had a plan: it was to hook up with the filmmakers of *The Romance of Transportation*. Despite his experience, Potterton

Colin Low and Roman Kroitor develop a device to control the acceleration and deceleration of camera movement over still photographs. They use the "Kroitorer" apparatus to shoot black and white stills taken during the Klondike gold rush of 1898. The final film, City of Gold, *wins 17 international awards. The duo are instrumental in the development of Imax technology in the late sixties.*

was not assured a job. Instead, he had to bide his time working for Jack Snow, a Sparks Street jeweller who needed commercial advertisements for his store. The NFB eventually hired Potterton to make a film for the Royal Canadian Air Force.

Envisioned as a simple cel animated film instructing air crews about the dangers and side effects of hyperventilation at high altitudes, Potterton's directing debut, *Huff and Puff* (1954), was so funny that marketing officers argued for its general release three years after the film was produced.[33] Potterton was teamed with Grant Munro, noted for his wit and comic timing. In fact, some of the comic shtick can be attributed to Munro's horrible experience researching the film.

Huff and Puff was Gerald Potterton's directing debut. Produced for the Canadian Air Force, it was never released to the public.

It would have been sufficient for Potterton and Munro to research the statistics and listen to the testimony of air pilots, but producer Frank Spiller insisted that one of the directors should experience firsthand the effect of hyperventilation at high altitudes. Potterton had served in Britain's Royal Air Force and was an experienced airman, but as the senior partner on the project, Munro was assigned to ride with Canadian fighter pilots. It was an unforgettable flight. By the time the plane landed, Munro had vomited eight times into his helmet, and his legs had ballooned from G-Forces. Not to mention the little scare he received when the pilot thought one of the engines was on fire. The lesson was learned. The film conveys with great success the dizziness and confusion a pilot can experience under stress.

Its resounding success, however, is primarily due to Potterton's clever design and deadpan humour. It launched Potterton's directing career. Despite repeated requests by the NFB's distribution people, the air force would not sanction a general theatrical release. *Huff and Puff* never found a wide audience.[34]

Gerald Potterton works on
Fish Spoilage Control.

Potterton worked back and forth between Canada and Britain in the fifties and his enthusiasm for British commercials infected the NFB. He persuaded Low to let the new cadre animate a series of short sponsored films for the Department of Labour and CBC TV. They were fabulous training films — 30 second exercises intended as fitness projects to build creative muscle.

Following his *Huff and Puff* debut, Potterton animated *Fish Spoilage Control* (1955) for the Department of Fisheries. The title says it all — how fishermen must keep fish fresh between the time they bring in their haul and put it on the table. And it speaks volumes about the NFB's talent for making the mundane seem magical.

Potterton's devilish bacteria are a convincing graphic reminder that fish rot is harmful, even deadly. After expounding on the multiplication of tiny micro-organisms, the film ends with a hungry restaurant patron lipsyncing this terrible line: "Fresh Fish, Delish." It was the second time an animator at the NFB tried lipsync. Potterton doesn't even remember how he learned it. "I probably cribbed from a 'How-to' book," he jokes.[35] Of course, NFB animators got much more proficient at marrying dialogue and lip action. It helped that the new generation already had some commercial experience, and passed it along.

As an instructional film for the fisheries industry, *Fish Spoilage Control* surprised everyone with its festival legs. The film had a degree of sophistication, and the director never underestimated his audience. Rather than choosing traditional jigs or pop tunes, he allowed composer Eldon Rathburn to use a contemporary jazz score. This musical choice caused Mulholland to pen another memo, this time to executive producer Tom Daly: "I don't know many professional fishermen, but I would be willing to hazard a guess that they were comparatively simple fellows with an ear more attuned to a western hit parade than progressive jazz, and in cartooning perhaps more old fashioned than that displayed in *Fish Spoilage*."[36]

Fish Spoilage Control
was the second lip sync film produced at the NFB.

It was not the first nor the last time the animation unit was questioned for its highbrow tastes. The government clients preferred a more conservative approach to their propagandizing shorts. They registered complaints, but the studio frequently dug in its heels, refusing revisions. The animators were often vindicated by fan mail, strong box office numbers, and film awards. Good press silenced opposition.

The public service announcements produced after the war often spoofed icons of the time. Hollywood feature films were a popular target of the NFB animators. It's a Crime, a PSA warning against seasonal unemployment, parodied The Third Man, an espionage flick starring Orson Welles and Joseph Cotton.

Parody was a favourite tool, and like today, Hollywood and British features provided great fodder. The NFB fifties gang indulged in post-modern, self-referential jokes long before and R*en & Stimpy* made waves on television. Koenig and Potterton were the earliest Canadian pop culture satirists.

Do It Now: Don't Wait for Spring, a series of films addressing the scintillating subject of labour shortfalls, was fashioned after Peter Sellers' *The Goon Show.* Potterton's personal favourite was a short produced for the Department of Forests entitled *Money Burn* (1964). The writers added up the government's forest fire bill, which turned out to be three times the budget of Elizabeth Taylor's *Cleopatra* — the most expensive film made at the time. *It's a Crime* (1958), a film animated by Potterton and directed by Koenig, is a spoof of *The Third Man*, an espionage flick starring Orson Welles and Joseph Cotton. Their debonair thief gains insight into the economy when cracking vaults. Based on his inability to earn a living during the cold weather, the thief deduces that the problem is due to seasonal unemployment. Following a personal investigation, he offers sage advice to employers. Hailed by the *Globe and Mail* critic as "entertaining and original," *It's a Crime* suffered the same fate as *Huff and Puff* — poor distribution. The film's sponsor, the Department of Labour, planned to send the film on a service club and civic organization circuit. But at its premiere at the Stratford Film Festival, the 13-minute cartoon drew such critical applause that plans were made for TV and theatrical bookings. Despite its entertainment value, the film's message had no impact on its target audience. Unemployment rose 10 percent in the following year.

Gerald Potterton effectively mined the humour of Stephen Leacock for the hilarious short My Financial Career *(1962).*

The film that best exemplifies Potterton's dry wit and versatility is the wildly popular, *My Financial Career* (1962), based on a short story by Canadian humourist Stephen Leacock. Potterton replaced the bulbous-nosed characters popularized by Koenig in favour of a stylized format borrowed from French graphic artist Jan Lenica (Monsieur Tête). The eyes became dots, the nose triangular, and the body rimmed by a thick black pencil. The heavy outline lent itself to paper cutouts, so Potterton temporarily abandoned the cel approach. *My Financial Career* was the first of Potterton's many films nominated for Academy Awards. Eighteen years later, Potterton turned to Leacock for inspiration once again and brought to life the neurotic and nervous Melpomenus Jones.

It was soon clear to even US network executives that Potterton had the right stuff for mainstream audiences. Just two years after directing *My Financial Career,* another short entitled *Christmas Cracker* was up before the Academy Award judges. Potterton landed a deal with Paramount to direct a half-hour TV special based on the same premise. Frustrated by his inability to find the perfect object to place on the top of his Christmas tree, Potterton's animated character rockets himself into space to capture a live star to bring back to earth. His simple line-drawn cartoons mirrored shorts by George Dunning and Richard Williams in England. It shows the convergence of cartoon taste between artists who travelled across the continents.

Potterton gradually drifted into live action filmmaking. *The Ride* (1965) and *The Railrodder* (1963) were storyboarded as animated films but shot in live action. But he never completely abandoned his animation roots.

Derek Lamb was also part of the cel vanguard at the NFB. He has always drawn a parallel between magic and animation. Lamb's own father, an amateur magician, taught him the sleight-of-hand trick when he was a boy. The lessons stayed with him, says Lamb, because in the world of animation, a little of the hocus-pocus — "now you see it, now you don't" —applies.[37] Like true magicians, animators must use timing and alter perception to maintain the illusion. *The Last Cartoon Man* (1973), a film Lamb directed with Jeff Hale, illustrates his philosophy. In the film, a man performing on stage is able to dazzle his audience with amazing feats; he can remove a nose, eyes, arm and even a head. The thesis is simple: animation is the ultimate magic act.

While camping out at Montreal's YMCA in 1958, Lamb attended a screening of Norman McLaren's films. Like those before him, Lamb could not resist the call of animation's very own Pied Piper. He practically parked himself on the studio's doorstep and begged for an audience. When freelancer

Derek Lamb's
The Last Cartoon Man

Christmas Cracker *was supposed to be a short vignette included in an NFB holiday package but it was released separately after it was nominated for an Oscar Award. The director, Gerald Potterton, was approached to direct a similar narrative for Paramount.*

Cameron Guess abruptly departed the studio to claim an inheritance, Lamb was waiting in the wings.

Animation teams of more than three people were practically non-existent at the NFB, but by the early sixties, the NFB equivalent of the "Rat Pack" were assembling groups for larger pictures. *The Great Toy Robbery* (1964) required 12 artists. The principals included Jeff Hale and Cameron Guess who returned to the NFB to co-direct and animate the film. The rest of the team included Lamb (writer/designer), Verrall (background artist), and a group of painters and in-betweeners whose job it was to draw the intermediary frames based on the animator's key drawings.

In a take-off on the old westerns of the twenties, poor Santa Claus is robbed by three robbers who hide out in a bar and greedily play with the toys. Santa and the Sheriff are shot at when they try to recover the stolen gifts.

The film is pure cartoon camp. In a take-off on the old Westerns of the twenties, poor Santa Claus is robbed by the three robbers who hide out in a bar and greedily play with the toys. Santa and the sheriff are shot at when they try to recover the stolen gifts. A klutzy Dudley Do-Right character, who bears a resemblance to the handsome, square-jawed, guitar-strumming writer himself, inadvertently saves the day.

The Great Toy Robbery was originally produced as part of a holiday package that included Potterton's *Christmas Cracker*. Programmed as nonsensical, cream-puff filling, the film expanded as the ambitious team members reworked their idea. By completion time, it was evident the film should be launched separately. NFB distribution sold it to Columbia in Canada to screen before Stanley Kubrick's

Dr. Strangelove. Its extravagant budget and popularity caused a bit of a tiff in the studio. Low viewed it as a learning experience for the young animators and delighted in watching a strong creative team emerge. Wolf Koenig, a rather utilitarian producer/director, found its lack of depth an embarrassment. Moreover, the team's disorganization and the constant revision made him uncomfortable. In Koenig's eyes, Lamb, Guest and Hale were out of control.

The new A-team was short-lived. They split up during the production of *I Know an Old Lady Who Swallowed a Fly* (1964). Lamb had originally planned to work with Hale on an adaptation of Alan Mills' lively song about an old lady who dines on a menagerie of insects and mammals, but a dispute ended their association. Acting quickly, Lamb cornered Kaj Pindal — another cel enthusiast — at a party. Over drinks in the kitchen, he insisted Pindal pick up where Hale had left off. *The Old Lady* was already over-budget and behind schedule, but Pindal jumped into the fray. He even set aside development on his own project, *Peep*. Together, Pindal and Lamb overcame the production red tape and completed the film.[38]

The Old Lady is a delightful adaptation with plenty of playful animation. A memorable scene features the dear old lady swallowing a chortling cow that wiggles and jiggles and tickles inside her. Pindal was already a favourite of the studio's honchos. With this film, he became heir apparent to the cel throne.

Kaj Pindal has a recognizable graphic style. Over the years, he has drifted towards economy of design and lines. His trademark is spaghetti legs, rounded torso, and happy face smiles. In his quest to achieve "pencil mileage"[39] — the most movement with the fewest lines — Pindal created *Peep*, a barnyard chicken. Peep underwent a multimedia transformation in the nineties — from black and white film to CD-ROM. It probably best exemplifies the childlike energy and exuberance that Pindal injects into his films.

Pindal is the son of a painter, who dabbled in renaissance-stylized landscapes. However, Pindal eschews pastoral scenes and embraces contemporary themes.

Described as having a "cool modernist" style, Pindal is clearly in his element in the film *What on Earth!* (1966), featuring an abstract aerial view of a world populated by cars.[40] His work on director Terence Macartney-Filgate's *The Hottest Show on Earth* (1977) deals with the perceived energy crisis of the seventies.

Kaj Pindal's poses.

Kaj Pindal's Peep *is so simple in design that he could animate it on a roll of toilet paper.*

Kaj Pindal started his career at the NFB animating a technical film about Jet Engines *for the Royal Canadian Air Force. His funny cartoons quickly made him a popular animator in the studio.*

Pindal's first love was comics, but he quickly discovered Walt Disney's short films. As a young artist working for an advertising agency in Copenhagen in the late forties, Pindal regularly snuck out of work to watch movies. Following every feature was a cartoon. One day, Norman McLaren's *Fiddle Dee Dee* replaced what was usually a Popeye short. When the projector stopped and the lights came on, one patron jumped out of his seat and demanded his money back. The guy next to him also leapt to his feet, but not in protest. He argued that it was the best darn thing he'd ever seen. Suddenly everyone shouted out their preference. "From that time forward, I became very interested in the [films] of the NFB," says Pindal.

Back in the forties, cartoon production was cloaked in secrecy. Learning to animate was like decoding spy dispatches. The secret was partially unscrambled for Pindal by former Disney director David Hand, who was lured to Europe by J. Arthur Rank with the promise that Rank would eventually produce feature films. When the feature films didn't materialize, Pindal and a group of other Danish artists invited Hand to Copenhagen to teach them the ropes.

The first contract Pindal landed as an independent was an information film explaining the workings of a ship's marine diesel engine for the German shipping company Burmeister and Wain. The film simplified combustion through a series of diagrams and arrows. It was his ticket into the NFB. In the fall of 1957, he made a technical film about jet engines for the Royal Canadian Air Force.

Pindal proved to be more than just adept at making training and educational films. He was a very funny guy. He made a series of sponsored films under the title *Stop, Look and Listen. I Know an Old Lady Who Swallowed a Fly* was really the first time Pindal exercised his comedic chops.

Pindal and Lamb thrived both inside the NFB and outside its doors. Lamb left the institution in 1964 after run-ins with new executive producer Wolf Koenig. His last two projects — *The Great Toy Robbery* and *I Know an Old Lady*

Who Swallowed a Fly — are unadulterated silly entertainment with high production values and big budgets. Koenig strongly believed in functionality. Each film should serve a greater purpose. For him, Lamb's films were escapist nonsense.

Although he left on a sour note, Lamb's work was not finished at the NFB. Ironically, he too came to embrace the notion that the NFB served a higher purpose, and should engage the public in some kind of debate.

He may have made some crazy shorts in the sixties, but Lamb eventually proved that he was first and foremost an educator and purveyor of ideas. He proved it by producing two animated films to teach street children in the Third World about AIDS prevention, and by making shorts for *Sesame Street* and *Masterpiece Theater*. And he proved it during a successful term as executive producer of the NFB's studio A between 1976 and 1982. Even Koenig must have been proud ... if only from a distance.

I know an old lady who swallowed ... a pig?

The Great Toy Robbery and *The Old Lady* were programmed during a period when the studio was operating on auto-pilot. For years, studio head Colin Low had been distracted by his own films — some of them completely out of the animation realm. He was studio head in name only. By 1964, Grant McLean, head of English Program, wanted someone who would avoid the scandalous budget overruns by keeping a closer eye on directors. He gave Low an ultimatum: "Either manage the animation department or do films." Low's response: "If you put it that way, I guess I better go do the films."[41]

As early as 1954, Low had become less interested in making animated films. Exhausted by *The Romance of Transportation*, and eager to try his hand at actuality filmmaking, Low took Wolf Koenig home with him to Alberta and shot *Corral* (1954), a visual poem about a cowboy and his horse. *Corral* was the progenitor of the cinéma-vérité film. Breaking with tradition at the NFB, Low insisted that the film have no commentary, and the soundtrack consisted only of sound effects and music. It was a radical departure for an agency steeped in propaganda.

Later that year, Low and Roman Kroitor began experimenting with innovative ways to film photographic stills. At first, Low brought in mathematician Brian Salt to calculate very complex acceleration and

Outside the NFB, Derek Lamb and Kaj Pindal reunited to make the AIDS prevention film Karate Kids.

Kaj Pindal illustrates his working relationship with Derek Lamb.

Many of Pindal's characters look suspiciously like his NFB collaborator, Derek Lamb.

deceleration camera movements. With Kroitor, he worked on a tracing device named "The Kroitorer" that could plot specialized pans, close-ups and tilts over a relatively small photograph.

The result was *City of Gold* (1956), a film made from old black and white stills of Dawson City during the Klondike gold rush of 1898. It won 17 awards from the likes of the British Film Academy and the International Film Festival at Cannes. The smooth tracking over photographs has been imitated by many other cineastes. But Low became bored with his invention after two films.

"There was a certain amount of rebellion amongst the animation group. They moved away from the stodgy, pedagogical aspects of [filmmaking], and looked for a livelier and experimental expression," says Low. Once they learned a technique they quickly shed it. "Don Mulholland (NFB head of English Programme) used to complain about us and say: 'You guys invent this wonderful stuff, and then drop it and start something else. Why don't you stick with what you've got? It would be cheaper!'"

By 1956, Low immersed himself in the production of *Universe*, a film that explores the astronomical wonders of the world, using stop-frame, multiple exposure techniques, and model animation. At the time of its release in 1960, *Universe* was a benchmark in the special effects industry. So impressed was director Stanley Kubrick, he approached Low, Wally Gentleman and Sid Goldsmith (also animators on the film) to work with him on his feature film *2001: A Space Odyssey*. Gentleman went to Los Angeles, Low and Goldsmith stayed behind.

Kubrick expressed interest in one particular pan across a star field. Using a 40 exposure shot, the filmmakers were able to simulate the gaseous and luminous effect of the galaxy. The laborious superimposition of images was accomplished manually. In some shots, the identical camera movement had to be repeated 40 times without error, which meant many late nights for the filmmakers. Reflections off a revolving crenallated tin plate created the solar heat flare effect. Low developed the idea after noticing the play of light across his ceiling caused by a simple reflection off his cup of tea.[42]

Science documentaries were a mainstay for Low and Goldsmith. Low used 3-D computer effects in his Imax films *Transitions* (1986) and *Emergency* (1987).

When it was clear to Grant McLean that Low had no plans to cut back his workload, he launched an executive search to replace him as head of Studio A. Low waved good-bye to the animation studio and proceeded to make *Labyrinth*, a highly technical multiscreen film considered a big-screen precursor to the Imax and Omnimax formats.

🍁 🍁 🍁 🍁 🍁

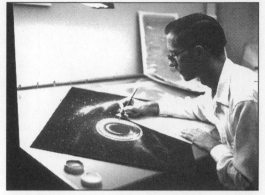

Sid Goldsmith

Having launched himself into the documentary orbit in the early sixties with the acclaimed cinéma vérité film *Lonely Boy* (1962), Koenig returned to save the animation unit from a fate worst than death — a bureaucratic manager. He managed to thwart McLean's plan to hire from the distribution sector by persuading the powers-that-be to try both himself and Bob Verrall as a tag team. Verrall functioned as a senior producer and art director under Wolf, and although they frequently disagreed about details, Verrall says they were in "profound agreement about the general direction of the program."[43]

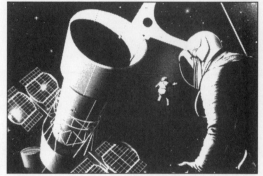

Universe was a benchmark in special effects animation. One pan across a star field was achieved through 40 exposures.

As the new studio chieftains, Koenig and Verrall had to inject fresh creative juices into the mix, and to save it from the budget axe. Koenig believed that the only way to keep the unit operating effectively following the 1965 budget rollback of 33 percent was to find new funding from government departments. Rather than waiting for bureaucrats to suggest campaigns, the new execs developed their own public service spots and pitched them to ministries with deep pockets. And so began the weekly train treks from the new Montreal studios to the nation's capital, where the various federal agencies were based.

Koenig had much success selling his cartoon characters in Ottawa. "Bureaucrats like to laugh just like everyone else, and they soon realized that these films worked," says Koenig. "Once people laugh and open their mouth, the message goes in and there's nothing anyone can do about it. It's like breathing in a fly."

It was not always easy to get the studio artists interested in propaganda films. Low remembers how tough it was to sell sponsored campaigns internally: "You kind of introduced the idea, sometimes gently and sometimes roughly." Koenig was

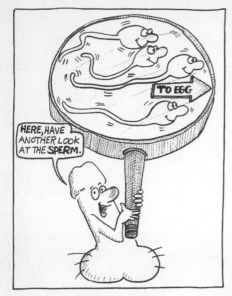

Ottawa bureaucrats balked at Don Arioli's proposal for a sex education film starring Jimmy Penis and Vicki Vulva.

The legendary Chuck Jones circulated the Jimmy and Vicki storyboard among educators in the US. Eventually Arioli went to work for Jones as a writer.

particularly inventive in massaging ideas and making them palatable to both animators and clients alike. Despite grumbling by some filmmakers who wanted to work exclusively on personal films, the sponsorship era did not drain the NFB of creativity. On the contrary, some of the funniest toons ever made in Canada include a series of anti-smoking clips for the Department of National Health and Welfare, a film promoting fire safety, and a silly short selling the notion of national unity to French and English Canadians.

The dynamics created by this strange liaison between artist and paper pusher led to some interesting results. "The NFB was set up by Grierson in such a way that the arrogant artist and the blockhead bureaucrat were pitted against each other," says influential storyboard artist Don Arioli.[44]

The animators became experts at effectively injecting a little satire and self-deprecating humour into the films, and the civil servants were the conservative sounding boards for new ideas. Whenever they could, animators tested their clients' limits. Arioli jokes that as a government-financed film studio, the NFB got away with many tricks because it already had a "Fuck-you" budget to spare. A private organization could not have pushed through the jokes and ironic script without losing all its backing. There were occasions, however, when the studio was reined in. Whereas a playful attack on smokers showing a dog pissing on a cigarette butt was acceptable, a direct sex education film starring Jimmy Penis and Vicki Vulva was not.

Jimmy and Vicki are legend at the NFB. So is their creator, Don Arioli. Recruited in 1966 from Film Design in Toronto, Arioli was the studio's best storyboard artist. A colleague described him as a "wordsmith, salesman and tap dance artist," and his style dominated the sponsorship era.[45] Arioli decided one day to make a sex education film after his young daughter inquired whether it hurt when mommy and daddy made love. Arioli wanted to set the record straight, so he drafted a script for Health and Welfare that showed how the birds and the bees, the horses, and even the humans, did it. Although department officials secretly loved the concept, they wouldn't approve it until Arioli covered Adam and Eve with a blanket. Incensed at this request, Arioli returned with an even more outrageous board. "I figured, if they wanted it to be abstract and isolate the act, why not go all the way and abstract it to the point were it was just organs involved," says Arioli.[46] Jimmy and Vicki were born, and although they were never brought to animated life, they became a cult storyboard and circulated for years.

If Lamb and Hale were Colin Low's boys, then Don Arioli was Koenig's. Arioli quickly asserted himself as the government's court jester. He became the ultimate pitch man of the sixties and seventies. Arioli drew and performed every concept for NFB's clients. Koenig and Verrall alternatively played the straight man role. On more than one occasion, Arioli would sketch a storyboard on the train going to Ottawa, and revise it on the train back. His inability to meet deadlines would drive Koenig mad — but not mad enough to dump him. Some of the NFB's best ideas were born on that Montreal-Ottawa track, including, *What On Earth!*, *The Drag, Tax Is Not a Four Letter Word*, and *Propaganda Message* (1974), a film directed by Barrie Nelson.

Propaganda Message takes a poke at Canadian identity and government. Rather than making a sappy film about unity in English and French Canada, the animators decided to gently mock some of the Canadian clichés — the beaver, snow, parliament hill, to name a few. The title, *Propaganda Message*, was a sophisticated way of telling the audience: "We know that this is a little government goodwill film, but hey, aren't there some good points to Canada?" It is an evocative example of how no cow was sacred at the NFB — not even nationalism.

Winnipeg-born Barrie Nelson was a hot young star in Hollywood when Koenig and Verrall first called him up to direct a Manitoba Centennial public service announcement, and to work on *Propaganda Message*. His animation in John Hubley's films *Herb Alpert and the Tijuana Brass* and *A Windy Day* (1968) had earned him a solid reputation in the field. His "Hubley-styled" approach carried into the films he directed for the NFB during the seventies. In *Propaganda Message*, Nelson adopted the anti-realistic backdrops favoured by Hubley. The colours look as if they were mopped directly onto the screen, and spill beyond the contours of the characters.

Propaganda Message is an evocative example of how no cow was sacred at the NFB — not even nationalism.

With this newly sponsored-film cash cow, Koenig and Verrall were free to hire expatriates such as Nelson. They also endeavoured to hire other international stars such as Carlos Macheorri (Spain), John Hubley (US), Les Drew (UK), Mike Mills (UK), Zlatko Grgic (Yugoslavia) and Bretislav Pojar (Czechoslovakia). Pindal and Potterton continued to direct some wonderful shorts for the new studio heads.

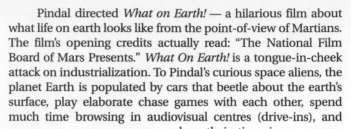

Pindal directed *What on Earth!* — a hilarious film about what life on earth looks like from the point-of-view of Martians. The film's opening credits actually read: "The National Film Board of Mars Presents." *What On Earth!* is a tongue-in-cheek attack on industrialization. To Pindal's curious space aliens, the planet Earth is populated by cars that beetle about the earth's surface, play elaborate chase games with each other, spend much time browsing in audiovisual centres (drive-ins), and when their time is up conveniently remove themselves from society by checking into a dismantling plant (car wrecking company).

Although Pindal directed the film, and his creative stamp is evident, *What On Earth!* was actually animated by Les Drew, another British expatriate who left school at 15 years of age, and joined Halas and Batchelor in 1957. It wasn't until 1964, when the NFB was in a position to hire new freelancers, that Drew made the trans-Atlantic trip. Drew was not an ideas man, but he took Pindal's layout and smoothed out the edges. The film is testament to Drew's years as a commercial artist. The flow and timing exceeds that of Pindal's earlier films.

Drew directed numerous sponsored films including *Tilt* (1972), an exposition arguing for the redistribution of resources in the world; *In a Nutshell* (1971), a film about the Canadian International Development Agency; and *Man: The Polluter* (1973), a film co-produced by the NFB and Zagreb Films. He also directed four young animators (Pino Van Lamsweerde, John Weldon, Blake James and Robert Doucet) on the production of the *The Energy Carol* (1975), a film starring the irascible Ebenezer Scrooge who takes audiences on a trip to the spirits of energy past, present and future.

After years working on Pindal's films, Drew directed and animated the popular *The Old Lady's Camping Trip* (1983), a fire and outdoor safety video for Fire Prevention Canada. Lacking the confidence to design his own characters, Drew mimicked Pindal's style, but three years later, he would cast off the design

Arioli was the resident storyboard artist and court jester of the sixties. The "every man" conceived for Arioli's films was in his own image — short, round and balding as seen in director Ron Tunis' The House That Jack Built *(above)* and Man: The Polluter *(below).*

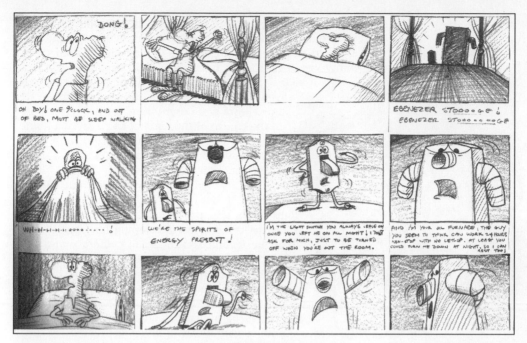

shackles, and create his own characters for a video about accident prevention.

Drew's most imaginative character is Wally the Safety Dog, the star of *Every Dog's Guide to Complete Home Safety* (1986). Wally is a delightfully pompous pet whose self-appointed mission is to ensure that everyone in the home sticks to basic safety rules decreed by the National Safety Council. In creating his protagonist, Drew struck a balance between patrician concern and madcap confusion. Poor Wally knows better, but his family remains blissfully ignorant of hazards in the home. One of Canada's largest mining firms, Inco, bought 5,000 videos for its employees. No doubt many other Canadians exposed to the film bought a dog.

Michael Mills, the whiz-kid of British commercials, arrived in Canada shortly after Drew to animate *Tax Is Not a Four Letter Word* (1966). A high school dropout in London, Mills was directing commercials by the time he was 18. By age 21, he had accrued credits on 150 spots and directed episodes for the TV series *The Lone Ranger.*

Success had burned Mills out. After seven years in the commercial field, he craved adventure. So when Les

The storyboard from The Energy Carol *directed by Les Drew. Scrooge is a chip off the Don Arioli block of design.*

Les Drew mimicked Pindal's style but later developed the delightfully pompous Wally the Safety Dog.

Drew offered a contract for the NFB, he jumped. An experience in Canada was just the tonic for a jaded animator in his mid-twenties. "When I came to Canada, I asked them how long I had to do it," says Mills. "They told me one year. I almost fell over. I was hoping for maybe three months." As Mills discovered, the NFB didn't work at a commercial pace. "That's part of the charm of the place. I came from a high-powered commercial background, and suddenly I was back in art school again. I went from one extreme to another."[47]

Mills tried to fit into the corporate culture of the NFB, but old habits die hard. He worked long hours and processed film in his cupboard when the lab delayed developing his pencil tests. When the technicians found out, there was a big meeting, and Mills was forced to stop. Just seven weeks into his one-year contract, Mills was halfway through the film. He was told to slow down. One contract led to another. His second NFB credit was *Dynamite* (1970), a hilarious anti-smoking public service announcement involving an explosives man so desperate to light up a cigarette he chases a burning fuse all the way to the bomb and gets blown sky high.

The NFB was famous for its outrageous series of anti-smoking clips. Michael Mills' construction worker tries to light his cigarette by chasing a burning fuse along the ground until he reaches a stack of dynamite.

Years after quitting the institution, Mills still harbours a love-hate relationship. His beef is with the bureaucracy. He also argues that the lack of pressure and deadlines can be self-defeating: "Every artist is a lazy son-of-bitch. You've got to push yourself. Left to my own devices, I could be totally idle. I could sit in the NFB cafeteria for six months."

Although his sabbatical from England was only to last a year, the NFB had some "leftover" money in its budget to produce an educational film, and Mills stayed on to work on his story idea about evolution. Taking creative licence with animal physique, Mills neatly conveys Darwin's theory of natural selection. Rather than working on cel, Mills chose to work on paper using self-matching colours. It was an optical assembly job. *Evolution* (1971) was also drawn on an uncommonly small 3x4 inch paper radius. He worked on a close field so that everything would naturally stay loose. Large drawings accommodate detail. The small field forced Mills to draw a looser style, and out of the experience he developed his "shaky line," akin to New York cartoonist R.O. Blechman.

Despite the film's didactic intent, *Evolution* entertained Academy members who later nominated it for an Oscar. Mills' shaky design was also copied in Canada. Not only did Sesame Street animators imitate his style, but Mills borrowed the look for some of his later commercials. In 1972, Mills took a leave of absence to direct *The Happy Prince*, a half-hour TV special for Potterton Studios. He never returned.

Zlatko Grgic, a talented Yugoslavian filmmaker, was recruited by Verrall and Koenig after they saw his film *Scabies*, a dark parable accurately foretelling the collapse of the Soviet Empire. He worked on several shorts including Arioli's

Michael Mills drew his film Evolution *on a small 3x4 inch field. The restriction forced him to draw in a loose manner. He later refined that for his commercial work.*

storyboard *Hot Stuff* (1971). Some clever improvisation by Gerald Budner and Grgic turned Arioli's funny layout into a little masterpiece. It all started in the studio session when Budner, an animator himself, began ad-libbing voices for a snake and the cat. Arioli got a bit annoyed with Budner's banter, but Koenig loved the asides, and insisted that they remain. Grgic had complete freedom to improvise. The cat never interacts with the main character because it never existed in the layout. In the end it serves as an animated Ed McMahon — a comic visual sidekick.

The fantastic collaboration with Grgic led to a large-scale collaboration with Zagreb Films, the Yugoslavian production company where he worked. It was a filmic match made in heaven. Eight of Grgic's colleagues worked as animators on *Man: The Polluter* (1973), a film that shows man's capacity to foul his own nest and ignore it.

Grgic lived in Zagreb until the early eighties when the studio collapsed. He moved permanently to Canada to work in advertising and teach at Sheridan College. Although the bulk of his films were produced at Zagreb Film, Grgic had a huge impact on the Canadian scene.

The comical cat in Zlatko Grgic's film Hot Stuff *was invented after Gerald Budner ad-libbed in the sound studio. Budner's witty asides amused producer Wolf Koenig so much that he asked Grgic to invent a character and insert it into the film. Grgic's sourpuss sidekick remains an NFB favourite.*

For years, the NFB was involved in an anti-smoking crusade with the Canadian Department of National Health and Welfare. Smokers made great targets for humour, and Carlos Marchiori had a field day with *The Drag* (1965). It had one of the shortest production schedules in the history of the studio. Koenig and Verrall knew only one man who

Carlos Marchiori produced his spot, The Drag, *in just two weeks. Despite the hasty production schedule, the film was nominated for an Oscar award in 1966.*

could meet the two-week delivery deadline imposed upon them. That man was Carlos, but all they knew was that he was living somewhere in Tokyo. Verrall spent one night on the phone tracking him down and making reservations on the next plane back to Canada. Two weeks later the clip was delivered.

The Drag begins with a smoker reclining on the psychiatrist's couch recollecting how he became hooked on the weed and how he's tried to break the habit. Marchiori combined cel animation with a pastiche backdrop of magazine clippings to brilliantly skewer tobacco companies and advertising. The film was given a nod for an Oscar.

The NFB's studio had a field day with subsequent anti-smoking shorts such as *King Size* (1968) by Kaj Pindal, and *Where There's Smoke* (1970), a series of films by 12 directors and animated by Pindal, Michael Mills, Blake James, Al Sens and Wolf Koenig.

During this period, the executive producer baton was passed between Koenig and Verrall. The dynamic duo ran the studio together between 1964 and 1967, until Koenig left to pursue live-action films. Verrall continued in the position until 1972, when he passed it back to Koenig, and was bumped upstairs to be director of English Production.

Low's critique of the Koenig "era" was simply that his successor loved to convert everything into a cartoon. "In some cases, it didn't fit either the style or the sponsor," says Low. Many of the characters in the large budget films looked and sounded similar. The "every man" conceived for Arioli's films were in his own image — short, round and balding. They stammered, muttered, grumbled about the new metric system, having to buy a bra for the wife, and Canada's aid packages to Third World countries. Arioli initially voiced his own characters in films such as *The House That Jack Built*, and *Hot Stuff*, but George Geertsen's gentle whine was favoured in other sponsored shorts including *In a Nutshell* (1971) and *Ten: The Magic Number* (1973).

By the early seventies, the private sector's challenge to the NFB's industrial monopoly took its toll. Independent film companies wanted those lucrative contracts. Studio A's cavalier attitude toward bureaucrats gave the government another good reason to take its business elsewhere. Ministry officials entertained more tenders.

The era of artist as propaganda messenger was winding down. The last straw was the battle between the Department of External Affairs and Studio A over the film *What the Hell's Going On Up There?* (1977). External Affairs wanted a film for foreign consumption that could neatly summarize the Canadian constitution and issues such as Quebec independence. But the film had more bite than the government bargained for. Its mix of satirical cartoons and acerbic interviews with Canadian authors and personalities such as Margaret Atwood, Mordecai Richler, Marshall McLuhan and Quebec independantiste Pierre Bourgault proved to be a little too nationalistic and anti-American for the embassies to stomach. Many refused to take the film.

Memos flew fast and furious between Canadian embassies, External Affairs and the NFB, but Lamb refused to make significant changes to the film. For the most part, *What the Hell's Going On Up There?* sat on the shelf. In 1981, External Affairs replaced the film. This time, they bypassed the NFB and hired a commercial company to produce the short. The government's decision was a great blow to the NFB. It lost both production monies and its important role selling Canada abroad.

A police dog burns out in Kaj Pindal's Caninabis.

The sponsorship era at the NFB inevitably led to battles between bureaucrats in Ottawa and NFB artists. Kaj Pindal was able to show a dog peeing on a cigarette in the anti-smoking film, King Size.

The self-parody of the early sponsored shorts served Canadians well. Later generations of animators have maintained the NFB's critical edge when producing commercials. In the spirit of these government-employed wise guys, animators such as Marv Newland (*Hooray for Sandbox Land*) and Danny Antonucci (*Lupo the Butcher*) have managed to push the envelope of acceptable commercial material, and carve out a distinctive style. Canadian audiences are more apt to digest a little satire with their public service announcements, and perhaps as a result Canadian artists have the stomach to dissect the dominant American culture and expose its contradictions.

Cold War Paranoia

In the 1950's, the animation studio produced a mixed bag of educational films and sponsored shorts. The Defence Department and Atomic Energy were regular clients. In this Cold War climate, it was mandatory for animators to get security clearance from the Royal Canadian Mounted Police. Sidney Goldsmith worked on so many government projects that his office was fitted with a steel door that was locked at all times. Some of the security measures were over the top. Grant Munro was assigned to produce an air force training film in 1951. It required a graphic depiction of what a bomber sees when he looks through his sights to line up a target. In order to draw it properly, Munro was blindfolded and then driven to a building in Ottawa. He was escorted into a room where they removed his blindfold long enough for him to peer into the viewfinder. "All I could see was an 'x,' " says Munro. "They blindfolded me just so I would know how to draw an 'x.' "

chapter 4

Hockey & Other Canadian Themes: The NFB Matures

If there is one subject that can define, unify and divide Canada, it is hockey. The calling is so strong that Canadian animators such as Steve Williams and his cohorts took the game with them when they descended on Industrial Light and Magic outside San Francisco. They organized hockey leagues and kept a table-hockey set within easy reach of their computer keyboards. It should come as no surprise that one of the most successful shorts in the history of the NFB, *The Sweater* (1976), is about a Quebec boy's love of the game. In his heavily accented English, writer Roch Carrier narrates the tale of a young Montreal Canadiens fan who becomes disconsolate when forced to play ice hockey wearing the team sweater of the rival Toronto Maple Leafs. Sheldon Cohen's film manages to both underline the tension between English and French Canada, and celebrate the shared passion of the two solitudes for the sport.

The Sweater illustrates how the NFB stretched itself thematically during the seventies and early eighties. How-to shorts were supplanted by films with cultural concerns. The shift in content was not premeditated. The NFB was unceremoniously pushed into a new reality by an aggressive private sector lobby that wanted the NFB to stop working on government contracts. Restrained from bidding on public service assignments, the studio increased its focus on ideas generated by the animators themselves. It was a hard blow to storyboard king Don Arioli, who thrived on commercial challenge. However, the door opened for a new generation of animators who wanted nothing to do with the cartoony character used to promote government services. The third wave of artists was able to experiment with complex stories and various graphic styles.

Wolf Koenig ushered in the sponsored era in the early sixties, but by the mid-seventies, he accepted that film should not be seen simply as an informational tool. After years of programming sponsored works, Koenig began to green-light projects that drew from the well of literature and music. "Film is a means of reflecting back to the community what it is, and without the knowledge of who you are, you can't act," says Koenig. The films of the seventies began bridging the information/cultural divide. Story adaptation was the preferred device.

Yvon Mallette adapted E.B. White's short story about the Pruiett family of Barnetuck Bay who lived a secluded and quiet life on an island until one cold winter day someone on the

Yvon Mallette scores a festival hit with his adaptation of E.B. White's short story about the Pruiett family of Barnetuck Bay.

mainland reported that the family was in distress. The rescue parties met a tragic end, and everyone's lives were turned upside down. Mallette's style fell somewhere between cartoon and illustration. *The Family That Dwelt Apart* (1973) was nominated for an Oscar, in part because the narration, read by E.B. White himself, struck just the right note of irony and wit. Two years later, Cohen successfully interpreted a CBC radio reading of writer Roch Carrier's short story, "The Sweater." Literary adaptation was a successful formula.

Caroline Leaf, a talented freelance artist contracted by the NFB, wanted desperately to animate Kafka's *Metamorphosis,* but Koenig insisted that she mine the work of Canadian authors for her next project. Leaf dutifully obliged. It was a compromise that led to a masterpiece. Leaf took Mordecai Richler's short story, "The Street," and crafted a film using oil-on-glass technique. Textured images wiping across the screen give a rhythmic account of a young boy growing up in a Jewish neighbourhood of Montreal. *The Street* (1976) became a favourite abroad, earning numerous awards and an Academy Award nomination. It became a benchmark for Canadian animation. Leaf's ability to animate camera moves, make seamless transitions, and create interesting perspective, show the power of illustrative form. In many ways, she paved the way for a new generation of animators. Even Frédéric Back, who is much older than Leaf, cites her as an influence.

Hockey serves as an analogy for linguistic strife in Canada in Sheldon Cohen's film The Sweater.

Before employment equity became a catch phrase — and the NFB hired its own equity watchdog — Koenig practised it. In addition to Leaf and Janet Perlman, Koenig hired Lynn Smith for a series of anti-smoking spots. He gave Evelyn Lambart the budget for *The Lion and the Mouse* (1976), a cutout film based on Aesop's fables, and brought master puppet animator Lotte Reiniger into the studio to direct *Aucassin and Nicolette* (1975), a timeless tale of love won and lost using her famous silhouette puppets. Up and coming female animators such as Joyce Borenstein, Gayle Thomas, Anastasia Michailidis, Micheline Lanctôt and Veronika Soul found support through the studio. The influx of women animators meant an increase in abstract styles and techniques.

Koenig precipitated change in the studio, but he became distracted with his own animation project in the Far North. He fell into the same hole that his predecessor Colin Low had toppled into. His long absences caused morale to plunge. Derek Lamb, Koenig's old nemesis, was recruited to come back and run the studio at the end of 1975. Lamb picked up where Koenig left off, completing films that were already programmed, including Sheldon Cohen's *The Sweater*, Caroline Leaf and Veronika Soul's *Interview*, and two films by Perlman — *Why Me* and *The Tender Tale of Cinderella Penguin*. Koenig had an eye for talent, but Lamb had a way of challenging his staff to squeeze the most out of them. His five-year stint would produce some of the best animation to come out of the NFB studio. The proof was on the podium; the NFB won two Academy Awards and landed three more nominations during his tenure.

A protégé of Colin Low, Lamb had left the NFB in the mid-sixties to work with Halas and Batchelor in London. He moved on to Harvard University, where he set up an animation course. Back at the NFB, Lamb threw himself into brainstorming and storyboarding. He was rigorous and demanding, and he liked to include outside experts in his encounters with artists. Geneticist David Suzuki was brought in to do *The Hottest Show on Earth* (1977), and UN consultants were used during research on Eugene Fedorenko's Oscar-winning film, *Every Child* (1980).

During development of Janet Perlman's *Why Me* (1978), Lamb recruited a host of psychologists and doctors. They were consultants, informing the filmmakers about patients' reactions after learning they had a terminal illness. The final film takes viewers on an emotional rollercoaster ride. The main character is informed by his doctor that he has just minutes to live. In a rapid-fire exchange with his doctor, Nesbitt Spoon runs the gamut of feelings, from despair to acceptance. At one point Nesbitt declares: "Well, it's a good thing my condition isn't as bad as it could be." That tragicomic line was supplied by one of the film's doctor-consultants, who once treated a terminal patient in denial. "None of us could ever dream up such a response," says Lamb.

In a rapid-fire exchange with his doctor, Nesbitt Spoon runs the gamut of feelings, from despair to acceptance when he learns that he has only minutes to live in Janet Perlman's film Why Me.

John Weldon drew the underground comic The Pipkin Papers *while working as an insurance actuary in the sixties. The comic helped him land a job as an assistant animator at the NFB. Pipkin Papers now fetches $50 from San Francisco collectors.*

Weldon vents his disdain for bureaucrats and guidance counsellors in Spinnolio, *a film starring an inert wooden puppet.*

Lamb's rigorous agenda had its opponents: "I would say to our animators over and over again: 'We are the best in Canada. But we need to talk to smart people who know what they are talking about.'" Lamb felt the NFB's old *modus operandi* of drawing first, and worrying about the story later, should be reformed. It was too hit and miss. He wanted to know that the stories worked, and the films had something to say; but that proved to be a tough battle. Lamb clashed with a number of animators including NFB storyboard artist Don Arioli. They didn't see eye-to-eye. Lamb wanted Arioli to write more relevant scripts.

Sparks also flew between Lamb and John Weldon, a young humourist with a flair for writing. In Weldon's case, the battles ignited a creative streak that resulted in an Oscar for the studio. "John's a great guy, but like us all, he can be lazy around the edges, and not take an interesting idea all the way," says Lamb. His frankness cost him a friend. On the other hand, it found him a wife. After completing two films together, Derek Lamb and Janet Perlman got married.

John Weldon worked briefly as an insurance actuary before becoming an animator. On the side, he created the underground comic *The Pipkin Papers* and wrote plays. Weldon was not a trained animator, but his rough comic-book drawings and sardonic wit made him an ideal candidate for sponsored work. Hired by Robert Verrall to paint and trace on the film *Hot Stuff*, Weldon leap-frogged from contract to contract. His directorial debut was *You've Read the Book — Now See the Movie* (1975). His mission: to make tax palatable.

Weldon thrived during the sponsorship era, but under Lamb's supervision his career soared. His first independent film, *Spinnolio* (1977), not only offers a sociological reading on the Pinocchio fable, it also gives new meaning to the term dead wood. In Weldon's version of Pinocchio, a group of school kids drag a wooden puppet named Spinnolio to school. Over time, Spinnolio graduates school and advances up the corporate ladder to become a career consultant. Spinnolio passively reclines, yet pulls in a regular paycheque until one day, he is replaced by a computer, and is literally dumped into the streets. By the time the good fairy arrives to grant Spinnolio the gift of life, he has been adopted by bums. Poor

Spinnolio starts his life as a drunk —
not exactly the stuff of fairy tales.

Weldon brandishes two daggers in
this film — one for bureaucrats and the
other for career planning consultants.
The vindictiveness he directs towards
the banal and benign stems from a personal experience with a career counsellor during the sixties. He sarcastically
attacks bureaucracy and mediocrity,
but also criticizes the holy grail of technology. Spinnolio foretells the human
cost of the post-automation era.

"In 1974, people began contem-
plating what they would do with all the
leisure time that was supposed to be
coming their way because of the new technology. What they
didn't realize was that it would translate into unemployment," he says.[48]

Weldon is a crusader for everyman. The characters in
his films ask broad ethical questions about genetic engineering (*To Be or Not to Be*) or the cult of personality in politics
(*The Lump*). Citizen Weldon, however, is at his very best
when he mines his own guilty conscience. *Special Delivery*
(1979), a murder mystery involving an unshovelled sidewalk
and a postman, reflects Weldon's innate fear that one day the
post office will come after him because he neglects his yard.
The macabre short won an Oscar in 1979. Weldon attributes
the film's success to the fact
that its protagonist is an
average, irresponsible
schlump, who gets away with
murder and still lives happily
ever after. "The NFB doesn't
make films like that any-
more," sighs Weldon.[49]

A banjo enthusiast,
Weldon revived the folk song
tradition in the animation studio when he animated to the
McGarrigle sisters' rendition
of *The Log Driver's Waltz*
(1981), a delightful ditty about
a young woman who sings
about the grace and daring of
her favourite logger. Music
has since become an integral
part of Weldon's storytelling.
He writes and composes
songs for many of his films.

*Spinnolio is a satirical take on
the fabled tale,* Pinocchio.

In the film Special Delivery,
*John Weldon creates a cartoon
alter-ego – a man who lives in
constant fear that he will one
day be punished for his
slovenly habits.*

Music has become an integral part of John Weldon's films. Today he performs most of his own material, but for The Log Driver's Waltz, Weldon called upon the musical talents of the McGarrigle sisters.

The idea of animating to music came to him long after he joined the NFB. It was probably around the time Chris Hinton bought a mandolin, and Weldon took out his old banjo.

Over the years, Weldon's lyrics have overtaken his visuals; he is more songwriter than animator. In *The Lump* (1991), Weldon manipulates unsightly puppets on metal fishing line sinkers, paying little attention to movement and flow. Weldon's intention was to make a folkish puppet film, but the hapless puppets are overwhelmed by the decorous backdrops such as a swimming pool of inlaid gold tile. The overdone backgrounds overshadow the characters.

The combination of media and colours of *Scant Sanity* (1996) is also hard on the eye. However, his commentary, sung by Bowser and Blue, remains provocative. It revisits the futility of aptitude tests given by counsellors. For *Scant Sanity*, Weldon draws on a personal experience with a counsellor who officially informed him that he was a lunatic and should seek help. Instead, Weldon took the guy's unofficial advice and joined an artistic institution. But he can't help toying with the notion that perhaps he really went to the insane asylum and is just wandering around thinking he is an animator. There is, after all, a fine line between genius and madness.

Many animators and graphic artists let colour and design speak volumes. But for Weldon, the medium is not the message. His latest films are almost "animated radio" — a term once used by Chuck Jones to describe the satirical prime-time series *The Simpsons*. Like many series, Weldon's style is derived from comics, but his films have an intellectual weight rarely seen on television.

There remains a quiet battle of wills between the graphist and the cartoonist at the NFB. While Weldon embraces the "cartoon," Ishu Patel flatly rejects that term for his work. "If you are a cartoonist you get hooked on one particular theme. In other words, humour is your basic subject matter. If it can't be dealt with humourously then you won't do it. I'm more interested in creating emotions, exploring the spirituality, fantasy, sensuality and the supernatural."[50]

Ishu Patel arrived at the NFB in 1970 on a six-month scholarship that he stretched into a year. Ever since a wooden box laden with NFB films arrived in his village school in India, Patel had dreamed about working for the NFB. The small collection of films shipped to rural areas of India contained gems by Norman McLaren. It was not the kind of fare the kids were accustomed to. "To their surprise the first film was not a live-action film or a cartoon with which they were familiar. Instead it was a fast-moving, lively abstract film with great music. Three minutes after it ended, everyone shouted: 'Oh no, the projector's broken again.' It was not true, the film was only three minutes long. They all wanted to see it again and again. The film was *Blinkity Blank*."

Patel is a talented graphic artist who trained at the National Institute of Design in Ahmedabad, India, and Allgemeine Gewerbsschule in Basel, Switzerland. In 1970, he received a scholarship from the Rockefeller Foundation to study animation in North America. He chose to spend his scholarship year at the NFB in Canada, where he made *How Death Came to Earth* (1971), an adaptation of an Indian folk tale created using cel and cutout figures. His first sponsored films at the NFB were functional vehicles for External Affairs dealing with issues related to reproduction, puberty and venereal disease. With his hat trick of education shorts, Patel proved himself to the executives in charge. Koenig permitted him to make *Perspectrum* (1974), an experimental essay on colour and geometry.

Patel's palette expanded during Lamb's regime. His strategic use of back light creates lush films that border on the meta-physical. *The Bead Game*

Visualizing other spiritual dimensions is Ishu Patel's intent in Afterlife.

(1977) is a dazzling short produced by manipulating thousands of beads into the shapes of various animals. Patel's assembly and disassembly builds feverishly during the film, concluding with an image of annihilation as the accumulated beads shatter.

Patel planned to score the film using Indian music, but executive producer Derek Lamb counselled him to use a percussion soundtrack which would underscore the war the-sis. "I've never seen anyone get involved as much as Derek did, but he never forced anyone," says Patel. *Bead Game* won a British Academy Award and was nominated for an Oscar.

In *Afterlife* (1978), Patel undertakes a spiritual journey using accounts of near-death experiences. By sculpting Plasticine across opaque glass, and illuminating it from

Fantasy and the fantastic are the stuff of Ishu Patel's films. The resplendent birds symbolize envy in his film Paradise *(above).* Divine Fate *(below) is a parable about renewable resources.*

beneath, Patel is able to simulate a dreamlike state. He constructs another magical kingdom in a subsequent film, *Paradise* (1984). Shafts of coloured light streaking through perforations cut into a black-paper back-drop create a bejewelled city — a paradise. There is a dark morality tale to be told. In this fair kingdom, a plain blackbird bedecks itself with rich plumage. But as the film implies, vanity and envy are not liberating emotions. The faux pea-cock is locked away to be admired. Patel is telling us that our obsession with beauty and perfection can create gilded pris-ons for our souls.

Visually resplendent, Patel's films are sometimes criti-cized for their intellectual coldness. There is no viewer/char-acter bond with either the misguided bird in Paradise or the starving masses in *Divine Fate* (1993), a parable about renew-able resources. *Divine Fate* visually instructs without offering an emotional outlet. The message it telegraphs is a simple one: you can take from the earth as long as you give some-thing back. The weakness of the film is that it never goes beyond hypothesis. It never descends to earth to directly con-nect us with the wretched humans it portrays.

During Lamb's reign, his hands-on approach proved successful for both Patel and Eugene Federenko, the director of the Academy Award-winning short *Every Child* (1980). Produced at the invitation of the United Nations to celebrate UNICEF's Declaration of Children's Rights, *Every Child* is the story of a baby who mysteriously appears on the doorstep of a busy executive and is subsequently bounced from household to household along the street. The film highlights one of the ten principles of the Declaration: every child is entitled to a name and a nationality. Both poignant and funny, the film is exemplary in its sensitive treatment and artistry.

The film's success was due to the collaboration between Fedorenko, Lamb and the comedy troupe Les Mimes électriques. This creative nucleus brainstormed story and characters over several weeks. When it was time to be presented to the NFB's programming committee, Lamb arranged to transfer the storyboard to projection slides and have the troupe perform the soundtrack, complete with sound effects and music. "I didn't want people thumbing through a 50-page drawn script and just getting off on the drawings. I wanted people to see it as a film," says Lamb.

Despite all his best efforts, one member of the program committee announced that he would not vote for the film because the performers entertained him, not the storyboard. Lamb pacified him by promising to include the troupe in the film. This concession solved a major creative problem — how to open and close the film. Les Mimes électriques performed in the studio during the recording of the soundtrack, and the footage used to create the opening and closing cues. Audiences loved the device. Not only could they enjoy the troupe's performance, but they were also privy to behind-the-scenes production of an animated film. The film achieved a perfect balance between humour and pathos.

Near the end of his tenure, Lamb faced some difficult decisions; budget cutbacks and a recent ruling by the Public Service Staff Relations Board (PSSRB) that stipulated that 99 percent of the freelancers, working on back-to-back contracts, were employees by definition. Already top-heavy, the NFB was forced to expand its roster of employees. A huge chunk of the unit's annual budget was now ploughed into salaries. The PSSRB decision and continued cuts to the NFB's parliamentary allocation effectively wiped out resources to hire new freelancers.[51] While long-time contract employees such as Gayle Thomas, John Weldon, Ishu Patel, Gerald Budner and Meilan Lam were guaranteed employment, the new kids on the block — Eugene Fedorenko and David Fine — were shown the door. Fine moved to the United Kingdom to train at London's National Film and Television School. Fedorenko was forced to teach to make ends meet.[52]

Lamb publicly argued against the cutbacks and the government's callous disregard for talented artists such as Fedorenko. His plea fell on deaf ears. Compounding fiscal issues, Lamb faced internal opposition from the new director of English Programme. Peter Katadotis replaced Ian McLaren in 1979. Lamb and his new boss clashed over the issue of NFB sponsorship.[53] Katadotis supported the government's desire to hand over all sponsored jobs to the private sector. Lamb did not agree. He believed that the filmmakers

An unwanted baby is bounced from door to door in Eugene Fedorenko's provocative and funny film honouring UNICEF's Declaration of Children's Rights.

The release of Ludmila Zeman and Eugen Spaleny's film, Lord of the Sky, *was delayed after the filmmakers were accused of cultural appropriation.*

worked most effectively when their projects alternated between sponsored clips and personal projects.

Lamb's position was weak, particularly because he did not have the full support of his own staff. Many animators felt sponsored vignettes violated the integrity and artistic purity of their own work. Exasperated by the continual infighting and pettiness within his own unit, Lamb decided to step down. He wanted Michael Scott, executive producer of the prairie region to step up to the Studio A plate, but Katadotis had another man in mind.

Doug MacDonald, a former teacher and NFB producer of filmstrips, was management's chosen one. Although he lacked animation experience, many Studio A staffers acquiesced to his appointment. "They figured they would have a cozier life with him," says Lamb. "No challenges, no surprises, just nice, pleasant, annual work reports. I left the Board in 1982, sick at heart about it all."

Former executive producer Robert Verrall was also upset with the decision, but kept quiet, because his son, David Verrall, was the acting executive producer in the studio. Today, he no longer minces words: "I knew Doug for years as a stupid producer in Studio G — a jerk. I couldn't believe Katadotis sent him up to animation."[54]

The burden of cutbacks and change fell onto MacDonald's shoulders. The discretionary funding available to the studio dropped to 5 percent of the total allocation. MacDonald now had more directors than money for films. To add to the unit's woes, the sponsorship creek had dried up, and MacDonald was without a creative paddle.

MacDonald was a safe choice, but not a particularly inspiring one. From the start of his tenure, he looked to internal committees for thematic solutions. Rather than develop good literary material or original stories, MacDonald handed out children's storybooks as he would a class assignment. Lamb warned that this strategy would diminish the animator's role to one of interpreting other's work and thus undermining the studio's own creative talent.

MacDonald believed his studio had a number of solid animators, but they were weak with narrative. They needed structure and focus. There wasn't enough money in the budget to hire outside directors or writers to assist, so MacDonald

demanded that his staff themselves animate storybooks. "Some of the very talented animators were not strong writers and needed a bridge," says MacDonald.[55]

In the past, the tried and true veterans like Don Arioli and Kaj Pindal supplied the structure or glue. MacDonald correctly assessed that their look was tired. Unfortunately, he had no firebrands to lead his own charge. Instead, MacDonald distilled his philosophical approach into a simple administrative list.

"One by one he told us what he expected of us during the time he was there, and the kinds of films we could do," remembers Gayle Thomas.[56] "He had a list from one to seven — Canadian artists, Canadian literature, I can't remember them all. Then the very last number was wild idea or great idea. And I said: 'Great that's the one I'll pick.' And he replied: 'You can't do that. That's very extraordinary. We won't be doing very many films like that.'"

From Les Drew, MacDonald asked that he continue the accident prevention theme that was so successful in *The Old Lady's Camping Trip*. From others, he sought Canadian content. Patel is still smarting over MacDonald's suggestion to use maple leafs in his film *Paradise*.

MacDonald was keenly aware of the studio's legacy, but he was not prepared to climb out on any shaky limbs. After all, Katadotis had appointed him because he had a track record as an administrator, not because he was an artist. The organiza-

Les Drew borrowed Kaj Pindal's design for The Old Lady's Camping Trip.

The NFB adapted a series of lacklustre children's books including The Dingles *(above) and* Blackberry Subway Jam *(below).*

Pies is the antithesis of Sheldon Cohen's previous film The Sweater. Pies *is a morality tale about two feuding neighbours told in bold black and blue imagery.*

tion once criticized for harbouring Communist and bohemian elements had ushered in the small "c" conservative era. Producer David Verrall, hired by Lamb in 1979, adopted the role of agitator and pushed for the bold and riskier projects. "It was not our most expansive period," says Verrall, diplomatically.[58]

The stellar reputation of the studio faded during his tenure, which produced beautifully animated but lacklustre films such as *The Dingles* (1988) and *Blackberry Subway Jam* (1984). Sheldon Cohen's *Pies* (1984) was one successful adaptation from a short story by a Saskatchewan writer. *Pies* was the antithesis of *The Sweater*. The bold black and blue images produced using ink on cel tells the story of two feuding neighbours — both new immigrants — who attempt a domestic truce. On the pretense of friendship, one woman invites her neighbour over for afternoon tea and serves manure pie. After engaging in pleasantries, the malicious neighbour feels twinges of guilt, and in an act of contrition eats a slice of the offensive pastry herself. *Pies* horrified a lot of people because of its content, and the fact that it dealt with racism.

MacDonald also favoured adapting legends — a popular thematic choice of Evelyn Lambart. Adaptations were less flavourful when tackled by Françoise Hartmann in *Summer Legend* (1986) and *The Long Enchantment*, a film made with tapestry-like cutouts and pencil on frosted cel. Gayle Thomas' *The Phoenix* (1990), based on the story by Sylvia Townsend Warner, lacks the tenderness of the *Boy and the Snow Goose* (1984) or the graphic impact of her earlier film, *Sufi Tale* (1980). Even Thomas felt she was just illustrating someone's story and didn't enjoy the process as much.

MacDonald ran into the political correctness wall with Ludmila and Eugen Spaleny's film *Lord of the Sky* (1993), inspired by Haida and Tsimsian legends. In his quest for the community's and educator's stamps of approval, MacDonald found himself caught up in a bureaucratic nightmare. The beautiful paper cutout animation sat in the vaults until the dust finally settled because people worried about the possible appropriation of a Native legend.

The acrimony created by MacDonald's arrival led to the departure of Caroline Leaf and Janet Perlman. Ishu Patel did not make a film for six years. The studio was divided.

The gulf between the public and private sector widened during the 1980s and 1990s. Once upon a time, filmmakers such as Michael

Mills, Kaj Pindal, Gerald Potterton, and Les Drew traversed comfortably between commercial studios and the NFB. They picked up sponsored contracts, and occasionally they had a film of their own greenlighted. That bridge had collapsed. Increasingly, animators drew lines in the sand. NFB animators began to see themselves as "artists" and quietly condemned those who had "sold out" by accepting jobs in the commercial arena.

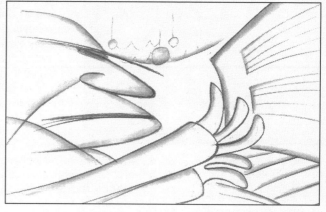

The commercial community showed its contempt for the cloistered group of NFB artists in a passive-aggressive manner. It provided little support for the NFB following the release of the Applebaum-Hébert report in November 1981, which recommended that the NFB be turned into a training centre and stripped of its production role. Darts posted on bulletin boards are not infrequent. This one was found in the lunchroom of a large commercial house in Toronto. The pin-up read:

George Geertsen captures the rhythm and movement of Madame Bolduc's music.

> "*Top Ten Reasons Why NFB animator* _____ _____
> *took 8 years to finish her film.*
> *1) Because she thought NFB stood for 'No Film Before its Time.'*"

Poor direction did not stamp out the creative soul. It never really can. Staff animator George Geertsen made the delightful *La Bastringue Madame Bolduc* (1992), Robert Doucet further explored sketch/illustration with *Dreams of a Land* (1987), and Weldon remained consistently funny.

Patel's assistant on *Paradise*, George Ungar, received a budget to make his own film, *The Wanderer* (1988), using monochromatic oil on glass. Based on Michel Tremblay's short story *The Devil and the Mushroom*, the film is a dark tale of a stranger who arrives in town and feeds on the townsfolk's weaknesses — greed, gluttony, envy and lust. The stranger's

Storyboard panels from The Wanderer, a dark parable of a strange man who steals into town and arouses the most base instincts of the quiet community.

George and Rosemary by David Fine and Alison Snowden.

arrival unleashes their passions, and chaos ensues. The dramatic tension created at the start of the film is not fully exploited, but Ungar's bacchanalian transformations are beautiful.

Canadian-born David Fine and Briton Alison Snowden (former students of Britain's National Film and Television School) were recruited to make *George and Rosemary* (1987), the pilot film in producer Eunice Macaulay's *65 Plus* series. In the hands of this talented duo, what could have been a didactic little story about geriatric love, became a charming film that captures some of the idiosyncrasies of the elderly. Known for their oblong faces and button noses, Snowden and Fine's characters can project both innocence and naughtiness. The *65 Plus* series did not proceed, but as a solo effort, this film stands on its own.

In 1983, MacDonald established the Opportunities program to give recent animation graduates the chance to prove themselves. MacDonald and producer Eunice Macauley scouted student festivals and managed to cobble together funding over the next decade to hire a handful of hopefuls including Wendy Tilby and Craig Welch.

When Barrie Angus McLean joined the NFB as executive producer in 1992, he sought outside financial sources. His savvy move was to back David Fine and Alison Snowden in their film *Bob's Birthday* (1995) commissioned by Britain's Channel 4. On the eve of his 40th birthday, Bob arrives home and has a heart-to-heart with his wife Margaret. Meanwhile invited surprise party guests remain crouched behind couch and curtains and listen to the conversation. Mid-life crisis meets major faux pas in this short by the talented husband and wife team. After two tries at the bat, the duo finally hit a home run on Oscar night. Their win couldn't have come at a more opportune time. Oscar's gold-plated figure became a Teflon shield used to defend the middle-aged studio from further cutbacks.

McLean's second strategy was to negotiate a broadcast pre-sale to a Canadian cable network, Bravo. The extra money was not enough to seriously underwrite the costs of the films. Instead, McLean used the sales as collateral of sorts. With a broadcast commitment, he could twist the arms of the NFB's money men to ensure the films received continued support.

"A critical mass of people was needed in the studio to keep morale and energy high," he says.[59] The balance between staff animators and freelancers was also critical to life in the studio. In order to preserve this integrity, the producers committed three times the normal production output a year through pre-sale agreements. Personnel remained stable, but tempers did not. The pressure to complete 14 films in just a few years frayed nerves. The studio skated on thin ice, psychologically.

The Id and Ego battle it out in No Problem.

While McLean may have outmaneuvered managers inside the NFB, journalists criticized the Bravo deal as the work of a poor salesman. One critic argued: "In its rush to reach viewers, however, the NFB appears to have sold its best wares for cheap."[60]

Freelance animators made seven of the 14 films intended for broadcast. It was a second film for many of the independents, including Tilby, Welch, Heidi Blomkvist and Brian Duchscherer.

Craig Welch was the last filmmaker to slip into the NFB under the Opportunities program. Welch took a few turns in the career path until he ended up as a mature student at Sheridan College. When most of his younger classmates drew dinosaurs and rocketships, Welch made

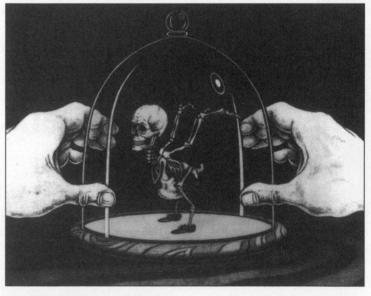

Craig Welch does a stylistic backflip for his second film How Wings Are Attached to the Back of Angels.

Disconnected, a film about common problems in daily life. *Disconnected* impressed NFB producer Eunice Macauley enough to bring him into the studio to develop a storyboard. His response was the cel animated short, *No Problem* (1992), a film about the internal war between id and ego. Welch's debut film is thematically linked to Weldon's but his style is pure cartoon.

Chapter 4

76 ....

A defective batch of cels result in an unusually innovative background in the film The Alchemist *(above and below). Assistant Jennifer Small accidentally discovered that she could literally Xerox photographs of cityscapes directly onto the cels. The technique can never be duplicated.*

Welch did a stylistic backflip for his second film under McLean. *How Wings Are Attached to the Back of Angels* (1996), is replete with cross-hatching and rendering of the human anatomy and strange instrumentation. It is a complicated approach requiring every ounce of knowledge Welch gathered from earlier industrial design studies and his short-lived years as a painter in Toronto. The film is about a man who obsessively controls everything around him. With logical precision, he attempts to understand an enigma — angels and flight. In the end, his obsessive nature costs him everything.

Independent animators rarely change their style from one film to the next; however, Welch changes mood and technique with each project. His stylistic range is unparalleled in the unit.

Heidi Blomkvist adapted a Peter Desbarats' poem, *Lucretia* (1986), using pencil on frosted cels. Her second film, *The Alchemist* (1992), has severe narrative problems, which unfortunately overshadow her interesting character style and the innovative Xeroxed backgrounds created by Jennifer Small. A flawed batch of animation cels actually soaked up the ink giving the film an airbrush effect. The technique will never be reproduced again.

Long-time staffer Bob Doucet based his film, *The Legend of the Flying Canoe* (1996), on the Quebec folk legend *La Chasse-Galerie*. The film is a dark tale about a lumberjack who makes a pact with the devil on New Year's Eve. A magical canoe can fly through the cold winter night to reunite family and friends for a festive evening. There is one condition. The men can never touch a cross or speak the Lord's name.

The Flying Canoe was the culmination of 20 years of filmmaking. A graphic artist in Montreal, Doucet joined the NFB's graphic department in 1965, after Yvon Mallette left his post to pursue directing. After years of assisting filmmakers such as Michael Mills, Doucet received a big break when the NFB commissioned him to do a vignette for its series on history, geography and culture.

The vignette series gave many filmmakers an opportunity to flex their creative muscles. Weldon made *Log Driver's Waltz* (1981), his first musical film. Doucet finally had the freedom to experiment with styles and discover his niche. That niche turned out to be films pertaining to Quebec history, crafted in a loose illustrative style.

Doucet came into his own with *Dreams of a Land*, a colour pencil sketch based on the journal of famous explorer Samuel de Champlain. His rendered style was further refined in *The Flying Canoe*. Its only drawback is the digitized colour system implemented in the studio. The spectrum of colours and subtle shading is sacrificed at the altar of technology in this case. The heavy magenta and special effects weigh down the illustrative images.

Luckily, the digitized colourization applied to Les Drew's latest offering, *Shyness* (1996), works better because of the flat cel characters. The twisted Dr. Frankenstein of Mary Wollstonecraft Shelley's novel is a kindly, benevolent inventor in Drew's cartoon version. Drew's Dr. Frankenstein helps his monster overcome their debilitating shyness. The film is as predictable as a self-help book, but Drew creates the entertaining sidekick character Trevor, who provides most of the comic relief.

Animators considered McLean a more expansive and supportive executive producer, but he had his share of duds. Thomas' *Quilt* (1996) is an uninteresting graphic exercise on computer. Munro Ferguson's *How Dinosaurs Learned to Fly* (1996), is a borderline preschool project. The film received much attention when distributors selected it as a feature film preview to run in theatres, but it does not have the comic timing and sight gags of Janet Perlman's *Dinner for Two* (1996).

Shyness, as well as George Geertsen's film, *Words* (1996), both suffer from an NFB malaise. The well-intentioned shorts are overcooked edu-tainment products. The filmmakers themselves are caught between making films that are to meet the educational mandate requested by their bosses, and the artistic legacy passed on to them. Continually struggling for self-justification, staff animators are clearly conflicted.

The NFB has been in decline for many years because of rudderless leadership. Film Commissioner François Macerola succeeded in reinforcing the institution's corporate image on Parliament Hill, after navigating through a tricky policy strait. However, at the end of his tenure, Macerola's loyalties were divided. He signed an expensive Imax co-production deal with his future employer, Lavalin Inc., and had started negotiations to make the NFB's technical services available to Lavalin's new audiovisual project.[61]

After creating Wally the Safety Dog, Les Drew invented a group of terribly reclusive monsters for his film Shyness.

The next film commissioner, Joan Pennefather, warded off government vultures trying to peck away at her budget, by currying favour with the Minister of Culture Marcel Masse. Ignoring protests, Pennefather stepped aside on Oscar night to allow Masse to accept the NFB's special Academy Award in 1989. Unfortunately she did not articulate a vision to bring the institution into the next century. When she departed in 1994, public sympathy was at an all-time low.

The NFB survived many attacks from the government and the private sector, but years of shaky leadership weakened its pillars. Tragically, the NFB is slowly being dismantled.

Like all departments, the animation studio is affected by the seismic tremors rocking the NFB. Just before stepping down as executive producer of Studio A in September 1996, Barrie McLean stated: "I think it's a sad time at the NFB, because we've had to limit and cut our activities, not because of a lack of money — there's more money in the world than there's ever been — but because we lack people with the courage and humanity to stand up for products which have a social responsibility. They've bowed down before a belief that corporate identity driven by marketing is more important than a cultural identity driven by a sense of social responsibility. I'm sorry to witness the decline of this once great institution." In his office on a rainy summer day, Barrie McLean's words rang like a requiem.

NFB Academy Award Nominations and Awards

Neighbours 1952*	Sand Castle 1977*
The Romance of Transportation in Canada 1952	Bead Game 1977
	Special Delivery 1978*
A Chairy Tale 1957	Every Child 1979*
My Financial Career 1963	The Tender Tale of
Christmas Cracker 1964	Cinderella Penguin 1981
The Drag 1966	Paradise 1984
What On Earth!1967	The Big Snit 1985
The House That Jack Built 1968	George and Rosemary 1987
Pas de deux 1968	The Cat Came Back 1988
Walking 1969	Blackfly 1991
Evolution 1971	Strings 1991
The Family That Dwelt Apart 1974	Bob's Birthday 1994*
Hunger 1974	La Salla 1996
Monsieur Pointu 1975	
The Street 1976	*Oscar award winners

The dates listed are the actual years these films were made.
The Academy Award presentations were held the following year.

chapter 5

The French Revolution

For two decades, animation in Canada was the domain of English-language practitioners. French folk songs were embraced, but Quebecois ideas were not. Norman McLaren's protégé, René Jodoin, was asked to form an animation division in the NFB's French Production in 1966. He paid homage to his old master by forming a non-traditional film unit that embraced puppet animation, scratch-on-film and multimedia. Celluloid cartoons remained in the realm of Studio A.

Mainstream and experimental merged in the seventies when Jodoin and his successor Robert Forget were swept up with the brave new world of computer graphic imagery. Jodoin had caught a glimpse of the future; it was in the primitive computer drawings from Nestor Burtnyk's lab at Ottawa's National Research Council. Jodoin instinctively knew the medium would change animation forever, and he collaborated with the research team. For the next decade, Jodoin boldly charted a separate course for the French animation studio.

Those who know him well — like filmmakers Pierre Hébert and Francine Desbiens — see him as the keeper of Norman McLaren's legacy at the NFB, and an innovator in his own right. Even after retirement, he continued to experiment.

"René Jodoin is an innovative thinker, a true visionary," says Desbiens. She adds: "He always had a clear vision of the studio's future, which helped those around him know exactly what to expect. He had a frugal approach to cinema, which contrasted sharply with the path taken by English animation in the late sixties. UPA had enormous influence over English animation, but our inspiration comes from the NFB films of the forties. He taught us to make do with scraps."

Jodoin himself credits the old master for many of his innovations. McLaren showed him how to make films for next to nothing, a lesson that served the French animation team well. For the most part, Jodoin provided key technical support for documentaries, particularly map sequences and titles. It was a defining era.

That shaped Jodoin's vision of animation. He saw it as a craft, a somewhat experimental one at that. He remained faithful to this initial vision throughout his career.

L'heure des anges combines Bretislav Pojar's puppets with exquisite pinscreen backgrounds by Jacques Drouin.

Jodoin met the father of Canadian animation in 1943 when he was recruited from Montreal's École des Beaux-Arts to make up the first animation team assembled at the NFB. McLaren was instantly impressed with the contemplative introvert. "He revealed himself to be a thinker, and an interesting one," said McLaren. "He was knowledgeable on the subject of motion, and it was clear that he had a wider view of the possibilities of animation than just cartoons."[62] Jodoin absorbed McLaren's philosophy, and shared his passion for mathematics and motion. Together they attempted to make an animated film featuring characters in constant, unchanging motion. In their 1948 experiment, Jodoin and McLaren wanted to see whether or not they could hold the attention of an audience by animating moving spheres that never change their rate of speed. There were no cuts, just one continuous flow of movement. They aborted the film in 1948, but Jodoin completed it 20 years later.

Jodoin's fascination with geometric puzzles and precise calibrations continued. He directed *Four Line Conics* with mathematician Trevor Fletcher. *Dance Squared* (1961) demonstrated the subdivisions and permutations of a square, and *Notes on a Triangle* (1966) revealed an ingenious series of transformations, strictly within the concept of triangularity. *Rectangle & Rectangles* (1984) and *A Matter of Form* (1985) also rely on symmetry.

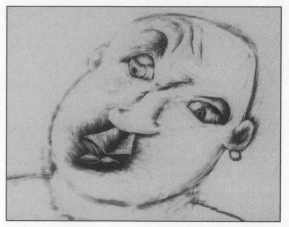

The French Programme had already gotten off the ground at the NFB in 1964. Francophone filmmakers were all grouped together within a single structure — except the animators, that is. Some, like Pierre Hébert, were in the English Programme; others worked outside the department, with the encouragement of Jacques Bobet, the executive producer at the time. But as a result of internal pressure, the French animation studio was finally created.

The French Programme provided fertile ground for women animators such as Caroline Leaf who directed Entre deux soeurs.

René Jodoin was fascinated by geometric puzzles that moved.

Marcel Martin, director of French Programme, made one demand: René Jodoin would have to head the new studio. Once Jodoin agreed, money was siphoned away from the English animation studio to help establish its French counterpart. The start-up budget was a modest $50,000, and was used to assist filmmakers working on educational fare. French animation soon evolved into a full-fledged production unit. "Strangely enough, it was [like] my early days with the NFB all over again," says Jodoin.

As department head, Jodoin's golden rule was to keep animation technically simple, to give directors a greater margin of manoeuvre. The intent was to emulate a painter alone in his studio with a canvas. To succeed, he believed each filmmaker must develop the individual tools that give each film a unique aesthetic. His philosophy was about to be tested on a larger scale.

Among the first filmmakers to join the French team were Bernard Longpré, Pierre Moretti and Pierre Hébert, a seasoned independent filmmaker who directed five short films under English animation's umbrella. Later members included Francine Desbiens, who left her permanent job at the NFB's photograph library to become an animation apprentice,

*European auteur,
Paul Driessen, was
embraced by the NFB's
French animation
department. He produced
Une vielle boîte
in the studio.*

and students Jean-Thomas Bédard and Viviane Elnécavé.

The goal of the unit was to nurture and safeguard cultural creativity. But Jodoin was not interested in creating a Quebecois ghetto. He was open to a vast array of styles, techniques and backgrounds. His progressive approach is the reason Quebec became a hotbed of experimental films.

Caroline Leaf is indicative of the liberal tastes embraced by the NFB's French animation studio. An American immigrant, Leaf normally would have worked in the English unit. The fact that she did significant work with the French studio proves that the language division at the NFB had become, in the case of animated films, an aesthetic division. The studio enabled her to perfect the sand-on-glass experiments she started at university, and to interpret the Inuit legend, *Le Mariage du hibou* (*The Owl Who Married a Goose*, 1974). Indeed, Leaf's visual experiments in a film like *Entre deux soeurs* (*Two Sisters*, 1990), involved etching on 70-mm film and rephotographing it on regular 35-mm, was philosophically more in tune with French animation.

Improvisation was key. The studio forged a name for itself because of the quality and technical diversity of the product. Styles ranged from scratch-on-film to the early pinscreen experiments that resemble animated engravings. Jodoin led the way with his three films based on abstract shapes. Along these same lines, Pierre Moretti produced *N'ajustez pas* (*Do Not Adjust*, 1970), and *Variations graphiques sur Télidon* (*Graphic Variations on Télidon*, 1981). Pierre Hébert followed McLaren's lead by etching on film *Souvenirs de guerre* (*Memories of War*, 1982).

The ghost of Norman McLaren hovered in the French workshops. Pixilation — the technique used in McLaren's film *Neighbours* — was frequently used in the French Studio. Bernard Longpré used it in *Dimensions* (1966), as did Roland Stutz in *Taxi* (1970). The most unusual stop-motion technique was employed by André Leduc in *Monsieur Pointu* (1975) in which objects are moved by manipulators wearing black costumes and hoods to make them invisible to the camera.[63]

Experimentation was the mantra. Suzanne Gervais developed her own multiplane animation method using cutouts with *L'Atelier* (*The Studio*, 1988). Ron Tunis neatly blended watercoloured drawings with interviews with children in *Moi, je pense* (*This Is Me*, 1979) and Robert Awad and André Leduc married the documentary and animation forms in *L'Affaire Bronswik* (1978). Jacques Giraldeau's *Opera Zero*

(1984) uses a complete grab bag of tricks including cutouts, drawings, xerography, prints, photography, etching and engraving techniques to illustrate William Shakespeare's stark line: "(Life) is a tale told by an idiot, full of sound and fury, signifying nothing."

The only animator who remotely resembled a traditional cartoonist was Paul Driessen, another Dutch import who directed numerous films in both the French and English animation units. But when he fooled around with the tried and true methodology, he was a

The pinscreen technique achieves the look of monochromatic etching.

stylistic leader. In the film, *Une vieille boîte* (*An Old Box*, 1975), Driessen discovered an animation shortcut by placing his backgrounds on cels over his characters drawn on paper.

No one in the world wanted to tackle the formidable pinscreen apparatus built by Alexandre Alexeieff and Claire Parker. Not even Norman McLaren, who bought one of the contraptions in 1972. For a year, it collected dust in the English animation studio until Jacques Drouin knocked on McLaren's office door and shyly asked if he could see it. "I found that it looked like a white cushion stuck with thousands of headless, black, pointed pins. Norman pressed the surface of the screen with his finger, leaving behind a white print. I then grasped that this mysterious invention was a sort of bas-relief on which one could model images."[64]

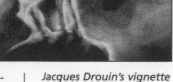

Jacques Drouin's vignette for the 1990 Ottawa Animation Film Festival.

Drouin's first three "exercises," set to music by Maurice Blackburn, were so strong that Jodoin funded a full-fledged pinscreen production. The monochromatic etching was perfect for Drouin's hallucinatory film, *Le paysagiste* (*Mindscape*, 1976), in which an artist steps into his own painting — his personal universe of memory and imagery.

Experimentation and collaboration hit a high note when Drouin teamed up with Czechoslovakian filmmaker Bretislav Pojar to animate *L'Heure des anges* (*Nightangel*, 1986). The film combines Pojar's 3-D puppets with exquisite backgrounds animated on the pinscreen board. Although Alexeieff invented the pinscreen to do pure black-and-white chiaroscuro imagery, Drouin adapted it for colour.

Co Hoedeman, a puppet animator from Holland, was re-routed from the English unit to French animation by Wolf

Co Hoedeman experiments with 2-D cutout puppets in 3-D environments in Charles et François.

Koenig in 1965. From the start, he avoided constructing elaborate dolls favoured by the Czechoslovakian masters, and sought alternative materials. Using twisted wire puppets, he produced *Maboule* (*Oddball*, 1969) a simple allegorical film about superficial beauty. In a subsequent film, *Tchou–tchou* (1972), Hoedeman turned to wooden construction blocks because he was fascinated with how children can create imaginary worlds from concrete shapes. Liquid latex and sand were his tools of choice to build the stars of his Oscar-winning film, *Le Château de sable* (*Sand Castle*, 1977). By cleverly mixing metaphor and material, Hoedeman neatly offers a visual twist to the Sisyphus myth by illustrating how hard it is to construct something tangible from nature and have it wash away with the tide. Audiences also read it as a biblical parable inferring the act of creation.

Later in his career, Hoedeman inserted flat 2-D puppets into 3-D environments with interesting results. "I was always looking for escapes, or a different approach," he says.[65] The most successful film of this genre was *Charles et François* (1987) a film about aging and death. Less successful is *L'Ours renifleur* (*The Sniffing Bear*, 1992) a film warning Native children about the dangers of glue-sniffing. Although the texture provided by homemade paper cutouts is interesting, the story is thin.

Pierre Hébert, who created several abstract minimalist works within the more structured English studio in the sixties — *Opus 3* (1966) and *Autour de la perception* (*Around Perception*, 1968) — pursued his daring approach at the French studio. In 1971, he made *Notions élémentaires de génétique*, a disconcerting abstract piece based on Mendel's laws of cross-breeding.

During the eighties, after a militant period spent making films inspired by Bertold Brecht's notions of distancing and epic drama — *Entre chiens et loup* (1978) and *Souvenirs de guerre* (*Memories of War*, 1982) — Hébert continued his experimental phase with "extended cinema" performances. At these live shows, he etched on loops of 16-mm film while musicians improvised in front of the screen. The experiments developed into a series of performances titled *Conversations*, featuring simultaneous improvisations with a musician, a writer and a dancer. The multidisciplinary show is captured in the film *La Lettre d'amour* (1988). In it, the filmmaker assembles and completes loops etched at live public performances.

Hébert's contentious films are part of a major trend at the French studio: using animation to address social issues. Like NFB founder John Grierson, animators in the French unit embraced a utilitarian vision of cinema. Norman McLaren precipitated this wave with the film *Neighbours*, a powerful satire of war. Jodoin and his compatriots forcefully defended this socialist agenda.

"McLaren was in the habit of saying he was a civil servant," says Hébert. "This term is appropriate because it stresses that filmmakers are responsible to the public more so than to a political power. In fact, this civic duty is part of the NFB's philosophy. We're continually reminded of that in all kinds of ways." [66]

Hébert's *Memories of War*, and Bretislav Pojar's *Balablok* (1973), revisited the resounding theme of *Neighbours*. This cinematic triad perfectly illustrates the expressive potential of animated film and the possibilities provided by technical diversity. *Neighbours* draws satirical force from McLaren's decision to use pixilation. The film's terrifying violence results from having real bodies in confrontation. When revenge impels two neighbours to attack each other's wife and child, a real baby is assaulted while nursing at its mother's breast. The effect is shocking.

René Jodoin was not interested in creating a Quebecois ghetto. He hired English animators whose work was philosophically in tune with the NFB's French Animation unit. Ron Tunis the director of The Animal Movie *(above)*, was recruited to direct Moi je pense.

Similarly in *Souvenirs de guerre* (*Memories of War*), Hébert draws on the intrinsic features of the etched line to denounce violence. The etched line is of course a tear in the emulsion of the film. For this reason, the line itself conveys aggression, which the filmmaker channels to create images devoid of beauty. In the film, Hébert contrasts these images with sequences using cutouts reminiscent of the illuminations of the Middle Ages. In this way, he creates breaks in the narrative that cause viewers to step back from the reality they are facing. And finally, in *Babalok*, the stylization of the shapes and movement in the cutouts allows Pojar to illustrate the costs of intolerance, and refute the logic of war. All three films demonstrate the power of animated films to explore complex issues.

A raging controversy over the traditional seal hunt in Quebec is the impetus behind Nathaël et la chasse aux phoques.

Films of the French animation unit attack social inequities, violence, waste and intolerance. They are tougher, more severe, more political than their English counterparts. Quebec's Quiet Revolution had a sobering effect. Robert Awad and André Leduc's *L'Affaire Bronswik* pokes fun at advertising and consumerism. Less amusing is Peter Foldès' grotesque computer animated film, *La Faim* (*Hunger*, 1974). Foldès' villain is a gluttonous man who stuffs himself with roasted meat and pastries until his bloated form is cannibalized by starving children.

Using clippings from popular magazines, Jean-Thomas Bédard's *Ceci est un message enregistré* (*This Is a Recorded Message*, 1973), compares man's unbridled consumerism to the terrible atrocities of mankind.

Pierre Veilleux questions the responsibility of institutions, and fantasizes about escape from urban decline in his films: *Dans la vie* (1972) and *Une âme à voile* (1982). André Chapdelaine and Yvon Larochelle's *Nathaël et la chasse aux phoques* (*Nathael and the Seal Hunt*, 1989) shows the Îles-de-la-Madeleine community grappling with their traditional seal hunt and the outrage it provokes off their island.

Pierre Hébert coupled computer animation with film etchings in La Plante humaine.

Pierre Hébert's magnum opus, *La Plante humaine* (*The Human Plant*, 1996), addresses the fundamental gap between human life and the ultimate survival of the planet. In his first full-length film, Hébert creates a protagonist who is bombarded with shocking images that swamp his own reality and reveal

how man is at odds with his environment.

Preoccupied with cultural identity, music also became a thematic link between films in this studio. Staff composer, Maurice Blackburn, a close associate of Norman McLaren, set up his office in French animation, and even directed a film in 1968. Talented freelance musicians such as Eldon Rathburn, Pierre Brault, Normand Roger, Denis Larochelle and Alain Clavier also collaborated extensively with the studio's

filmmakers. The experimental works in the French department demanded such complex sound concepts that producers eventually founded a "Sound Conception" workshop in the late seventies.

The composers took complete responsibility over the soundtrack of the film, says Roger. Even though the musician did not do the sound effects or editing, he would overview, and direct the soundtrack.[67] Blackburn forged this new unwritten rule not because he preferred to work this way, but because there were many young filmmakers with no experience in sound.

The seventies brought a renewed interest in traditional music. As a result, many directors wove folk songs and melodies into the fabric of their films. The film composers drew from the well of traditional songs by Quebecois fiddlers and singers to create new soundscapes. Since scoring Frédéric Back's Oscar-winning short *Crac!*, Roger has frequently been called upon to write music with a Quebecois flavour. Notable contributions outside the French studio include Sheldon Cohen's *Le Chandail* (*The Sweater*) and Robert Doucet's *La Chasse galerie* (*The Legend of the Flying Canoe*).

Paul Cormier — or rather Monsieur Pointu as he was known on stage — was filmed twice by director André Leduc: once in a humorous take-off of his performance, and a second time in a playful interpretation of his song *"Chérie, ôte tes raquettes"* (1976). With partner Bernard Longpré, Leduc highlights the political tensions in Quebec by illustrating the separatist tendencies of a violin and accessories that refuse to be guided by the musician. Every element dances to its own beat.

Composers such as Norman Roger had an enormous impact on both the English and French animation departments. French folk songs were married with French folklore in Robert Doucet's The Legend of the Flying Canoe.

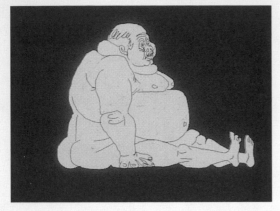

Hunger is one of the earliest computer-animated films to be made in Canada.

Music underscores provincial icons in Jacques Giraldeau's *Zoopsie* (1973), where his papier mâché character wanders in a mythical snowy Quebec filled with bleeding sacred hearts and religious statues.

Music is not an afterthought in French animation. In many ways it's the guts and the glue of these films.

Once based in the NFB science division, Jodoin eagerly explored the creative avenues opened by new computer graphics programs. In the early seventies, he developed ties with the National Research Council of Canada in Ottawa.

The collaboration led to the production of Peter Foldès' *La Faim* (*Hunger*, 1974), a striking piece that marked the beginnings of computer-assisted animation. The film racked up 14 awards, including an Oscar nomination. "With computers, I realized we could produce longer films with a different aesthetic without needing to hire a huge technical crew," explains Jodoin. "I also wanted to impose my vision early so that we could use computers as artistic tools. I believed we had to approach computers just as we did any traditional technique."

Robert Forget, who replaced Jodoin at the helm of the French animation studio in 1978, set up a computer animation centre that kept the NFB at the technological forefront. Forget and his team produced their first computer-animated segment, *Transitions* (1987), for the Vancouver International Exhibition; followed by *Emergency* (1988), an Imax film about the drama of emergency medicine.

During the late eighties, the French program branch developed FLIP, a tool for filming and colouring traditional animation. Using the system, animator Marc Aubry directed *Si seulement...* (*If Only...* , 1987), featuring two drunken cartoon characters who dream of a tropical paradise that is already under their very noses. To celebrate the NFB's 50th year, Marc Aubry and Michel Hébert used the in-house software to make *L'Anniversaire* (*Anniversary*, 1989).

The path followed by Forget attracted some criticism from defenders of traditional techniques. They would have preferred to see the studio set more modest goals, in line with the concerns of Jodoin — who considered the computer a tool in the hands of directors, rather than in the hands of computer specialists. At the time, Forget defended his decision to invest in computer technology by insisting that the NFB was concentrating on film special effects: "Today, if you want to transfer synthesized images on 35-mm film or larger sizes like Imax, the place the world goes is the end of the corridor, the NFB's French animation studio."[68]

The statement was dated the moment he uttered it. Given the speed of technological innovations, and the scope of research required, the NFB could not compete against the private sector for long. Its accumulated knowledge was immediately sucked into Montreal's private sector and exploited.

Daniel Langlois, hired by the NFB in 1979 to apply a 3-D system to the NFB's first stereographic 3-D Imax computer film, went on to found Softimage, one of the world's leading 3-D computer software producers.

Notes and sketches from the NFB computer-animated film L'Anniversaire.

After years working on the NFB's paint program, Terry Higgins joined Discreet Logic, a company that successfully markets 2-D effects and post-production services. Discreet Logic's packages — Flame, Inferno, Flint and Riot — are now used in Hollywood productions.

The dogged pursuit of computer graphics technology was curtailed after Forget stepped down and Yves Leduc took over the French animation studio in October, 1989. Educational films such as Jean-Jacques Leduc's *Les Miroirs du temps* (*Mirrors of Time*, 1990), signalled a change in style. The NFB gracefully bowed out of the technology race, and the computer specialists once again became support technicians for the artists.

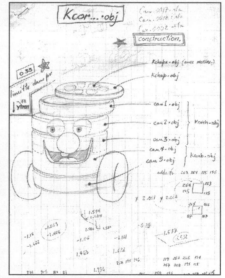

Says Pierre Hébert, who replaced Yves Leduc as studio head in the fall of 1996: "The French animation studio had a novel role to play in computer use. It's one of the rare places in the world, if not the only, where it's possible to combine computers with the full range of traditional techniques." Hébert should know: in 1996, he completed the feature film *La Plante humaine* (*The Human Plant*), using computers coupled with etching on film.

The French studio also provided fertile ground for women filmmakers. Indeed, the proportion of films by

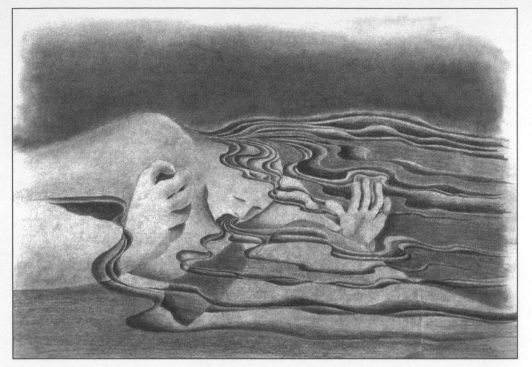

Clorinda Warny's beautifully rendered Premiers jours.

women has been much higher here than at the NFB's documentary and fiction studios. This situation, Francine Desbiens believes, stems from Jodoin's open-minded and non-discriminatory approach. There was never a political decision to hire women artists. Their numbers were a progression.

In 1967, Clorinda Warny (*L'Oeuf*, 1972) arrived from Belgium after spending two years working for Belvision (*Astérix*). But she quickly settled in and mentored Desbiens, Suzanne Gervais and Judith Klein.

It's difficult to define a common aesthetic to these women filmmakers. And it's almost impossible to measure their exact contributions to the language of animated film. Yet they clearly had an impact on a range of themes. Above all, films made by women helped animation in Quebec become more introspective. These films also focused more closely on the relationships between people and the realities of families.

A striking example includes Warny's *Premiers jours* (*Beginnings*, 1981), which artfully merges people and landscapes while exploring life cycles. *Beginnings* is breathtaking. The filmmaker paints in a single swirling brushstroke the ages of the Earth, the cycle of human life, and the passing of seasons. Through the juxtaposition of cross-fades, this world sweeps by, creating a series of strange but lasting impressions and brilliantly duplicating the logic of dreams. The mind is engulfed by a melange of both clear and hazy images.

The same kind of allegorical narrative and originality is found in the work of Suzanne Gervais and Michele Cournoyer. Gervais explores internal landscapes, particularly in *Solitude* (1983), in which she introduces a voice-over narrative. Her work is an ongoing reflection on art's ability to get to the bottom of things. This desire to delve into her characters, to tunnel beneath surfaces, has had considerable aesthetic repercussions on her six films, the most important being her novel approach to movement. In *The Studio* — a film that examines an artist's reflections through her relationship with her male model — the abrupt, disjointed movements match the film's timeframe, which is broken and unclear. Gervais fragments surfaces so as to penetrate them more easily and uncover their essential core. The film *Expectations* (1993), in which a pregnant photographer observes the world through her pregnancy, pursues the same kind of reflection on the relationships between the woman-artist and the world around her.

As for Cournoyer, her narrative explorations are conveyed through the use of rotoscoping and morphing. Two films, *Dolorosa* (1989) and *La Basse Cour* (*A Feather Tale*, 1993), enabled Cournoyer to perfect her style. In these short shorts, she uses surreal morphs to create new meanings In this way, *Dolorosa* might be likened to haiku, the Japanese 17-syllable poems that reflect life. The four-minute film is the literal and thoughtful illustration of a simple metaphor — the withering of the body. Using strong lines and simple shading, Cournoyer presents an aging woman for whom the body is a wilting flower, and youth as fleeting as the life of a rose. It's a clichéd metaphor, one that might have faltered if not for the subtlety of the tone and the quality of the line. Through rotoscopy, the lines are endowed with true musculature and give the character an undeniable physical presence. In a few short seconds, the old woman emerges, a troubling figure in her helplessness, rebellion and nostalgia. The withering feeling is strong, and the woman's anguish palpable.

Artist Suzanne Gervais ponders her relationship with a model in the film L'Atelier.

Michele Cournoyer's A Feather Tale *explores the world of the subconscious.*

With its more secretive and complex approach, *A Feather Tale* creates a world drifting between sleep and reason. Once again, the territory explored is the body, and the story unfolds through a series of metamorphoses and metaphors.

Other filmmakers — Francine Desbiens (*Variations on Ah! vous dirai-je maman*, 1985), Luce Roy (*Oniromancy*, 1987) and Viviane Elnécavé (*Luna, Luna, Luna*, 1981) — further developed the woman's approach to animated films in Quebec. Another talent is Caroline Leaf, whose work with the French animation studio is characterized by *Entre deux soeurs* (*Two Sisters*, 1991). In this disconcerting film, a visitor disrupts the lives of two sisters, one a famous, disfigured writer, the other a woman whose life is spent preserving the isolation that protects her sister from strangers' stares.

Soon after Thérèse Descary was named producer at the French animation studio, she put together the series *Droits au cœur* (*Rights from the Heart*, 1992). In doing so, she broke with NFB convention. Traditionally, producers did not initiate projects at the French animation studio; directors did. Over the past 30 years, only a few films originated with producers. The other exception is *Les Miroirs du temes* (*Mirrors of Times*), which owes its life to Robert Forget. *Rights of the Heart* is the first example of such an elaborate series being developed by a producer at the studio. In fact, Descary was able to deal with the new economic climate of the nineties and bank on a series that would meet traditional concerns while being marketable worldwide.

With *Rights of the Heart*, Descary drew inspiration from the United Nations' Convention on Children's Rights, which came into force in 1990. Several films in the series picked up awards at festivals, including Diane Chartrand's *L'Orange* (1992); Michele Cournoyer's *Une Artiste* (1994); and Jacques Drouin's *Ex-enfant* (*Ex-child*, 1994).

"The studio's worth lies mainly in its diversity," says Pierre Hébert. Indeed, a surprising number of its films are hard to classify, such as the absurd and sophisticated humour of Claude Cloutier's *Le Colporteur* (*The Persistent Peddler*, 1989), and the comic cockroaches scurrying madly about in Martin Barry's *Juke-Bar* (1989).

The leeway granted to filmmaker-initiated projects at the studio explains in large part this profusion of unclassifiable films. Many have noted the technical diversity of the animated films made by the NFB. Indeed, this great diversity is often used to distinguish Canadian animation from the work of other production studios worldwide. Technical diversity is especially apparent at the French animation studio, where it translates into a variety of styles and themes.

Michele Couroyer crafted the film An Artist *(above), and Jacques Drouin directed* Ex-child *(below) for the French animation series* Droits au coeur.

Thanks to the NFB's unique structures, animated films in Quebec have developed outside the laws of the market, thereby preserving the innovative spirit left behind by Norman McLaren and embraced by René Jodoin. Partly because of the language barrier, francophone animators, unlike many of their anglophone colleagues, have not been inclined to draw their inspiration from American animation techniques and aesthetics. These reasons might explain the technical diversity that marks Quebec animation. The importance of social documentary in Quebec productions is another distinguishing characteristic.

Still, the French filmmakers profited from cross-pollination thanks to the proximity of their anglophone counterparts. The English-speaking animators also gained from this symbiotic relationship. However, audiences did not benefit from the same close relationship, because the NFB's French and English marketing departments were worlds apart — two solitudes for the most part. Rarely did the best French animation films get shown in English Canada, despite the fact that animation so often lends itself to translation. Only in recent years have video compilations made French animation more accessible to anglo audiences. Vive la difference. Long live creativity.

Claude Cloutier exhibits his cartooning skills in the film Le Colporteur.

From Test Tube to Television

In the late 1960s, Nestor Burtnyk, at the National Research Council of Canada, assembled a team to develop techniques that would allow an animator to work on a computer without having any knowledge of programming. In 1970, he developed the "key-frame animation" technique patterned on conventional cel animation. Figurative animation could be gener-

ated using free-hand drawings. Marceli Wein joined the team to continue its development. His PhD project was on weather radar systems, but his experience with photographic screens helped the team with playback and filming display.

Through an informal arrangement with the NFB, freelance filmmaker Peter Foldès was given a contract to experiment on the Systems Engineering Laboratories model SEL-840A and a modified IDI display. Together with Foldès, the NRC tried to perfect the animation system.

With his first film *Metadata* (1970), all key frames were drawn with the mouse. Foldès found that drawing with a mouse required movement of the arm from the elbow, not the wrist, much like painting.

On the second film, *Hunger/La Faim* (1974) Foldès drew all key images on a Computek graphics tablet equipped with standard animation registration pegs on the tablet. The key frame interpolation approach involved mapping an image in one key frame to the next one, on a stroke-to-stroke basis.

Throughout the production of the film Foldès would fly in from Paris for a week, then further development would proceed for the next three weeks. When the work on the computer was completed, each scene was filmed on several 35-mm black and white film sequences to be combined and coloured optically into the final composite. It took a year for the NFB to carry out tests on the optical printer and to merge the separate sequences to produce a satisfactory result.

The NFB's computer animation got another boost in 1982 when it hired University of Waterloo Math graduates Doris Kochanek and Ines Hardtke. The computer graphics program at Waterloo had taken off after Kelly Booth from Lawrence Livermore Labs joined the faculty of mathematics in the mid-seventies and was joined by John Beatty and Richard Bartels.

Kochanek and Hardtke implemented the basic ideas from the NRC system but on more modern SGI workstations and more importantly, implemented spline interpolation instead of linear interpolation.

Terry Higgins, another Waterloo alumnus working for the NRC and the NFB, wrote a paint program that used a virtual frame buffer image memory with 128 bits per pixel. The pixel bits were used for masking and for blending. Higgins went on to head up research and development at the Montreal software company, Discreet Logic.

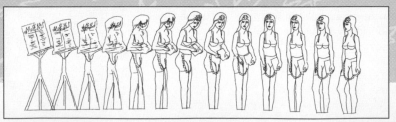

chapter 6

Hewers & Drawers

I get mighty annoyed when I hear the Film Board being touted as the father and mother of all things creative in Canadian cinema. Nonsense. Compared to you, the Board was lolling around a government oasis while you were hacking your way through the commercial, uncharted, forest primeval.
— Munroe Scott's eulogy for Budge Crawley (1987)

frank "Budge" Crawley is a legend in Canada — the original producer. He was a man who could shoot, edit, and strike a hard bargain. His Ottawa-based company, Crawley Films — founded in 1939, and laid to corporate rest in 1988 — shepherded such diverse properties as the classic short *The Loon's Necklace* (1948) and the Oscar-winning documentary *The Man Who Skied Everest* (1975). Crawley also serviced the first animated series in Canada.

Tales of the Wizard of Oz (1961) was a limited animation series, produced by New York's Rankin/Bass, and distributed by Videocraft International. Rankin/Bass were known for their syndicated puppet show, *The New Adventures of Pinocchio*. The 130 five-minute cartoons ordered from Crawley Films marked the first time Rankin/Bass tackled a cel animation series.

Animation was supposed to be a profitable diversion for Crawley. He moved into the genre only as a means to subsidize his $1.37 million live-action series, *The RCMP*, produced for the Canadian Broadcasting Corporation (CBC) and British Broadcasting Corporation (BBC). Unable to secure a big US sale for his series, Crawley was losing money. In order to ensure the future of the show, he signed the *Tales of the Wizard of Oz* service contract.

Rather than earn a tidy profit, the first season proved to be a money pit. Local animators were slow to deliver, and Crawley drafted a handful of New York artists to speed up delivery. Their presence must have created waves in the studio: they charged double the going Canadian rate.

Unlike most animation projects today, *Tales of the Wizard of Oz* had no supervising director; only Tommy Glynn, the floor manager. Each animator was responsible for his own mini-episode. Canadians Barrie Nelson and Bill Mason took 24 apiece. The shows reflected some of the social preoccupations of the time. The Tin Man, Straw Man and the lion are drafted into the army, and the Wizard builds a rocketship.

Midway through the second season, Crawley was offered a renewal. Fearful that his company would continue to lose money on the series, he declined another run. He did, however, make the TV special *Return to Oz* in 1964.

Budge Crawley (left) produced the Bass/Rankin series Tales of the Wizard of Oz, *and the TV special* Return to Oz *(below) in 1961 and 1964. It was the first animation series ever made in Canada.*

When the Videocraft deal ended, so did Budge Crawley's interest in animation. He had put Canada on the cartooning map, but he was simply not interested in developing a specialized studio. Still, *Tales of the Wizard of Oz* paved the way for other north-south deals. Commercial animation had arrived.

Branch plants opened in other cities across Canada. A television station in Vancouver expanded its facilities in 1965 to service Hanna-Barbera and King Features Syndicate cartoons. Two years later, Toronto's Al Guest Studios launched *Rocket Robin Hood*, the first animated joint venture that met Canadian content requirements. Montreal was the home of Potterton Studios, the first company in Canada to develop an original TV special for a US network.

And so began another cartoon adventure. Thirty years after Budge Crawley cut his deal with Videocraft, Canadian companies had hacked their way to the front of the supply lines. All of the original firms founded in the sixties are extinct, but they have been replaced by a group of corporate giants that have stormed the US and Europe. Toronto's Nelvana and Montreal's Cinar and Ciné-Groupe no longer wait for handouts from US studios. They license properties, pitch new concepts, and build libraries. Once upon a time, Hanna-Barbera, Filmation and Ruby-Spears ruled the airwaves. Today, Canadian companies are king of the hill.

For a few short years in the midsixties, Vancouver was the Canadian service hub for Hanna-Barbera. Canawest Film Productions, a modest commercial unit attached to KVOS-TV in Bellingham, was offered a contract by H-B to produce seven half-hour shows based on the Beatles songs. Most of the key supervisors were brought in from the US. Canadians were to supply the facilities and cheap labour.

The Canadians who travelled from Winnipeg and Ottawa to find work were unimpressed with the American directors and animators working on the shows. "Some had been out of the business for years and came back to get a share of the loot," says Barrie Helmer, a Winnipeg animator who headed up the Canadian crew at KVOS. "The young ones were simply oppor-tunists — assistant animators claim-ing to be directors, in-betweeners claiming to be animators, and some with no qualifications at all other than the right connections."[69]

The highest position offered to seasoned local animators was that of assistant. However, the American crew bailed out before com-pleting the job, and the remaining Canadians finished the last episode on their own steam. The Canadian-crafted show treated the Beatles as separate personalities rather than interchangeable ciphers. No one at H-B's studios could tell the difference.

The Fab Four.

Two years after *The Beatles* aired, H-B came courting once again — this time with a handful of shows including: two episodes of *Sampson*, five episodes of *Moby Dick*, 54 episodes of *Abbot and Costello*, and 12 episodes of *Wait Till Your Father Gets Home*, a situation comedy for both H-B and Global TV.

At its peak, Canawest employed 90 people. But when H-B started shipping animation to the Orient, the great expec-tations fizzled. Like Crawley, the owners of Canawest were not interested in building a full-fledged animation studio.

Canawest's contribution to the industry was primarily psychological. Local animators learned that they could complete — at least artistically — with their US counterparts. Business acumen was another matter. Vancouver animators were out of the starting gate early but they never really capitalized on their early lead in the industry, and eventually contracts slowed to a trickle.

By the early nineties, American feature films such as *Space Jam* and *Anastasia* generated an avalanche of work for West Coast animators. Dynamic new studios such as Bardel Animation, Studio B Productions, and Natterjack were thrilled with the service work, but found themselves too busy to develop and market original ini-tiatives. They became a victim of their own success.

Vancouver's commercial studios have now start-ed to carve a niche in the industry. Herve Bedard of NOA Network of Animation adapted the Belgian comic book *Billy the Cat* into a series, and developed the 3-D computer

Chris Delaney, the namesake and founder of Delaney and Friends.

In Nilus the Sandman, *pixie dust turns real life boys and girls into cartoons.*

animated series *Cybersix* (1998). Financed with the help of Japan's TMS-Kyokuichi, *Cybersix* was adapted from a comic book by Argentinean artists Carlos Trillo and Carlos Meglia, and stars a cross-dressing vampira.

Gord Stanfield broke away from his service contracts long enough to develop the "My Little Pony" look-alike, *Kleo the Misfit Unicorn.*

Natterjack produced *Max and Moritz* (1997) with a German partner, and Studio B finally signed deals for three productions to be aired in year 2000. *D'Myna Leagues* is a series that mines the baseball legends of W.P. Kinsella; and *Yvon of the Yukon,* an explorer frozen in the tundra until a pissing dog thaws his 300-year-old body.

Delaney and Friends has had the most success. After stockpiling money from a job on Nelvana's *Care Bears: The Movie* in the mid-eighties, Chris Delaney opened a Vancouver shop with two local partners. Commercial jobs and service contracts were his bread and butter. Delaney received his first big break in the form of a butter campaign for the Dairy Bureau of Canada.

Delaney invented original characters like Christopher the Christmas Tree.

"The butter commercial was great because we just won every kind of award there was," says Delaney.[70] "So everyone said: 'Oh, these guys are good.' We were probably good before, but they believed it now." Not only did Delaney's list of clients increase, so did his clout.

After the spot aired, Delaney was offered a co-production deal with Toronto-based Cambium Productions for their property Nilus the Sandman in *The Boy Who Dreamed Christmas* (1991). Live-action stories segue into animation tales featuring a sandman whose pixie dust turns boys and girls into toons. Nilus evolved into a full-fledged series in 1997 — the first of its kind in Vancouver.

"We didn't want to do jobbers, producing for DIC Entertainment or someone else because there's very little money in it," says Delaney. He adds: "We thought we wanted to do our own stuff. We took the longer, harder route, trying to develop a profile for ourselves, and raising our own money to do shows."

One such show was their direct-to-video film, *Christopher the Christmas Tree,* which sold to YTV and the US home video market.

Since 1996, Delaney and Friends has developed several feature film projects and another direct-to-video film, *The Littlest Angel* (1997). Unlike some of the more raunchy independent animators who've start- ed companies in Vancouver's fashionable Gastown, Delaney has positioned his company squarely in the "family enter- tainment" category.

But a handful of shows does not an industry make. Vancouver is still fight- ing an uphill battle to compete against the Toronto-Montreal corridor.

The Mungo Brothers from Studio B's D'Myna Leagues.

In the post-Expo 67 euphoria, commercial production in Montreal blossomed. Gerald Potterton cut his ties with the National Film Board and rented a huge space in Place Bonaventure for his new firm, Potterton Productions. A one- hour NBC-TV special, *Pinter People*, was Potterton's first film under the company banner. An interview with the playwright Harold Pinter is expertly woven into ani- mated adaptations of Pinter's early works, and sketches inspired by dialogue recorded in a London pub. With a visual flourish, Potterton was able to literally draw the sounds and scenes that influenced this great writer.

Following *Pinter People*, Potterton was approached by distributors Anthony and Oliver Ungar to rework a beautiful but flawed 70-mm Russian epic entitled *Dr. Applelite 66*. The film itself was unwatchable, but the Ungar brothers wanted to exploit the gorgeous film footage. Their idea was to construct a story around a bunch of cartoon characters directing a live-action pirate film.

Potterton obliged by rounding up a talented crew including Jack Stokes (*Yellow Submarine*) and NFB animator Mike Mills. Halfway through production, Ungar's Commonwealth United went belly-up, and Potterton was forced to find financing to complete it. The finished film, renamed *Tiki-Tiki* (1970), had a limited release. A print remains in the vaults of the Cinematheque Quebecois.

The cartoon folks in Pinter People *are inspired by real- life characters recorded in a London pub.*

Storyboard panels from
Pinter People.

Tiki-Tiki *is a strange cinematic
concoction. Potterton made a
film about making a film,
only his director was a cartoon monkey, and the scenes
of the monkey's film were
cut from an ill-fated Russian
feature film entitled*
Dr. Applelite 66.

With partners Peter Sander and Murray Shostak, Potterton undertook a series of high calibre made-for-television films based on Oscar Wilde's and Hans Christian Andersen's classic stories for children. When the first half-hour, *The Selfish Giant*, was nominated for an Oscar, *Reader's Digest* approached Potterton with a buyout offer worth $3 million. Although Shostak was eager to sell his shares, Potterton and Sander resisted. Instead, *Reader's Digest* purchased *The Selfish Giant* (1971) for distribution, and financed another four half-hours. *The Happy Prince* (1974) directed by Michael Mills was the official US entry at the 1976 Cannes Film Festival.

Most of the money fronted by *Reader's Digest* was spent on *The Happy Prince, The Little Mermaid,* and *The Christmas Messenger*. There was so little cash remaining after those productions that Potterton animated the final special almost entirely on his own.

Even under financial duress, Potterton delivered strong films. *The Remarkable Rocket* (1975) illustrates the plight of a supercilious firecracker who brags about his superior pyrotechnic capability but is passed over for all the big fireworks displays. When his fuse is finally lit, it's by a bunch of kids on a bright summer day. The pompous rocket shoots into the sky unnoticed.

Potterton Productions built a solid reputation for animation in the early seventies, but both Potterton and Shostak longed to make feature dramas. The business looked promising at first. Potterton's directorial debut, with *The Rainbow Boys* (1973), received both decent reviews and reasonable distribution in Canada. The second film, *Child Under a Leaf*, was a flop, and drained the company's coffers. According to Potterton, Shostak was so preoccupied with wooing the film's star, Dyan Cannon, that he did not keep a tight enough rein on the budget.

"If we had stuck with animation, the studio might have survived," says Potterton. "But you could say if Richard Williams hadn't spent all his money on *The Thief and the Cobbler*, he'd still be in business. I don't have any regrets." Williams is another Canadian animator who lost his studio pursuing his own feature film dream.

Potterton sold his shares in the company, and the corporate entity that bore his name atrophied. His career as an animation director did not. Potterton proceeded to work as an associate director on *Raggedy Ann and Andy* (1977) with director Richard Williams, and was supervising director for Ivan Reitman's animated rock-and-roll film, *Heavy Metal* (1980).

Ivan Reitman was already a Canadian success story with two Hollywood hits to his credit: *National Lampoon's Animal House* (1978), and *Meatballs*

Potterton Studios produced a handful of award-winning television specials sponsored by Reader's Digest *including* The Happy Prince.

(1978). With a deal from Columbia Pictures under his arm to produce an animated film, he approached Gerald Potterton to oversee the entire production.

Potterton was initially unenthused about the idea of adapting a sciencefiction magazine for the big screen, but eventually accepted the project because he liked the comic book's range of styles.

Heavy Metal was a concept-driven project targeting young rockers and comic book fans alike. The goal was to take the highly stylized illustrated science fiction magazine and blend it with a heavy metal music soundtrack featuring Black Sabbath, Devo, Cheap Trick, Nazareth, Stevie Nicks and Blue Oyster Cult. Animators were to be teamed with comic book stylists such as Juan Gimenez, Mike Ploog, Howard Chaykin, Christos Achilleos, Angus McKie and Richard Corben. The formula was appealing in pitch form. In reality, hammering diverse styles into a cohesive whole would prove difficult.

Thematic considerations aside, there were plenty of worrisome obsta-

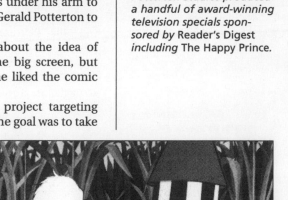

The Remarkable Rocket was based on an Oscar Wilde story.

cles, including a nine-month production timeline. Also, Potterton Studios did not have the production capacity to stickhandle the entire project. Instead, production was farmed out to six companies on two continents.

Atkinson Film-Arts in Ottawa handled the "Harry Canyon" and "Gremlins" sequences; Boxcar Films in Montreal animated the "Captain Sternn" story; Potterton's makeshift

Gerald Potterton's model designs based on Moebius' character, Arzach (Potterton misspelled it on his model sheets).

Montreal unit oversaw the "Taarna" finale; and five other segments were animated at Halas and Batchelor and TVC in London, England.

As if production logistics were not challenging enough, there was no script to start with. The original version was discarded because *Heavy Metal* designer/illustrator Jean Girard/Moebius refused permission to use his characters. Moebius' Arzach was supposed to serve as the linking device between the various sequences. Now writers Len Blum and Dan Goldberg were forced to create the character Taarna and develop a narrative link between the disparate stories. Their solution was a behaviour-mutating energy source in the form of a fluorescent green orb that resurfaced in each episode. Taarna's mission would be to destroy the malignant sphere.

Production hit another wall when Mike Mills, the animation house originally hired for the opening and closing sequences, threatened to sue Reitman for non-payment of work. Numerous script rewrites forced Mills back to the drawing board several times. Frustrated with the skyrocketing bills, Reitman challenged Mills by withholding some payment and threatening to countersue. The case was eventually settled out of court.

The original "Soft Landing" sequence, and a final epic struggle, are buried in Mills' Montreal studio. Instead of settling the fourth round of production costs, Reitman called Jimmy Murikami at TVC in London to create a totally new "Soft Landing" which looks as if it were lifted directly from the pages of *Heavy Metal*. In keeping with the strong graphic feel of the comic, Murikami used cutout photographs of a

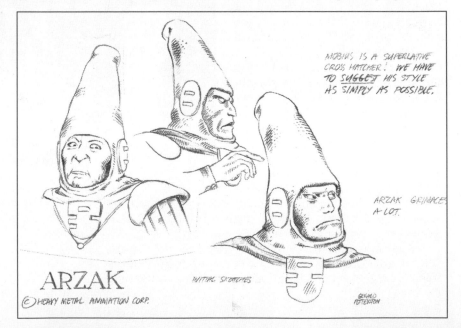

Corvette and driver to create a hyperrealistic introductory scene. The Corvette was airbrushed and fused to highly stylized backgrounds. Murikami successfully delivered the impression that audiences were getting what they paid for — a fantasy magazine come to life.

The best segment in the entire film is "Gremlins," directed by Barrie Nelson in Los Angeles, and finished by Atkinson. Gremlins was a catch-phrase used by RAF and USAF bomber crews when referring to inexplicable glitches in airplane machinery. Dan O'Bannon exploited aviation lore for *Heavy Metal*. It was retooled from his live-action feature script, *Alien*. The story of an army of demonic creatures ripping apart a B-17 bomber plane was reworked by the film's writers and layout artists no less than five times.[71] The conclusion is more frightening than O'Bannon's original script. The plane's surviving pilot parachutes out of the possessed bomber only to land on an island littered with downed war planes and avenging ghosts.

Drafting a realistic plane was a technical challenge. Barry Atkinson constructed a scale model of a B-17 bomber. The model was photographed on black and white negative film that was blown up, transferred onto animation cels and painted. The accidental application of a matte paint gave the plane's hull an unexpected texture. The shading and rendering was more believable.

Pino van Lamsweerde, a long-time commercial director in the country, directed the Harry Canyon story. The animation team of Paul Szuchopa and Julian produced the short Captain Sternn story, one of the more cartoony segments of the film. It was voiced by SCTV regulars Joe Flaherty and Eugene Levy.

Only the final "Taarna" sequence was produced in the Montreal studio by Potterton and a crew of 11 designers, 30 animators and 54 assistants. Directed by John Bruno, "Taarna" was to be the film finale — the ultimate showdown between

When Moebius refused to sign onto the production, the writers created the Amazonian vigilante Taarna.

Storyboard for Michael Mill's original "Soft Landing" sequence. After a legal tussle with Reitman over revisions, Mills' animation was buried in his own basement and never made it to the big screen.

Animation drawings of Taarna by George Ungar.

good and evil, and the last word on Amazonian might. Taarna is the last of a warrior race, who must avenge the barbaric slaughter of her people and destroy the corrupting powers of the force.

Reitman contracted British-based fantasy artist Christos Achilleos to design the film's ultimate heroine. The denouement is an elaborate choreography between special effects people and background artists, creating beautiful travel pans and multiplane camera shots to give the illusion of depth and space to Taarna's flying scenes.

Reitman and Potterton deployed their talent strategically in the "Taarna" episode. Top-notch animators from abroad, including Yugoslavian animator Zdenko Gasparovic and Portuguese artist Jose Abel, worked alongside Canadian notables Norm Drew, Danny Antonucci and George Ungar.

With its pool of local talent, *Heavy Metal* enhanced the profile of Canadian animation; but the production also exacted a toll on the industry. Vic Atkinson collapsed during production and was hospitalized. Potterton also required much recuperative time-off. The excitement generated by its modest theatrical gross may also have indirectly contributed to the near collapse of a promising young Toronto-based company named Nelvana.

Heavy Metal raised expectations at home. Visions of box office sugar plums danced in the heads of Nelvana founders Michael Hirsh, Patrick Loubert and Clive Smith, who were deep into production of their own project, *Drats* (renamed *Rock & Rule*). After a string of strong half-hour TV specials, and a stint servicing some animation for mega-producer George Lucas, Nelvana's principals approached the film in a kamikaze manner.

Originally conceived as a musical Pied Piper aimed at a younger audience, the film was restructured and repositioned to also attract the target audience of *Heavy Metal*. Not only did Nelvana believe they could cater to kids, they also wanted the film to attract hard-core music fans among teenagers and adults. Nelvana wasn't target marketing; it was marketing to all targets. In doing so, the trio set themselves up for a big fall. The failure of *Rock & Rule* (1983) did not decimate the company, but it dramatically changed its charted production course. Despite forging a solid reputation as a supplier of original cartoons, Nelvana was forced into the ball-and-chain production cycle of TV series and Saturday-morning cartoons, to pay off its heavy debt to *Rock & Rule's* investors.

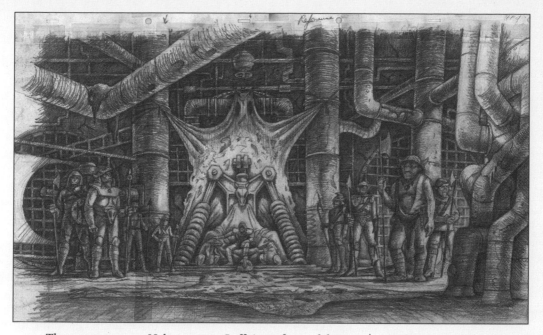

The precursor to Nelvana was Laff-Arts, formed by a gang of film students including Michael Hirsh, Patrick Loubert, Jack Christie and Peter Dewdney, who had trained with claymation expert Mark Chinoy.

In 1971, Hirsh and Loubert co-authored *The Great Canadian Comic Books*, and proceeded to sell CBC a documentary TV show. Convinced that Laff-Arts was an unprofessional moniker for a serious company, Loubert and Hirsh decided to "change their name and clean up their act."[72] Hirsh and Loubert formed a new company and christened it "Nelvana" as a tribute to the indigenous World War II comic, *Nelvana of the Northern Lights*. Clive Smith, a director recruited from Cinera, became Nelvana's third partner. Nelvana wanted for projects and funds in its early years. To make ends meet, Smith was even forced into a pencil suit and chased by thugs down Toronto's Queen Street, during a very, very, low-budget production for CBC's children's department.

A breakthrough came in the form of the animated half-hour TV special *Cosmic Christmas* (1977). Rather than bringing in talent from abroad, Nelvana lured Frank Nissen from Cinera to do layout and design. Dave Thrasher, Robin Budd, Charlie Bonifacio, Vivien Ludlow, Bill Speers, Wendy Perdue and Ken Stephenson formed a tight-knit crew. The

George Ungar's design sketches for Heavy Metal.

Mr. Pencil, one of the first characters designed by Clive Smith for Nelvana.

Nelvana took its name from a wartime comic produced in Canada.

The TV special Cosmic Christmas *marks Nelvana's first foray into the US market.*

success of *Cosmic Christmas* was largely due to appealing and eclectic designs by Nissen and Smith, and some secondary character studies drafted by Bonifacio and Budd.

The film stars a winsome boy named Peter who shows a trio of aliens the meaning of the Bethlehem star. The geometric morphology of the cosmic wise men stands in sharp contrast to the cartoony Canadian goose Lucy, who romps with an alien mascot, and the lethargic chief of police, Snirk.

Unlike the output of the large US studios — Filmation, Ruby-Spears and Warner Bros. — Nelvana's early TV specials sported an unconventional, non-uniform look. During the seventies, Nelvana unabashedly served up raw talent and rejected the assembly line look of the larger units. "I think that the sense of community among animators made its way into the film," says Bonifacio.[73] Their skill did not go unnoticed. During production of *The Devil and Daniel Mouse* (1978), mega-producer George Lucas contracted Nelvana to animate a 10-minute segment in his *Star Wars Thanksgiving Holiday Special* (1979) for CBS.

Nelvana was well served by its stable of artists, but its current corporate girth is due to the deft stickhandling of Michael Hirsh, the company's self-appointed business manager. The late-seventies was the era of the Canadian tax shelter, and Hirsh sought international pre-sales to sweeten his investment packages. Licence fees from the CBC were just

not enough. For an upstart television company, cutting deals in 1976 meant calling up a friend who had a friend, who knew a guy who rode the Long Island train with an executive at Viacom. It was a tenuous connection, but it got Hirsh through the door.

Jamie Kellner, the executive who rode the Long Island train, was in charge of first run syndication at Viacom. He bought *Cosmic Christmas* on the spot, and sold it to 185 stations in the United States. Kellner particularly liked the original story and novel use of music.[74]

When the show received a healthy national rating, Viacom lobbied Nelvana to turn *Cosmic Christmas* into a series. The offer precipitated the first disagreement between the partners. Hirsh pushed to do the series, but Loubert and Smith opted to build their catalogue with high-quality specials. "We lost an opportunity to establish ourselves as creators of properties as compared to great adapters," says Hirsh now.

While Hirsh worked on fresh business angles, Loubert fashioned himself as the story and ideas man, and Clive Simith concentrated on directing. Smith's greatest strength is his ability to marry soundtrack to visuals.

The Devil and Daniel Mouse, the story of a mouse's determined struggle to break a devil's pact, was a strong sequel to *Cosmic*

Frank Nissen became Nelvana's head designer/animator and invented characters such as Lucy the Goose in Cosmic Christmas.

Nelvana serviced George Lucas' TV series Ewoks *and* Droids.

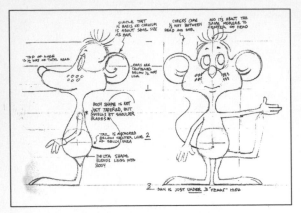

Nissen shows a more functional approach with Daniel Mouse.

Christmas. Writer Ken Sobol gave a new spin to the classic tale, *The Devil and Daniel Webster,* and even evoked the tragic memory of Janis Joplin with his character "Funky Jan," who makes a meteoric rise to superstardom.

Adroit drawers such as Greg Duffell, Dave Thrasher and John Collins infused energy into Nissen's often mathematical approach to layout and design. Nissen was an innovative artist, but the animators gave the characters their organic soul. Thrasher worked on a marvelously morphing Beelzebub that could shape-change from a vulture to a cat, fish and rhinoceros while retaining its characteristic blubbery visage. Duffell animated the great weasel sidekick scenes, while Bob Fortier invented magical acts that included a dancing microphone.

Breaking in a new character is akin to breaking in a new pair of Levi's, according to animator Charlie Bonifacio. Nelvana broke in their brand of jeans with a roster of top-notch sequels — *Romie-0 and Julie-8* (1979), *Intergalactic Thanksgiving* (1979), *Easter Fever* (1980), *Take Me Up to the Ball Game* (1980) and *Herself the Elf* (1982).

While the company continued to develop its one-offs, Hirsh kept in touch with George Lucas, and cogitated about a feature film. Their bid for feature stardom was *Drats* — conceived as the next generation of *The Devil and Daniel Mouse.* The film's characters live in a post-nuclear city inhabited with drats — humanoid rodents that have survived a holocaust. In this futuristic world, Mok is a musical superstar who wants to resurrect a demon that will give him all-consuming powers. But he needs a certain female singing voice to conjure up his evil energy source. The heroine whose voice holds the key to his supreme power is Angel, a singer who jams in a rock band with her boyfriend Omar. When Mok can't win Angel over with his snaky charm, he kidnaps her, and stages a concert at the Ohm Power Plant. The demon is called up and Angel the heroine must contend with it. "If I

Dave Thrasher animates the marvelously morphing Beelzebub in The Devil and Daniel Mouse.

can sing it up, I can sing it back," she exclaims before vaporizing the demon.

The promise of a feature film project was an adrenaline rush for local talent, and a lure for artists who had left to work abroad. Robin Budd quit after *The Devil and Daniel Mouse* to work as a designer for the hot US commercial company Colossal Pictures. He returned to design and animate the main character, Mok. Chuck Gammage, another talented animator working for Warner Bros., jumped on board this feature vehicle. It was the greatest collection of Canadian animators to work in a single studio since Al Guest produced *Rocket Robin Hood*.

Nelvana's instinct for signing hot musical acts was inspired, but the company still lacked clout. Early in development, they had hoped to sign the young Bruce Springsteen as Omar's alter-ego. They settled on a top eighties music act, Cheap Trick. Mick Jagger was the template for the villain Mok Swagger, but their queries to the mega rock star provoked a nasty response from Jagger's business manager, Prince Rupert of Loewenstein, who warned Nelvana not to use Mick's likeness or name. After the Jagger brush off, Nelvana approached and was rejected by David Bowie, before finally settling on Iggy Pop and Lou Reed. Despite stern warnings from Loewenstein, Budd's cartoon megalomaniac retains an attitude and bearing that is unmistakably Jaggeresque. Budd says he also copied the mannerisms and acerbic wit of actor Peter O'Toole.[75]

Animator John Collins struts his stuff in Nelvana's special Easter Fever.

Deborah Harry, the undeniable star of Blondie, was signed as a big musical ID to headline the lead character. Rising pop artist Prince was passed over in favour of the tried and true act Earth, Wind and Fire.

Nelvana faced hurdles signing musical talent and recruiting animators with experience, but the fundamental production problem lay in the graphic schizophrenia induced by management's indecisiveness.

Everyone had a say about everything. The company would have huge meetings with lots of people, but no one knew what the final decision was; it always seemed open–ended.

Rounder designs and canine-like visages that had been conceived by Dan Haskett were scrapped for more realistic human characters. Haskett's snouts were shaved off, and the greasy hair and cigarettes of the lead Omar were erased. Eventually, Nissen took over the lead to ensure his vision of a sexy, pouty hero. Mylar — the business manager of the band — went through several transformations, first at the capable hands of Greg Duffell and John Collins, and later Gian-Franco Celestri. Even Angel's hairstyle and length changed over the course of the film. The improvisation was endless.

Dan Haskett's early canine-like designs of the leads in the feature film Rock & Rule *are scrapped.*

Chuck Gammage's Schlepper Brothers.

The mix and match of characters worked well in Nelvana's half-hour specials, but the incongruous characters in *Rock & Rule* only underlined the weakness of the script. Nissen achieved realistic body shrugs and gestures with Omar, but the sullen, often petulant lead is irritating. Angel becomes the true hero of the show, but the audience is left wondering why she even cares about Omar. Too much time is spent in unnecessary travel to and from Ohm Town and Nuke York. In the end, both Omar and Angel play second fiddle to the outrageous cartoon antics of Chuck Gammage's Schlepper brothers and sister Cindy, Charlie Bonifacio's inquisitive Dizzy, and Robin Budd's diabolical Mok. Visually, all the characters take a back seat to the elaborate special effects created by Keith Ingham, and Nelvana's capable camera operators Lenora Hume (later vice-president of Walt Disney International Animation) and Dennis Brown.

With a big pot of money to play with, Smith upped the ocular ante by embellishing every scene with shadows, highlights and even glint off Mylar's toothy grin. Colours were modified by running two camera passes across scenes while experimenting with black window mattes and varying exposures. The crew created additional effects using pinpoint mattes, filters, and a unique combination of slitscan and streak photography to elevate two-dimensional artwork to three-dimensional space. Bob Fortier's hypnotic holograms (echoing Ishu Patel's work) added some delightful eye candy to the film, not to mention the frighteningly nebulous creature conjured up from another world.

Smith hoped to finish the film in one year. It took three. By the time the film was ready for release, Earth, Wind and Fire, Blondie and Cheap Trick had burned off the charts.

In the end, *Rock & Rule* (released as *Ring of Power*) catered to everyone and no one. MGM/United Artists opened the film in Boston for a one-week trial.

"It was guaranteed to fail because there was no advertising budget," says Hirsh. "They buried it in their vaults after the abysmal response. *Rock & Rule* was never released theatrically. The $8.4-million price tag — $3 million over budget — brought Nelvana to the brink of bankruptcy."

For the loyalists who dreamed Nelvana was destined to become the Disney of the North, the failure of *Rock & Rule* came as a heavy blow. "*Cosmic Christmas* triggered a real hope, a promise," says Budd. "People were really disappointed because it was obvious that with *Rock & Rule* a dream was dying."

But rather than fold, Hirsh went to the marketplace and cut the deal he thought Nelvana should have made years ago: he took on series work. After years of carving out a niche in original programming, Nelvana accepted the yoke of subcontract and service production. "In a matter of six months I brought in what amounted to 100 hours of television," says Hirsh. It was a lot of bad television — 65 half-hours of the TV series *Inspector Gadget*, a computer show, and the fitness series *20 Minute Workout*.

The goal now was cash flow. In order to stave off its creditors, Nelvana also executed the first attempt by a corporation to use cartoons to sell toys; they produced several episodes of *Strawberry Shortcake* for American Greetings Corp. and Kenner Parker Toys. Based on the *Strawberry Shortcake* deal, they were contracted to do

The many faces of Mylar.

Mick Jagger is the template for villain Mok Swagger. Robin Budd returned to Nelvana's fold to animate the character.

Nelvana hitched itself to service productions such as Strawberry Shortcake.

Nelvana's fortunes turn once again when its feature film Care Bears: The Movie *rakes in $25 million. Theatrical exhibitors reawaken to the lucrative children's market.*

some Care Bears shows, and the first of two Care Bears movies. Nelvana's unspoken corporate motto became Toons R Us.

The sugar-and spice-and-everything nice *Care Bears* won adoring fans under the age of eight. From their fluffy white clouds, the bears descent to the "Forest of Feelings" and onto Earth, where an evil spirit has convinced a young wannabe magician named Nicholas to cast spells on the village kids who made fun of him. The indefatigable *Care Bears* prove that getting even is wrong. The sunny toys spread joy and goodwill with frighting speed and efficiency. Inspired by the vocal performance of Jackie Burroughs as the pernicious spellmeister, Collins introduces at least one edgy character into the cast

Care Bears: The Movie earned $25 million at the North American box office in 1985, making it the highest grossing non-Disney feature ever released at the time. It proved that movies could simply be a lucrative merchandising appendage. Its success led to a spate of other movies for young kids — another theatrical *The Care Bears Adventure in Wonderland* (1987), and one featuring the royal pachyderm, *Babar: The Movie* (1989). Unable to repeat the box office score of the first Care Bears movie, Nelvana settled on steady series work.

Television work transformed the studio. Gone was the "holistic" managerial approach. Nelvana started to pay animators by the foot of animation generated, rather than the hours incurred. Like their American counterparts, they discovered how to save money by shipping animation to the Orient. Nelvana stalwarts either changed jobs or moved on.

"I would have starved if I was paid by the foot, so they had to let me start to direct," says Bonifacio. Collins also directed segments for *Strawberry Shortcake* and the *Care Bears*. Promising young artists such as brothers Dick and Ralph Zondag (now a director at Disney) were funnelled into layout and posing.

The doors to the American networks were opened by George Lucas, who commissioned Nelvana to produce *Droids* and *Ewoks*, two Saturday-morning cartoons for ABC-TV. Even for a firm with a solid reputation, breaking into the US market was tough.

"(The networks) weren't interested in anything different and new, they were interested in reliability," says Hirsh. "Lucas was in the position to force us in." Although the shows didn't perform well, ABC liked Nelvana's participation and bought *Care Bears* — the series — from them the following year. Once Nelvana wedged its foot in the network door, it sold more product. ABC-TV purchased *Little Rosie* (1990), and Fox hired them to produce *Eek! the Cat* (1992) and *Jim Henson's Dog City* (1992-94).

Steven Spielberg's Amblin Entertainment hired Nelvana to do *An American Tail* series, and *Family Dog* (1992) for CBS; and the network in turn bought Nelvana's independently developed, *Cadillacs and Dinosaurs* (1993-94), a series based on Mark Schultz' comic books and a story edited by Steve de Souza (*Die Hard I* and *II*). With follow-up series such as Jim Lee's *Wild C.A.T.S. Covert Action Teams* (1993-94)and *Ace Ventura*, Nelvana also became a regular supplier to CBS.

Hirsh decided that in order to keep the infrastructure afloat, he would have to do more than just service work for the networks. In the late eighties, he waded further into European partnership after successfully co-producing the *Babar* (1989-91) series with France's Canal+ in 1987. The series was strong, but Nelvana's output deal with the Brizzi Brothers Studio in France fell through after its partner was bought out by Disney.

Rather than train another studio for someone else to acquire, Nelvana started a studio with Canal+ as partners. Le Studio Ellipse was operational by March 1990, and Nelvana continued to option classic European characters such as *Rupert Bear* (1991-97), *The Adventures of Tintin* (1991-92), and *Little Bear* (1995-98). By the fall of 1998, Nelvana rules the CBS Saturday-moning airwaves when it was announced that it would produce six animated series for the network. Every single show from 7 a.m. to noon was theirs. Not only did Nelvana bounce back from the brink of bankruptcy in the early eighties, it also successfully went public on the Toronto Stock Exchange in 1994. The new battle would be to retain its talent.

Nelvana had built a reputation on skilled young artists. Restricted to posing and layout tasks, however, the troops showed signs of discontent. Initially, Nelvana tried to maintain a balance by handing over a few episodes — or at least a few

Babar: The Movie *does not hit its target in the theatrical marketplace. Nelvana refocuses on TV series.*

Nelvana options classic European characters such as Rupert Bear, Tintin, *and* Little Bear *(below).*

Tintin

show openers — to artists. But the look of the episodes done in-house was so radically different from those done in the Orient that Nelvana had to abandon that practice. "The shows done in the Orient looked from beginning to end exactly the same; they were very flat and they didn't have the little spark the animators here would bring to it," says Collins.[76]

Budd was the director for *Beetlejuice* (1988-91), a series created by US director Tim Burton. In its first season, it won an Emmy award, and was picked up for syndication. Budd's kinetic approach was so astonishing that his episode "Pest o' The West" was accepted into official competition at the Ottawa•90 International Animation Festival.

When *Beetlejuice* was syndicated, the workload and pressure proved too much for Budd, so he "ducked out" of the series. But not before Nelvana appeased both its client and Budd. Nelvana gave Budd several months to animate the snappy one-minute introduction, the ultimate teaser to lure kids to the show. It was one of the many goodies the company parceled out to Budd to keep him on the payroll.

Those who stayed did so out of a sense of fraternity. "My relationship with Nelvana has been like one of the younger brothers growing up," says Bonifacio. "I wasn't an owner, but I was there when they started. At one point, Patrick called me his conscience because I would often write letters about how the animators were feeling about things, what the mood in the studio was like, and what people would really like to be doing. I felt very much involved in the company. In a sense, I felt patriotic about wanting this Canadian company to do well." But he, too, quit after Nelvana announced it would adapt the biblical tale of Noah's Ark, sans its religious essence.

With Disney Television poised to open a studio in its own backyard, Nelvana dangled the feature film plum as a way to attract animators. It worked.

"I was threatening to quit, and they said, 'don't quit, we're starting a feature department,'" says Budd. Frank Marshall and Kathleen Kennedy (*Jurassic Park* producers) came to the rescue. Under contract with Paramount Pictures, Marshall and Kennedy offered to raise the development financing for three feature film ideas. Not only did the Kennedy-Marshall deal clinch Budd's contract, but Gammage, Bonifacio and Nissen returned to the fold.

The film with the most promise was *The Thief of Always,* based on Clive Barker's story and designed by Budd. Nelvana had arrived at the Leica-reel-and-soundtracks stage before the bad news hit. Kennedy and Marshall had left Paramount. Nelvana was once again out on a limb. "It's dead, dead, dead. It died an ugly death," says Budd. For six months they waited for the production thumbs up. Paramount did not respond. Nelvana shopped it elsewhere, but there were no takers. Smith, however, went on to direct the feature *Pippi Longstocking* (1997).

By the end of the century, Nelvana had come to a crossroads. The company had solidified its role as a steady network supplier; but it had taken 15 years for Nelvana to return to its roots — supporting original ideas. In 1996, Nelvana tried a refreshing kids' series entitled *Stickin' Around* (1996-98), created by Robin Steele, who did Stick Figure Theater shorts on *MTV's Liquid Television.*

Two years later, Nelvana added a couple of auteurs to its roster. After years of animating popular shorts for the NFB and Channel 4 in Britain, David Fine and Alison Snowden hooked up with Nelvana when their development deal with Universal fizzled out.

For years, they had stuck to independent films funded through the NFB or Channel 4 in Britain. After all, independents working in television were considered "sell-outs." The stigma no longer applies. Fine says that independent animators working in Canada "pooh-poohed TV series work because it was generally seen as kids' animation." The trend among cable networks to program more adult animation has changed the perception.[77]

Bob and Margaret was spun out of the duo's Oscar-winning short *Bob's Birthday* (1995). It is literally an animated sitcom based on a horribly normal British couple who elevate the mundane to sublime comedy. In a cultural landscape littered with gross-out shows like *South Park*, Fine and Snowden have perfected a kinder, gentler form of adult animation.

The success of *Bob and Margaret* had an in-house effect on Nelvana. Proprietary characters are slowly making a comeback. After three decades, the corporate agenda of Hirsh, Loubert and Smith has come full circle.

After it solidified itself as a network supplier, Nelvana once again supported original projects such as Stickin' Around *created by Robin Steele and Brianne Leary.*

In late 1999, Nelvana signed a $40 million deal with PBS, the US public broadcaster. Nelvana's shows such as Franklin *(below) dominate the American broadcast scene.*

Auteur animators break into prime-time TV with the hit series Bob and Margaret.

Sebastian Grunstra's drawings for Atkinson Film-Arts' first TV special, Little Brown Burro.

Nelvana's closest competition in the 1970s and early 1980s was Atkinson Film-Arts, a breakaway group from Crawley Films. Vic Atkinson had more hands-on animation experience than Nelvana's principals, and he had a stable of mature directors and designers to call upon.

Pino Van Lamsweerde, a noteworthy commercial animator, directed a number of Atkinson's half-hour specials including the company's maiden film, *The Little Brown Burro* (1977), and *The New Misadventures of Ichabod Crane* (1979). The addition of European-trained background artists Michel Guerin and Sue Butterworth created an unbeatable troika. One of Atkinson's best TV specials, *The Trolls and the Christmas Express* (1980), was directed by John Gaug, who later moved to New York as a graphic artist and illustrator.

Atkinson helmed a small ship and avoided risky series work. But by 1981, he was ready to call it quits. Hospitalized after overseeing two segments of *Heavy Metal*, Atkinson returned only long enough to supervise production of *Christmas Raccoons*, a CBC special developed by Kevin Gillis and Gary Dunforth, writers on Bruno Gerussi's *Celebrity Cooks* series.

Atkinson didn't stick around to see the show spin off into a prime-time animated series. He sold his shares to partner Bill Stevens because he didn't like the commercial direction the studio was taking: "I've been in this business a long time, and I won't produce garbage. I never will."[78] Stevens says the disagreement was about growth and financial risk. If he was going to mortgage his house to invest in expanding the studio, then he wanted more control over the employees.[79] The cordial split later ended up in the courts when a cash-strapped Stevens stopped his corporate alimony cheques to Atkinson. The payments were eventually resumed.

Atkinson's personal story has a happy ending. After quitting the company he built, he joined his son Lee, and drew over 1,000 images for the Corel Draw software package. The Atkinson family had grown since their "Gore Galore" days when father and sons made Super-8 horror flicks using prosthetic limbs stuffed with chicken guts.

After buying out his partner, Stevens proceeded to buy out his former boss, Budge Crawley. Encumbered with a hefty

Hewers & Drawers

.... **117**

debt of $1.2 million, Crawley unloaded his company for $1. It was no doubt an enormous ego boost for Stevens to buy out both his mentor and former employer, but it stretched his finances. Asked why he shouldered the additional burden of Crawley's debts, Stevens said: "That's where I started, and that's where I had loyalties." He also thought a live-action unit might pad out the cyclical cash-flow problems inherent in animation production. It didn't.

Under the new Atkinson-Crawley umbrella company, Stevens serviced two Care Bears specials and formed a limited partnership deal that included four CTV specials: *The Bestest Present*, *The Body Electric*, *The Velveteen Rabbit* and *Rumpelstiltskin*. By 1984, Stevens was turning the company around. He cut a deal with the Worlds of Wonder merchandising house to produce the series *Teddy Ruxpin* with DIC in France; and he signed a co-production deal with China to produce two animated half-hour specials, *The Nightingale* and *The Rocking Horse*.

Ottawa-based producer Merilyn Read approached Atkinson-Crawley with the rights to Laurent de Brunhoff's storybook character, Babar the Elephant. With company lawyer Mark Rubenstein, Stevens helped finance one of the most expensive specials at the time. *Babar and Father Christmas* cost $600,000 to produce.

Raising money through public offerings was easier in the eighties. "As long as you were Canadian and breathing you got funding money from Telefilm," says former legal counsel Mark Rubenstein.[80] Tax shelters were also lenient and there was little accountability. "Under the tax system then, it didn't matter if the show made a cent," he adds. "Their incentive was tax relief."

The Trolls and the Christmas Express — *one of four holiday specials by Atkinson Film-Arts.*

The New Misadventures of Ichabod Crane.

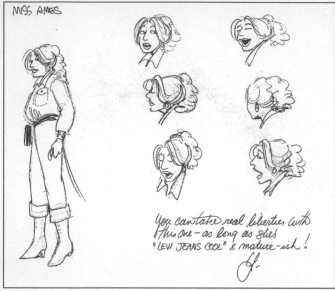

MISS AMES

You can take real liberties with this one – as long as she's "LEVI JEANS COOL" & mature-ish!

Cartoonist Lynn Johnston did all her own model sheets for the CTV specials based on her comic strip, For Better or For Worse.

VINNIE

Projects such as *The Velveteen Rabbit*, and Lynn Johnston's *The Bestest Present* CTV special (based on her comic strip *For Better or For Worse*) were successful. But Atkinson-Crawley's attempt to produce adult entertainment fell flat. *The Body Electric* was a TV half-hour featuring a couple of futuristic punk kids in space getting into trouble. The obnoxious special was scored by Canada's most obnoxious band — Rush. The studio went through three directors during production. Even the music track was out of sync.

Atkinson-Crawley Films benefited from a string of service deals for the *Raccoons*, a project co-produced by Kevin Gillis and former real estate lawyer Sheldon Wiseman.

What began as seasonal CBC one-off special events — *Christmas Raccoons* (1981) and *Raccoons on Ice* (1982) — grew into series proportions. The stars, Bert, Melissa and little Ralph find themselves constantly pitted against the snarling, cigar-chomping Cyril Sneer, a nasty aardvark. That includes winning a hockey game to save Evergreen Lake from Sneer's development plans. Sneer's Brezhnev-like bears are pitted against an all-star Canadian team.

Raccoons is a case study in how to build a franchise from scratch. Wiseman raised the $700,000 budget by selling shares to 22 investors. The special was then pre-sold to CBC and the New York syndicator Time Buying Services (TBS). The second installment, *Raccoons on Ice*, was budgeted at $855,000. By the time *Raccoons* became a series, the budget per episode was a high $415,000 and commanded unprecedented licence fees.

Quality and merchandizing aside, *Raccoons* profited most from an executive shuffle within CBC. When Nada Harcourt, CBC's executive producer of children's programming, was promoted to head of drama, she took the series with her. It became the first animated TV series to hit prime time in Canada, and the first local show purchased by the Disney Channel in the United States.

Raccoons was Atkinson-Crawley's financial artery in the early eighties. But in 1995, Gillis suspected that the company was over-charging, and withheld payments. In turn, Stevens pulled the plug on production, a move that threatened the delivery date. The dispute was temporarily solved by a cash injection by the producers. A divorce was imminent. Wiseman and Gillis wanted to control price and delivery.

In 1986, Wiseman and Gillis set up their own studio on Hinton Avenue. They named it Hinton Animation Studios. It recruited much of its staff from the Atkinson-Crawley team.

Bill Stevens orchestrated other business ventures, but cash flow was erratic after Hinton was formed. Jamie Oliff, now a hired gun at Disney, says that an activated Crawley intercom inevitably meant trouble: "The minute the speaker system came on we walked out the door and headed for the bar. We knew there would be no paycheque that day."[81] Cartoonist Lynn Johnston's stuffed bunny was held ransom when subcontracted work was not paid for.

Meanwhile, Stevens enjoyed his plush Fairmount Avenue office building in downtown Ottawa. It became a bitter joke to the animators who were working in dilapidated quarters. They crafted cartoons about the office politics and stuck them on their bulletin boards. They also joked that his band, "Stevens and Kennedy," took up too much of his time. Many in the studio felt that Stevens was more preoccupied with arranging the next charity gig for his (18-piece) orchestra than he was running the company.

Raccoons was the first Canadian series picked up by the Disney Channel.

Hockey great Mike Bossy autographed an animation cel of the Raccoons on Ice *special.*

Bill Stevens brokered many deals including the special The Velveteen Rabbit.

It was a hand-to-mouth operation. Stevens was often in the position of trying to bail out the company by accepting unappetizing service jobs such as *Dennis the Menace.* In a last ditch effort to stabilize cash flow, Stevens prepared a public offering to raise $6 million under a new entity — The Crawley Group. Three days before he was to make a presentation to Montreal investors, the stock market crashed. The offering went on the back burner.

A messy service stint finally brought the house of cels crashing down in 1988. The French animation firm Belkopi contracted the Montreal firm Via le Monde to produce animation for its series *Ys le Magnifique.* Via le Monde in turn contracted Crawley Films. After producing nearly 10 half-hour episodes, Belkopi was closed down by its owners, and Atkinson-Crawley Films owed $2.17 million.

With accrued debts of $4 million, Stevens was forced to sell his offices and shut down. "I was mortally wounded, I couldn't fight anymore," says Stevens. Employees were owed weeks of back pay, and discovered that their insurance coverage had lapsed. Exhausted, Stevens was no longer capable of finding another project to bail out the studio.

As the company's spirit flickered, many of its employees left to join the Hinton studio, and the

Raccoons

Raccoons' gang. Lesley Taylor jumped ship, as did directors Paul Schibli, and Sebastian Grunstra. Animators Nik Ranieri and Jamie Oliff took their leave as well.

Hard times continued in Ottawa. Less than five years after setting up the Hinton studio, Wiseman and Gillis also had a falling out. They clashed over the expansion of the studio. Gillis' pet project was *Raccoons,* but Wiseman wanted to add an ambitious feature film to Hinton's production slate.

Wiseman signed Paul Schibili to direct *The Nutcracker Prince,* an offbeat adaptation of the famous ballet. The quirky approach was soon dumped after Warner Bros. signed on as the US distributor and Cineplex Odeon bought the Canadian rights. The animators in Ottawa were not up to the challenge of crafting a theatrical feature. The top dogs had already moved on.

Just as *The Nutcracker Prince* wrapped production, Gillis learned that the Royal Bank had called in Hinton's loans. The *Raccoons* series was well within its budget, so Gillis concluded that money was being siphoned from the series to pay for the under-funded feature. Worried that he would not see final payments for his work as producer of *Raccoons,* Gillis hijacked

Cadet Rouselle
©Copyright National Film Board of Canada

Teamwork — Past and Present
©Copyright National Film Board of Canada

Evolution
©Copyright National Film Board of Canada

The Last Cartoon Man
Courtesy of Derek Lamb

The Drag
©Copyright National Film Board of Canada

Paradise
©Copyright National Film Board of Canada

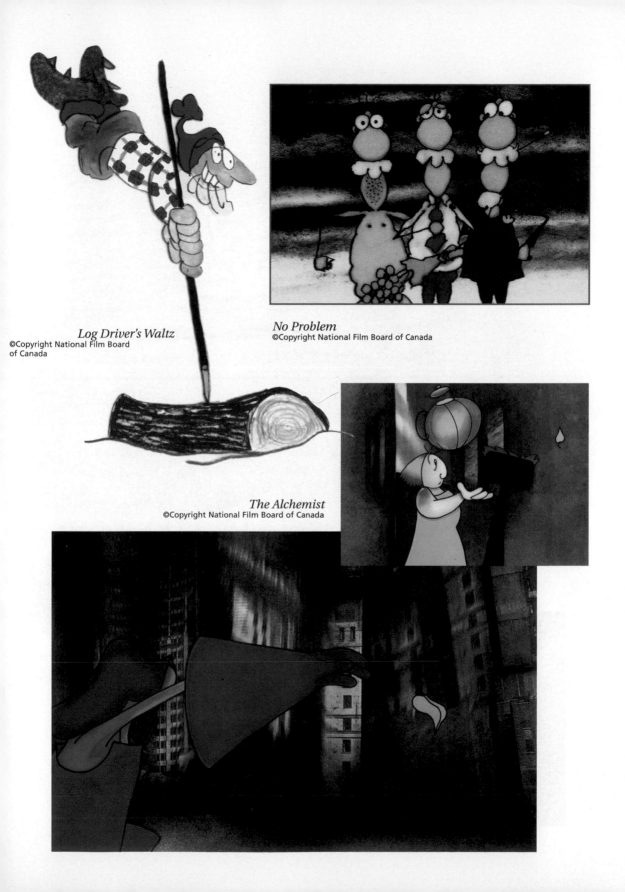

Log Driver's Waltz
©Copyright National Film Board
of Canada

No Problem
©Copyright National Film Board of Canada

The Alchemist
©Copyright National Film Board of Canada

Premier jours
©Copyright National Film Board
of Canada

Legend of the Flying Canoe
©Copyright National Film Board
of Canada

The Artist
©Copyright National Film Board of Canada

Karate Kids

Characters ©Copyright Derek Lamb and Kaj Pindal
Karate Kids ©Copyright Street Kids International
and National Film Board of Canada

Yvon of the Yukon
©Copyright Studio B Productions

Return to Oz
©Copyright 1996 Golden Books
Publishing Company, Inc.

Heavy Metal

Easter Fever

Mok from *Rock & Rule*

Cosmic Christmas

Rome-0 & Julie-8

Caillou

Raccoons

Little Lulu

"The Faster Life Gets,
The More Sense Milk Makes"
Image supplied by Michael Mills Productions
Used with permission by Dairy Farmers of Ontario

LifeSavers *"The Good Times Roll"*
Image supplied by TOPIX•Mad Dog
Courtesy of Carder Grey DDB Needham and LifeSaver Company

The Old Lady and the Pigeons
©Copyright Les Productions Pascal Blais and Les Armateurs

Teletoon station ID
Image courtesy of
Cuppa Coffee Animation Inc.

the master copy of the
final episode of the series. He
slept with it under his bed, using
it as leverage against his partner. In
desperation, he also undertook a late
night raid of the Hinton Studio to recover
material from the series.

The Royal Bank retaliated by seizing
Hinton's equipment. The Wiseman-Gillis partnership dissolved. Five months later, Wiseman was back
in business on his own. He rented the studio's assets from
the bank and opened his own unit — Lacewood Studios.

The Nutcracker Prince pulled in $2 million in theatrical
revenues in Canada. Even though it opened in 906 screens
across the United States, Warner Bros. scarcely matched the
box office receipts of its northern neighbour. It was an unmit-
igated disappointment.

Wiseman blames his US partner: "Warner Bros. had no mar-
keting plan or tie-ins."[82] It was not the hit they were hoping for.
Nevertheless, Lacewood picked up where Hinton left off, develop-
ing half-hour specials such as *Blue Toes: The Christmas Elf, The
Woman Who Raised a Bear as Her Son* (1989), *The Teddybear's
Picnic* (1991), *Tooth Fairy, Where are You?* (1989), *The Railway
Dragon* (1991), *The Teddybear Christmas,* and six one-hour spe-
cials based on the *For Better or For Worse* (1991) comic strip.

A strange production pattern continued despite the various
company closures. Some of Crawley's model sheets and designs
found their way into Lacewood's premises.[83] Even the production tics of one studio were inherited by the next. Schibli's
unusual dopesheet formula was passed down and adopted
by local animators. Freelance artists from outside the
nation's capital found the doping methodology rather
bizarre, but copied it anyway.

Five years after closing Hinton, Sheldon
Wiseman's company was in trouble again. After
Lacewood defaulted on a $2.5 million debt, its creditor,
Paragon Entertainment, launched an aggressive takeover bid. By
August 1997, Lacewood Studio had become Paragon
Animation. A year later, even Paragon went belly-up.
Ottawa's lively production scene was decimated.

The cyclical work in Ottawa convinced one freelancer, Gord Coulthart, to open his own shop. He
formed Funbag Animation Studio, in 1993, with pro-
ducer/director Don Spencer and Rick Morrison.
Coulthart decided he could make a better living taking subcontract work on Nelvana's *Tales from the
Cryptkeeper*, and Film Roman's *The Simpsons.*

On a chilly winter day, Coulthart can be found in
his office sketching poses for one of his clients. He co-

*Funbag Animation developed
many new concepts including
Old Goat (below) which was
made into a seven-minute
short for Hanna-Barbera.*

"Everyone who
lives here is
in my way!"

Cinar focuses on established properties such as Little Lulu *(top) and* Arthur *(second from top). The success of* Arthur *on the Public Broadcasting Service (PBS), has led to three other shows on PBS —* Caillou *(below),* Wimzie's House *and* Zoboomafoo.

founded the company but still works in the animation trenches. In their spare time, the employees head out for a beer and propose off the wall cartoon ideas to pitch south of the border. Funbag's offerings over the years have included *Mouthy Marge, Whacked out Mountie, Living with a Goof* and *Truly Sucky Adventures*. One Coulthart favourite was the character Old Goat — a curmudgeon with the motto: "I'm older than everyone and I hate you!" They finally scored with the TV series *Toad Patrol* with Edward Sarson Productions for Teletoon.

While Ottawa's animators are retrenching, Montreal once again has become a flourishing animation hub. Its star company, Cinar, has a production line-up that rivals Nelvana's. Micheline Charest is the poster girl of Canadian animation. She is the public face of Cinar — one of the fastest-growing entertainment firms in Canada. She beat Nelvana to the stock market in 1994, and her company's stock doubled in value two years after its public offering on the NASDAQ. With all the press, and annual revenues hitting $67 million in 1997, it's no surprise that Charest made the top-20 list of *Hollywood Reporter*'s "Women in Entertainment."

Therein lies the rub. Cinar is better known for its distribution prowess and business affairs than its originality. With the exception of *Smoggies!* (1989-90), produced with director Gerald Potterton, Cinar has rarely ventured into the scary, scary world of novel character design. It prefers tried and lucrative adaptations such as *The Busy World of Richard Scarry, Madeline, A Bunch of Munsch* (1991-92), *The Little Lulu Show* and *Arthur*, the children's series based on Marc Brown's books.

Cinar, however, wisely sidestepped service ventures and quick-hit deals with US networks. While Nelvana shovelled out tens of hours of shows for toy manufacturing companies, the wife/husband team of Micheline Charest and Ronald Weinberg concentrated on building a library with a long shelf life. Early on, they focused on highly recognized literary-based properties. Their strategy paid off; by 1997 its stock price had multiplied.

When Charest and Weinberg first decided to break into the film industry, they borrowed $10,000 from their families and hit up a wealthy acquaintance for another $65,000 to land the theatrical rights for Robin Hardy's cult horror flick, *The Wicker Man* (1973). With the film in the trunk of their car, the couple toured art houses in the United States and raked in $250,000. When their partner pulled the plug by repossessing the film, they joined a small distribution company in New York that sold American films to Russia and former Soviet bloc countries.

With the advent of cable television in the United States, the partners realized they could reverse the usual flow of distribution and sell animation from Eastern Europe to the new cable systems. They packaged a series of Czech films for Nickelodeon and brokered the sale of the Japanese series *The Adventures of the Little Koala*. Distribution was their first corporate building block. They became the Canadian distributor of Mattel Toys' show *Captain Power and Soldiers of the Future*. The company hit pay dirt when it pre-bought the Japanese series *The Wonderful Wizard of Oz* (no relation to Crawley's *Wizard of Oz* series) for $20,000 per episode and resold it for twice that amount to RCA Video Productions. Rather than contracting out versioning to other sound houses, Cinar built its own post-production facility in Montreal.

For his part, Potterton had long ago thrown in the corporate towel, but he couldn't resist brokering a deal or two on the side. While working on titles for the *Wizard of Oz* package, Potterton approached Cinar about a show he had developed with France's Initial Groupe starring the Smoggies — a group of environmentally conscious trolls. On Potterton's urging, Initial Groupe engaged Cinar as a co-partner on the series.

"We dropped it in their laps," he says. *Smoggies!* was the first original production Cinar tackled. It would also be one of their last.

Had Potterton possessed more business acumen, he might have accrued a fortune in the eighties. Instead, he introduced Charest and Weinberg to Christine Larocque, the former production supervisor of *Heavy Metal*. With Larocque as full partner, Cinar opened Crayon Animation in 1989. Financed through a $1-million tax shelter offering, Cinar launched an ambitious production slate including a package entitled *My Favourite Songs*, *C.L.Y.D.E.* (1990-91) and *Madeline*. Potterton worked on a few *Favourite Songs* and *C.L.Y.D.E.*, but drifted off to toil on his own productions.

When the Crayon partnership eroded, Larocque sold her shares back to Cinar. Cinar scrambled to find a studio replacement. After some fierce lobbying on Weinberg's part, Lacewood's able production manager, Lesley Taylor, moved to Montreal and took over the running of Crayon. She promptly

Smoggies!, a series starring some environmentally conscious trolls, was the first original production tackled by Cinar.

HUCKLE IN SUN SUIT (COSTUME)

Sc ⑨ - ⑰

The character designs of The Busy World of Richard Scarry. *Cinar has built a business making cartoons for young children.*

lured Ottawa regulars to Montreal. Bill Speers (*The Teddybear's Picnic*) directed *Bunch of Munsch*, based on a series of books written and drawn by Robert Munsch, and Graham Falk did design work on *Baa Baa Black Sheep* (one of the *Favourite Songs* installments). But the Ottawa gang did not stay, and Cinar eventually found artists in Montreal. While Taylor cut new and cost-effective deals with companies such as Phil Cartoons in Manila, its best shows — the early *Madeline* series and the Robert Munsch classic, *50 Degrees Below Zero*, were in-betweened and painted in-house.

There has been an ebb and flow of artists at Cinar. Lacking Nelvana's track record, Cinar had a hard time recruiting. Art director Chris Wren and directors François Brisson and Greg Bailey laid the creative cornerstones. They were the masters of adaptation magic. It's not an easy task, especially when authors insisting upon creative control don't understand the problems inherent in transferring their drawings to animation.

For example, Huck Scarry interceded on behalf of his father Richard Scarry, offering design input on the show, *The Busy World of Richard Scarry*. At times, it was a difficult collaboration. Scarry's characters are flat and animators found it difficult to move them. In the storybooks, the creatures' hands are drawn to look like little clubs. "There are no fingers, they kept the fingers really short, so we never really get to have a solid hand for expression," says Bailey. "It's kind of a loss, and one of the restraints of the series."[84]

Little Lulu was much easier to tailor. She had a big black hole for a month, and no teeth. Cinar's most popular show, *Arthur*, ran head to head with PBS's *Barney*. The storybooks had all the ingredients for a successful video conversion: a flexible author, good stories, great writing and appealing rounded designs. Cinar has also produces the TV series *Animal Crackers, Wimzie's House* and *Caillou*.

Nelvana and Cinar became quite savvy at acquiring properties, particularly rights for popular literary characters in Europe. Montreal's Ciné-Groupe also signed European characters and comic books, but their shows have not had the same global appeal.

Ciné-Groupe was created as a service and production house in 1979 by Jacques Pettigrew, a former news cameraman at Radio Canada, and Yves Michaud. After producing a live-action film entitled *Rien qu'un jeu*, Pettigrew decided that animation was the most profitable route. In 1983, the company started developing the series *Ovid and the Gang* with Kid Cartoons in Belgium.

Ovid is a genial platypus who survives various encounters in the forest, including a stranger who wants to capture him for a Metro zoo. The 65 episodes of *Ovid and the Gang* took four years to complete. Pettigrew chalked up plenty of frequent flyer points criss-crossing the Atlantic. Director Jean Sarault supervised storyboards in Belgium, which were shipped to Canada to be animated, returned to Belgium for colour rendering, and sent once again to Montreal for final post-production. It was a headache at times, but it worked.

Ciné-Groupe joined forces with Belgium artists to produce Ovid and the Gang.

Ovid and the Gang generated more work with the Europeans. Unfortunately, it also led to one of the sorriest co-productions ever attempted in Canada. *Bino Fabule* (1987) is a stop-motion/live-action science fiction fantasy starring Bino, "a new wave scientist" from the planet Karmagor and his sidekick, a tortoise astrophysicist. Developed as a series, director Rejeane Taillon reworked her concept into a feature film when it was apparent that Telefilm Canada and its Quebec counterpart would green-light this star-crossed feature. The film fails miserably in all categories: poor story, clumsy character design, and limp special effects. *Bino Fabule* is a Playdough nightmare in motion.

A collaboration with Zagreb Film brought better artistic results, but also provided harrowing experiences for Ciné-Groupe executives. The respected Yugoslavian animation unit had won many international prizes, but they had never tackled a commercial series. Neven Petricic went to the Cannes Film Festival with some interesting designs and storyboards starring a family of flying bears, a concept rooted in Yugoslavian folklore. At Cannes, Petricic met Pettigrew and the two entered into a joint venture for *Little Flying Bears* (1989-90). After completing the first four episodes, it was clear that there weren't enough stories to tell about bears in a forest, so Ciné-Groupe inserted two children into the scripts.

In the fall of 1990, halfway through the second cycle, the Croatian-Serbian war broke out. "We heard stories of animators on the front lines in the morning, then at their table in the afternoon," says Pettigrew.[85] "We were pulling our shows out of Yugoslavia in the trunks of Fiat cars heading to Frankfurt." Louis Duquet, the Canadian overseas line producer, spent many evenings in the bomb shelter with the animators. They were literally in the animation trenches. Nevertheless, it took

Bino Fabule *a strange 3-D sciencefiction fantasy feature film, stars a strange cast of characters that look like Playdough rejects.*

Final episodes of Little Flying Bears *were animated in war-torn Yugoslavia.*

Sharky and George: Crime Busters of the Deep

Duquet about four months to convince the general director of Zagreb Film that the shows had to be completed elsewhere. In December, Duquet packed up the remaining shows and drove out through neighbouring Slovenia.

Ciné-Groupe remained faithful to its Belgium partners. It co-produced the series, *Spirou* (1993-94), based on a French European comic book character, and *Sharky and George: Crime Busters of the Deep* (1991-92) who "always get their fish."

Having invested in its 3-D animation unit, Toonteck, Ciné-Groupe ran into trouble. In 1994, Montreal's film company, Cinepix, bailed out the company by acquiring 55 percent of the business. Cinepix was subsequently bought out by Lion's Gate Group. After struggling for its life, Cine-Grope produced a new film based on the *Heavy Metal* comic. After years of conservative TV series, Ciné-Groupe decided in 1997 would be the Year of Living Dangerously. They had embarked on a Canadian cultural initiation rite — the making of a feature film.

When Budge Crawley produced the first animation series in Ottawa, Canada was considered by New York heavies to be a backwater. It took three decades for the industry to build a sturdy foundation. The Canadian commercial landscape is littered with companies that made and lost it all. Those who survived — Nelvana, Cinar and Ciné-Groupe — now support a growing web of animation studios, which are filling up Saturday-morning schedules on both sides of the border.

Canadians carved out a piece of the turf for themselves by slowly infiltrating the US market — by beating Americans at their own game. But now, the reverse is also happening. Lenora Hume, once Nelvana's cameraman, became Disney's vice-president of international animation. She has spearheaded the move to open Disney branch plants in both Vancouver and Toronto. Not surprisingly, she recruited many of her Nelvana contemporaries, including Bill Speers, Charlie Bonifacio and Ken Ingham.

Rather than wait for the talent to move south, the south is travelling north. The spectre of branch plant production looms, but for now, Canadians are no longer mere minions. They are sitting in the directors' chairs and producers' offices. Canadian animators were once considered the gypsy kings of the animation world. Now, with so many options in their own backyard, they finally have a place to call home.

chapter 7

A Hard Cel: The Evolution of the Commercial

n the corporate world, animation has traditionally been a tough sell. Animators have received little respect and even less remuneration from advertisers. But a truce has been brokered in the long-running civil war between animated spots and live-action commercials. Animation still holds the kids' commercial territory and is making gains in the adult demographic market after decades of hard slogging.

In the 1950's, Winnipeg's Phillips-Gutkin-Associates, the largest animation house in the country, barely survived in an era when boys were boys and a promotional spot for Labatt's beer featured a friendly bartender named Gus rather than bikini-clad babes. Using posterized graphics and limited animation, they flogged products for Kellogg's and Milko, and occasionally won less lucrative contracts for household goods such as floor wax.

Animation in Canada has come a long way, baby! Through experimentation and ingenuity, the spectrum of styles has expanded dramatically. Flat 2-D cartoons are a thing of the past. Once ghettoized in the 13-and-under category, animation is not only used to promote milk products, it energizes sophisticated "adult" campaigns peddling running shoes, beer, cold medicines, and soft drinks. Now, many advertisers view animation as an ideal vehicle for the soft sell.

Budge Crawley had a corner on the commercial-industrial market in Canada in 1948. Handed steady commissions from government agencies like the National Film Board, Crawley Films thrived during the war. By its ninth birthday, it was the country's largest private film enterprise, though it was not the largest private animation studio.

Two new rivals emerged in the late forties: Winnipeg-based Phillips-Gutkin; and Toronto's Graphics Associates, a company formed by ex-NFB staffers Jim MacKay and George Dunning. Unlike Budge Crawley, a documentary man, they had trained in graphic arts and animation. MacKay and Dunning had spent years in the animation department alongside Norman McLaren before establishing their own studio.

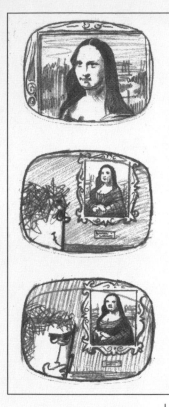

Storyboards from Phillips-Gutkin — one of the first animation houses in the country.

Wacky Bird for Windsor Salt.

Phillips-Gutkin-Associates was formed in 1948 by catalogue fashion photographer John Phillips and Harry Gutkin, a freelance illustrator for the *Toronto Star* and *Maclean's* magazine. The Winnipeggers' debut marked the beginning of a new advertising era in the country, which coincided with the birth of CBC-TV.

Operating out of an office in a third floor walk-up on Winnipeg's Main Street, Gutkin hired British animators Dennis Pike and Jeff Hale, and recruited local boys Barrie Nelson, Blake James and Barrie Helmer. The one-room office quickly expanded to take up the entire floor. The logistics of their operation were daunting. Most of their clients were based in Toronto, Montreal or New York; making a deal over a cup of coffee cost hundreds of dollars. In addition, the only motion picture film processor was located in Montreal. Phillips-Gutkin had the graphic artists, but post-production was practically a double-blind experiment.

In 1954, the company landed a large contract to produce animated commercials for *Libby's National Movie Night* on CBC. It was a big break which led to more work. Tight budgets, ranging from $1,200 to $4,000 per spot, meant the company had to take shortcuts: substituting full animation with postering and collage techniques. The posterized low-end spots included a series for Simoniz Floor Wax (Leo Burnett Advertising) and Mackenzie Diamonds (Brooks Advertising).

Bigger budgets meant better animation and lip-syncing. Although the company leaned towards the more popular UPA design style in spots for Chrysler cars (Ross Roy), it occasionally aped Hanna-Barbera for the Kellogg's cereal ads and an endorsement for Security Storage. Gutkin designed several appealing characters including a worldly water tap for Hydro Electric Power of Ontario (Foster Advertising) and Wacky Bird for Windsor Salt (J. Walter Thompson). The bird was born on the back of a napkin during a Toronto luncheon meeting and was brought to life by actor Jack Little, who voiced a number of commercials for the company. It won consecutive awards in 1959 and 1960 at the Art Directors Club in Montreal and Toronto.

When the CBC banned animated spots aimed at children, Phillips-Gutkin was knocked on its backside. Kids were the target audience for many of their commercials. Competition in Toronto was growing, and the company suffered two major financial setbacks in close succession. One costly error involved a mistake at a film lab. The company was also stuck with the cost of redrawing a series of animated commercials for Shirriff desserts. The original spots, based on the agency-boarded work, were drawn from characters from a popular game show on American TV. After the spots were completed, lawyers correctly pointed out that Shirriff could be sued for copyright infringement. Although the mistake was made by the agency, Phillips-Gutkin shouldered the financial burden. To add insult to injury, the agency blamed Phillips-Gutkin, and refused to send more work its way.

The studio set its sights on producing animated films for TV programs. Harry Gutkin met with British commercial producer John Halas in 1960 to discuss the possibility of collaborating on an animated television series entitled *T. Eddy Bear*. T. Eddy was a monocled, stuffed toy that would venture each week to a new and exotic part of the world. According to Helmer: "The studio embarked on the production of *T. Eddy Bear* with no knowledge of any of the shortcuts and devices that were to become the mainstay of made-for-TV animation. At first we worked on it during slack periods — funding was always hard to come by — but eventually the whole studio was engaged full-time to achieve a pencil test."[86]

T. Eddy Bear, a monocled pompous bear, is the first Canadian cartoon developed for a proposed TV series. It was never aired.

Both parties eventually lost interest. It was just as well. Poor T. Eddy had no plot line. The only entertaining scene — the pompous T. Eddy wiping his monocle while lecturing at the camera — was an inside joke. Animator Barrie Nelson drew it as a caricature of his boss Harry Gutkin.

The reign of Phillips-Gutkin came to a slow and painful end when video replaced film and competition for low-end commercials intensified. Increasingly, the "gravy" national advertising accounts were no longer awarded to advertising agencies outside Central Canada. Agencies consolidated campaigns in their Toronto and Montreal offices.

In 1963, Barrie Helmer left Winnipeg and joined Canawest Studios in Vancouver. Hale, Pike, Nelson, James and Mason joined Crawley films for the launch of the *Tales of the Wizard of Oz* series.

For newly independent Jim MacKay and George Dunning, Toronto was Mecca in the Canadian advertising industry. They waved good-bye to the NFB in Ottawa and formed Graphic Associates in 1949, focusing on animation, design and filmstrips rather than commercial photography or live-action production. It was a creative choice, but not a profitable one. Their portfolio is distinguished for its economy of design, minimal backdrops, and bulbous-nosed characters popularized by the UPA studio in the United States and NFB cartoonist Wolf Koenig.

Graphic Associates produced the first Canadian colour commercial for a Buffalo TV station in 1950. It also gave both Richard Williams and artist Michael Snow their first jobs in the industry. Graphics Associates gained international recognition. After four years of scraping by in Toronto, George Dunning was hired by UPA in New York in 1955, and later moved to Britain to establish a local office. When UPA closed its British operations, Dunning stayed and set up TVC — a company that remained in business until the late nineties. Dunning would later direct *Yellow Submarine* (1968), and his company became the Godfather of the animated commercial in the U.K.

MacKay was courted by another animation company that had opened its doors in Toronto's West End one year earlier. Reg Batten and partner Arthur J. Rank owned Batten Animation. The men knew nothing about the industry, but had acquired a former gambling hall after its manager was found in a ditch riddled with bullets. Gearing up to become a leading-edge production house, the partners bought the second Oxberry camera to come off the assembly line, and hired Julian Rothman, and assistant NFB film commissioner Ralph Foster, to run the studio.

Foster was considered a persuasive man. He convinced a reluctant MacKay to abandon his own firm and work as their creative director. Stylistically, MacKay continued to pursue the minimalist design he had perfected with Dunning. In a public service announcement for the Canadian Wildlife Service, he drew characters using a thick black marker. It was a simple drafting approach. No fuss, no muss. His Tri-Nut Margarine spots were vintage fifties — modelled after UPA characters. An ad for the *Toronto Daily Star* was clearly influenced by the popular Canadian short, *The Romance of Transportation.*

Background artwork was also minimized, or even eliminated. Sometimes the animation team simply sponged paint on cels to serve as a textured backdrop, as in the Alpha-Bits commercial. They pared the body of an entire car down to a simple prop in a Department of Transportation spot warning drivers about the dangers of speeding. The commercial fea-

George Dunning's first piece of professional graphic design was this self-promotion brochure.

tures a man zipping across the screen holding onto a steering wheel. Other popular shorts include a series produced for Labour Canada entitled *Do it Now, Don't Wait for Spring.*

Batten Films had a rocky history. Internecine battles between the owners and the managers led to the sale of the company to Spence Caldwell — the "C" behind CTV, Canada's largest independent TV network. MacKay stuck it out for only one year, and then rented his own space in the Gooderham distillery building in downtown Toronto. He named his reincarnated firm Film Design.

MacKay hired some remarkable young talent in 1958 after his company was flush with cash from a commission to animate six-minute inserts for the CBC-TV children's series *Mr. Piper.*

Don Arioli also started his career at Film Design. In the early sixties, Arioli published a humorous 1960's "zine" with Les Nerenberg. A vocation in animation wasn't high on his priority list when he approached MacKay about doing a little work for Film Design. Arioli actually owed MacKay five dollars, and offered his meagre services to pay off the debt. "He's a charming little bugger, and we got along well," says MacKay. "He just did a little of everything. He charmed the girls in the ink and paint department, and he started doing storyboards."[87]

Arioli's big break came when Wolf Koenig chose his storyboard, "The House That Jack Built," among all others submitted by Graphics Associates for a film about union diversity. To make the film, Arioli moved to Montreal and joined the NFB. He never left. *The House That Jack Built* (1967) was nominated for an Oscar.

Just before MacKay decided to re-establish his own business, another aggressive young man entered the market. Al Guest, a transplanted Winnipeg animation cameraman and former editor at CBC Television, opened his doors in 1957 as Spectrum Productions, and produced spots for the public network on an animation stand he built

The Tri-Nut Margarine spot directed by Jim MacKay for Toronto's Film Design.

Al Guest and partner/wife Jean working on the series Ukalik.

Ralph Bakshi was one of the directors of Rocket Robin Hood. *Bakshi invented great gags including laser beam blasts from the eyes.*

himself. His first contract was for a pair of commercials for Buckingham Cigarette through MacLaren Advertising. Spectrum Productions changed names several times, but by 1964, it had become Al Guest Animation. Enlisted artists Manolo Corvera and Barrie Shaw-Rimmington worked alongside the office's pet alligator, Peaches.

Some of Guest's early commercials were rather experimental. A series of ads for Prudential Life Insurance were animated with string, and another pool of spots were inked directly on tissue. A pair of public service announcements for the Department of Transportation entitled *Snowplow* and *Garbage* picked up awards, but the bread and butter was the usual collection of clients such as Kraft Peanut Butter Teddy Bears and Kellogg's characters.

By 1967, The Guest Group was the reigning king of Canadian animation. Its offices occupied three floors in a University Avenue building. One floor was devoted to commercial work. Another two were fully occupied by animators working on the *Rocket Robin Hood* series. Guest took the plunge into serial work in 1967 by cutting a $1-million deal with US producer Steve Krantz to make 52 half-hour episodes of *Rocket Robin Hood*. The series took England's most famous thief and transported him 1,000 years into the future, to a time when Sherwood Forest was a floating, solar-powered asteroid. *Rocket Robin Hood* was a thinly disguised service contract. However, by making a sale to the CBC, Guest was able to pass the show off as Canadian content.

When the show ran into trouble one year into production, Krantz sent Ralph Bakshi to Toronto to oversee production and direct several episodes. Bakshi can be credited with inventing visual gags such as laser beam blasts from the eyes. The series also took on a darker, grittier visual tone thanks to input by comic book artist Gray Morrow, who served as the series layout artist during Bakshi's reign.

When Guest threatened non-delivery because his cash flow had dried up, things got ugly. Bakshi devised a plot to rival any Saturday-morning cartoon: he grabbed a pile of storyboards and film cans, jumped into a taxi, and fled across the border to Buffalo. A warrant was issued for Bakshi's arrest in Canada, but it was too late.[88]

Bakshi and Krantz finished the series in New York by mixing backgrounds from their *Spider-man* series. Financially unable to launch a legal suit in the United States, and bereft of product, Guest liquidated his company and fled to England. Guest would later return to produce *Ukalik* (1975), a half-hour fantasy based on Inuit art, and *Captain Nemo* (1976), a series of five-minute films. Despite his vast experience, he never regained a toehold in Canada.

The animation community in Toronto quickly regrouped. The largest post-Guest house to open was Cinera, run by Vladimir Goetzelman. An art director for Guest since the 1950s, Goetzelman picked up where Guest left off. He hired many of Guest's then-unemployed staff. For more than a decade Goetzelman resisted serial projects, preferring to focus on commercials and service work such as a group of commemorative spots for the American Bicentennial. Having witnessed Guest's burnout, he remained skittish about doing a series. After 15 years in the business, Cinera would only produce one television special, based on Johnny Hart's comic, *B.C.: A Special Christmas* (1980) aired on HBO. It would take a second wave of Toronto animation houses to venture into television specials and series.

Goetzelman hired untested designers with a natural aptitude. Frank Nissen, Bob Fortier and Marv Newland — later to become Canada's top animation directors — passed though his doors. "Animators were few and far between so Vlad was just looking for somebody who could animate, who could put the thing

Toothbrush Family *spot from Al Guest's reincarnated studio.*

Storyboard from Cinera's HBO show *B.C.: A Special Christmas.*

(Storyboard panel labels:)
PETER STRUGGLES UPHILL WITH ROCK

(CHOP CHOP STILL IS HEARD DOWN IN VALLEY)

DROPS INTO WAITING BOX

(CHOP CHOP CONTINUES)

Cinera produced numerous commercials in the sixties and seventies.

together. And whatever design idiosyncrasies you could offer was just a plus," says Nissen, a former art college graduate from Los Angeles.[89]

Nissen designed and animated one of the company's most stylized commercials: a cat food spot featuring Miss Mew who is chatted up by three male cats. The spot is starkly designed, with no anthropomorphic clothes covering the cats, and no backdrops. Only the occasional marker — a manhole or piece of fence — travels across the screen to convey movement. One cat is introduced simply as a smile illuminated in the black. Subsequent Miss Mew commercials filled out the background and added props like hats and aprons, but the client returned to Nissen years later to repeat his minimalist approach.

In addition to more conventional fare for Bell Long Distance, Q-Tips, Shirriff's Mashed Potatoes and Del Monte chocolate pudding, Cinera produced some psychedelic commercials for Lowney's. The animators borrowed heavily from Dunning's *Yellow Submarine* in a spot promoting Cherry Blossom chocolates. Floating lips tuck into the chocolate-covered coating to the cherry centre, surrounded by colourful flower-power images. The sexual imagery is underscored with a Beatles imitation soundtrack. One of their most comic efforts was a spot for Uniroyal steel-belted tires, featuring the comic strip character B.C. navigating through the snow on a single wheel.

Marv Newland, and his replacement Bob Fortier, were the animators with counterculture roots. Both worked on the alternative "newspaper" *Guerrilla*, and occasionally did artwork for the *Roxy Movie Theatre* playbill, a second run, alternative cinema on Toronto's Danforth Blvd. When Newland left Toronto for Vancouver, he recommended Fortier to Goetzelman.

Business was good until the industry was rocked yet again by a Quebec law banning animation in commercials aimed at children under 13. As a result of financial setbacks caused by the new advertising law, private companies lashed out at the National Film Board. Its monopoly on government contracts made it a prime target. The new animation society made it a priority to topple the NFB's Studio A enterprise. Veteran animator Dennis Pike argued: "In Canada the government is obliged to have all its work done by the Film Board, and if you do get a government film to do you can be pretty damn sure that the Film Board is not interested in it. They put it out to tender and you know full well that it's a bitch."[90] The commercial directors eventually won the battle. By the early eighties the NFB had weaned itself off sponsored clients.

The attack on the NFB did not save Goetzelman's business. His ship was leaking. Star animators drifted off to work for the competition or to start their own firms. Nissen became Nelvana's key animator before moving to Disney in LA, and Fortier and Newland now operate their own shops in Canada. Cinera did not end with a bankruptcy, but with a whimper. Goetzelman remains bitter about the growth of an industry he helped create. "[Nelvana and others] all got into business by raiding Cinera Productions," says Goetzelman. "I trained everybody in this town. I didn't want to do it over and over again."[91]

Goetzelman bowed out just as the industry was becoming interesting. The feature film *Who Framed Roger Rabbit* attracted a whole new audience to animation in the late eighties. Advertisers jumped on the bandwagon to exploit the new interest. Once the demand for copycat spots was satiated, the industry settled into a productive and eclectic period. But not without a push from commercial directors.

Bob Fortier is one of the best, and perhaps the most successful creative director-owners of an animation shop in Canada. Like many young artists in love with "the quality of line," Fortier looked to cartoonists like Duncan Macpherson of the *Toronto Star* for inspiration as a teenager. His passion for cartoons and comics has served him well. He easily references classic cartoonists like John Held Jr. and casually offers his own sketchbook doodles to snare clients looking for cutting-edge graphics. Over time, his company also bridged traditional cel and post-production wizardry by forging alliances with effects houses in order to bring gloss and texture to flat 2-D animation.

In 1979, Fortier joined Nelvana Animated Commercials (NAC). Nelvana's early commercial incarnation lasted less than four years. His departure precipitated its closure. "The feature *Rock & Rule* was draining (Nelvana's) resources... I didn't like the direction the company was heading in," he says.[92] Clive Smith eventually resurrected the commercial division and renamed it Bear Spots.

In March 1983, Fortier opened Animation House. The industry was still in its infancy but Fortier preferred to cut his own path: "Once you've run your own studio, it's tough to go back and work for somebody else." His first commer-

Bob Fortier changed the Animation House logo many times over the years.

Animation House gives Kellogg's™ gang a new 3-D look.

cial under the company banner was less than impressive; in fact, it wasn't even animated. The Labatt Classic beer spot consisted of camera pans and tilts over a painting of a 19th-century brewery. The staid approach was not a harbinger of spots to follow.

Animation House succeeded because, like other good animation houses, it was able to reinvent existing characters such as the Quik bunny, Nabisco's Shreddies and TONY THE TIGER™. Animation House gave the dated Shreddies characters a new retro look in keeping with the early nineties animation style. It also gave TONY, the ageless tiger, a European facelift, and the Quik bunny an Asian makeover. But the company entered the spotlight with its live-action/animation work. After the surprise hit *Who Framed Roger Rabbit*, every creative art director in the world wanted his own shorter commercial version. The animation inserted into live-action footage is often referred to as "2 and a half D" animation. Classical 2-D animation is now fleshed out because the characters can cast shadows, cause reflections, and have more body tones.

Famous since 1937, the Kellogg's™ Rice Krispies™ gang were dragged into the 3-D live-action world by Fortier and effects house Command Post. In the first spot, "Child's Play," Pop!™ is snatched off the cereal box by a mischievous kid. The trio jump into a television set in a second commercial dubbed "Tube Trouble." In a visual 2-D/3-D twist for Nabisco, Fortier built latex green "Gobblin' Goblins" puppets complete with armatures and accessories, who chase Nabisco 2-D heroes Eddie and Freddie Shreddie up and down Escher-like staircases.

Agencies frequently turned to Fortier when they wanted to replicate the success of TV cult favourites. His design impulse lends itself to underground comic books. He prefers to describe it as: "imagery cartoon drawing, one step above graffiti."

Although clients coveted the demographics, they were not prepared for the accompanying satire. "I tell clients there is an acidity in such animation; not only in the drawing style, but in the attitude of characters," says Fortier. Nevertheless, after requesting "edgy," many would pull out a buzz saw to smooth out the ragged humour.

In his benchmark spot for Junior Caramels, Fortier managed to both appease the client and retain his personal touch. The ad features an overloaded family car crashing down a precipice with the tag line: "Your cousins from Idaho had to cancel their annual visit. What a shame. Moments like these are made for Juniors." Teenage angst is highlighted in a second spot with the running commentary: "The school sent home all the notes you forged during the year." Fortier's caricature was called upon again for Young & Rubicam's Dorito's Cheetos in a script that eliminates one of his protagonists with a mouse trap. Murder is not usually the stuff of advertising, but black comedy survives here.

There is a little experimental whimsy in all creative souls, even in those whose feet are firmly planted in the world of marketing. Fortier's can be found in his company's logo. The insignia, which evolved from a scratch-on-film symbol, pays homage to Canadian experimental animator Norman McLaren.

The non-traditional approach McLaren practised rarely surfaces in the commercial world. "The frustration with those techniques is that they exist in a very delicate world, and oftentimes the advertising industry wears very heavy boots," says

The distinctive look of animator Bob Fortier as applied to a Junior Caramels spot.

Fortier. "So you have to have a very sophisticated creative team behind you, and a very sophisticated client." Fortier encouraged clients to try multimedia approaches, and hired stop-motion artist Philip Marcus Has and alternative media specialist Hubert Den Draak to round out his traditionalist team.

Fortier gave up some of his independence in 1998, when the company was acquired by Balmur Entertainment, singer Anne Murray's management and publishing company.

While Fortier has consistently led the pack in traditional animation, the digital leader in the nineties was TOPIX Computer Graphics and Animation (later renamed TOPIX•Mad Dog). TOPIX was, and remains, a pioneer in Canada. Founded in 1987 by Chris Wallace, Don Allen and James Snelling, TOPIX has been a pioneer in Canada.

Two creative people controlled the "look" of TOPIX 3-D production: William Cameron started with TOPIX in 1989 as a director and designer. His overlay of images, numbers and symbols dominated Canadian broadcast graphics during the early nineties.

Harold Harris, the man behind MuchMusic's station ID, Mickey Mouth, was TOPIX's key commercial animator and director until he left in 1998. For years, Harris alternated between

TOPIX lets the good times roll in a commercial for LifeSavers.

Show IDs for MuchMusic by TOPIX.

the music industry and the animation w o r l d . H i s résumé includes stints at Potterton Studios, Michael Mills and the National Film Board — where he worked as an ink and paint artist for John Weldon. Along the way, he aspired to be a rock star, but gave up after age 30. Not surprisingly, TOPIX's first commercial hit is a result of his ability to choreograph a note-accurate performance in the LifeSavers commercial, "Good Times Roll." The commercial raked in over 25 international awards and put the company on the international map in 1990. It also spawned several look-alike campaigns including the "Oreo Scoreo" cookie campaign for McCann-Erickson (1992).

Rock 'n roll LifeSavers aside, TOPIX discovered a niche in the marketplace by deftly combining graphics, software development and creativity. TOPIX was able to undercut its competitors by designing a system that could compete with the standard 2-D effects product on the market.

With its cheaper system, TOPIX became a top contender in the broadcast design and 2-D compositing arena. In the early nineties, it rendered 90 percent of all animation — logos, station IDs, titles — at Citytv/MuchMusic stations. Its "nimbling" innovations were used on MuchMusic's Cliptrip, FAX and R.S.V.P., and its incorporation of text and design for MediaTV was repeatedly mimicked.

Two years after its Lifesavers hit, TOPIX made another splash with a Post SugarCrisp commercial for McKim Baker Lovick/BBDO, which married 2-D and 3-D animation. TOPIX animators mirrored the effect of the ballroom scene in Disney's *Beauty and the Beast*. The goal was to seamlessly insert the 2-D cel animated Sugar Bear into a 3-D environment, and match colour and lighting. A "roaming" camera added to the complicated calibrations.

In 1995, the company opened a high-end post-effects division called Mad Dog Digital. It was used with compositing prowess by director Floria Sigismondi on David Bowie's "Little Wonder" rock video. Sigismondi also morphed a moth in Marilyn Manson's music video "Tourniquet."

The equipment has changed over the years, but code-crunching is still part of everyday business. Colin Withers, technical director at TOPIX, released free on the Internet a cloth plug-in program he designed for a Post Honeycomb "Craver" campaign (Grey Advertising 1996-98).

TOPIX's Comdisco "the Face of Technology" spot won a silver Clio Award in 1998.

TOPIX is a hybrid of a traditional animation studio, and a post-production/special effects shop. Its success spawned imitators in the industry. Animation houses teamed up with post and effects houses such as Command Post, Dan Krech Productions, Calibre Digital Design and Spin Productions in order to deliver extra shadows, highlights or difficult compositing scenes. The line separating an animation house and an effects house is blurring. Dan Krech and others now produce directly for agencies, and everyone in the business is taking equity in TV series. The boutique business has grown into a mall.

In 1990, TOPIX was the new kid on the block with its 3-D animation and 2-D compositing prowess. By marrying organic animation and 2-D wizardry, Adam Shaheen's production house, Cuppa Coffee, has become the next big thing. MuchMusic immediately embraced Shaheen and partner Bruce Alcock as its favourite new designer for station IDs and bumpers. The station manager remained unfazed even when the Cuppa Coffee crew, working late into the night, accidentily shot the station's "French Kiss" show opener upside down. Everyone had to cock their heads to one side to watch the spot. It was later flipped in post-production. TOPIX got its start making cheap spots for the music station, and so too did Cuppa Coffee. One year after opening its doors, the company was inundated with orders from Disney Channel, Turner Classic Movies, ProSieben Germany, TSN (The Sports Network) and Teletoon.

David Bowie's "Little Wonder" music video.

Cuppa Coffee broke into the business doing show openers for MuchMusic's "French Kiss" program.

Cuppa Coffee's retro approach includes stop-motion.

Animation House capitalized on its underground graffiti look, but Cuppa Coffee takes a retro animation approach. Cuppa Coffee works with wire-framed puppets, scratch-on-film, papier mâché and wooden blocks. It's as if Rankin/Bass stepped into a time machine and discovered Inferno 2-D.

Cuppa Coffee flaunts its use of textiles and fabrics. Texture is the company's signature. Rather than just drawing on regular bond paper, the directors choose brown garbage bags or fine Japanese papers. Rather than seamless pictures, materials literally collide with one another. It's trash TV at its best. Competitor Bob Fortier characterized this multimedia cut-and-paste trend as the "primitive movement" backlash.

When Shaheen started as an illustrator in the business, there was either cel animation, CGI, or NFB shorts on the CBC at odd hours. "I thought the three disparate groups could work united. We'd bring eclectic artists and learn on the job."[93] Alcock moved on a year later, and Shaheen recruited indie talents such as Justin Stephenson, Julian Grey and Steve Angel. A stream of young animator/artists, including Ann Marie Fleming, flowed through the studio.

The company's innovative commercial for Shoppers Drug Mart promoting the Toronto Raptors' "Slam Seats" made critical waves in 1995. In the spot, a wire-framed dinosaur rips apart a paper city that subsequently goes up in flames. The animators built a Toronto skyline by gluing colour laser prints of cityscapes on tinfoil so they would crumple effectively. The set itself was backed by a bluescreen to permit composite time-lapse clouds and colour corrections to match sky with the paper metropolis. Mad Dog Digital's post-production team added plenty of smoke and mirrors. The technique was "an integration of two almost mutually exclusive techniques — stop-motion and post-production layering," according to Stephenson.[94]

A paper dinosaur trashes the city of Toronto in the Shoppers Drug Mart "Slam Seats" promotion.

In a 1996 opener for Turner Classic Movies, filmed actors are digitally regurgitated on the screen. The effect was created by scanning every third frame of film into a Macintosh computer, spitting out the images on a laser printer, and physically cutting out the actors. The paper cutouts were placed next to a copper and brass globe of the world and manipulated. To create a stop-motion effect, a digital camera was set up to double each exposed frame. The final digital footage went to Spin Productions where Inferno digital compositing artists added 25 layers of effects. With such teaser campaigns, Cuppa Coffee lowered the commercial limbo stick.

Experimentation is the key to success, says Shaheen. "We are a company of happy accidents." It is also a company of unhappy exits. Senior directors Julian Grey and Steve Angel broke away in 1997 to form Head Gear Animation.

Operating as a separate company under the TOPIX umbrella, the whiz kids of the advertising world built and animated a complete 3-D Willy Wonka candy factory. The spot designed to promote Nestlé's Willy Wonka Nerds and Sweet Tarts is full of strange inventions.

A sophisticated illustrative approach for an Exquisine commercial.

Montreal has been the epicentre of the Canadian animation scene for years, but studios focusing on commercial spots did not spring up until the mid-seventies. One of the earliest commercial houses, Potterton Productions, was geared towards high-end TV specials and feature films, rather than commercials. Three ambitious employees broke away to set up their own companies: Paul Sabella and Julian Szuchopa formed Boxcar Films, and Michael Mills set up Michael Mills Productions, now the oldest Canadian animation house still operating.

If Animation House is rock 'n roll, then Michael Mills Productions is classical. Whereas Fortier's team is a multimedia master, favouring the quick edits and collage effects of rock videos, Mills is still a bit of a purist, always seeking sophistication. In a "Stella" Exquisine commercial for Backer Speilvogel Bates, Mills and his animation team translate what appears to be a sketch from a fashion designer's notebook into movement. The controlled, colourful strokes of a fashion model's face mimic the assured draftsmanship of a seasoned stylist.

Michael Mills' campaign for the Milk Marketing Board was so popular it ran for six years.

The feathery rendering of this Canada Savings Bond spot mimics Frédéric Back's illustrative style.

Mills' distinctive "shaky line" style was called upon by corporate big-shots like Bell Canada (above) and the Montreal Jazz Festival (below).

Mills' years at the NFB may account for his appreciation of arthouse techniques. He clearly has an eye for talented auteurs in his field, and is one of the commercial leaders advocating the soft sell. The commercial that best exemplifies this savvy approach is the award-winning Milk Marketing Board spot for McKim/Watt Burt. The watercoloured commercial, which features a man astride a hamburger, resembles the illustrative style of Ryan Larkin. Its intended market was the "on the go" white-collar crowd.

"Originally, the client came to us with hardlined linear drawings," says Mills. "I thought it had to be softer, like water colour, and they let me experiment." The six-month marketing plan turned into a six-year campaign. The advertisers discovered that the spot not only appealed to its target audience, but also happily crossed into other socioeconomic groups. The client ordered two more versions with varying colour backdrops.

Mills returned to the softer illustrative approach in his Sudafed commercial for Burroughs-Wellcome, and a Canada Savings Bond spot, which has feathery renderings reminiscent of Frédéric Back's award-winning approach.

Over the years, Mills developed his own distinctive caricature. His big-nosed men, drawn with a nervous line, are frequently requested by advertising clients. It is animation's answer to a style made famous by *New Yorker* cartoonist R.O. Blechman. J. Walter Thompson called upon Mills to produce two corporate messages for Alcan — one promoting the recycling of aluminum cans, and the other highlighting the company's participation in the 1990 Montreal International Jazz Festival.

Mills was a rebel from the National Film Board of Canada. He left in 1973 and never looked back. The next year, he formed Michael Mills Productions. Consistently ranked among the top five animation houses in Canada, Mills directed another short film

that put him in contention for an Oscar. Animated by Bill Speers, John Gaug, Jim Hiltz and Rick Bowan, *History of the World in Three Minutes Flat* (1980) was given a nod by the Academy in 1981 and won the Golden Bear Award at the Berlin Film Festival. The film starts with an ominous voice confessing: "I had seven days, blew six ... here goes." In exactly three minutes, the film humorously depicts famous events in the history of the world including the downfall of Adam and Eve, the escape of the Jews from the Egyptian Pharoahs, a group of monks singing, "It's been dark here for ages," and a mischievous "Lennie" Leonardo da Vinci. The film was the ultimate corporate calling card.

International accolades attract clients, but it was Mills' improvised rearscreen projection method that proved to be a cash cow for many years. Mills devised a simple way to combine live-action and animation by projecting animation plates of the backgrounds and characters using a rearscreen projector owned by the NFB. He produced a pool of live-action/animated commercials for the Bank of Montreal using a technique that was the exclusive domain of special effects houses in Los Angeles. For years, his major competition, Cinera, was unable to replicate it. Before computer graphics became affordable, Mills had a decided edge over his Canadian competitors.

For many years the only competitive threat Mills faced was from companies located in Toronto. A couple of amateur

History of the World in Three Minutes Flat, an independent short directed by Michael Mills, became his company's ultimate calling card.

Pascal Blais' young company took off after he directed the Diet Coke spot starring the famous French character, Astérix.

Kellogg's™ MINI-WHEATS™ cereal spot by Productions Pascal Blais.

NFB animator Cordell Barker makes his mark in the commercial world by animating for Chlor-Tripolon.

groups — Disada and Les Film Quebec Love — were around in the early seventies, as were Boxcar Films, and puppet master Koos Hillenaarra of Kohill Productions. The first real challenger to appear on the Montreal landscape was Les Productions Pascal Blais.

Pascal Blais was self-taught. Barely out of his teens, the clean-cut kid directed commercials for Kohill before starting his own enterprise at age 23 with partner Bernard Lajoie.

Blais' father was a producer and director .... "Don't waste your time on that stuff. It's way too complicated, and there's no future to that."[95] They encouraged him to consider cutouts or object animation. But Blais wasn't interested. The French animation studio was not for him. He would have to forge his own path.

The combined trust of director Yves Simoneau and art director Yvon Paquette of Arsenault Paquette resulted in his agency's first big break. Simoneau and Paquette lobbied their client to hire Blais for the Diet Coke live-action/animation spot starring the famous French Astérix character. "I don't know what convinced them to try me, but they had to convince the publisher of Astérix, who made it a condition that everything had to be done through their studio in Paris." The company was on a roll.

Until 1990, Blais directed everything that passed through the studio. But it was time to diversify. Blais was heading towards a serious burnout, and he had backed himself into a creative corner. At one point, he was forced to turn down a great job, with an unlimited budget, because he could not find an animator to replicate the illustrative style the agency demanded. That's when he decided to represent top notch directors with different styles. "A lot of studios still work in the old fashioned

way where there is a man who is the front figure who will go to all the meetings of the clients, and the client thinks he does everything," says Blais. "I thought we'd be better off working like a live-action company, so I went out and got the best directors I could find, with different fields of expertise and different techniques." He now markets their expertise alongside his own.[95]

Cordell Barker was the first director added to Pascal Blais' roster. Blais loved the looney style Barker perfected in the NFB short *The Cat Came Back*. He convinced Cossette to hire him for the Chlor-Tripolon ad. The result is a delightful wheezy bee suffering from a pollen attack. Barker has also invented a doodle character for the long-running Bell Intermax series.

Plasticine artist Anthony La Molinara animates those notorious allergy instigators.

Plasticine artist Anthony La Molinara was also roped in to sculpt anthropomorphized allergy perpetrators — ragweed and pollinating trees — for a pair of clever Claritin commercials. Others on his roster at one time included: Denis Lavois, the animator behind the stop-motion animation for the Jos. Louis cream-filled biscuit; Greg Duffell (former director at Lightbox Productions), who is animating wacky Warner Bros. characters; Caroline Leaf, Gerald Potterton, Martin Berry, and Oscar winner Ferenc Rofusz. The great Russian animator Alexander Petrov (*The Cow*) was originally hired to animate an Imax film *The Old Man and the Sea*, but while his camera was being rigged, he brought to animated life great masterpieces of art by Renoir and others for the Labatt Bleue beer spot "Gallery Rave." It remains a seminal moment in advertising: the wedding of art to commerce.

Pascal Blais underwrote director Sylvain Chomet's film The Old Lady and the Pigeons.

In 1997, Blais helped finance Simon Chomet's 24-minute film, *The Old Lady and the Pigeons*. An eccentric Parisian man seeks food and comfort by disguising himself as a pigeon to visit an elderly woman passionate about birds.

It has been a long and rocky road for commercial houses on Canada's West Coast. In the early sixties, Lou Parry's Capilano Studios specialized in maps and diagram work, and Al Sens operated a small scale

Spots for Lowney's candy (above) and Texaco (below) by Canawest Film Productions.

International Rocketship delivers innovative spots for Nickelodeon.

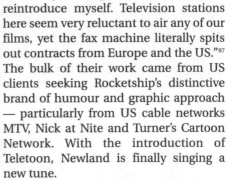

studio working primarily for CBC. The first truly commercial studio was Canawest Film Prod-uctions, a wholly-owned subsidiary of KVOS-TV in Bellingham, Washington. The station founded a production arm in 1960 to do station promos. But within three years, it was bidding for commercials in the private sector, an exception in the industry.

When Barrie Helmer joined KVOS in 1963, the company was producing a handful of commercials. "Colour TV was an exciting rumour for most of us, and 90 percent of TV production was in black, white and 12 shades of grey," says Helmer.[96] A surviving reel of commercials includes bulbous-nosed characters for the Treasury Branch of the Province of Alberta; a UPA stylized short for Coronation Foods, and a take-off of Rocky and Bullwinkle for Lowney's candy.

When agencies seek adventure they approach International Rocketship, and spin-off firms such as a.k.a. CARTOON, which gained a reputation on the festival circuit with outrageous shorts like *Anijam* and *Lupo the Butcher*. Initially, Canadian broadcasters and clients were too conservative to sign them on. After two decades of innovation, director Marv Newland was frustrated by their conventional attitude: "Every time I go to Toronto I have to reintroduce myself. Television stations here seem very reluctant to air any of our films, yet the fax machine literally spits out contracts from Europe and the US."[97] The bulk of their work came from US clients seeking Rocketship's distinctive brand of humour and graphic approach — particularly from US cable networks MTV, Nick at Nite and Turner's Cartoon Network. With the introduction of Teletoon, Newland is finally singing a new tune.

There is a collegial sense of competition among Rocketship's staff. When clients request ideas, "Everyone cuts loose and does boards," says Newland. In the spring of 1995, Rocketship was approached by Nickel-odeon to produce a series of 3-D shorts (two 15-sec-

ond spots and one 20-second bumper) for its NoggleVision primetime slot, where viewers search the house to find those cool 3-D goggles in time. In this instance, animators Andy Bartlett, Alan Best and Shelley McIntosh were given the thumbs up. Asked how the animators figured out 3-D animation, Newland offers a *Reader's Digest* account of the process: "We're smart."[98]

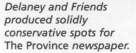

Delaney and Friends produced solidly conservative spots for The Province *newspaper.*

On occasion, Rocketship has performed for local clients. Newland brilliantly interpreted Scali, McCabe, and Sloves' copy for Earl's Restaurant. The chalk-rendered spots feature either a pig, cow or chicken each recommending one of his other barnyard rivals to hungry patrons visiting Earl's. The B.C. Dairy Foundation twice turned to Rocketship for its unorthodox style. Their first spot features Jersey cows in lip-sync, and in the second, a rolling pinball traverses strange pastures where a cow jumps over a buttery moon.

Delaney and Friends is the straight man to Rocketship. In the boom and bust cycle of regional production, Delaney produced staid, solid spots for *The Province* newspaper and Purex toilet paper. Their watercoloured "Butter Lambada" spot for the Dairy Bureau of Canada catapulted them to the A-list in 1990. After a campaign — reminiscent of Frédéric Back's fanciful films — was launched in May, retail sales for butter jumped dramatically. A wave of fan letters poured into the Dairy Bureau and the Marketing Board. This letter from Helena Jenson of Toronto is a client's dream: "Although I am now in my 71st year and have been continually told [otherwise] by the media and my doctor, I shall continue to use butter much against their advice."[99]

Canadian production houses are the tortoise to the American hare. For years, Canadians copied, mimicked and plagiarized their southern counterparts. Today, the maple leaf has the upper hand over the stars and stripes in two areas: Canadian houses cull ideas from the numerous experimental artists in their backyard, and they have a decided edge in computer animation. Companies such as TOPIX•Mad Dog, Animation House, Toronto and International Rocketship now promote signature styles and techniques. And they have proven beyond a reasonable doubt that animation cels products.

TOP SPOTS

Behind the scenes for six innovative spots that put Canada on the commercial map.

LifeSavers: "Good Times Roll," 1989
Production house: TOPIX Computer Graphics and Animation, Toronto
Director: Harold Harris • Producer: Stephen Price
Animators: John Mariella, Bob Munroe, Paul Griffin
End graphic: Louis Fishauf, Reactor Art & Design

"Can you make a LifeSaver play the piano?" That's the assignment from Howard Alstad, art director at Carder Gray DDB Needham advertising agency. The client requests that there be no eyes and no arms, "none of the anthropomorphic things you usually get," recalls TOPIX producer Stephen Price. Other parameters are minimal — no props, and black background sans environmental effects. No boards are drafted.

Harris, a former musician, throws out ideas — all very loose — and the spot begins to take shape around a Stevie Ray Vaughn "The joint is rockin' and nobody's knockin' tune. Pre-production takes place in producer Ted Rosnick's studio with a honky-tonk piano player searching for musical phrases that would fit with the leaping LifeSaver choreography.

Three or four animators, including Paul Griffin (now a CGI animator at Industrial Light and Magic) take a scene and try different animation riffs. "In the course of producing a 30-second commercial, we probably produced eight of them, and threw away seven," says TOPIX president Chris Wallace.

"The lighting was pretty much a fait accompli, since it was against a black piano and very dramatic," says director Harold Harris. "We concentrated on getting the right action, and the right camera moves."

	File	**Edit**	**Region**

1|1|000	0:00.00	0:00:00:00	4
1|2|455	0:00.72	0:00:00:21	♪
1|3|044	0:00.77	0:00:00:23	♪
1|3|089	0:00.80	0:00:00:24	♪
1|3|131	0:00.84	0:00:00:25	♪
1|3|174	0:00.87	0:00:00:26	♪
1|3|222	0:00.91	0:00:00:27	♪
1|3|265	0:00.94	0:00:00:28	♪
1|3|297	0:00.96	0:00:00:28	♪
1|3|330	0:00.99	0:00:00:29	♪
1|3|359	0:01.01	0:00:01:00	♪
1|3|365	0:01.02	0:00:01:00	♪
1|3|385	0:01.03	0:00:01:01	♪
1|3|395	0:01.04	0:00:01:01	♪
1|3|401	0:01.04	0:00:01:01	♪
1|3|414	0:01.05	0:00:01:01	♪
1|3|417	0:01.06	0:00:01:01	♪

The piano presents another challenge. Senior animators take the MIDI information from the soundtrack and translate it into keystrokes and guitar licks using a program created by Bob Munroe. The team also builds a CGI piano on SGI's Personal Iris boxes running Wavefront software. They construct it to look like a player piano that has been shot by a wide-angle lens. Bob Munroe (now at C.O.R.E.) writes a program with key stroke information so that the 3-D virtual piano can play itself.

Nestlé Nescafé: "Café State of Mind," 1994
Production house: TOPIX Computer Graphics and Animation, Toronto
Director: William Cameron • Producer: Sylvain Taillon
Live-action production house: Imported Artists
Director: Richard D'Allessio

Nescafé wants to create three spots for its instant European-style coffee products. The McCann-Erickson Agency strategy is to take specialty java away from the hip café crowds and deliver it to the ordinary folks including senior citizens and staid bean counters.

The idea is to juxtapose the fifties beat feeling with present-day voices, by suggesting that by drinking café au lait you're transported to a simpler era — but one that is still cool and relaxed.

McCann-Erickson's art director Michael Wurstlin makes a prototype of a TV graphic. Borrowing from his "Café State of Mind" print campaign, he takes a black and white photo of a saxophone player and sticks it onto coloured paper. A torn-out, full-coloured head is glued on top of the musician's body. The effect resembles the Blue Note album covers of the fifties. But there is one hitch; nobody has a clue whether or not this graphic can be animated.

The challenge for producer Sylvain Taillon is two-fold: how to keep the spot interesting and add motion. In their first test, TOPIX shoot both black and white and colour film of the actors doing the exact same movements. A wide shot of the entire body is shot in black & white, and medium close-ups of the face are shot in colour. Director William Cameron is aware the gestures are out of sync, but decides that "it doesn't matter." The technique does, however, need refining. He decides to bring an old Photo-Stat machine out of retirement in the basement. It prints on animation style paper with peg holes, for an interesting staggered effect.

Cameron reshoots the actors' bodies using a fairly static camera. The film frames are printed and cut with an exacto blade, stuck under a video camera and reshot into the computer. Former Cuppa Coffee types — Bruce Alcock and Steve and Tom Hillman — are enlisted for the exacto blade work. The digitally enhanced coloured heads are adhered in the post-production phase with the help of Adam Putter working on Discreet Logic's Flint. They now look as if they are literally ripped out of a magazine and attached to the bodies.

The music is written on set. The players jam through the actual shoot. Wild audio is also recorded. The two recordings are recombined to make the final music tracks. "For a spot that's so intricate to put together, there was a lot of ad-libbing," says Taillon. The end result is a spontaneity rarely achieved with planned special effects shoots.

Richard Unruh of Third Floor Editing does the rough cut, selecting which takes of bodies will go with which heads. Unruh cuts two spots for each commercial that eventually airs. "It wasn't until we started putting the two rough cuts together that we knew how it was working," says Cameron. "Until then there was this constant nagging suspicion that this was going to end up looking grotesque."

By the time Cameron is ready to complete the last installment of the three-part campaign, he has devised a swifter, digital way of doing the organic blade work. Cameron also decides to discard the static black and white camera work. In the last reshoot of the campaign, overhead shots and additional camera elements are introduced. "If we hadn't done it in the traditional way to begin with, we never would have known how to get that organic look using digital means," says Cameron.

The Dairy Bureau of Canada: "Just Butter It," 1990
Production house: Delaney and Friends Productions, Vancouver
Animation director: Chris Delaney • Animator: Norm Roen

The Dairy Bureau of Canada wants a butter campaign that will put the brakes on the decline of butter consumption in a health-conscious and calorie-wise age. The mission is to counteract the cholesterol backlash.

According to focus groups, animated commercials will not sell dairy products. Jim Burt, art director at Watt Burt Advertising, begs to differ. He overrides research naysayers and decides to seduce butter-lovers back with a lyrical animation campaign that shows a butter knife dancing romantically with a food partner. He wants a pastel-hued soft sell done in a painterly style, which culminates with copywriter Graham Watt's killer tag: "Butter, it doesn't take much."

Montreal illustrator Nina Berkson is commissioned to do preliminary sketches of Burt's storyboards. Burt wants to avoid making butter look greasy, and asks for a "gossamer art style." Berkson gives a dreamy, yet realistic look of the butter-knife character. It is reminiscent of the films produced by Montreal Oscar-winning animator Frédéric Back.

Jim Burt calls in animation director Chris Delaney who produced the award-winning Ontario Milk Board spots featuring line-drawn neon characters. "We realized it would be a unique approach to animation and advertising, because nobody — in advertising — had really animated a series of watercolour-painted images. Most ad animation up to that point was your Saturday-morning cereal-type stuff. We thought it would break some new ground, but I don't think any of us had any idea of how successful it was going to be," says Delaney.

Execution-wise, Delaney decides the campaign needs the finesse of an individual animator with sensitivity to rhythm, and who is versed in non-Disney styles.

Delaney hires Vancouver-based animator Norm Roen because of his organic drawing. Every image Roen draws looks as if it is approached as an individual rendering. The first "Butter Lambada" spot shows a knife dancing with a slice of bread to the rhythm of the Lambada melody. Ironically, the popularity of the lambada music causes the next creative struggle. The Dairy Board requests that all subsequent spots use the same song. Burt, however, convinces them to keep a distinct musical flavour for the next installments. When butter consorts with corn, Burt chooses a hoe-down country theme. Asparagus and butter sways to Montreal blues/jazz singer Ranee Lee's version of "You're Nobody til Somebody Loves You."

In addition to its critical success, the campaign's impact could be measured in practical terms: it broke a 25-year butter sale record. Sales of the client's product jumped by 10 percent in Ontario and 5 percent nationally during the six months the ads ran. "Just butter that!" crows Delaney.

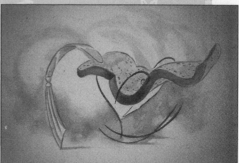

Cartoon Network: "Hi-Ball," 1992
Production house: International Rocketship, Vancouver
Producer: Michael van den Bos
Directors: Russell Crispin and Dieter Mueller
Animator: Danny Antonucci

The Cartoon Network, the Atlanta-based Turner Broadcasting's 24-hour cartoon channel, wants a package of animated show openings for its inauguration. Forty-nine versions of the spots are needed for the show titles. Miriam Tendler of Corey McPherson Nash Advertising in Massachusetts contacts Rocketship producer Michael van den Bos to develop a concept for the series of 20-second bumpers and station IDs. The checkerboard logo must be incorporated into the spots, and they should interact with the characters. The other stipulation is that the project should "embody high energy and zaniness."

Michael van den Bos meets with the Rocketeers chosen as likely suspects to work on the project. He discusses the brief and throws out a storyboard deadline. Everyone goes away and works up ideas, which are duly faxed off to the agency. The winning character and concept is director/assistant animator Russell Crispin's original court jester "Hi-Ball" — an annoying entertainer who is always getting the royal crap kicked out of him. The agency thinks he would be a good icon for the launch of The Cartoon Network.

Storyboards are developed with some input from the client. Storyboard approvals move into layout and animation. Once comments and the thumbs up are given at the pencil test stage, tweaks are made and colour production commences.

Van den Bos lends his own lungs to the first spot. He voices Hi-Ball's screams, while Doug Parker talks the normal talking voice. Crispin, who had never directed anything of this scale before, co-directs the master opening spots with veteran director/animator Dieter Mueller.

While commercial animators are considered chameleons, the style of this spot is pure Crispin. "That was just him at the time, his hand to paper," says van den Bos. "If we're doing straight commercial work, the design is usually driven by the agency, but not this one."

Danny Antonucci, noted for his snappy cartoony style, animates the masters, and brings his ebullience to the spots. "It didn't need a delicate hand, it needed somebody who could zip that character around, whack it about, and infuse it with life," adds van den Bos.

Junior Caramels: "The Visit" & "Dear Teacher," 1989
Production house: The Animation House
Animation director: Bob Fortier
Animators: Lesley Hedrick, Pat Knight
Producer: Jo-Ann Cook
Post-production: Command Post

Warner Lambert wants to pitch its Junior Caramels to the savvy Gen-X crowd. Hip humour and edgy illustration are the catch-phrases used.

The J Walter Thompson agency asks animation director Bob Fortier to adapt their billboard illustrations for animation. Problem: The print cartoons are concepts designed to work as a single panel. Fortier must adapt the ideas to last 15 seconds or 360 panels. In addition, the client now requests that candy product in the advertisement look realistic, and not cartoony like it was in the print campaign. Fortier believes any realism compromises the style, but he complies. Junior Caramels — the TV spot — is still a dead-funny and stylistically breakaway campaign, despite client intervention.

Fortier credits this pool with paving the way for his "edgy" cartooning style. Requests for his edgy look are made by MTV and a Pepsi spot. The style also proves that animation can work for products with an older audience.

"Things like Jr. Caramel turned the corner on that. Now anything goes," says Fortier. Even Molson Canadian beer turns away from bodacious babes to animation for its "Project X" campaign.

Molson Canadian: "Project X," 1995/1996
Animation director: Bob Fortier • Animators: Bob Fortier, Lesley Hedrick
Producer: Jeanine Sinopoli • Production house: The Animation House
Live-action house: Spy Films, Toronto • Director: Pete Henderson
DOP: Sean Valentini • Producer: Suzanne Allan
Post-production: Mad Dog Digital, Toronto
Producer: Sylvain Taillon • Flame artist: James Cooper

Agency MacLaren McCann puts out a call to animation houses asking for the artwork submissions. Any medium is welcome. On the strength of his doodle book, animation director Bob Fortier gets the job.

"Make it more fucked up," is how Fortier paraphrases the creative request. MacLaren McCann producer Deb Narine arrives at Animation House with a slew of poems written by Mark Fitzgerald. They are formulated as if written in a stream of consciousness. Art director Kerry Reynolds' strategy is to film all kinds of "extremely Canadian" activities. Her request is to use animation to augment an intense audiovisual experience.

"No one had a clear vision, which is what attracted me," says Fortier, "They wanted it raw, sketchy and rude." The pool is one of the few spots that Fortier actually animates himself. "I couldn't turn it over to a team," explains Fortier, "the sketches were mine. The live-action crew were shooting all over North America and desperately wanted me to join them." But Fortier refuses to go on the shoot. He orders the DOP to leave some space on the frame where he can animate. Then he locks himself in his garage and doesn't come out until he has animated segments for all four spots. The result is a Ralph Stedmanesque loose animation with a guerrilla-graffiti random violence to it. "There wasn't a direct relationship between the animation and the live action. I was flying blind. They were shooting while I was drawing. It was stream of consciousness animation." Fortier animates on paper with a 6B pencil. There are no preliminary drawings and no in-betweening. Everything became a key drawing. "Whatever came off the pencil stayed. Because it grew out of my sketchbook style, the freedom was amazing," says Fortier. "It turned into a real art piece."

The animation is a hot property on websites, postcards, T-shirts. And, Fortier says that if you freeze frame, there's a busload of nude women in one spot, whose nipples ran afoul of B.C.'s regulatory threshold. Curiously, says Fortier, "the B.C. government made us take the nipples off the naked ladies."

by Mary Maddever

chapter 8

Geeks From the Prairies

Prairie geeks in search of an identity. That's how one Canadian critic described characters in the films produced in the grain capital of Canada, Winnipeg. The description could apply equally to the filmmakers themselves — an eclectic group of musically inclined, socially dyslexic artists with a taste for the absurd.

Winnipeg has a long but spotty track record in the field of animation. It was home to the Canadian pioneers of puppet animation in the late 1920's, but the field lay dormant until Phillips-Gutkin-Associates opened its commercial shop in 1948 to produce limited animation spots. By the early seventies Kenn Perkins was running the sole outlet for animation.

Two introductions in the summer of 1968 gave Kenn Perkins an entrée into the animation field. One was a fortuitous encounter with NFB director Grant Munro at The Pony Lounge in Winnipeg. The other was a meeting with a senior designer at the Museum of Man and Nature in Manitoba who reacted to Perkins' bald plea for regional favouritism by hiring him. Munro took Perkins' portfolio back to Montreal and enrolled him in a six-week training course at NFB. Back in Winnipeg, Perkins beat out Ottawa animation veterans and landed the contract to produce *A Brief History of Astronomy* for Winnipeg's Man and Nature Museum.

In November, 1969, the local agency, Foster Advertising, hired Kenn Perkins to produce three, 60-second commercials for the Manitoba Telephone company. When the bank refused him a loan, Perkins turned to his client for an advance. With a deal in place, Kenn Perkins and Associates was officially launched.

Brad Caslor was Perkins' second employee. Caslor was recruited after the studio was handed a contract by Perry Rosemund of CBC Winnipeg to prepare Canadian segments for the original *Sesame Street*, produced by the Children's Television Workshop in New York. The *Sesame Street* deal lasted for four years. CBC discovered it could cut overhead costs by hiring independent artists directly. A succession of talented neophytes — Caslor, Chris Hinton, Neil McInnes, John Paizs, Bill Stewart and Cordell Barker — shuffled through Perkins' studio during the seventies.

With the exception of *Sesame Street*, the work was laborious and unfulfilling. Hinton recalls that each Monday morning, K-Tel, a high-velocity direct sales company, would have a new product — a patty stacker or a record — to advertise on television the following weekend. The never-ending, gruelling schedule resulted in high staff turnover. Caslor left to set up Credo Group with entrepreneur producer/director Derek Mazur two years after joining Perkins.

As a high school student, Cordell Barker used to hang around Perkins' studio learning animation skills by osmosis. He spent a summer volunteering until he became afflicted with a common teenage ailment — lack of cash blues. Barker was ready to accept a paying job as a car mechanic when Perkins countered with an offer to work as a cel painter. It was a tough choice: animation versus mechanics. One paid more, but the other was considerably more cool.

Barker undertook an apprenticeship of sorts. It wasn't long before Perkins promoted him to animator on *Sesame Street* interstitials and the weekly K-Tel spots. For three years he slugged it out and learned the craft. At age 21, he too left the company. He took with him the K-Tel account and lived on that for many months.

Winnipeg was not a region noted for its creative commercial campaigns in the late seventies. Barker found himself on a tread-mill, repeatedly cranking out graphic jobs with no character animation. Eventually, he threw in the towel to work as a bar-tender, blending alcohol rather than paints. He soon found salvation at the National Film Board.

Brad Caslor brings visual pizzazz to an otherwise staid historical vignette about Fort Prince of Wales.

When the NFB opened a satel-lite production centre in Winnipeg in the spring of 1976, it became a lifeline for those who wanted to take the independent route. Small con-tracts were awarded to a chosen few with a flair for story and design. The NFB shipped hometown boy Mike Scott back to Winnipeg to fulfill its plans to decentralize operations. It was never Scott's intention to foster a distinct line of animated heroes. But that's what happened after he scoured the locale looking for filmmakers who could start immediately. "When I arrived, there was a small film community and only a few peo-ple who were accomplished. There was this crazy group of animators ready to be serious filmmakers," says Scott.[100] Caslor and Sesame Street regular, Richard Condie, showed the most promise.

Condie was already in the middle of his first indepen-dent short, *Oh Sure*, when Scott arrived on the scene. Scott gave him the opportunity to complete the film and start on a second funded entirely though the new regional centre. Simultaneously, he contracted Credo Group to produce three Canadian vignettes for the NFB. Caslor couldn't write, storyboard, direct and animate all three contracts, so he lured Hinton away from his former boss to work with him.

Caslor is a more meticulous drawer, but there is a kinetic affinity between the two. Caslor helmed *Fort Prince of Wales* and *Spence's Republic*, and Hinton directed *Lady Frances Simpson*, but they animated interchangeably on each other's film. The commercial training wheels were still on, but the pair pedalled fast and furious. It shows. The films crackle with energy.

The regionalization experiment did not engender good-will towards the rest of Canada. Contempt for Eastern busi-nessmen is a resounding theme in Caslor and Hinton's ani-mated sponsored short *Blowhard* (1978). The film is replete with sarcastic digs aimed at Central Canadian companies profiting from government grants and tax loopholes while engaging in unscrupulous business practices.

Chris Hinton's imprimatur is evident in the historical clip Lady Frances Simpson.

Produced by Credo Group for the NFB's Renewable Society series, the film features J.B. Edwards, an entrepreneur who is sent to the sleepy prairie town of Blowhard to tap its natural resources — fire-breathing dragons. According to his Eastern partners, J.B. possesses the qualities to get the job done. He has "imagination, initiative and a complete and utter lack of integrity." The town prospers and J.B.'s company gets rich, but the exploited dragons start dying off. As a result, the town lurches into an energy crisis. While Blowhard's message is to promote conservation and resource management, its underlying theme is: Prairies good, Central Canada bad.

Blowhard did nothing to improve strained relations between NFB's regional office and Montreal headquarters, but it did establish Credo Group as a serious independent production house in Winnipeg. Twenty years after completing *Blowhard*, the company has grown to become Manitoba's biggest supplier of movies and TV series.

Detached from the Montreal–Toronto epicentre, Manitoba artists are not haunted by the ghost of Norman McLaren, nor are they affected by Studio A's backlash against Hollywood-style 'toons. Whereas many Montreal-based animators took their cue from the intellectual European animation coming from the Eastern Bloc countries, the Manitoba artists felt free to borrow from their southern neighbours. Culturally, they are a hybrid between the cerebral European tradition and American athleticism. By straddling the divide, the Prairie animators have become an unexpected bridge, proof that intercontinental sensibilities can cross over.

Brad Caslor definitely favoured his American brethren. He spent six years crafting a film tribute to the old Tex Avery and Bob Clampett classics. When the NFB commissioned Credo Group to make *Get a Job*, Caslor's intent was to make an earnest educational short for the unemployed. Scott hoped the film would eventually receive sponsorship money from the federal government. It was supposed to be an introductory film for Canada Manpower to run in its training programs, but after Ottawa pulled the plug on negotiations, Caslor was able to vent freely. In the end, "people were surprised at the energy of the film," says Scott. "The Warner Bros. style was something no one (in Canada) had any skill at." Conceived as a send-up of Disney's "How To" cartoons starring Goofy, it remains one of the most entertaining films in the NFB catalogue. The ensemble cast supporting Bob Dog is vintage screwball classics — from *Who Killed Who?* to *Red Hot Riding Hood*. The bulldog henchmen of the MGM and Warner Bros. golden era populate the film.

Brad Caslor is one of the country's best natural animators.

In keeping with NFB tradition, the film half-heartedly clasps a pedantic theme to its narrative heart. The characters parading through the film instruct Bob Dog how to draw up a plan, organize a résumé and assume a rigorous job search schedule. The lyrics, written by Caslor, Mazur and Jay Brazeau, are grafted to toe-tapping fifties classics.

The bureaucratic programmers had asked for a tool to inspire downtrodden job-seekers; however, by identifying with the plight of the unemployed, Caslor offers a hilariously jaded message to the government's target audience. The film portrays the daily humiliation of the jobless and the intimidating experience of knocking on doors. Finally, the only job available for Bob Dog is the one offered by dad — not exactly a motivational video for the pogie masses.

Like the Warner's stars Caslor emulates, Bob Dog has his share of sight gags. He is trampled, elongated, shaken and booted across the frame. The superior squash and stretch

Brad Caslor used to dream about living in the forties and working for Warner Bros. Get a Job *is a fitting tribute to Tex Avery and Bob Clampett's classics.*

Bob Dog is pursued by well-meaning job experts.

Richard Condie tried several professions before he settled on a life in animation.

action of Caslor's characters would have made Avery proud. His superb cartoon impersonations show Elvis and the Andrews sisters belting out lyrics that literally force Bob Dog to make a thorough job search.

American in its influences, *Get a Job* is not without references to Canadiana. Having spent many a late night toiling over K-Tel plugs, Caslor could not resist a "J-tel" commercial lampoon. In his classic film, Bob Dog's television set features a record promotion. The songs featured on the special J-tel album include: "Water Cooler Blues," "Teen Foreman," "Work Around the Clock" and "You've Gotta Have a Plan."

Caslor is one of the country's best natural animators. Fans love his slick movement and slapstick antics. With one film, he raised the professional bar in the region, and then left the business. He now works as a storyboard artist and film editor.

If Caslor was classic, then Richard Condie was eclectic. A former astrophysics student, teacher, social worker and musician, Condie sampled many professions before settling on animation at the age of 27 — and even then it was by default. Condie gave up on teaching when he realized that 30-odd students would be staring at him from behind rows of desks all day long. When his band won the first round of a music competition, he failed to

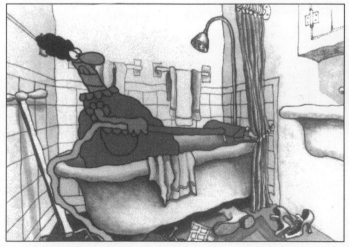

show up to compete for the second round because he was paralyzed by self-doubt. Then he discovered that as an animator, he could chain-smoke and drink Coca-Cola all day long, accompanied only by his paper and pencil. It was the perfect vocation for a reclusive guy.

In 1978, the NFB commissioned Condie to make *John Law and the Mississippi Bubble*, an economic tale about the introduction of paper money into France. It was the second animated project out of the Winnipeg studio. When the film did not perform well on the festival circuit or in rental offices, Condie turned his magnifying glass on himself, and made a semi-autobiographical short about creative frustration entitled *Getting Started* (1982).

Getting Started was the first in what was to become a series of shorts about human foibles. Unlike Hollywood's gravity-defying gags, Condie's world is pure slice-of-life: procrastination, cheating at scrabble and housework. The daily irritants between squabbling couples are transposed into Condie's cartoon land as strange behavioural tics: removing and shaking a pair of eyes, or sawing the armrest of a living-room chair.

Richard Condie's world is pure slice-of-life. In Getting Started *(above) procrastination gets the better of Condie's hero. In* The Big Snit *(below) cheating at scrabble and bizarre idiosyncrasies are the order of the day.*

In his Oscar-nominated short *The Big Snit* (1985), Condie's over-the-top personality traits transform a domestic dispute into sublime comedy. The visual gags even inspired a British couple to open a bar called the Big Snit in London. The pub owners supplied saws and eyes to their customers while projecting filmclips on the walls.

Unlike Condie's earlier films, *The Big Snit* reads like a post-modern fable. A surprise ending adds further subtext to the film. The bickering couple eventually kiss and make up, only to step outdoors to discover a bigger snit happening outside — nuclear holocaust. The narrative evolution of Condie's films reflects the intersection between Condie's personal views, and the NFB's social agenda.

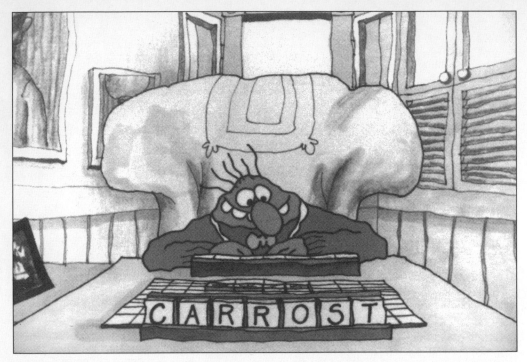

The Big Snit characters exhibit behavioural tics such as removing and shaking a pair of eyes.

Cock-eyed and orthodontist-needy.

For years, Condie was hired by an organization with a long history in sponsored films, and a mandate to adapt Canadian culture. The NFB made dramas, documentaries and animated films — and the cross-currents were strong between the units. Condie started *The Big Snit* shortly after Terre Nash released her anti-nuclear protest film *If You Love This Planet* (1982). Unlike Nash's sobering treatise about the devastating effects of nuclear bombs, Condie chose a more subtle weapon — humour. Yet, the effect was the same: a damning indictment of nuclear proliferation.

With subsequent films, Condie successfully tackled broader social issues. *The Apprentice* (1990) is an esoteric tale of mentoring and youthful impetuousness. *La Salla* (1996), is about temptation, fate and order in the universe. Condie's character in *La Salla* frolics happily in a bizarre fun room where he can paint a pastoral scene by shooting cows out of a miniature cannon, or play with an odd assortment of toys such as a fish on wheels. A forbidden door tempts him from time to time, but he refuses to open it. The character of the film appears to be the master of his own fate even if it means succumbing to temptation and ruining his ordered life. "Moments ago I had everything. Now there's a cow in my nose," sings the baffled man.

Condie's universe is governed by obsessions and existential notions. It is undoubtedly the most philosophically complex film in his repertoire. This film also places him squarely in the European corner with the likes of Paul Driessen, who has posed similar cognitive puzzles with such shorts as *The Same Old Story* (1981), a film in which a man reading a story is living the same narration told in the book.

The Apprentice is an esoteric tale of youthful impetuousness.

The Condie stamp, which has become synonymous with the term "Manitoba Animation," is an exaggerated cartoon style. In graphic terms, it could be billed as a National Film Board genetic experiment gone wonky: mutations of the buggy-eyed/bulbous-nosed characters favoured in the sixties. Cock-eyed and orthodontist-needy, Condie's characters are the creative manifestation of cabin fever. Their appeal is so great, Condie has long been hounded by broadcasters around the world. He prefers to remain in Winnipeg and control his work.

So hands-on is Condie, he even prefers to personally voice his own characters and lends his lungs to others. His imprimatur is evident in Cordell Barker's NFB short *The Cat Came Back*. Condie joins Barker as one of the voices belting out the *Cat* soundtrack. The camaraderie among the Prairie artists is exceptional. This may be due in part to the simple fact that most of the films were scored, recorded and mixed in the basement of Wayne Finucan, a former drummer for the Canadian band The Guess Who. Over the objections of Montreal, Scott insisted that local facilities should be used where possible. As a result, a small community of artists contributed to the films. "There was a special energy to these films," says Scott. Actor Jay Brazeau is a regular voice on Manitoba's animation soundtracks. He has gone as far as to spend the day drifting in a canoe crafting a silly libretto for Condie's opera bouffe in *La Salla*.

Cordell Barker hams it up in studio.

Insanity is endemic in the Prairie toon. *The Cat Came Back* (1988) is loosely adapted from a 100-year-old folk song about a poor man who can't get rid of his cat no matter how hard he tries. Each dastardly plot to lose the furry feline leads

The Cat Came Back (1988) is loosely adapted from a 100-year-old folk song about a poor man who tries one dastardly plot after another to rid himself of a pesky cat.

to personal misfortune. With each round of the chorus — "the cat came back the very next day, the cat came back, he thought it was a goner, but the cat came back, it just wouldn't stay away" — the protagonist gets progressively crazier until he dynamites his whole house — and himself — to smithereens.

Barker had originally developed his own storyboard about a nasty old man and a cat. "It was over the top and mean-spirited in its intended humour, and when I think back on it, it wasn't funny, it was a gross out," says Barker. Instead, Ches Yetman, the studio's new executive producer asked Barker if he would consider animating the song "The Cat Came Back." Children's entertainer Fred Penner had popularized the ditty in Winnipeg, and Yetman felt Barker could easily roll his ideas into this new treatment. Later, Yetman backed Barker's decision to record a rougher track using untrained voices to give the song an "around the campfire" authenticity. *The Cat Came Back* works in part because it sounds like a lusty old folk song sung by drunken hobos.

Visually, *The Cat Came Back* shows Prairie artists' ability to balance European balletic movement with Warner gags. Barker's tortured toon has both great sight gags — such as a rail dolly riding over women and a cow tied up on the track — as well as Paul Driessen-like reflexes.

Barker's protagonist has the solid, square body and stubby limbs seen in Driessen's work. The squareness makes the character more difficult to move around the screen, but adds comic appeal. Yet, the Hollywood influence is evident in the full-blown coloured backgrounds, its joke-laden narrative, and physical expressiveness. Driessen prefers a more deadpan approach.

Barker reprised his cat characters for a British advertising campaign, but pared down his style for other commercial work. Unlike his Winnipeg contemporaries, Barker has been a prolific and popular commercial artist directing commercials for Nike, Chlor-Tripolon and numerous spots for Bell Intermax. For the Intermax run, Barker abandoned full-blown cel animation in favour of winsome stick figures married to live-action footage. He often works for Les Productions Pascal Blais, a company that has frequently called upon auteur animators for specialized ad campaigns.

Chris Hinton no longer lives in Winnipeg, but stylistically he remains a member of the Prairie clan. Thanks to Perkins, who hired him before he completed his third year of studies at Sheridan College, Hinton spent his formative years in the region. "Kenn hired me on the basis of one line test, but I don't think I had a shred of skill," says Hinton.[101] Instead of a normal walk cycle, Hinton attached a ball and chain to his character's ankle. His initiative captured Perkins' attention.

Once in Winnipeg, Hinton followed Caslor to Credo Group where he animated a few *Sesame Street* spots and contributed to the NFB vignettes and *Blowhard*. Hinton's early *Sesame Street* spots were of high quality, considering the small budgets allotted. He put hundreds of drawings into his early films.

Back in Montreal, Hinton took a break from cel animation to scribble on paper. "When you are working with cels the whole idea is to control things very carefully and keep them on the ground and in perspective. I was trying to get away from that." *A Nice Day in the Country* is purposefully primitive, with childlike renderings produced by a thick black kindergarten crayon. Hinton drew as fast as he could and didn't erase a thing. Having mastered the cel

A Nice Day in the Country was rapidly scrawled using a thick black kindergarten crayon.

Espresso is a film about the odd effects of coffee consumption.

Blackfly is based on a song about a man driven crazy by Northern Ontario's blood-sucking insects.

cartoon, Hinton now likes to see how much he can scribble and still make a character believable. The energy and spontaneity are captured on-screen.

Since that late night experiment, Hinton animated *Watching TV* (1996), a black satirical short about society's fascination with violence on the tube, and its stupefying effects. Everything is blown apart by a gun. There is no context given to each rapid-fire incident. It doesn't matter. Violence is gratuitous. The Hintons rented a TV set following the birth of their third child. After wasting a winter in front of the set, Hinton returned it, went up to his studio and scribbled his storyboard in 30 seconds.

Espresso (1999) is a violence of a different kind: coffee drinking. He finds the coffee break an odd contradiction; a routine but dangerous act that excites the brain to new heights of reckless action.

Like his contemporaries, Hinton has found his greatest success in adapting folk songs. His Oscar-nominated film *Blackfly* (1991) is based on Wade Hemsworth's song about a man driven crazy by Canada's most pesky creatures. Being bushwhacked in the fly-infested North Ontario was a theme Hinton could relate to. There has always been a lot of screaming and distemper in the animation from Middle Canada.

While Hinton's characterizations and love of the folk tune bear a strong resemblance to *The Cat Came Back*, Hinton's structural approach differs. Barker took more liberty in developing a little story out of the repetitive chorus of the 100-year-old song. Hinton, however, wanted to construct a film based solely on the images derived from Hemsworth's lyrics rather than developing a completely new narrative.

Many animators have a talent for music, but Winnipeggers excel in this area. Richard Condie was a concert pianist who wrote scores for several documentaries despite the fact that he cannot read music. Hinton learned how to play the violin in later years. And Barker, well, he dreams of playing the violin. On occasion, the three of them join NFB Montreal animator John Weldon in his backyard for impromptu jam sessions.

The artists from this region rely heavily on a strong musical soundtrack, on sound effects, and make playful use of songs in their films. The comic timing and clever use of sound distinguishes this region from all others. It is reminiscent of the early NFB era when Norman McLaren, George Dunning and a host of other staffers animated songs for the World War II newsreels. NFB composer Normand Roger has relied heavily on traditional Quebec reels and folk songs to score NFB shorts over the years. George Geertsen's best effort features the music of Quebec singer Madame Bolduc. There is clearly a symbiosis between the animation genre and regional minstrelsy.

Prairie artists stand out as a reminder of how cross-pollination of graphic styles can give rise to new artistic approaches. They are a graphic recombinant, blending such diverse styles as Warners Bros. and Paul Driessen's tremulous line drawings. The community is so small it's easy to trace its influences. Credo Group's foundation is grounded in animation, as well as the very original and funny director John Paizs, who animated *The Dreamer, The Nine To Five Crack* and *Ho Down* before moving into drama with his stunning feature debut. *Crime Wave* (1986), a dark comedy about a B-movie adventure, is considered by many critics to be one of Canada's greatest films. As with Caslor, the K-Tel commercials cranked out by Perkins provided creative fodder for the B-movie vignettes Paizs inserted in his first film.

Since the late seventies, the NFB's regional studio has operated

Director John Paizs' move from cartoons Nine to Five Crack *(above) and* The Dreamer *(below) to live-action films.*

John Paizs' live-action cartoon Crime Wave.

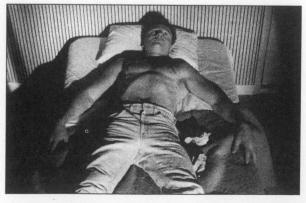

much like a benevolent benefactor to Condie, Barker and Caslor. Unfortunately, the nurturing environment may have stifled the very souls it hoped to develop. There are no new "Manitoban" protégés on the horizon. The baton has not been passed to the next generation. If the animation community in Manitoba implodes, the loss will be significant. Prairie geeks are a unique breed: an odd composite of Old World and New.

In some ways, the Manitoba artists have contributed to the blending of animation styles prevalent on the cable stations. Had the animators accepted the plethora of offers lobbed in their direction they might have been in the forefront of change on the television sets around the world. Instead, their influence is indirect. By setting themselves above the commercial din, they challenged broadcasters to find bankable surrogates. When the producers vaguely describe a "look" or a "concept," the animation by the Prairie geeks may well be in the back of their minds.

Secretly, many have wished for a "Big Snit" hit for commercial TV. As a result they have looked for a fusion of styles and characters replete with idiosyncrasies. Having opted not to ascend to the altar of television, this group of artists has not attained the cult status awarded to or *Ren & Stimpy*. Instead, they remain iconoclasts frozen on the prairie steppes.

Les Ames, Kenn Perkins' first employee, was the calligrapher who wrote the new Canadian Constitution in 1982.

The first animated Imax film, *Primitti Too Taa*, was made by Winnipeg filmmaker Ed Ackerman. Using only a typewriter on Imax film stock, Ackerman crafted a clever dadaist poem for the big screen experience.

chapter 9

Give Us Your Sick, Demented & Lewd: Animators of the Wet Coast

ack in the 1960s and 1970s, disenfranchised youth churned out underground comics. The best of them raked over the detritus of American pop culture and reconstituted it in darkly humorous pen and ink illustrations. Now the medium has changed, even if the sentiment has not. Today's renegade drawers have channelled their energy into animation. The shorts are a backlash against the 1980's corporate culture that has degraded cartoons into mere vehicles for feel-good cuddly toys or plastic action heroes come to animated life.

Stifled by the conservative production slates of Ontario's large commercial companies Nelvana, Cinar and Animation House, a group of animators migrated to the West Coast. The cost of production discourages a true underground scene, but Vancouver boasts the next best thing — animators with attitude. The West Coast practitioners parallel the grunge music scene. They are nihilistic and draw violently.

Danny Antonucci, J. Falconer, Mike Grimshaw and Dieter Mueller are the artists pushing the envelope of good taste with their shorts: *Lupo the Butcher, Dog Brain, Quiet Please* and *Butterfly*. This West Coast fraternity has no intention of catering to the superheroes, or Care Bears pablum, so prominent on Saturday-morning television. They deliberately bypass politically correct catechisms and indulge pubescent pastimes such as petrified body fluids, burping, boogers, blood, guts and gore — and not necessarily in that order. As a result, they have become the front-runners of the new trend in raunchy television; the creators of cel characters more violent and gross than *Beavis and Butt-head*. Compared to Lupo and Olaf, Beavis is as innocuous as the lead in *Leave It to Beaver*.

Built by commercial pioneers, Vancouver is the North American hub for outrageous cartoons. The launch pad is at International Rocketship, a company that cultivates debauched animators. Over the years, founder Marv Newland has underwritten the hard costs of freelancers within his orbit. Rocketship's high octane artwork has hooked MTV and Nickelodeon, and occupied centre stage on Spike and Mike's Classic Festival of Animation. It took years, but the company built a cult following on college campuses. Today, the best shorts are downloaded onto QuickTime and passed around like comic books during the sixties.

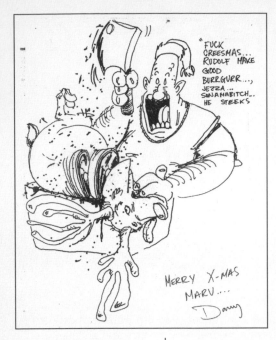

"FUCK
CREESMAS...
RUDOLF MAKE
GOOD
BURRGURR...,
JEZZA...
SUNAHABITCH...
HE STEEKS"

MERRY X-MAS
MARV....
Danny

Lupo the Butcher is
a one-gag cartoon
full of good ole
blood 'n guts gore.

A typical Al Sens
character.

These contemporary 'toons shock Al Sens, granddad of the West Coast scene. Their apolitical approach seems gratuitous for a man who has spent a large part of his career producing left-wing shorts. Still, he talks about the design and bravado of his young successors with parental pride. Hell, he's hired some of them himself on occasion.

Sens' office is papered with hundreds of yellowing thumbnail sketches. "Animators are like wolves, they have to piss in their corner to claim it," says Sens, pointing to the territorial markings that have accumulated on his walls.[102] Embossed on the dusty drawings is Sens' signature. Recent renderings belong to members of the new generation of Vancouver animators who freelance for him. The room is virtually a West Coast animation archive — each layer revealing a trail of talent.

A cartoonist for *Maclean's, Colliers* and the *Saturday Evening Post*, Sens turned to animation in order to expand ideas beyond the comic strip format. In 1958 he set up shop and started producing black and white commercials. Sens' first film, *Puppet's Dream* (1959), is a simple silhouette film laced with religious iconography. He expanded this metaphysical theme in his follow-up film *The Sorcerer* (1961). In it, a red wizard spits out magical symbols, causing a strange metamorphosis in the peasants. It serves as a metaphor for people led astray by fancy talk or commercial images. Today, it would be interpreted as the spellbinding effect of the mass media.

Low on cash, high on chutzpah, Sens teamed up with rod puppeteer David Orcutt. Together they travelled towns through British Columbia's interior to screen their works in local halls. Persistence paid off when they landed a distribution deal with a Los Angeles–based company. Sens never made the big leap to the US although Warner Bros. invited him to LA after *The Sorcerer* screened at the Annecy Film Festival in 1962. He maintained roots in Vancouver and continues to make a living from his animation camera and stand. Sens now has 18 films to his credit.

While working for the CBC in the early sixties, Sens discovered an animation shortcut: he would spit on the acetate cels, rub off the ink and draw the next image. This hasty erase method leaves ink smears that records as a ghostly afterimage on celluloid. Italian animation historian Giannalberto Bendazzi dubbed Sens' haphazard appliqué the "spit technique." He used this method for his films *The Peripatetic Patient* (1962) and *The Playground* (1964), two acerbic shorts concerning the nature of man.[103]

In the former film, Sens depicts a troubled character pacing back and forth across the screen. The latter includes dark gags depicting aggressive females with enormous breasts and a penchant for gun play. *The Playground* was a thematic turning point for Sens. He abandoned his mystic motif and struck a political pose.

Sens' repertoire of cartoon characters expanded to include a long-billed duck, a wolf, a Cheshire-grinning cat, and a cow. All of them star in Problems on an Imaginary Farm.

Over the next 30 years, Sens would make 14 films, broaching the subject of industrialization – *Man and Machine* (1969), *The Bureaucracy* (1975), *Problems on an Imaginary Farm* (1977), *A Hard Day at the Office* (1978), *Political Animals* (1991) and *The Landlord*. Not a man to hide his political colours, Sens prominently positioned a picture of Latin American revolutionary Che Guevara in the backgrounds of two of his films, and condemns the human race in rambling prose. In *The Bureaucracy* he argues that so-called Western democracies have a tendency to impose ego and personality upon everything.

As Sens drifted to polemic tracts, his repertoire of cartoon characters grew to include a long-billed duck, a wolf, a Cheshire-grinning cat and a cow. All of them star in his politically-charged *Problems on an Imaginary Farm*. These characters recall the "rubber hose" era of ani-

Al Sens' backdrops are papered with his politics as evident in A Hard Day at the Office.

mation, a period in the 1920's and 1930's when characters were drawn without knee and arm joints. The result is a loonie toon that appears slightly out of control.

The rubbery look percolated down to other West Coast artists, most notably Marv Newland. When Newland opened the commercial production house International Rocketship in

Some of the motley crew from International Rocketship.

Al Sens and Marv Newland share a passion for rubber-hose charac-ters as shown in Newland's Black Hula.

1975, the loose limb design was his trademark. Surprisingly, Newland and Sens did not really connect until the mid-eighties, but the two innovators are now fans of each others' work. Newland acknowledges Sens' influence, but Sens doesn't buy the trickle-down theory: "I've stolen more things from Marv than he's stolen from me. It's been reciprocal, at best."[174]

Newland made *Black Hula* (1988) as a tribute of sorts to Vancouver's old-timer. The film's cynical evolutionary theme — from fish to man to machine — is near and dear to Sens' own heart. The evil newcomers who introduce machines to paradise some-what resemble the square black and white characters from Sens' spit days. But Newland is clearly influenced on other fronts. *Black Hula* is a dark take-off on *Betty Boop's Bamboo Isle* cartoon. Betty isn't anywhere to be seen, but the Natives with the stretched smiles are. Newland's Natives look as if they passed through a sixties prism. Newland has no doubt navi-gated the underground straits of comic book artists, and drawn inspiration from their graphic approach.

Newland's self-initiation into the world of animation was born out of sheer desperation to finish college. He made his first animated film at the end of his final academic year.

Newland needed a final film to graduate from the Los Angeles Art Center College of Design in 1969. The student film he scripted called for a sunset, but it rained for two weeks straight and he was unable to shoot. With only a few weeks remaining in the term, Newland drew *Bambi Meets Godzilla*, a 30-second short featuring a monstrous foot squashing an angelic fawn. The film has an amateurish look, but its ghoulishness clearly appealed to the sicker side of the Canadian psyche. It became a cult favourite on campuses across the country.

Marv Newland's festival favourite Bambi Meets Godzilla.

West Coast production was scant in the mid-seventies when Newland returned to Vancouver after a stint working for Cinera Productions in Toronto. KVOS-TV, a CBS network affiliate in Washington state, had a contract with Hanna-Barbera to service their Saturday-morning shows — executing the storyboards sent from California. They serviced the likes of *Wait Till Your Father Gets Home*, *Gidget*, *The Beatles* (King Features Syndicate) and *Abbot and Costello*. The station's production arm, Canawest Film Productions, operated two animation stands and a camera in Vancouver, and it recruited people out of the art schools to train them on shows. Barrie Helmer, Norm Drew, Tom Ashcroft and Carlos Sanchez were the experienced few who helmed the series.

Canawest's foray into Saturday morning series spawned a few small animation houses. Norm Drew set up his own company in 1974 and worked for *Sesame Street*; he produced the animated titles for the TV variety show *The Irish Rovers*; and produced *Chika's Magic Sketch Book* for CBC-TV. Mal Hoskin and Wayne Morris set up Synch Pop Animation Studio in 1974. Malcolm Collette, a young graduate of the Vancouver School of Art, formed Marmalade Productions to do a series of vignettes for the Province of Alberta's 75th anniversary. After years of producing corporate videos and commercials, Telefilm Canada — eager for more projects on the West Coast — encouraged Marmalade to produce a half-hour CBC special *Tales of the Mouse Hockey League* (1986). Eight months and $560,000 later, Marmalade finished production and began

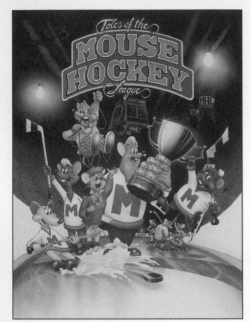

Tales of the Mouse Hockey League *was the first indigenous TV show to be produced in Vancouver. Dreams of a West Coast series were dashed after Telefilm pulled its financial stake in the show.*

"I'd rather spend two months making a commercial to make a profit than spend 10 minutes talking to any banker. Trying to explain what I do for a living is hell on earth." Marv Newland on why it took him five years to raise the capital for his first independent short, Sing Beast Sing.

developing a series after the CBC ordered four more episodes. Having sold the half-hour program as a pilot outside Canada, Marmalade tried to pull in the rest of the financing. Telefilm's refusal to further back the series left Colette high and dry. The company went bust.

The animation revival on the West Coast in the eighties was largely due to the dogged determination of Marv Newland.

Newland never really intended to become a commercial producer, but he quickly discovered that it was easier to subsidize his own shorts through the revenues that commercials brought in. "I'd rather spend two months making a commercial to make a profit than spend 10 minutes talking to any banker. Trying to explain what I do for a living is hell on earth," says Newland.

It took five years before Newland could raise capital for his first independent short, *Sing Beast Sing*. Conceived during a long and boring road trip across the Canadian prairies, the film stars Vern, a prop man, who pulls a cactus across a room and deposits it beside a piano. At the keyboards, Toledo Nung Beast starts belting out the Willie Mabon's blues song, "I'm Mad."

Toledo is a mutant half-man/half-octopus with the mannerisms of Ray Charles. As ole' Toledo pours out his heart, the camera repeatedly dollies back and forth across the room. It pans past a duck roasting a chicken on a tabletop campfire and rests on a catatonic Black-Eared Dog. The images are strange and mundane at the same time. There is always an expectation that something will happen, but the camera is slow to reveal change, however slight. When Toledo finishes the song, the prop man returns to remove the cactus. The props deflate, and poor Toledo crawls out of the picture.

Newland has a deadpan approach. Rather than seeking laughs in story or character development, he builds his jokes into the movement and attitude. The absurdity lies in what you see, not hear. "The jokes aren't in-your-face, they leak into the films," he says. Newland's comedy lies in his ability to confound expectations. Action takes place offscreen, objects move into a still frame, and sequences cycle throughout. It is an approach adopted by his disciples.

The Ottawa Animation Festival rejected *Sing Beast Sing* in 1980. Unfazed, Newland proceeded to do a little guerrilla marketing. He convinced Paul Gratton, then programmer of the Byway Theater in Ottawa, to screen his short at the repertory cinema just a few blocks away from the festival. He then papered the festival with flyers and even paid the taxi fare to the Byway for a group of Bulgarian animation students. Turned away at Ottawa, the film went on to win awards at the Chicago International Film Festival and Journées Internationales du Cinema d'Animation in Annecy, France. The Central Canadian snub reconfirmed the West Coast's sense of alienation.

In the studio's infancy, Newland both designed and animated many commercials. When the budget permitted, he hired Dieter Mueller to animate his storyboards. Mueller, who joined the studio in 1977, has remained a close associate and took over Rocketship's commercial operation in 1998. He is the creator of Chloe the Sea Cucumber, a favourite Rocketship animated character.

Marv Newland's hero "Hogey" in Hooray For Sandbox Land.

When International Rocketship finally landed a contract to make a sponsored short about road safety for the Insurance Company of British Columbia, Newland roped more talent into his studio. He hired two ex-Sheridan graduates, Danny Antonucci and J. Falconer. The new hires called themselves the "Rocketeers." Over the years, Rocketship's commercial contracts have not only underwritten the hard costs of Newland's personal shorts, but they subsidized the cost of several other freelancers.

Hooray for Sandbox Land (1984), a rather esoteric public service announcement intended to teach kids about the rules of the road, best represents Newland's personal style. Once a comic strip artist himself, Newland likes to revisit the classic animators of the thirties. Toylike in design, Newland's *Sandbox Land* lead characters, such as Hogey and Nagel, have the rubber energy of Ko-Ko the Clown. They move as if they had elastic connective tissue. Newland is also influenced by Paul Driessen's after-flow kinematics. It is an extra wave or motion that defies physical laws, even traditional cartooning precepts, for that matter.

Dieter Mueller, creator of such films as Butterfly, *is now at the helm of Rocketship TV, the new commercial division of International Rocketship.*

Foska, the star of Anijam, *is a favourite character at International Rocketship.*

Unlike any other commercial house in Canada, favoured characters or designs occasionally find their way into commercials. By producing shorts — however sporadically — International Rocketship continues to set challenging benchmarks for its stable of animators, and an array of artistic designs for potential clients. Clients request custom-designed characters from Rocketship. Some elements of the independent shorts find their way into the commercials. A snappy Levis 501 spot stars a character who wears black, heavy-rimmed glasses, as does Foska, a recurring character in Newland's own films. But, for the most part, Newland has avoided cannibalizing his own shorts to feed the commercial engine.

International Rocketship blasted off in the international scene with the release of *Anijam* (1984), a 20-minute film version of the *cadaver exquis* (exquisite corpse) surrealists' technique. It is virtually a jam session among 22 of the world's best animators. As producer, Newland had one rule. The first and last frame of each segment had to contain his bespectacled Foska character. Apart from that, animators were free to do whatever else they chose. It is a film historian's delight — a controlled experiment in which 22 auteurs interpret the identical character. Paul Driessen's Foska melts; Brad Caslor's is caught in an explosive gag; Kaj Pindal wrests humour out of a ticking bomb; and Zlatko Grgic gets great comic mileage out of a funny skit involving a reflection in a mirror that plays tricks.

Pink Komkommer (1990), the second film anthology produced by International Rocketship, solidified the company's international reputation. Billed as the first animated pornographic film, *Pink Kom-kommer* didn't turn out to be as hard core as Newland secretly hoped. The artists behind the project's conception are the same two who play out their raunchy fantasies on screen. Newland's involves little fetish fairies who make a surprise landing in a poor unsuspecting lad's house, and whip his fuzzy bunny slippers. In Driessen's

Billed as the first animated pornographic film, Pink Komkommer *features little fetish fairies who descend upon an unsuspecting lad in fuzzy pink bunny slippers.*

sacrilegious clip, God himself is pleasured by a cherub, and Adam and Eve get kinky with a snake. The most erotic submission belongs to Sara Petty who draws luscious vulvas and ribbonlike penises that fold and blend in a kaleidoscope of colours. The other five artists use parody rather than titillation. Janet Perlman draws a playful mime character that silently gestures the facts of life. Alison Snowdon and David Fine's contribution involves silly activities at a nudist colony. Stoyan Dukov animates an S & M circus trainer; and Chris Hinton cleverly incorporates the soundtrack into a little vignette about an old lady who awakens from a nap, pours tea, scolds her parrot and hugs her cat.

International Rocketship's logo is hidden on the T-shirt in this MTV station ID.

Newland has had an enormous impact on the Vancouver scene, not only for his design sense, but his support of independent theatrical cartoons over the years. Since 1980, Newland has directed five of his own films and underwritten the hard costs of at least 15 others. All the while, he instituted an open door policy. Any of International Rocketship's loyal freelancers can pitch the president an idea. If Newland thinks the idea is sound, and his company is flush, he will bankroll it.

The approach has paid off in both creative and corporate terms. In the last decade, International Rocketship gained

Danny Antonucci's notorious Lupo the Butcher. *Lupo eventually starred in some spots for MTV and Converse running shoes.*

recognition for its shorts thanks to animation festivals worldwide, and exposure through Spike and Mike's Festival of Animation, a touring animation compilation that screens at first-run art houses and repertory cinemas in North America. Now commercial clients are requesting "the look" or "the edge" of the shorts, says Newland.

The popular syndicated cartoonist Gary Larson approached Rocketship in 1992 to direct a television version of his panel, Far Side, for CBS-TV. The rapport between Newland and Larson was evident from the start. It was a twinning of sorts between two artists who prefer limited dialogue, non-recurring characters, and scenes that draw humour from incongruous settings and situations. Newland recruited Dieter Mueller, J. Falconer and Dennis Heaton to join him at Larson's home in Seattle where they fleshed out the series of sequences. The sketches and notes that came out of that brainstorming session became the backbone of a script and storyboard.

The non-sequitur stories range from Frankenstein cows to a scene depicting a wolf watching home movies. Visual cues link each animated strip. A scene featuring the crash of an airliner carrying insect passengers cuts to a shot showing an automatic wiper cleaning a bug-splattered windshield. By refusing to voice characters and by juxtaposing segments, Newland has faithfully adapted Larson's vision to the TV screen.

The most famous Newland disciple is Danny Antonucci, creator of *Lupo the Butcher*, and MTV's *The Brothers Grunt*. Antonucci raised eyebrows and collected fans when he made *Lupo the Butcher* in 1986. Lupo is a stereotypical Italian-Canadian butcher undone by his over-the-top emotions. It's good old blood 'n guts, a one-gag cartoon that's near and dear to adolescents' hearts. Stupid jokes aside, the character design is what makes this cartoon so interesting.

Lupo is fashioned after Max Fleischer cartoons and has the rubber-hosed limbs, zipper mouth and beady eyes favoured by Newland and Sens. The film gained promotional steam when the rock group Guns 'n Roses projected it during their 1987 concert tour. It also spawned a new festival genre. Unable to include Lupo in its more classic animation touring package, Spike and Mike created a "Sick and Twisted" tournee of animation. Launched in San Francisco, these late night screenings drew a larger crowd than Spike and Mike ever predicted. Cable executives used to scout talent at the screenings. Antonucci was one of the lucky few offered a series at MTV.

It's not surprising that other animators tried to emulate Lupo's success. Spike and Mike hired Bardel Animation to make *Brian's Brain*, an opening short for their Outrageous Animation video package. But perhaps the most derivative of Antonucci's style is Paul Boyd, a hot animator hired to work on *Tales from the Far Side*. He completed a hack-em whack-em short entitled *Chili Con Carnage* that is pure Lupomania.

Rod Filbrandt and Mike Grimshaw's troublesome baby from Quiet Please.

Antonucci has left the Rocketship orbit, but Dieter Mueller, Dan Collins, Mike Grimshaw and J. Falconer still consider themselves freelance Rocketeers. While still working part-time as a plumber, Mike Grimshaw produced the au courant blues short *Beat*, before embarking on the Sick and Twisted festival track. *Beat* became the cartoon trailer for the feature *Wired*, a film based on John Belushi's life. Unfortunately, *Wired* sank and *Beat* drowned alongside it. Disillusioned and drunk, Grimshaw and partner Rod Filbrandt decided one evening that they could produce a film to surpass Lupo's grossness quotient. To prove their point, they drafted a storyboard/practical joke and mailed it to producers. Their proposal, *Quiet Please* (1989), is a perverted version of the old Baby Huey films. It stars Olaf, a brutish babysitter who kicks and pisses on Elmo, a squalling baby. The only reaction came from Spike, of Spike and Mike's Festival of Animation, who bluntly informed them: "Nobody's going to laugh at this shit."[105]

Vancouver Film School students, Liam Hogan and Trevor Watson, directed Below the Belt. *The film was screened in Spike and Mike's Sick 'n Twisted Animation Festival.*

Using twisted logic, they surmised that if Spike hated it then they must really be on to something. Grimshaw started animating the short on his own. *Quiet Please* was also launched at the new late-night series later dubbed *The Sick 'n Twisted Festival*.

The second nasty of Grimshaw's career was *Deep Sympathy* (1991), a film commissioned by Spike after he made some good money on *Quiet Please*. Described as *Deep Throat*

"J" HAS GONE HOME BECAUSE HE CANNOT DRAW ANYMORE. HE WILL BE IN TOMMOROW MORNING

A bulletin board sketch by J. Falconer.

Dan Collin's austere film, Waddles, *is dramatically different from the films made by his colourful friends at Rocketship.*

in the funeral parlor, the short was inspired by a bilious letter written to Ann Landers by a woman whose undertaker husband requested that she lie in a cold bath for a half hour and remain immobile while making love. Grimshaw gives new meaning to the words "Dead Head" in his second installment for the Sick and Twisted folks.

The film's popularity has been dismissed as a politically correct backlash. What was a therapeutic wank for some animators is clearly tapping into a North American need for a cathartic gross-out genre, a purge of conservative cobwebs. However, the response by some diehard fans has even unnerved Grimshaw on occasion. There are always people who interpret them literally. Most of Grimshaw's independent work went underground, but Mike Judge and Danny Antonucci hired him to write episodes of *Beavis 'n Butt-head* and *The Brothers Grunt*.

Dieter Mueller, the dean of International Rocketship's corral, has animated one independent short, *Butterfly* (1982), which was selected for the Cannes Film Festival. It was the first Rocketship short to make a profit. The first in the one-gag wonders from the Rocketeers, Mueller designed a Dr. Seuss-like creature that gobbles down a beautiful butterfly as it flits across the screen. Mueller remains Rocketship's principal commercial director and animator responsible for Labatt Blue's spots, BC Lotteries Corporation, Dairyland, MTV Music Television, Nickelodeon interstitials and Ha!TV Comedy Network.

J. Falconer has two shorts to his credit. His first indie short sponsored by Rocketship, *Dog Brain*, answers the one question everyone asks about their pet: "What is my dog dreaming about when it twitches its hind legs while sleeping?" Falconer's answer is simple: dogs dream about ... sleeping.

Friends since the eighth grade, Falconer and Antonucci share the same sensibilities, although Falconer says his work is considered cute. He has been a major player in the *Far Side* cartoon, storyboarding and animating the one-hour special. The only other short animated by Falconer is a "discussion starter" short for one of the National Film Board's educational packages. David Fine and Alison Snowden (*Bob's Birthday*) wrote the film *Deadly Deposits* (1992). It was a fruitful collaboration. "In a way it felt like an independent film because I had complete control," says Falconer.[106]

Only a handful of women braved the testosterone-laden land of the Rocketeers. Debra Dawson has consis-

tently worked as a designer and sometimes director on the hipper spots for Much Music and Nickelodeon, as well as Gary Larson's *Tales From the Far Side*. Dawson has a couple of shorts as a director under her belt: Sesame Street's *Doug the Monster* and *Pollen Fever*. She clearly has one foot in the trenches of underground comics à la Mary Fleener and Montreal's own Julie Doucet.

Citizen Harold *pits an average denizen against the government monolith.*

There is always one exception to the rule — even at a studio like Rocketship. Dan Collins' personal films are quite unlike anything else coming out of the region. Collins eschews the explosive gags of his contemporaries at Rocketship. Instead, he is a contortionist of colourless graphics. *Points, Dry Noodles* and *Waddles* are geometric films that wrestle with weight, balance and shape. "Form interests me. How you can combine movement and line. How you use timing. I like to use a black line on a white background because I think it makes it more tactile. I don't use colour because I can never think of any reason to use it."[107]

While Rocketship cornered the market on cool, some interesting films have emerged from graduates of Emily Carr Institute of Art and Design (ECIAD) and the NFB's Pacific Centre office. John Taylor and Hugh Foulds were the impetus behind the formation of animation departments at the two institutions. After attending a summer animation workshop in Montreal in 1970, Taylor and Foulds returned to Vancouver full of "piss 'n vinegar." Taylor founded the

Vancouver School of Arts animation club, and he managed to talk the college into buying an old Bell and Howell projector and a couple of cameras rigged on stands for an animation course. Two years later, the NFB asked him to set up an animation department in its new Pacific regional office. The agency soon tried large-scale cel films such as Al Sens' satire about bigotry and intolerance, *The Twitch* (1973). The film employed local animators Hugh Foulds and Wayne Morris.

Sens and Foulds have borrowed heavily from one another. Both seem to favour heroes with widely spaced eyes, bulging noses and two-humped hats. Bureaucracy and the underdog is a shared theme. Foulds' first film for the NFB, *Citizen Harold* (1971), pits an average denizen against the monolithic-government. When Harold encounters obfuscation by friendly but unhelpful officials, he considers direct action, but collapses into apathy. Official zoning laws and red tape also bind a frustrated couple trying to build their country dream home in Foulds' third film commissioned by the NFB, *For Lands Sake* (1976). Unlike Sens, Foulds offers no fables or moral tales. His characters flounder in their situation, and we smile as they rail.

Stephen McCallum captured the West Coast ambiance in the film From Flores *(above). Outside of Rocketship's circle, independents preferred crosshatching and watercolours as in Martin Rose's paper cutout and pencil-rendered film,* Trauna Tuh Bel Vul *(below).*

Ernie Schmidt tried the satirical approach with his film *TV Sale* (1975), a rather uninteresting film that fails in its attempt to make a biting comment about channel surfing across North American television.

Perhaps the earnestness of the NFB's first films was too much for the laid back West Coast scene, but the B.C. shorts never hit a chord with audiences elsewhere. *Twitch* did run as a short in local theatres alongside *Jaws*, but it did not get much play outside the province.

After limited commercial success with full-scale cel animation techniques, the NFB changed course and began sponsoring non-traditional, solo films. Bill Maylone, a dinosaur-obsessed model maker, made a vignette and short, *64,000 Years Ago* (1981), starring a hairy miniature mammoth and T-Rex. His wife Bettina pro-

duced two fabric films for the agency. Kathy Li directed *Sabina* (1991), Stephen McCallum took an illustrative approach with his film *From Flores* (1990) and Amanda Forbis drew elaborate paper cutouts for *Bach's Pig* (1988). "If Winnipeg is wacky and colourful, then Vancouver is all cross-hatching and water-colours," she says.[108]

Not surprisingly, many of the new NFB recruits are graduates from the ECIAD. Hugh Foulds' courses were the polar opposite to classes offered at Sheridan College in Ontario. Foulds clearly favoured students who wanted to make personal mixed-media films over those who wanted classical training in cartoon animation. Screenings of Czechoslovakian puppet artist Jiri Trnka were more popular than Disney or Warner Bros. showings. Foulds cultivated female artists such as Wendy Tilby, Amanda Forbis, Jill Haras and Kathy Li, who preferred to work directly under the camera.

Martin Rose was also a product of Foulds' curriculum. For the NFB's Pacific region, Rose crafted an elaborate paper cutout film *Trauna Tuh Bel Vul* based on a poem written and narrated by Earle Birney. With the rumble of his deep voice, Birney provides the rhythm of the train as it travels from Toronto to Belleville — the sound of the conductor's call, the whistles and the clanking. Using Birney as a guide track, Rose supplies changing perspectives on the rail car including great characters, flashes of landscape — skyline, thistles, dogs, cars,

While a student at Emily Carr, Amanda Forbis directed the lovely cutout film, Bach's Pig. She later won the Palme d'Or award in Cannes with Wendy Tilby for their animated short When the Day Breaks.

snaking tracks, and turning wheels. *Trauna Tuh Bel Vul* is a beautiful mood piece and one of the most creative films to originate from the region. After Foulds died in 1992, the baton was handed to Rose.

Despite the recent growth of regional service production houses for US series, Vancouver is still viewed as a centre for alternative animation. "We are probably a little less repressed than other places in North America," says Grimshaw. "The Prairies are known as the bible belt, Ontario is known for its film censorship, and the United States is a lot more restrictive about material than Canada is in general. And the West Coast, well, I guess there's just a lot of loose stuff sliding over the edge," he adds.

How Pink Komkommer *Came to Be*

Driving back from the Annecy Film Festival in France, Dutch animator Paul Driessen began hounding Newland about the subject of his next film. Newland said he didn't have one, but that answer did not satisfy Driessen, who kept pressuring him to name his latest project. Finally, Newland blurted out — it's a porno film. Driessen clammed up and contemplated Newland's response for the remainder of the drive.

The morning after arriving in Amsterdam, Newland received a call from Driessen telling him he had booked studio time to make the soundtrack for his film. Flabbergasted, Newland shouted into the phone: "It was a joke Paul, a joke!"

"Too late now," replied Driessen, "I've already talked Kommer Studios into giving us two free hours of studio time." With the vocal support of studio technicians and their girlfriends, the soundtrack was laid, so to speak.

Back in Canada, Newland appealed to the good nature of his animation friends to write letters of support for the project to the Canada Council. He figured Richard Condie's and Wendy Tilby's squeaky clean image would help sell a pornographic idea to the government agency. His ploy worked. Funding came through and the film was made. In a tongue-in-cheek tribute, he devised end credits that read: "The film was inspired by Richard Condie and Wendy Tilby." Of course, when it screened at Annecy, many people assumed that Richard and Wendy were now an item. "I thought they would never talk to me again," recalls Newland. They did, and Newland is now being lobbied by other independents who want to be part of his next anthology.

Sara Petty's contribution to Pink Komkommer.

chapter 10

Breaking Out of the Cel: Women Animators in Canada

People best suited for this purpose are skillful at lettering. Girls are usually steadier, happier and quicker at the work — they are neater and more methodical.

— Organization of a Cel Cartoon Film, NFB report
written by Colin Low, May 3, 1951.

animation studios have traditionally been boys' clubs. No girls allowed — except in the ink and paint departments. The club mentality kept the pubescent humour of animators alive. They, in turn, generated remarkable slapstick comedy and cartoon ribaldry. But it has also stunted the growth of female characters and styles. Toontown is still sexist. Even today's edgier animators, like John Kricfalusi, confine themselves to comic book fantasy land populated by descendants of the buxom Betty Boop.

Many women found traditional cel animation to be too claustrophobic. Those who got past the studio doors found themselves drawing 3-D Barbies or ravished heroines. Anne Marie Bardwell got her big break in 1979 when Nelvana asked her to replace Dan Haskett, a character designer working on the company's first feature film, *Rock & Rule*. Haskett's rubberhose-like design did not complement the rest of the film's characters, and director Clive Smith began searching for a replacement. Anne Marie's sketches of Angel, the rock 'n roll chick, impressed him. Despite her tender age (early twenties) and lack of experience (two years working for Hanna-Barbera after graduating from Sheridan College), Nelvana principals assigned Bardwell the lead. It was a significant part that would take almost three years of her life. But Ann Marie never saw the film through to completion. Loubert took her off the character after they quarrelled over what constituted "sexy." Ann Marie did not envision her heroine spread-eagled on a stage, bound and helpless before the villain and his monster creation. In the end, animation director Frank Nissen was asked to finish the scene himself.

A handful of other female animators slugged it out in Nelvana's studios. Elaine Despins completed her work as an animator on *Rock & Rule* and promptly quit. Tired of drawing yet another stereotypical female lead, she left the business for nearly a decade. In 1992, she returned

Rock & Rule's *art shows a vulnerable heroine.*

The naive characters in Janet Perlman's Lady Fishbourne's Complete Guide to Better Table Manners.

to the animation world to design characters for Ciné-Groupe's TV special *David Copperfield* (1994).

Bardwell has remained in feature animation, where she is still consigned to drawing female characters. Her résumé includes Holli in Ralph Bakshi's *Cool World* (1992), Anne-Marie in Don Bluth's *All Dogs Go to Heaven* (1989), Esmeralda in Disney's *Hunchback of Notre Dame* (1996), and preliminary work on Jane, in Disney's remake of the Edgar Rice Burroughs classic, *Tarzan*.

"Outside of Heavy Metal's Taarna (and of course she had to be a walking Barbie doll to be accepted as well as voiceless), women are not much more than prospective mothers, wedding partners or sluts," says Wendy Perdue, who left Canada to work at Warner Bros. in the United States.[109]

Whether silly, sassy or sultry, the hour-glass cartoon heroines still hanker after the macho male and still respond in predictable patterns. Bardwell is resigned to it, but takes solace in knowing that her male counterparts also struggle within the mold created for the male hero.

In Canada, few female independents tackle cel animation. The most successful woman working in the medium is Janet Perlman, director of *Lady Fishbourne's Complete Guide to Better Table Manners* (1978), *Why Me* (1978), *The Tender Tale of Cinderella Penguin* (1981), *My Favourite Things That I Love* (1994) and *Dinner for Two* (1996). Perlman developed the rounded character with the wide-eyed stare — a look also adopted by the animation team of David Fine and Alison Snowden. They are naive creatures who deliver devilishly funny lines and actions. Her strength as a director also lies in her ability to humorously juxtapose graphics.

In *Lady Fishbourne*, elaborate Victorian titles trick audiences into thinking a bland review of table manners will follow. Instead a dry-witted cartoon character discusses the finer points of flinging peas. The most incongruous mix and match attempted by Perlman was her selection of images in *My Favourite Things That I Love* (1994). The film is so full of kitsch imagery that fellow animators joked it was a film only Janet could love. The film received a special jury prize for "Best Bad Taste" at the Ottawa Animation Festival, and it won the Normand

Roger Palmare du Son for "Best Horrible Music" at the Annecy Animation Festival in 1995.

Perlman's most popular film is the heavily booked title, *The Tender Tale of Cinderella Penguin*, her new twist on an old children's classic. Using a medieval style of illustration, she retells the fairy tale of poor Penguin Cinderella who loses her magic flipper as she runs from her prince to meet the midnight deadline. Her famous weeble-shaped characters are so appealing that the American Academy of Motion Picture Arts and Sciences nominated the film for an Oscar.

With a few notable exceptions — Sylvie Fefer, Debra Dawson, Beth Portman and Ellen Besen — most women artists steered away from classical animation. They gravitated toward solo techniques, particularly work involving painting or paper manipulation under the camera. The popularity of paper cutouts is due to the work of pioneer German artist Lotte Reiniger, who made one film at the NFB, and Canadian Evelyn Lambart, who had a profound influence on her contemporaries.

My Favourite Things That I Love received a special jury prize for "Best Bad Taste" at the Ottawa Animation Festival.

Evelyn Lambart was a long-time assistant/collaborator of Norman McLaren. Given free rein, she preferred to craft allegorical films. Whereas McLaren drew elaborate doodles of birds and hens, Lambart cut animals out of heavy construction paper or metal sheets. It was a radical departure from the painstaking calibrations with her mentor. She never complained openly about working with McLaren; her desire to direct was latent. It took Lambart more than 20 years to undertake her own films. Finally shaking the yoke of "assistant," she proclaimed herself in a blaze of colour.

Evelyn Lambart craved the opportunity to direct. But she balked when executive producer Wolf Koenig approached her about taking the lead on her own film: "I had been so accustomed to helping Norman that I found it difficult [to work independently]," she says.[110] Lambart knew she had the ability to make a film, but it terrified her to bear the entire burden. In their creative marriage of convenience, Norman made all final decisions. Years of dependency had created insecurity.

The Tender Tale of Cinderella Penguin is one of Janet Perlman's most popular films.

Evelyn Lambart spent 20 years working as Norman McLaren's assistant before she finally made her own films.

The film community was slow to recognize her talent and boost her confidence.

Employed by the NFB in 1942, Lambart's contribution to McLaren's work went largely unappreciated for nearly two decades. During that time, Lambart claimed only two directing titles, one for an ingenious film about cartography entitled *The Impossible Map* (1947), and another for *Family Tree* (1949), a film about European settlement in North America. She shared that credit with George Dunning.

Between 1947 and 1967, Lambart worked primarily as McLaren's indispensable assistant, collaborating on 12 films including: *Begone Dull Care* (1949), *Around is Around* (1951), *Rythmetic* (1956), *A Chairy Tale* (1957), *Lines Horizontal* (1961), *Lines Vertical* (1962) and *Mosaic* (1965). She also made films with Colin Low and Bob Verrall.

It eventually became apparent to Lambart that her contribution to the unit was not fully appreciated after she approached Colin Low for a raise in 1955. Low, once her trainee, informed Lambart that she made the highest wage within her category. It hit home: she was not one of the boys; she was relegated to the role of assistant, not artist. It took years before the NFB physically credited her alongside McLaren for the films they made together. Perhaps the worst insult was to deny her a credit for animating the chair in the short, *A Chairy Tale*. The producers reasoned that they must maintain the illusion that the chair was still alive. Imagine not crediting McLaren with drawing on film because a producer wanted the audience to believe the symbols he crafted were real. The ludicrous slight was later corrected. Her name now appears on the credits.

The McLaren/Lambart partnership was a true amalgam of ideas and experimental tests. Lambart once convinced McLaren that the annoying dust particles sticking to fresh paint should not be viewed as a disaster, but rather incorporated as a textural element. Struck by her logic, McLaren began running and jumping on the floor to kick up more dust – even shaking the film out the window to pick up the dirt from outside. As shown in *Begone Dull Care*, everyday grime could look like electrical static.

Together they discussed the concept for *Lines Horizontal* and *Lines Vertical* while driving back from Lambart's cottage one day. Fascinated with the way hydro lines appeared to weave along the horizon as they travelled, McLaren quizzed Lambart about the possibility of reproducing the effect on film. They achieved it by ruling lines on film emulsion and having them move against a background of changing colours.

McLaren took the lead, but Lambart often navigated some of the tricky straits. Sometimes she animated complete sections, as she did in *Short and Suite*. She was called upon regularly to do the tedious and laborious colour corrections, remixes and creative changes he dictated through the mail. While travelling through the United States with his film *Begone Dull Care*, McLaren instructed Lambart that the blue section of the film was too dark, and the tail end music should be recut. He also informed her of his error in colour judgement with the film *Rythmetic*. He changed the colour plan at the end of the film from blue to red, and requested that Lambart execute it.[111] While conducting experimental tests for *Mosaic*, McLaren wrote to commend Lambart on the saturation of dots, colour, and crispness. "All your painstaking work and that whole method of getting colour has proved itself. I feel it will be so easy to adjust and modify hue saturation and light value," he wrote.[112]

After years slaving over mechanical calibrations, Lambart chose to work with paper and metal cutouts. Lambart believed McLaren was too wrapped up in his own physical dependencies to be aware of any creative slight to her. She once mused: "Norman always credited me; but the world credited Norman."

Many of McLaren's requests were simply mundane, like shipping pencil supplies to China or New Delhi where McLaren was posted for UNESCO. They were requests made of secretaries. Another artist might have balked. Lambart stayed. In all likelihood, she had fallen in love with Norman. It was a love unrequited. For years, McLaren lived with Guy Glover, a man he met at the ballet in London in the thirties. As time passed, Lambart's love evolved into a maternal bond. At times she felt stifled and craved her space, but she nevertheless kept McLaren supplied with Band-Aids and art tools, sent presents to his parents, and always brought plenty of hot tea to work.

In 1965, Lambart's contribution to McLaren's films was finally recognized. A retrospective of McLaren's films at the Annecy film festival honoured Lambart as well. That spring, Lambart allowed herself to bask in the appreciation. Her self-esteem grew.

Four years after the Annecy tribute, Lambart and McLaren were on the road to professional separation. For

After years of collaborating with McLaren, Lambart proclaimed herself in a blaze of colour with films such as The Hoarder *(above) and* The Story of Christmas *(below). She left abstract filmmaking behind and focused on fables and fantasy.*

years, McLaren had been in and out of the Allen Memorial Hospital after consuming toxic amounts of barbiturates and alcohol. Lambart writes in her diaries that she felt like a stranger: "He is so far from you on another planet and communication is only on remote matters."[113] By this time, she was no longer dependent upon him. At age 55, Lambart had two solo works under her belt — *Fine Feathers* (1968) and *The Hoarder* (1969) — and was crafting her third.

The filmic fables Lambart eventually tackled were liberating. *The Story of Christmas* (1973) notwithstanding, she preferred tales that involved animals: *The Lion and the Mouse* (1976), *Mr. Frog Went A-Courting* (1974), *The Town Mouse and the Country Mouse* (1980).

Under McLaren's wing, she proved that she could undertake mechanical calibrations. Post-McLaren meant a mathematical-free world. Protractors and rulers were exchanged for paper and scissors. With her newfound freedom came the opportunity to expand her palate and explore the world of narrative. "Norman and I didn't have the same feeling for colour," says Lambart. "He'd start to wiggle around in his clothes if he didn't like the colour I used. My own sense of colour was modified when I worked with him. I've always been partial to blue and red. Norman didn't like bright colours. He loved olive green and cool yellow." A popular combination was the contrast of complementary colours for dramatic effect — royal blue next to orange.

Lambart never blamed McLaren for her years of obscurity. There was no malicious intent or ego rivalry involved. In her diaries, Lambart wrote: "[McLaren] is one of those people on the thin line between genius and insanity. He doesn't live in this world at all. To live like an ordinary individual is for him a continual compromise." McLaren was too wrapped up in his art, and his own physical dependencies, to be aware of any slight to his creative partner. "Norman always credited me; but the world credited Norman," Lambart once mused.

The emerging female talent in the seventies can be partly attributed to Lambart. It is also the result of the support of two influential instructors: Derek Lamb, a former Harvard professor, and Hugh Foulds of the Emily Carr Institute of Art and Design in Vancouver. One notable Canadian director once referred to Foulds as a "sexist pig," but she routinely encouraged pupils to take his course because "he put out the best female animators in the country." Kathy Li, Tracy Lewis, Amanda Forbis, Wendy Tilby and Clare Maxwell are all former pupils. Both teachers encouraged women to explore new materials, and whenever possible shunted their prize protégés to the NFB.

The Town Mouse and the Country Mouse *is an animated Aesop fable about two mice who compare their different lives in the country and the city.*

Probably the finest animated literary adaptation ever produced is a film by Caroline Leaf, a prize pupil in Derek Lamb's Harvard class. Leaf lovingly condensed author Mordecai Richler's short story *The Street* into a classical piece of animation. The film is about a nine-year-old boy growing up in Montreal waiting for the day his grandmother dies so he can finally have his own bedroom. In telling the story, Leaf remained true to Richler's tender and humorous voice. But it was her optics and perspective that stunned the animation community. This young director animated her own camera moves — the zooms, the 360-degree rotations and the crane shots. In a way, she liberated other artists. She proved she could create optical tricks through sheer imaginary force, as well as mechanical calibrations.

Leaf insists her approach was due in part to her lack of experience: "I hadn't looked at enough film to have an idea that these were camera moves that I was making. And I didn't really know how to cut and edit, so rather than making a cut and risk that the two pieces would not fit together, I made the transitions between the scenes. It was the safest way for me to get from A to B."[114]

The intuitive sand-on-glass technique that Leaf improvised at Harvard in the sixties is still being taught to beginner art students. Harvard design professor Albert Alcalay intro-

While at Harvard University, Derek Lamb tutored animators such as Caroline Leaf (above) in the art of animation.

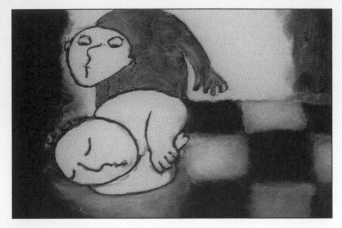

Caroline Leaf animated her own camera moves in the adaptation of Mordecai Richler's short story, The Street. *She proved that one could create optical tricks through sheer imaginary force.*

duced Leaf to Lamb's animation class. She remained, unsure of her ability to make images move. Lamb recalls: "[Caroline] seemed to hover around the edges of the class uncertain of this strange and unfamiliar medium. She would say in frustration: 'Oh, but I'm hopeless! I really can't draw at all.' Then, one day, I'd set an assignment. The class was asked to bring in objects or materials that could be animated on a lightbox as silhouette images. Everyone found interesting things, but Caroline brought in something quite special; a bag filled with beach sand. As you poured sand onto the glass and began shaping characters with it, there was born a new and original animation technique. From the first few motion tests it was obvious that she'd found her medium."[115]

Leaf's student film, *Peter and the Wolf* (1969), is a metaphor for light and dark, good and bad. The adaptation is with tonal efficiency. By adjusting the thickness of sand on the backlight glass, Leaf created half-tones and shades to evoke mood and perspective. White simply meant open spaces; darkness indicated closure. In *Peter and the Wolf*, Leaf's characters move in a two-dimensional plane. Only when she made *The Street* did she create a three-dimensional world.

Lamb made efforts to get Leaf hired by the NFB's English Programme unit, but it was the French animation studio at the NFB that eventually contracted her. Co Hoedeman, a Dutch-born animator working in the French animation studio, hired Leaf in 1972 to animate a traditional Inuit tale. Once again, Leaf applied her sand technique and made *The Owl Who Married the Goose* (1974). It is the NFB's best interpretation of a Native legend or story. The use of a patriarchal narrative voice often tramples a fanciful story. Leaf sidestepped this pitfall by relying entirely on an authentic recording of Inuit throat-singers to make the narrative soundtrack.

Between 1974 and 1977, Leaf would make two films simultaneously: *The Street* during the day for the NFB, and *The Metamorphosis of Mr. Samsa* at night with funding from the American Film Institute. The films use the same technique — tempera paints on glass — but they are a study in contrast.

Both *The Street* and *The Metamorphosis of Mr. Samsa* are literary adaptations; but whereas Leaf used Richler's staccato bursts of dialogue to her advantage, she avoided dialogue altogether in her adaptation of Franz Kafka's work. *Metamorphosis* is black and white, like Leaf's earlier films. Perspectives remain surreal in *Metamorphosis* because Leaf drew them as if they were images conjured up in Samsa's mind. Thus the point-of-view passes through walls, beneath closed doors and inside the beetle. As in earlier

works, Leaf visualizes *Metamorphosis* in black and white. Colour and 3-D perspective seep into Richler's story. *Metamorphosis* is mythic; *The Street* is firmly grounded in this world.

The Street has a depth not seen in her early works. In it, Leaf deftly uses transitions to evoke the passage of time and condense wordy passages. In playing with the tempera paints, Leaf leaves a trail of fingerprints and smudges as a subconscious reminder of the author's voice. *Entre deux soeurs* (*Two Sisters*, 1991), is an excerpt from a feature script she drafted about a stranger who enters the

lives of two sisters and alters their peaceful co-existence. It became an experiment on 70-mm Imax film. By scratching away the film emulsion, she created an etching in motion.

In 1996, Leaf received a Life Achievement award from the prestigious Zagreb Animation Film Festival for her "timeless and undisputed contribution to the art and development of animation."

Leaf's work had a huge impact on other female artists, most notably Wendy Tilby, a young student of Hugh Foulds' who also chose to express herself using paint-on-glass technique. Theatrical distributors bought *Tables of Content* (1986), Tilby's student film, and Doug MacDonald, then executive producer of Studio A, quickly contracted her to work on a film for the NFB.

Tilby chose similar tools, but has consciously tried to steer away from Leaf's style of storytelling and animation movement. *Strings* (1991), her first film at the NFB, requires audiences to visually connect the dots — to pick out visual clues that link her two protagonists. *Strings* was designed to feel two-dimensional. As a result, she limited the camera movements to pans and tilts. Despite employing graphic self-restraint, Tilby's characters are charming, and have more

A disfigured writer lives in complete isolation imposed upon her by an overprotective sister until one day a stranger arrives and disrupts their routine. The film, Entre deux soeurs, *was crafted by Caroline Leaf.*

colour and detail than Leaf's. In a similar vein, Prince Edward Island artist JoDee Samuelson expertly crafted the film *The Bath* under the camera. In both theme and style, Samuelson is disappointingly derivative of Tilby's work.

Like her film *Strings*, Tilby's third film, *When the Day Breaks* (1999), is about communal circuitry — the networks of pipes, wires and memories that tie us all together. It is the story of a young woman (Ruby) who collides with a man on his way out of a grocery store. When Ruby finishes picking up the milk she needs for breakfast and leaves the store, she witnesses a horrible accident. The man, whom she bumped into minutes before, is hit by a car and his groceries spill onto the street. Ruby returns home but her life is strangely altered by this encounter.

Wendy Tilby's beautiful paint-on-glass films, Tables of Content *(above) and* Strings *(below).*

"What we want to convey when you experience or witness the death of a stranger, it affects everything you see," says Tilby.[116] Her life has been touched, however fleetingly. Tilby strives to illustrate this connection by taking the viewer on a surreal tour through the physical infrastructure of homes in the neighbourhood, including the apartment of the man who died.

After more than a year of experimentation, Tilby and co-director Amanda Forbis developed an innovative new multimedia approach for *When the Day Breaks*. Shot entirely on Hi-8 film with actors, Tilby fed the footage through a video printer. The artists pulled selected frames off the printer and proceeded to Xerox and manipulate the characters beyond recognition. Because they used photocopies of actual film footage, the background moved in a weird pixilated way. The two photocopied and redrawn protagonists actually take on animal form — the man's head becomes chicken-like, and Ruby's head resembles a pig. It's an eerie combination of human and animal.

Tilby and Forbis have successfully straddled the gender issue, by turning their female into a pig. They found it difficult to design an interesting youthful character without adding prominent sex characteristics such as eyelashes or breasts. "It's hard to get just a person," says Tilby, who animated elderly women in her previous films.

The women in earlier designs looked miserable. Tilby and Forbis found it difficult to shape a whole personality. So instead they turned their character into a pig to give it a little "joie de vivre." They wanted her to start the day comfortable and happy, but after her encounter to return a little bruised. The film won the Palme d'Or for the best short film at the 1999 Cannes International Film Festival.

Many other female artists have chosen to express themselves through paper cutouts and collages — Bettina Maylone, Lynn Smith and Veronika Soul. Smith and Soul are both American citizens who worked extensively in Canada. The common denominator between them appears to be their desire to work independently using low-tech methods. Their characters also tend to be less representational than ones created by their cartoon-loving brothers. "I'm inspired by garbage, leftovers ... I like it when it gets stranger ... I guess that's what I can't stand about cartooning. It attempts to be real in drawing and it falls flat. There's no finesse, intellect, passion, mystery," says Soul.[117]

Wendy Tilby and Amanda Forbis created half-human/half-animal characters by using a new multimedia approach. The process involved printing video stills off Hi-8 footage, Xeroxing the images and finally painting and drawing on top of the photocopies. The final film, When the Day Breaks, *won the 1999 Palme d'Or award at the Cannes Film Festival.*

In her film *Pearl's Diner* (1994), Smith takes magazine clippings to construct a cast of characters who frequent a greasy spoon. It is her third collage film. Her first, *Teacher, Lester Bit Me*, is aurally assembled using snippets of dialogue from children in a daycare centre. The soundtrack was constructed in a studio, but the film has a cinéma-vérité feel. Perhaps, like Soul, Smith feels the need to rummage through leftover magazines to develop her characters. Theirs are media concoctions blurring racial and gender stereotypes.

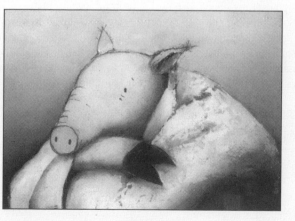

Smith is a contemporary of Caroline Leaf. The two crossed paths at Harvard under the tutelage of Derek Lamb, and then immigrated to Canada. She made several sponsored films at the NFB including *This Is Your Museum Speaking* and *Shout It Out Alphabet Film*, as well as three anti-smoking clips entitled *Circus, Uncle's Birthday* and *I Bet He Wished He'd Never Started*. The anti-smoking shorts, drawn on paper, reveal a comic side to Smith's personality.

Smith and Leaf collaborated for an entire year on a film for children. A shakeup at the NFB in 1982 changed their plans. Both Leaf and Smith found themselves at odds with Studio A's new executive producer. Although both directors had made wonderful films for kids including *Shout It Out Alphabet*, Doug MacDonald, the new executive producer, was insisting all concepts and scripts be vetted by teachers and educators. "It deadened the process," says Leaf. Smith never returned to the NFB, and Leaf made herself scarce during the MacDonald era. The studio's pedantic period put a damper on the gender equation.

Personality Software *looks ahead to a day when humans will be able to program a desired personality using specially designed software packages.*

The feminist wave that hit the female documentary filmmakers in Canada barely made a ripple in the animation studio. Evelyn Lambart, Canada's first lady of animation, was vehemently opposed to joining the separate women's studio at the NFB formed in 1974 — known as Studio D — and was not inclined to train others. "I always want to yell at them: 'Experiment for yourself,' " says Lambart. Films with caustic political humour were left to the real independents, who scrounged for funds through Canada Council grants and over-extended their credit limits. Sylvie Fefer made *A Short Story* (1985), a film about the body politic and self-image; *Personality Software* (1990), a futuristic morality tale about the future of computer-designed personalities; and *Brushstrokes* (1982), a short about artistic identity.

Joyce Borenstein sculpts clay on a backlight board to achieve a rare luminescence in The Man Who Stole Dreams.

Anne Marie Fleming, another Vancouver artist, made several multimedia films that incorporated animation techniques. Fleming made *Waving* (1987), a film about cross-cultural experience; *Red Shoes: An Interview in Exactly Five Minutes* (1990) about domestic violence; and *You Take Care Now* (1989), a personal film about rape. Fleming's approach is to combine animation with optically printed video. By mixing the two genres she's able to physically overlap the pained jumble of subconscious with more mundane documentary images. She has switched to stick figures in her most recent films.

Sexual reawakening is the intent of *Sabina* (1991), Kathy Li's erotic interpretation of Anaïs Nin's poetry. Sabina is a symbolic name for women of water – women afloat in their subconscious desires. Ribbons of colour lap over bodies and wind their way through the soul. In short, *Sabina* is a visual exploration of Woman's carnal

essences. Not the stuff of the familiar cadre of National Film Board artists.

Fables and fantasy are more the stuff of NFB filmmakers Evelyn Lambart, Joyce Borenstein, Gayle Thomas, Françoise Hartmann and Suzanne Gervais. The NFB hired Borenstein to make her first film, *Traveler's Palm* (1976), a visually resplendent work based on her Cal Arts student film, *Revisited*. The strange imagery was achieved by sculpting clay on a backlight board. Borenstein perfected the technique before others like Ishu Patel were recognized for crafting a similar approach.

Joyce Borenstein was one of the first artists to animate clay across a glass plate in her NFB film, Traveler's Palm.

She reworked the technique for *The Man Who Stole Dreams* (1987), and achieves a rare luminescence. But the film suffers from its conventional narrative approach. The film is based on Barbara Taylor's story about the nocturnal tricks hatched by a man who steals the dreams of the townspeople and attempts a profit-making venture by reselling them to restless villagers.

Borenstein is an animator who is still growing as an artist. *Colours of My Father* (1991) is a romantic ode to her father painter Sam Borenstein. In it Borenstein contrasts vivid images of her father's work with animated black and white scenes to represent her childhood memories. This exemplary artist-driven film was also nominated for an Oscar.

Borenstein also directed *One Divided by Two — Kids in Divorce* (1997). Although the subject matter is weighty, Borenstein works playfully with colours and design motifs. The film revolves around divorce stories as told by a group of youngsters aged 8 to 18. Borenstein's approach is to take select interviews and animate them. By interpreting their fears, anger and pain, she offers some insight into their psychological trauma.

Some artists thrive under the NFB roof. Borenstein in many ways has struggled to reassert her voice. In her downtown Montreal apartment, she candidly reviews her past work: "I've been on detour mode. I'm really ready to use the skills I've learned to get back to my own aesthetic — the aesthetic I was doing when I was 20, and doing more surrealist art."[118]

Gayle Thomas was a refugee of studio production. After working for Potterton Studios in Montreal, she moved to the NFB where she worked as an assistant on Michael Mill's short, *Evolution*. Impulsively, she turned to cutout animation after

The monochromatic
motif in A Sufi Tale.

The Boy and the Snow
Goose *offers the simple
adage: If you love some-
thing set it free.*

Françoise Hartmann's
Summer Legend *is clearly
influenced by the work
of Evelyn Lambart.*

doing some cel tests. "I liked the idea of filling up entire screens. I felt it was more of a visual experience," she says.[119] Thomas created a tonal polarity in her first film, *Snow*. Thomas later repeated this monochromatic motif in *A Sufi Tale* (1980), a film about superstition.

For years, Thomas resisted becoming "slave to a concept," and avoided straight-ahead narrative. Free association would best describe her film *A Magic Flute* (1977). When Thomas finally tackled storyline it was to animate her own children's tale, *The Boy and the Snow Goose* (1984). The feathery technique she employed involves shading on the front of frosted cels rather than taking the usual backpainting route. Her favourite orange and yellow colours dominate the film.

Phoenix (1990), based on Sylvia Townsend Warner's story is an unqualified creative disappointment. Drawn with wax pencils, the film lacks the energy and spirit of her earlier works. Forced to adapt another author's work, Thomas' frustration and lack of empathy for the poor bird are evident. Free to explore colour and shape in her film *Quilt* (1996), Thomas has returned to her love of design. The flaw in this film lies not in the story, but in the over-brightness and lack of hue of the computer-generated images.

Legend and lore are the ground tilled by Françoise Hartmann. Her biggest contributions to Studio A are *Summer Legend* (1986), an interpretation of Native folklore and *The Long Enchantment*, a medieval tale of a pony caught in an evil vizier's spell and of the young girl who frees it. The colourful paper cutouts are clearly reminiscent of Lambart's work. Here at least, tradition has been passed down.

Women working in non-traditional animation styles have had to break out of the cel mold and swim against the tide. For many years, the National Film Board provided a safe haven for a select few. As NFB budgets shrink, opportunities for women artists will diminish. What remains is a rich legacy of films and strong role models. Evelyn Lambart, Caroline Leaf, Wendy Tilby, Janet Perlman, Joyce Borenstein and others will inspire women well into the 21st century.

chapter 11

The Silent Minority:
Animation's Auteurs

C anada has nurtured a handful of artists who ignore established trends and create their own artistic standards. Their work breaks the mold, and defies classification. Norman McLaren embarked on the road not taken and led a handful of followers at the National Film Board down the experimental film path. He was an iconoclastic Pied Piper of animation who attracted many artists. Those who took their cues, and broke with conventional forms, include George Dunning, Ryan Larkin, Ron Tunis and Arthur Lipsett.

Across town in Montreal, another animation experiment was percolating at Radio-Canada, the French-language public broadcaster. Frédéric Back was given free rein to perfect an illustrative style that was greedily embraced and exploited by the commercial sector.

The NFB and Radio-Canada liberated a handful of artists from the pressures of commercial production, but not everyone sought such freedom. Some of Canada's best animators thrived in an environment burdened by deadlines and tight budgets. George Dunning left the NFB to work in the fast-paced world of commercial production. Richard Williams and John Kricfalusi also chose to work in the private sector but still managed to push their own creative vision.

NORMAN McLAREN

In the 1940's and 1950's, Norman McLaren was an underdog in a world dominated by cartoonists. He was the anti-animator of his time, preferring to work with symbols, texture and colour, rather than character design. McLaren's films had marginal release in North America, yet his impact on the commercial world is enormous. He proved beyond a reasonable doubt that animation was not exclusively visual gags involving mice, bunnies, pigs and ducks. By going beyond anthropomorphic character poses, he raised the craft from its pop culture status to artistic expressionism. Along the way, he pioneered five techniques: (1) hand-drawn films made without cameras; (2) pastel renderings; (3) pixilation stopmotion

Jean-Paul Ladouceur, George Dunning and Norman McLaren, (left to right) working at an NFB Steenbeck.

A Chairy Tale is a simple parable about power relationships.

technique, which involves altering the camera speed while shooting live-action characters; (4) synthetic sound; and (5) multi-imaging and stereographic animation.

If McLaren's art had been mediocre, he would still have made animation history for his innovations. Instead, he was heralded by French film critics as the man who revolutionized modern animation. Even Pablo Picasso, after screening one of McLaren's films in 1946, was moved to comment: "Finally, something new in drawing."

McLaren was not part of the mainstream, but he was — and remains — a major contributor of ideas that fed the commercial well. Over the years, he inspired a host of young artists trying to break new ground in animation. UPA co-founder John Hubley (*Moonbird, Mr. Magoo*) cites McLaren as one of his greatest influences. George Dunning, director of the feature film *Yellow Submarine*, was tutored by McLaren in the early forties. The animated renderings of *La poulette grise* and *A Little Phantasy on a Nineteenth Century Painting*, moved Ryan Larkin, Carolyn Leaf and Frédéric Back — animators who have used a variety of techniques such as charcoal, oil-on-glass, and pencil on frosted cel to craft their own pastel look.

If there is one tenet of McLaren's philosophy that has been absorbed by commercial artists today it is this: the physical medium should not be revered. Film should be treated as if it were steel. It should be

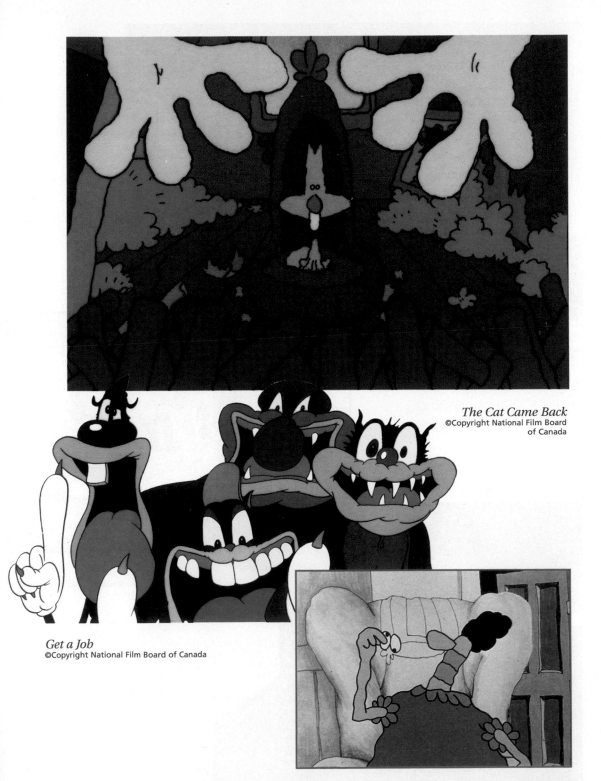

The Cat Came Back
©Copyright National Film Board
of Canada

Get a Job
©Copyright National Film Board of Canada

The Big Snit
©Copyright National Film Board of Canada

Pink Komkommer
©International Rocketship, Inc.

Anijam
©International Rocketship, Inc.

Trauna Tuh Bel Vul
©Copyright National Film Board of Canada

Rock & Rule concept art

The Town Mouse and the Country Mouse

Entre deux soeurs

Tables of Content

*Lady Fishbourne's Complete Guide
to Better Table Manners*

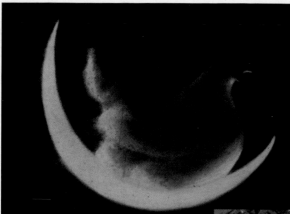

La poulette grise
©Copyright National Film Board of Canada

Crac!
©Copyright Société Radio-Canada

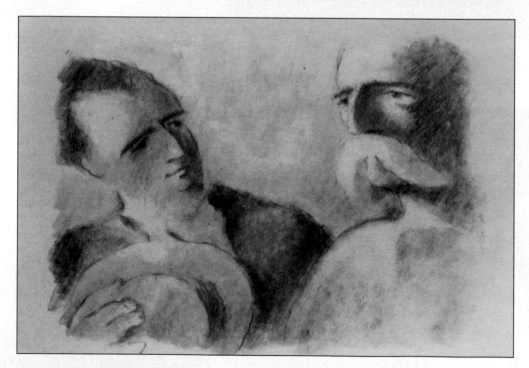

The Man Who Planted Trees
©Copyright Société Radio-Canada

Arabian Knight
©Copyright Miramax Films

Who Framed Roger Rabbit
©Copyright Touchstone Pictures/Amblin Entertainment

The Ren & Stimpy Show
©Copyright 1999 Nickelodeon

Beany and Cecil
Courtesy of Sody Clampett

Ed, Edd n Eddy
©Copyright 1999 Cartoon Network

*George Liquor
and Jimmy the Idiot boy*
©Copyright John Kricfalusi

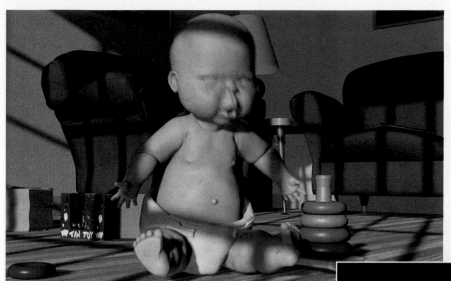

Tin Toy
©Copyright Pixar
Animation Studios

Car models by Alias/Wavefront

Bingo

The Mask

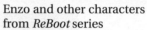

Enzo and other characters
from *ReBoot* series

Monster by Mistake!

Rolie Polie Olie

scratched, dirtied, pounded and painted to achieve effects. Today, commercial directors deconstructing and manipulating images using exacto blades or 2-D computer software programs are referred to as multimedia or compositing artists. McLaren was simply called an experimental filmmaker.

What makes McLaren a true master in his field is the complexity of his films. Unlike most animators, McLaren's artistry cannot be boiled down to a particular graphic style or image embossed on frames of film. It is all that is on the screen and in-between — the timing and composition of images — that make the film whole. "Graphism ... is of secondary importance," he wrote academic Georges Sigianos.[120]

McLaren believed film should be treated as steel; a medium to be scratched, dirtied, pounded and painted.

McLaren's filmic lexicon is inseparable from rhythm and music; he is a choreographer of light and movement. He summarized his philosophy thus: "Animation is not the art of drawings-that-move but the art of movements-that-are-drawn. What happens between each frame is much more important than what exists on each frame. Animation is therefore the art of manipulating the invisible interstices that lie between frames."[121]

McLaren films are about the unadulterated joy of movement, colour and shape. They are purely aesthetic. While most of his works do not offer conventional tales, each one begs a technical narrative. With every innovation comes an accompanying story — a discovery or invention. Queries from enthusiasts were so common that McLaren devoted much of his time to teaching, writing detailed explanations of his applications, and producing how-to films. He was a generous mentor as well as an artist. Says Don McWilliams, McLaren's assistant director on *Narcissus*: "He kept no secrets."[122]

Born in 1914 in Stirling, Scotland, Norman McLaren attended the Glasglow School of Art. Film schools did not exist at that time, so the young cinéaste had to form his own film club using a borrowed camera. "If McLaren had lived before there were moving pictures, he'd have invented them," his friend and colleague Grant Munro would later comment. [123] Lacking equipment and supplies, McLaren stripped an old 35-mm film of its

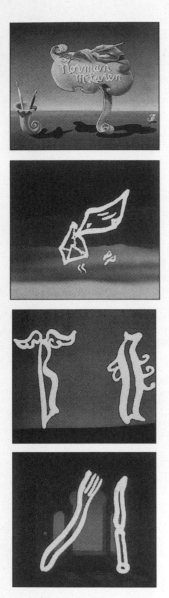

*Frames from McLaren's
Love on the Wing.*

emulsion and painted over the clear celluloid for his first project, *Hand-Painted Abstraction* (1933).

The enterprising Scot was "discovered" by documentary iconoclast John Grierson when two of his films — *Camera Makes Whoopee* (1935) and *Colour Cocktail* (1935) — were screened at the Scottish Amateur Film Festival in Glasgow. By adjusting the camera speed, McLaren was able to record the play of light across coloured paper in *Colour Cocktail.*

As the festival's adjudicator, Grierson awarded McLaren top prize, and offered him a job at the General Post Office Film Unit in London, England. But not before slapping him with a critical review: "You've got lots of imagination, trying all kinds of new things, but totally undisciplined, unharnessed. You don't know how to make a film and we're going to knock some discipline into you..."[124]

Despite its oppressive title, the General Post Office Film Unit had an impressive staff, including filmmaker Len Lye, poet W.B. Auden and the composer Benjamin Britten. Working alongside such an illustrious group of contemporaries did not intimidate the young artist. "McLaren developed in that world and proved to be one of the greatest experimentalists of them all," Grierson recalled.[125]

McLaren made five films at the GPO. His film *Love on a Wing* was labeled Freudian by the British Postmaster General and was never aired in theatres. Thankfully, McLaren did not abandon the technique that evoked the subconscious and made bureaucrats nervous. He drew directly on film for seven films that he produced while working in New York, selling his independent projects to the Guggenheim Museum of Non-Objective Art. He took the same approach for his first film at the National Film Board of Canada, *Mail Early* (1943), which ironically was also made for a national postal service.

McLaren's early years in New York and Montreal were spent perfecting his cameraless technique. He scratched, painted and stippled on film stock. With scant resources available, McLaren also experimented with hand-drawn soundtracks — first by painting directly on the film stock, and later by photographing cards bearing black and white stripes directly onto the soundtrack area of the film.

When management decreed that the NFB's animation studio should animate a series of folk songs, McLaren shifted gears. The jumpy, nervous lines of his scratch-on-film technique were unsuitable for sing-along shorts. Instead, McLaren found ways to transform painterly images into animation. *C'est l'aviron* (1945) was his first attempt at realism. The film's premise is simple. The bow of a canoe bobs up and down in the waves, travelling slowly past a craggy, surrealistic shoreline. McLaren started out by making a series of small paintings

on black cards. He super-imposed various card paintings on top of one another by exposing the film to one image, and rolling it back four or five more times to reshoot another. By using this continuous series of overlapping staggered zooms, McLaren was able to alter perspective and make the canoe appear to travel across a lake.

His new illustrative approach was labeled animated pastel. Haunted by the sunrises of the Scottish landscape where he grew up, McLaren experimented with the play of light on distant hills for *Là-haut sur ces montagnes* (1945). Rather than drawing hundreds of separate images to be shot individually by a cameraman, McLaren worked continuously on one painting and recorded each change he made to it. "In other words, do a painting, but put the emphasis upon the doing rather than on the painting — on the process rather than the end-product," he said.[126] He started with a piece of cardboard and coloured chalk, and ended three weeks later with a worn out piece of cardboard. *A Little Phantasy on a Nineteenth Century Painting* (1946), inspired by Arnold Boecklin's painting *Isle of the Dead*, and *La Poulette grise* (1947), capped McLaren's illustrative phase that bridged painting and animating.

In his trilogy of films — *Hoppity Pop* (1946), *Fiddle-dee-dee* (1947) and *Begone Dull Care* (1949) — McLaren achieved complete closure between the oral/aural and visual art forms. The cinematic triplet bubbles with life and energy. In practice, the craftsman choreographed colour, line and sound by taking musical measurements and building a cue sheet. The alchemy of sound and colour is magical. By making abstract symbols perform an interpretive dance to the music of Eugene Desormeaux and Oscar Peterson, McLaren literally allows "the eyes to hear and the ears to see."[127]

Despite the calibration involved in making these films, this trilogy appears to be more interpretive and joyous than his later efforts — *Lines Vertical* (1960), *Lines*

A Little Phantasy on a Nineteenth Century Painting (1946), is inspired by Arnold Boecklin's painting Isle of the Dead. *Rather than drawing hundreds of separate images to be shot individually by a cameraman, McLaren worked continuously on one painting, and recorded each change on film. He started with a piece of cardboard and coloured chalk, and ended three weeks later with a worn out piece of cardboard.*

In films such as Begone Dull Care, *McLaren literally allows the eyes to hear and the ears to see.*

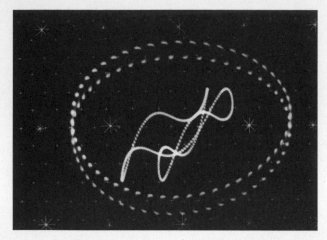

McLaren's technical achievements include 3-D stereographic films, Around is Around (above) and Now is the Time.

Horizontal (1962) and *Mosaic* (1965). The latter trio share a cold purity, an unemotional logic. They were also made at a time when McLaren was himself becoming more distant, a fact that his assistant Evelyn Lambert wrote in her diary.

Engraved in the film emulsion, a line mathematically divides until it climaxes with 17 criss-crossing lines in the first film, *Lines Vertical*. In *Lines Horizontal*, McLaren flips the premise and moves the lines horizontally. He believed that since gravity no longer exists once the lines run horizontally, viewers would perceive the films differently. Finally, in *Mosaic*, McLaren combined *Lines Vertical* and *Lines Horizontal* via a printer so that the lines do not move in two directions but instead pulsate across the screen.

McLaren's films always stimulate audiences, even if some find his work difficult to decipher. The cornucopia of shapes and colours is dizzying. McLaren joked that at least on one occasion he was called a Communist by a little old lady who couldn't fathom his art and believed it must harbour some hidden political message.

Only a handful of McLaren's films offer moral or conventional themes. The lack of narrative in McLaren's films never bothered his first patron, John Grierson. With a wave of his hand he dismissed the apolitical nature of his work: "I wouldn't trust Norman round the corner as a political thinker. That's not what Norman is for ... He's got joy in his movement, he's got fancy in his changes. That's enough."[128]

As Grierson once suggested, McLaren was one of the most protected artists in the history of cinema. Most of the time he led a fairly quiet existence shuttling back and forth between his Montreal home and the NFB studio. But McLaren was not always apolitical. As a youth back in Scotland, he was a card-carrying member of the Communist party, and in Canada he led an alternative lifestyle by co-habiting with his partner Guy Glover. Several times during his life, McLaren felt the need to address certain issues.

In 1950, after spending four months in China for UNESCO after Mao Tse Tung had come to power, he returned to the NFB to find it under serious attack by McCarthyite forces within the government. While supervising the film *Twirligig* (1951), NFB Film Commissioner Arthur Irwin threw out its director, Greta Eckmann, because of her Communist ties. Not long after, McLaren began a series of pixilation exper-

iments (using stop-motion camera), which culminated in the short *Neighbours* (1952), a powerful indictment of war. The combined experience of working in China during the revolution, and witnessing the expulsion of a valued colleague for her political views, finally moved him to strike a political stance.

Technically speaking, *Neighbours* was conceived by accident. By trying to retard movement through careful camera calibrations, McLaren was surprised to find that his actors looked like they were duking it out rather than performing balletic exercises. Once he discovered he could shoot a drag-em-out fight without having to actually film a violent event, McLaren developed his scenario.

Neighbours portrays two quarrelling friends who end up murdering each others' families during an absurd fight over a flower that grows along their property line. The film won the Oscar for best short documentary subject in 1952. Five years after completing *Neighbours*,

War Certain If No Peace. Peace Certain If No War. Jean-Paul Ladouceur and Grant Munro star in McLaren's film Neighbours. *Some colleagues believe McLaren produced the short after two animators were fired from the studio because of their Communist leanings.*

Blinkity Blank

McLaren directed another pixilated polemic — this time between a man and a chair. *A Chairy Tale* (1957) confronts the issue of power relationships. Management agonized over whether or not the chair should be painted black, lest audiences interpret it as a racial confrontation. The chair stayed white, and McLaren's allegorical brushstroke remained broad.

When asked why more of his films were not ideological, McLaren responded: "I feel I have not lived and experienced enough in my life to be able to make another film like *Neighbours*. Here at the NFB, I live a pretty sheltered existence, so to speak."[129]

McLaren may have been sheltered from economic hardships, but he waged a lifetime battle against his inner demons. His biographers refer obliquely to his personal suffering. No one mentions his attempts to alleviate his psychic "pain" through a wicked combination of alcohol and barbiturates. It is difficult to say how drugs affected McLaren's career. He often arrived at work feeling unwell and even passed out while editing on a Moviola. He also attempted suicide in the mid-sixties. With the exception of *The Head Test*, unearthed by Don McWilliams, McLaren's films do not mirror his torment. He exorcised some of the pain at home with his artwork.

Perhaps his cinematic smoke signals were too cryptic for us to comprehend. At least one critic came close when he commented, "Hell might well be an interrupted session in *Blinkity Blank*."[130] *Blinkity Blank* was a film McLaren designed to determine whether the mind can retain momentary images flashed onto the retina. This critic interpreted the black intervals as a horrible darkness threatening to suffocate McLaren's startling creations.

Whereas drugs and alcohol defeated more than one talented animator at the NFB, McLaren's work continued to evolve and mature. Colleagues have suggested that after producing the series of highly abstract minimalist films *Lines Vertical*, *Lines Horizontal* and *Mosaic*, McLaren stopped animating directly on film because his hands were too shaky.

If drugs were responsible for McLaren's decision to abandon this technique, then what a creative miracle it spawned. By the mid-sixties, McLaren was shooting live-action and exploring multiple-imaging effects on the optical printer. Using the printer, McLaren exposed individual live-action film frames up to ten times, leaving between them a span of five frames. The end result was a ten-fold exposure of the same image. While the visual impact is a strobe effect, the psychological impact of the technique is the ability of the brain to actually anticipate movement past and future.

The technical gymnastics produced two exceptional films, *Pas de deux* (1968) and *Ballet Adagio* (1971), which thematically tackle courtship and separation. The third and final film executed on the optical printer, *Narcissus* (1983), was to be McLaren's tour de force — both technically and thematically.

The film touches upon love of oneself, and love with one's own art and ability. Some have interpreted it as an open acknowledgement of McLaren's own narcissus, the personal revelation of a man who had lived a creative yet alienated life.

On the technical side, McLaren altered the shutter speed of the two cameras so that they ran slower than normal — one frame per second. The cameras' mechanical settings were calibrated to be 180 degrees out of phase with each other. This way each camera would capture on film the movement the other camera missed because of its slow shutter speed. There was one glitch. McLaren wanted each camera to film the dancers from the exact same position in relation to the dancer. He overcame the physical logistics by positioning the cameras at right angles from one another and placing a semi-silvered beam-splitting mirror between them. Precise choreography was key to ensuring that the dancer appeared in precisely the same position on the viewfinders of both cameras. Back in the lab, McLaren overlapped the blurs created on the optical printer by instituting a double chain of staggered mixes. Other interpretive passages included an upside-down sequence and a reverse-split-image shot.

For years, McLaren was a vocal advocate of do-it-yourself filmmaking. Ironically, at the end of his career, he no longer practised what he preached. *Narcissus* required the expertise of dancers, choreographers, a technician for the optical printer, three cameramen, an assistant director and three artistic counsellors.

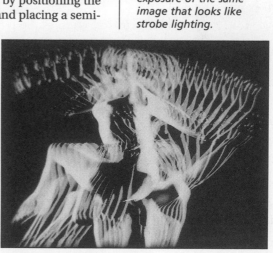

Pas de deux is an example of McLaren's experiments with multiple-imaging effects on the optical printer. Using the printer, McLaren exposed individual live-action film frames up to ten times, leaving between them a span of five frames. The end result is a ten-fold exposure of the same image that looks like strobe lighting.

The goal of *Narcissus* was to simulate a photographic blur, and impose metamorphosing backgrounds drawn in pastel. It was the greatest challenge of his life. But at age 64, and following years of substance abuse, this wall may have been too high for McLaren to scale. McWilliams notes that his sense of timing may have been unbalanced. Many critics considered it extraneous to his other dance films. It was not the high note he had hoped to ride out on.

McLaren retired from the NFB in 1984 and died four years later, leaving behind an impressive body of work including 98 short films. Most of the contemporary experimental animation exhibited on hip TV stations today are elementary exercises compared to McLaren's genius.

Oscar Who?

When *Neighbours* won an Oscar in 1953, McLaren was working on a development project in India. When the NFB cabled to inform him that his film had won an Oscar, he cabled back. "Great news. Who's Oscar?" He later commented: "I thought this Oscar ... I imagined (Oscar) as a great, big St. Bernard dog or something."[131] Before it won the Oscar, movie houses in Canada had

rejected it as "not very good."[132] It eventually opened in the Capitol Theatre of Ottawa and the Trans Lux Theatre on Broadway, New York. The simulated slaughter of wife and child at the end of the film was removed at the request of the US distributor. McLaren permitted the cut after he saw that there was no jump in the visual or the sound, and that the film worked smoothly. Later there were numerous complaints by people who had seen the original version. They worried that the climax of the film was now robbed of its message. It was put back in around 1968. In 1971, a group of parents in Edmonton balked about screening the film in the schools, arguing that it was a negative tool for teaching and that they didn't want their children to be captives of film violence. This time, the NFB did not back down.

Poulet Pour Vous?

Chickens keep popping up in McLaren's films. He used to see himself as a chicken, and his long-suffering colleague, Evelyn Lambart, as a horse.

GEORGE DUNNING

Director George Dunning's animated feature film *Yellow Submarine* won wide praise from critics when it was released in 1968. Journalists waxed eloquently about its phantasmagoria, puns, pastiches and visual non sequiturs.[133] The love-in was due to the simple fact that it looked like no animated feature film ever made. After a 30-year diet of Walt Disney product, Dunning threw the world a curve ball.

Al Brodax, head of King Features Syndicate's film department, wanted Dunning to adapt the ABC-TV series, *The Beatles* (1965–67) into a feature. Dunning was dismissive at first. He told Brodax that audiences would not pay to see a TV series on the big screen. But when Heinz Edelmann agreed to work as the film designer, the whole nature of the project changed.

Dunning was adamant that the film be more than just a showcase for The Beatles' songs. His sophisticated approach elevated the resulting film from trash TV to a cultural artifact that defined an era.

Yellow Submarine is set in Pepperland, a place where music, colour, love and peace are subjected to attacks by the Blue Meanies. Armed with their guitars and three new songs, the good Beatles waged battle with evil, and triumphed. With its psychedelic Pop Art look, and its flower-power storyline, *Yellow Submarine* became a visual anthem of the sixties counterculture.

When Edelmann arrived in England to begin work, he discovered there was no script to start with. The drawing team led by Jack Stokes took two songs — "Nowhere Man" and "Sergeant Pepper's Lonely Hearts Club Band" — and animated them while the script was quickly cobbled together.

The disorganization, and impossible nine-month deadline, eventually led to a legal dispute with King Features. At the height of production, King Features stopped payments to Dunning's company, TV Cartoons. Payments were quickly resumed when Dunning threatened to liquidate his company. But in the aftermath, *Yellow Submarine* not only pushed TVC (as it was later renamed) to the brink of bankruptcy, it wrecked Dunning's health.[134]

Yellow Submarine created a huge media stir, but Dunning never believed it was the pinnacle of his career. Its

With its psychedelic Pop Art look, and its flower-power storyline, Yellow Submarine *became a visual anthem of the sixties counterculture.*

The TV Cartoons' gang. Richard Williams (first on left) and George Dunning (second from right along the back row).

A TV Cartoons' commercial for Mother's Pride Bread.

flourescent, bold designs were the antithesis of Dunning's personal style. The absolute simplicity of line found in *The Flying Man* (1962) and *Damon the Mower* (1972) more closely reflect his own taste.

Dunning adopted a minimalist technique advocated by his mentor and colleague, Norman McLaren. A graduate from the Ontario College of Art, Dunning was only the second artist McLaren recruited to work in the NFB's new animation studio in 1943.

He cut his teeth doing film titles, but Dunning excelled at interpreting folk songs, which were frequently assigned to the animation unit during World War II.

One year after joining the NFB, Dunning made two films that show clearly his versatility as a graphic artist: *J'ai tant dansé*, a latticed paper cutout film, and *Grim Pastures*, a film that delivers its propaganda message through sparse line drawings.

Dunning's most popular short during his six-year tenure at the NFB was the metal cutout film, *Cadet Rousselle* (1947), based on a satirical French song about a hapless soldier. Extolled in *Film Digest Review*, *Cadet Rouselle* was considered "a step forward in the art of Canadian folklore."[135]

In 1949, Dunning and assistant Colin Low took a three-month leave of absence to work on a film about Baron Munchehausen. The ambitious film did not have the support of NFB executive producer Tom Daly, so Dunning defiantly moved over to Crawley Films to complete it.

Like *Cadet Rouselle*, the Baron Munchehausen characters were cut from metal. Dunning, however, envisioned a strange world for the Baron — a world in which gravity applied itself differently to each character, thereby confusing relationships and altering perspective. The visual brainteaser created a production nightmare, and the film was abandoned.[136]

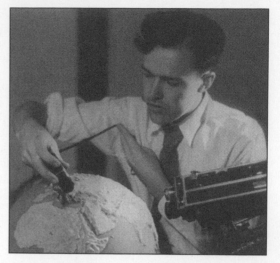

George Dunning was Norman McLaren's second NFB recruit. He later founded the influential British commercial house TV Cartoons.

A scene from one of TVC's British commercials.

Before quitting the NFB for good, Dunning co-directed *Family Tree* (1949) with Evelyn Lambart. The film chronicles the settlement of Canada, beginning with Jacques Cartier.

After a four-year stint working as a commercial director in Toronto with Jim MacKay, Dunning was recruited by Canadian expatriate Stephen Bosustow, president of UPA, to work on the *Gerald McBoing Boing* series. Bosustow had corresponded with artists at the NFB, having kept his eye on the best and brightest.

Less than a year after relocating to New York, Dunning was asked to move to London and set up a UPA satellite shop. When financial woes forced UPA to close its European operation in 1957, Dunning opted to stay abroad.

He convened an informal meeting in a London pub and invited John Coates, Richard Williams and Denis Rich for a drink and a pitch. His modest proposal was to form an independent production company. Coates left his lucrative job at Assoc. Redifusion (the first commercial TV station in Britain), and became a lifelong business partner. Williams and Rich became guns for hire.

TVC produced award-winning commercials for Sunblest bread, Mother's Pride Bread, the National Coal Board, The Ever Changing Motor Car and Golden Wonder Crisps. Dunning, now head of one of the country's top commercial houses, deftly stickhandled major accounts by charming clients.

In secret, he worked on his own projects. Only his patient cameraman, John Williams, and his steadfast assistant, Norman Kauffman, saw his experiments in the rough.

The Apple (1962) was conceived as a humorous film in the UPA style. But Dunning returned to his experimental roots with *The Flying Man* (1962). This film had a more impulsive element. Dunning placed his pencil drawings under a series of clear cels, then worked across the table, slashing colour onto each cel. Second and third strokes of colour were added until a complete series of cels was painted.[137]

The Flying Man captures the frustration of a man who wants to fly, but whose coat is eaten by a dog as he lifts off. It is about subconscious desires and realistic pitfalls.

The Flying Man is beautifully symbolic; *Damon the Mower* (1972) is pure poetry. Dunning's graphite drawings produced on a small flipbook are rearranged under a large camera field to reveal the frame registration numbers on the top of paper. The film is a play on the very medium itself. It both reveals the illusion of animated movement, while simultaneously creating a haunting image of death and regeneration.

The Apple (1962) was conceived as a humorous film in the UPA style (above). But Dunning returned to his experimental roots (below) with The Flying Man (1962).

Shakespeare in animation was to be his final statement; the ultimate experiment. When he died in 1979 of a heart attack at age 57, Dunning left behind a series of unfinished film sequences. The black and white pencil tests and coloured final scenes of *The Tempest* show his trademark elegant sweeping lines, and broad brushstrokes. As with *Damon*, *The Tempest* tests show an eclectic use of dialogue and sound effects.

His body of work is small, but Dunning pushed the boundaries of traditional animated films. He is also the undisputed father of British commercial animation.

ARTHUR LIPSETT

Arthur Lipsett was the original collage artist — the master of juxtaposition — able to clip snippets of our lives from newsreels, photographs and magazines and reassemble them to look like a frightening pastiche of our lives.

Before music videos and MTV, Arthur Lipsett physically demonstrated the powerful nature of montage in his film *Very Nice, Very Nice* (1961). However, his satirical use of sound bites and interviews pack a strong political bite, unlike the music videos of today. Whereas modern videos project musicians' values and image onto viewers, Lipsett's films hold up a mirror to society and challenge the viewer to interpret the patchwork of scenes.

Arthur Lipsett was the original collage artist, the first music video star before music videos were ever invented.

Arthur Lipsett always worked on the fringes of the animation and documentary units; nevertheless, his work influenced artists working in both studios. Lipsett was hired in 1957 to make public service announcements and advertisements. From the start, he veered away from the UPA stylized cartoons favoured by his colleagues Wolf Koenig and Colin Low.

For his first assignment, he pieced together a series of photographs. It was a technique enthusiastically endorsed by McLaren. During the sixties, he practised his photographic cut-and-paste craft. He was fearless about sticking his camera into the faces of people on the street, in the dance halls and in crowds. He was never without his equipment. Friends often found themselves staring into his lens. As a young animator, Derek Lamb cruised the Main (Montreal's St. Laurent Boulevard) with Lipsett. He is now immortalized in *Very Nice, Very Nice*, a film nominated for an Academy Award.

Very Nice, Very Nice, and the four other films Lipsett directed at the NFB, are time capsules of the sixties. The carefully chosen images alternate between militaristic images of mushroom clouds and rocket launchers to playful shots depicting family scenes or crowds. At times the images flash momentarily; sometimes the camera lingers on a face, an expression. The film is a composite of our lives in 1961 — our consumerism, militarism and humanity, or as Lipsett himself put it: "The complete spiritual disenchantment that afflicts many people in the super-machine age."[138] Despite its sophisticated theme, the film touched a nerve with many. "It's not just an interesting experiment," said Lipsett's boss Colin Low. "It works ... it moves people. It's not arty. Ordinary people enjoy and understand it."[139]

In this pre-computer animation period, Lipsett managed to simulate a morphing sequence simply by selecting soft focus close-ups and optically bleeding them into each other. His technique so impressed Hollywood director Stanley Kubrick that he wrote Lipsett offering to hire him for the titles of *Dr. Strangelove*. Lipsett turned him down. Years later, producer George Lucas queried Derek Lamb about Lipsett's whereabouts. Lucas and USC classmates Steven Spielberg and Francis Ford Coppola were also big fans of Lipsett's work. Lamb's reply was sad. Despite a spate of critically admired films, Lipsett quit the NFB in the early seventies. He worked very little, and by 1980, Lamb discovered him panhandling on the streets of Montreal. Five years later, Arthur Lipsett committed suicide.

RYAN LARKIN

Ryan Larkin saw his art as an act of growing things.

Walking

Ryan Larkin is a gifted animator who joined the NFB in the early sixties and directed two films using charcoal on paper — *Cityscape* (1964), a montage of urban drawings that shift and change, and *Syrinx* (1965), a sensual depiction of the Greek mythological god Pan. Larkin took a more literal approach to animation; each frame could be a sketch torn from an artist's notebook. Only Larkin managed to move his sketches with great fluidity.

Wielding his coloured pencils, Larkin took a mundane animation exercise, the walk cycle, and imbued it with personality. *Walking* (1968) is a study of weight, posture and stride, of people of differing shapes, gender and age. It is life-drawing class brought to life. *Walking* is the most frequently cited source of inspiration for animators of the "illustrative" style. The stagger frame effect Larkin developed with camera-man Claude Lapierre was later used by Frédéric Back to create lush water movement in *The Mighty River*.

In contrast to the tightly controlled exercise of the walk cycle, Larkin's final film *Street Musique* (1972), is a graphic stream of conscience. During production, Larkin called the film, Growing Things: "Like plants in a garden (or hair on a head), it's growing and growing and hopefully it will produce a fantastic blossom which I will then exhibit in flower shows

for everyone to enjoy." *Street Musique* is steeped in the graphics of the time including psychedelic fractal imagery.

Larkin's career at the NFB was meteoric. A protégé and friend of McLaren, he chose to work on pencil-and-paper during the era when cel animators ruled the NFB roost.

Unfortunately, drugs and depression forced Larkin into self-imposed exile in his home. Unable or unwilling to come into work, Larkin hibernated and worked on his drawings and music. For two years, the NFB sent paycheques to his home by cab. He was eventually fired.

Walking *is the ultimate training film: it is a beautiful study of weight, posture, and stride, and of gender and age.*

One of many sketches left behind at the NFB.

Larkin described Street Musique *as a graphic stream of conscience.*

FRÉDÉRIC BACK

The acronym NFB is synonymous with animation in Canada. One man tried to break the NFB's monopoly. As a young producer, Hubert Tison was handed one camera when he started work at Société Radio-Canada (the French-language arm of the Canadian Broadcasting Corporation). Inspired by an animation film festival in Romania in 1964, Tison was eager to build his own award-winning department. In 1968, he established an animation department, and recruited his secret weapon — Frédéric Back.

Frédéric Back was a late convert to animation. Born in Saarbrucken, West Germany, in 1924, and formally trained at the Fine Arts School in Rennes, France, under the famous illus-

Frédéric Back has been called "a true poet of animation." His films are living, breathing paintings in the spirit of Chagall, Van Gogh and Turner. Influenced by the Impressionists, Back took illustrative animation to the next level.

trator Mathurin Méheut, Back didn't start animating until he was 30 years old.

As a young immigrant to Canada in 1948, he started teaching at the École des Beaux-Arts in Montreal. But the call of a new medium seduced him. He joined Radio-Canada in 1952, just as Canadian television was hitting the airwaves, and temporarily turned in his paint and brushes to perform trick puppetry. In 1953, Back tried his first real animation experiments: "It was very basic animation," says Back, referring to his first short. "I worked almost three weeks without sleeping, and my animation stand was a board on a radiator. The camera was fixed on the pipes and you had to disconnect the refrigerator so the (camera) lights would not go down when the radiator went on ... so we had a lot of warm beer."[140]

The lack of funding drove Back to the NFB, where he did the illustrations for Denys Arcand's film on the life of Samuel de Champlain (1962). They did not offer him a job, so Back returned to television, this time Radio-Québec. "I hoped some day it would be possible to work on a short ... to speak out on an idea that was important for me."

Despite many promises, it became evident after one year that Radio-Québec would not create an animation unit either. So at the age of 44, Back returned to work for Radio-Canada, and prayed that Tison would help him finally realize his dream to animate. Tison delivered.

With partner Graeme Ross, Back made Radio-Canada's first animated film, *Abracadabra* (1970), a paper cutout film about four boys who recapture the sun after it is stolen by a wicked sorcerer. A naturalist at heart, Back tapped Algonquin and Micmac legends for his next two films, *Inon, ou la conquête du feu* (*Inon, or the Conquest of Fire*, 1972), and *La Création des oiseaux* (*The Creation of Birds*, 1973).

A naturalist at heart, Back tapped Algonquin and Micmac legends for his next two films, Inon, ou la conquête du feu *and* La création des oiseaux.

With his film *Illusion* (1974), Back made the thematic transition from Native fable to ecological parable. Man's relationship with nature is embroidered onto all of Back's films, but it was not until *Tout-Rien* (*All-Nothing*, 1978) that his command of the visual elements took hold.

In *Tout-Rien*, Back abandoned cutout animation entirely, and drew directly on frosted cel with coloured pencils. As an illustrator, Back had often used that technique, but because of the tight deadlines in the early years of TV, he rejected pencil drawings as too time-consuming for animation. With *Tout-Rien*, Back's art world came full circle. Having re-discovered his metier, he made history again. All of Back's last four films — including *Tout-Rien* — were nominated for Oscars. Twice he walked away with the golden statue.

Back's first attempt to draw directly on frosted cel with coloured pencils was Tout-Rien. *Back's last four films — including* Tout-Rien — *were nominated for the Oscars. Twice he walked away with the golden statue.*

Back has been called "a true poet of animation."[141] His films are living, breathing paintings in the spirit of Chagall, Van Gogh and Turner. Influenced by the Impressionists, Back took illustrative animation to the next level. The feathery brushstrokes, colour and passion of the master painters is equaled in the moving pictures of Back. His artistry lies also in his ability to stir our conscience and rekindle passion for the environment and a simpler era. "Films that are empty of content are just another kind of pollution. I'm opposed to pollution," says Back.[142]

His contempt for technological innovation is evident in *Crac!* (1981), a film centred around a wooden chair lovingly built by a French-Canadian farmer. The title *Crac!* is the sound that the wild cherry tree made when it was felled by the farmer's hands. The wood is carved into a sturdy rocking chair that becomes the focus of family life in rural Quebec. It sees the family through weddings and births. When urban sprawl reaches the farm, the old broken chair is discarded. It finds life

Crac! is a simple story chronicling the life story of a wooden chair lovingly built by a French Canadian farmer.

Back's feathery style in the film, The Man Who Planted Trees, *was the most copied commercial style of the late eighties.*

again in a museum of contemporary art when a guard restores it. The rocker is again a welcome amusement for young children who play on it while their parents tour the exhibits. At night, when the museum is empty, the chair beckons the paintings to join it in a nostalgic dance. For Back, the sturdy salt-of-the-earth chair represents the heart and soul of Quebec culture. It is also a subtle snub of contemporary non-figurative art.

"We've been through realism and hyper-realism in art and now we find it was a dead end. Looking back to the traditional painters we can accept that many were not great painters, yet they left us images of what life was like then. They witnessed and recorded their era."[143]

In telling the story of French shepherd Jean Giono, in his film, *L'Homme qui plantait des arbres* (*The Man Who Planted Trees*, 1987), Back certainly intended his film to be a testament to a simple man who spent a lifetime reforesting the alps. The film is an impressionistic masterpiece that salutes Monet and Van Gogh. Softly muted colours of blue, grey and green saturate to deeper hues as the film progresses. The evolution of palette illustrates the passage of time and changing landscape,

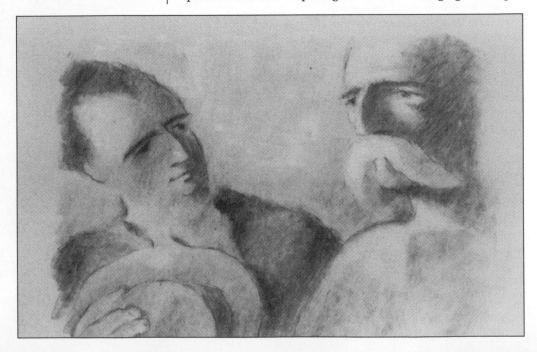

and the feathery pencil strokes evoke a dreamlike quality. "Because the text is so important, sometimes the drawing is minimal," says Back.

The restriction Back imposed on *The Man Who Planted Trees* is a sharp contrast to the use of colour in his previous film, *Crac!* Rather than the tempered, deliberate use of colour in *The Man Who Planted Trees*, the colours in *Crac!* reach a crescendo in the final dance scene. Colour spills over the lines in wild abandon to match the effusive fiddle music. "When I started *Crac!* I used the same kind of material, but I had no appreciation of the way I used colour," says Back. "In [the film] *The Man Who Planted Trees*, I started with a low level of colour and shape and created a kind of evolution of colour to contrast the beginning and the end."

Even the drawing style between the two films differs. Whereas the delicate wavy lines in *The Man Who Planted Trees* suggest a dream or a vision, the deliberate strokes that define the characters and the objects in *Crac!* carry the symbolic weight of an entire culture.

Back's last film, originally titled *Noah 2000*, was to be his final word on ecological annihilation. During storyboard stages, the biblical allegory turned into an ode to the St. Lawrence Seaway, one of the largest water reserves in the world. He couldn't resist giving it a Quebec nationalist reading. The decline of the seaway begins with the landing of the English settlers, and shows how their presence disrupts the balance of nature.

La Fleuve aux grandes eaux (*The Mighty River*, 1993), as it was eventually titled, became an exercise in drawing various states of water. The Inuit of northern Canada have many words to describe the various stages of snow. Back has developed his own visual lexicon for the water of the St. Lawrence. In order to make the waves and flow look realistic, Back further experimented with stagger mixing — a technique he used sparingly in *The Man Who Planted Trees*.

Sadly, Hubert Tison's dream of building a studio to rival the NFB animation unit ended when Back retired. Caught in a cash-crunch, the public broadcaster allowed Back to complete his final film before literally shutting off the lights of the studio. At its peak, Radio-Canada's animation unit employed nine people and supported artists such as Graeme Ferguson and Paul Driessen. Already, the studio is forgotten, and Back's work is frequently misreported in the press as belonging to the NFB.

The Mighty River, as it was eventually titled, became an exercise in drawing various states of water. The Inuit of Northern Canada have 14 words to describe the various stages of snow. Back has developed his own visual lexicon for the water of the St. Lawrence.

PAUL DRIESSEN

After Norman McLaren, Paul Driessen is probably the most influential artist to work in Canada. His anti-naturalistic designs, which feature two-dimensional movement and wiggly or "tremulous" lines, have found their way by osmosis into the work of animators in Montreal, Winnipeg and Vancouver. Even Frédéric Back, who at first glance does not appear to have a graphic relationship with Driessen, says he was greatly influenced by Driessen's unusual style.

Paul Driessen is probably the most influential artist to work in Canada. He has inspired animators from the St. Lawrence to the West Coast.

Today, Driessen divides his time between Canada and Europe. He directed seven films as a freelancer at the National Film Board (most of them in the French animation unit), as well as several for Radio-Canada, and he participated in a couple of independent compilations for Vancouver's International Rocketship.

A Dutch art school graduate and cartoonist, Driessen joined Cinecentrum, a small commercial animation studio in Holland headed by American animator John Hiltz in 1964. While apprenticing at the studio, Driessen met Canadian animator George Dunning, who ran TVC in London. Dunning offered Driessen a job back in the UK. When Driessen eventually landed in London almost two years after Dunning's offer, TVC was prepping for the Beatles animated feature *Yellow Submarine*. Driessen immediately started working on storyboard and later animated such memorable characters as the Blue Meanies. Art designer Heinz Edelmann's style and colour sense was close enough to Driessen's personal approach to keep it interesting. Driessen learned a lot about colour while working on the film, but the experience quenched any desire he had to work as a hired gun. With the odd exception, Driessen has divorced himself from the commercial world and works as an independent artist. He is one of the most prolific contemporary animators, with dozens of films to his credit.

Richard Condie, Cordell Barker and Marv Newland openly acknowledge the impact his shorts have had on their own work. One borrowed element is Driessen's weird kinetic style. When they move, his jointless characters appear to have an "afterflow" — a ghostly wave of the arm, hand, leg or body. The oscillating movement is not simply a delayed response like Warner Bros. cartoons in which every action, no matter how absurdly stretched or flattened, makes some logical sense. In Driessen's films, the undulating limbs serve an aesthetic purpose and do not follow the general laws of physics.

Driessen also has fun playing with perspective and cycles. For example, in *Sunny Side Up* (1985), what appears to be the reflection of a man on a small island is actually a person standing upside down, while his ego reflected in the water is right side up. It is an illusionary trick that becomes apparent only when the supposed reflection jumps in the water and drowns. In another short, *Home On the Rails*, a train passes through the home of an old lady who must get up every hour and open her doors so the train can pass through uninterrupted. At first the train enters from the right side of the frame; next it enters from the left. As a result, Driessen forces the viewer to imagine what lies beyond the frame — is there a switch somewhere or does the train travel on a circular track? Similarly, in his film *Sing Beast Sing*, Marv Newland has a creature pulling a wagon with a cactus across the screen and illogically re-entering the frame from the same side.

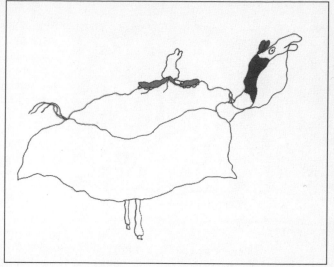

Driessen's anti-naturalistic designs feature two-dimensional movement and wiggly "tremulous" lines.

Using this technique, both films sustain the viewer's attention even though their cyclical nature evokes a sense of banality and boredom. Although the two filmmakers like to use cyclical motion, they do so for different reasons. "I set people up doing the cycle for a couple of times so you know what's happening, then I give the twist," says Driessen. "Marv just does the cycle because it's so bizarre. He does it because it's so weird to look at, and you don't know why he does it. That makes it interesting."[144]

In *David* (1974), Driessen actually forces the viewer to imagine the character itself. The protagonist is so tiny it can't be seen with the naked eye. The only way we know it exists is that it can call out, wave its hair in the wind so we can see the air currents, and make tracks in the sand.

Having created an imaginary world, Driessen believes it's up to the viewer to fill in the gaps. He has taken his play on perspective to absolute extremes in the film, *On Land, At Sea and In the Air*, by dividing the frame into sections. The three separate scenes relate to one another on both a visual and narrative plane, but this relationship is in constant flux. The

Killing of an Egg

Home On the Rails

David

film is like an audio-visual Rubik's cube you want to twist and turn. Eventually the frames merge in a surrealistic way.

In *Seasons* (1996), Driessen has divided the screen into eight units, each with a separate cycle of action. There are two levels of narrative operating — the main chase story that carries into the various panels, and subplots that cycle into each individual screen. When the two narratives collide, the whole cycle collapses and precipitates the start of a new season.

Driessen creates visual puzzles to tackle philosophical concerns. *Une histoire comme une autre* (*The Same Old Story*, 1981), features a storyteller who lives the very tale he narrates. It is an allegory about humans doomed to repeat the mistakes of their ancestors. Similarly, in *Killing of an Egg* (1977), a man preparing to eat a boiled egg is startled by a distress call emanating from inside the egg. He ignores the shouts, and cracks open the egg, crushing whatever is inside. When his own room begins caving in due to an outside force, the viewer instantly anticipates what is going to happen next. The crusher will suffer the same fate as the unseen creature inside the egg.

It was a theme later adopted by Richard Condie for his film *La Salla* (1996). Condie created a character who amuses himself in a toy laden room, but is constantly beckoned by a door of temptation. He has the choice of ignoring it or revealing its contents. When he does succumb, he learns that his world is simply a game in the hands of another.

These films carry existential messages. They suggest that humans are totally free and responsible for their acts, but that these individual choices can trigger a series of chain reactions that affect the lives of others. By encapsulating the riddle of life in his short films, and influencing the creative direction of others, Driessen has earned the title of auteur.

chapter 12

Richard Williams –
The Prophet

It has been written that Richard "Dick" Williams led animation out of bondage and into the promised land with the feature *Who Framed Roger Rabbit* (1988). When Williams was hired as animation director on the film, the industry had fallen on hard times. Disney's last successful film, *The Rescuers*, was already 10 years old. Directors Don Bluth and Ralph Bakshi were unable to parlay their talent into a blockbuster. The best animators were leaching into the commercial abyss.

Williams galvanized talented drawers, and he won back audiences who had previously dismissed cartoons as being just for kids. *Roger Rabbit* brought in US$150 million at the box office and it won an Academy Award for special effects. It marked a turning point in the industry.

Williams and his followers believed that he was a visionary — the man who could deliver animation from the evils of the Saturday-morning timeslot and resurrect it as a valid art form, not just an entertainment medium. But his quest to scale the artistic summit fell tragically short when his dream project — *The Thief and the Cobbler* — was seized by an insurance guarantor in 1994. After a lifetime of trailblazing work, the Prophet had failed to meet his production deadlines.

※ ※ ※ ※ ※

Richard Williams was born in Toronto in 1933. At 14 years of age he was already teaching animation to other children at the local YMCA. So obsessed was he with the craft that he left for Los Angeles and camped out for weeks at Disney Studios until his mother, a commercial artist, pulled a few strings and arranged a publicity tour.

It was his mother's hand at work again when Jim MacKay and George Dunning of Graphic Associates received a call from an ad agency asking them to look at a storyboard drafted by a gifted young man studying at the Ontario College of Art. He was clearly a natural. Graphic Associates immediately added him to their roster.

Richard Williams' first storyboard for Graphic Associates in Toronto. He was only 17 years old when he started working in the Toronto advertising industry.

One year after working for his first commercial outlet, Williams had a change of heart. He decided he wanted to paint. The Spanish landscape would be the subject of his canvas. There wasn't much art produced in those two years of dabbling with oils and brush, but Williams left Spain with a storyboard for an animated film about three men on an island, each with a fixed concept of truth, goodness and beauty. The allegorical treatment was entitled *The Little Island* (1958).

Back in England, Williams bundled up his storyboard and took it door to door seeking help to complete his film. One of the commercial studios he visited in the spring of 1955 was Gerry Potterton's small outfit on London's Saville Row. Potterton was working on a Guinness Stout commercial when 22-year-old Dick Williams dumped his drawings on the floor, and announced he was going to make an animated feature film. "We all laughed, but I was greatly impressed with his drawings," says Potterton.[146]

Williams eventually landed on George Dunning's doorstep in London. For the next several years, Williams free-lanced for Dunning's new TV Cartoons studio, animating and designing industrials and commercials. One of his most famous collaborations was Power Train, for the Ford Motor

Company. Dunning was impressed by Williams' ability to work all day in the TVC studio and all night on his own film. When *The Little Island* made its debut, it was considered to be the longest animated production undertaken by a single individual.

Even as a young man, Williams was not content to work under another person's shingle. By the early sixties, he struck out on his own under the banner Richard Williams Animated Films (later known as Richard Williams Studio). Although they were friends and associates, Williams never informed Dunning of his intention to set up his own shop. It was an acrimonious split.

Richard Williams made his first animated feature film, The Little Island, *at age 21.*

Dunning would go on to direct the feature film *Yellow Submarine* (1968) based on Heinz Edelmann's brilliant designs. Williams, for his part, received accolades for his work on film titles such as *What's New Pussycat* (1965), *A Funny thing Happened on the Way to the Forum* (1966), *Charge of the Light Brigade* (1968), *The Return of the Pink Panther* (1975), and his fabulous TV adaptation of Dickens' classic, *A Christmas Carol* (1972). The two never spoke after they parted company and the grudge endured. Almost 20 years later, Williams still aimed a few critical arrows at his old mentor. In

one interview, he sarcastically attributed his own artistic development to a revelation brought about by a screening of Dunning's feature: "*Yellow Submarine* convinced us we wanted to be finished with the kind of animation that is based on graphic tricks."[147]

Williams' long-term goal was to synthesize serious drawing and cartooning. In the late sixties, Williams experienced an artistic epiphany. He abandoned the graphic caricatures of *The Little Island* and *Love Me, Love Me, Love Me* (1962), a film about love's substitutions, and veered towards traditional realism as embraced by Disney. The revelation was precipitated by Chuck Jones, executive producer of the TV animation special *A Christmas Carol* (1972). Jones made a point of introducing him to veteran Warner Bros. animators Ken Harris and Abe Levitow, as well as to Disney's Hal Ambro. The matchmaking was inspired. Williams realized he had a lot to learn from the American veterans. He had a genius for stylization, but they were the experts at emotion.

Love Me, Love Me, Love Me *is a film about love's substitutions.*

The collaboration between Williams and the masters of animation is remarkable. Harris completely captures the crotchety Scrooge of Dickens' classic with his barking humbugs and sour grimaces. For his part, Williams constructs seamless transitions between hyperrealistic visages and flowing charcoal sketches or etchings. Each stylistic change serves a purpose in the film. The inventive, ever-changing backgrounds signal a shift in era and mood: from fully coloured rooms representing the present to inky shadows of Christmas Past. The approach compliments Dickens' narrative tale.

Williams' muscular direction is discernible in the opening shots of *A Christmas Carol*. His acrobatic camera shouts "Watch me" with its breathtaking sweep down London's Victorian edifices. The optical gymnastics create a vertigo sensation for viewers. It is a trademark of Williams' films. In *Who Framed Roger Rabbit*, Eddie Valiant plummets down a high rise with Bugs Bunny and Mickey Mouse in Toon Town; and *The Thief and the Cobbler* opens with a soaring vista of the desert.

Williams pursued accolades in Hollywood with the same determination that he pushed the envelope of style. He had an uncanny knack for upstaging the directors who hired him to do titles or sequences. A reviewer in the *Sunday Times* of London remarked: "One of the best things about the film *What's New Pussycat?* was the titles." Similarly, Pauline Kael in an unkind review of Tony Richardson's *Charge of the Light Brigade* stated: "The animation provides the only clear exposition we get of what's going on in the movie. It's too bad Richardson didn't leave the charge itself to Williams." Vincent Canby of *The New York Times* had a comparable reaction to Blake Edwards' *Return of the Pink Panther*. This time, Williams actually poured $40,000 of his own money into perfecting the opening cartoon sequence in Edwards' film, even after the director gave his approval. Williams indulged his own feeling of rivalry towards his clients.

Winning the Oscar in 1972 for *A Christmas Carol* did not satisfy his appetite for little golden statues. Five years after picking up one statue, he panted for yet another: "I'm crazy for awards! I have become worse and worse. I think it's because awards are like money or something. Some dreadful person I knew said that prestige is convertible to cash, and it just shows that if you can keep winning the awards you're still on the crest of the wave. The moment you stop it means you're not trying hard enough and I wet my pants every time one of our competitors gets in there — it means we are slipping. So I think the more awards the better." The press reports were more respectful. Williams even noted the appellation "wide-eyed Dick Williams" was replaced by "Academy Award-winning Dick Williams"[148] in later coverage.

Richard Williams' award-winning adaptation of the Charles Dickens classic, A Christmas Carol.

He truly took the media hyperbole to heart. He envisioned himself as Disney's successor; at the very most, the would-be creator of the best animation film to ever be made. *The Thief and the Cobbler* would be his magnum opus.

In order to surpass Disney, Williams knew he first had to learn the animation techniques of the old masters. He hired Art Babbitt, one of Disney's nine old men, to teach an intense one-month workshop in the summer of 1973. Every day for a month, Williams' Soho studio was closed and the employees poured into a rented projection theatre. Babbitt instructed young and old alike in the basics of animation.

Babbitt was the maestro, but he looked to Williams as Disney's heir apparent. In the seventies, traditionalists had few places to turn. Animation appeared to be a dying art form. At least Williams was trying to resuscitate it. Not only did he admire the work of the veterans, he spent his own money to bring them to England to pass on their knowledge. Babbitt overlooked the fact that Williams took perverse pleasure in pitting him against Ken Harris. He also ignored Williams' temper tantrums and idiosyncrasies. One of Williams' nastier habits was to make his junior staffers fully animate caricatures he had drawn of them, for television commercials. They all put up with the man they called a saviour.

At the very least, Richard Williams envisioned himself as Disney's successor; at the very most, the would-be creator of the greatest animated film ever to be made.

The old guard artists Harris, Shamus Culhane, Milt Kahl and Grim Natwick also taught and worked at the studio. "It made a fantastic difference immediately to some of the guys; guys who were not even assistants suddenly outclassed the animators," he says.[149] One genius "discovered" during these sessions was Russell Hall, a young assistant who had risen from the ink and paint department. Promoted to animator, Hall worked on numerous scenes for *The Thief and the Cobbler*, including the galloping stallions featured in the polo match. Years later, he became supervising animator for the

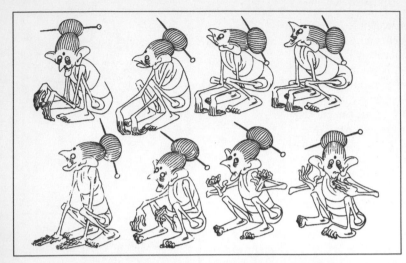

Clean-up guide for the Mad Holy Old Witch of the Desert Mountain, which was eventually cut from The Thief and the Cobbler.

The Thief and the Cobbler was conceived as an animated pantomime of the 1001 Arabian Nights. Over the years, Richard Williams rewrote the story around an honest cobbler and a Chaplinesque thief.

stupendous Jessica Rabbit of *Who Framed Roger Rabbit* fame.

When Williams spoke of relearning animation — going back to the classical era and pushing it forward — he was not referring to funnier sight gags. It was the mechanics, or rather the physics, of films that interested him. Williams did not simply wish to make entertaining theatrical shorts; he wanted to flesh out characters and ideas like any other dramatic film form. Rather than use dialogue to drive the narrative and develop personality, Williams sought conception through pure movement. In this respect, he diverged from the Disney format, and remained in sync with experimental animators such as the National Film Board of Canada's Norman McLaren, and his own mentor, George Dunning. He did not believe that a return to the old craft implied a wholesale acceptance of Disney's aesthetic notions.

Williams applied his philosophy of storytelling to his ambitious feature film *Nasruddin* (later renamed *The Thief and the Cobbler*). The film is a sort of animated pantomime of 1001 Arabian Nights, conceived as a visual reconstruction of evocative medieval miniatures produced in Persia. The idea sprung out of a series of storybooks Williams was asked to draw in 1964. John Culhane, a former *Newsweek* columnist, collaborated with Williams on developing the original script which starred Massa Nasruddin, a folklore character as popular in the East as Santa Claus is in the West.

But after his 1973 revelation, Williams discarded most of the drawings he had completed and started over. The Nasruddin character was excised from the script. The story was rebuilt around an honest cobbler and a thief, a Chaplinesque silent comic hero who quietly slips around the palace snatching valuables and eluding

captors. Williams decided that Nasruddin was too verbal and not suitable for animation. Other characters such as the villain ZigZag, the Grand Vizier, and the elderly nurse to the princess survived. Williams' revision starred Ken Harris, Emery Hawkins (Walter Lantz Studio veteran), and Grim Natwick, the magician behind both Snow White and Betty Boop.

As he ad-libbed his way through the storyboard, Williams' favourite character, the thief, was promoted from sidekick to star. Drawn by Ken Harris, the thief is not a traditional Hollywood hero or romantic lead. Instead, he serves as a catalyst for much of the film's action. His sole impulse is to steal shiny objects, and his mere presence creates a new plot twist. He is the progenitor of mayhem.

The film opens with the stealthy Persian pickpocket caught in the act of thievery by an apprentice cobbler. Their courtyard tussle over the attempted purse snatch disturbs a procession led by ZigZag, the king's evil right-hand man. Sentenced to jail by the conniving head of state, the poor cobbler is given a temporary reprieve by Princess Yum Yum, who requests that he mend her slipper. Yum Yum and Tack the cobbler start flirting. But when the persistent thief penetrates the palace's inner sanctum and grabs the princess' ruby-inlaid backscratcher and bejewelled shoe, the film diverges into another elaborate chase scene across checkerboard halls resembling Escher-like optical illusions.

ZigZag, the Grand Vizier is possibly the most inventive villain ever created. The evil one's hands had an extra digit and each finger sported three rings.

The romantic lead, the cobbler, is silent and a shoemaker's nail dangles from his mouth. He is an unlikely love interest of the beautiful princess.

Escaping yet again, the thief's next target is the three golden balls perched at the top of the city's minaret. By successfully capturing the city's protective orbs, he unwittingly aids ZigZag in his treacherous plot to rule the kingdom and marry the princess. With the city's golden globes in hand, the Vizier marshals the forces of the one-eyed barbarians to conquer the king and his subjects.

The cobbler, who has fallen in love with the princess, confronts the hordes preparing to ransack the palace. By flinging a simple tack into the centre of the maelstrom, the cobbler ignites a chain of events that results in the defeat of the brutish army and the killing of ZigZag by his crocodile companions. The cobbler wins the day and the hand of the princess.

The Thief and the Cobbler was history in the making. Everyone at Richard Williams' studio during the seventies and eighties knew it. To be able to animate a scene from the film was like winning an animation scholarship. Most high-budget feature films are done on "twos," meaning every picture is shot twice. Much of *The Thief* was done on "ones." That translates to 24 pictures per second, instead of the usual 12. Not only was Williams churning out twice the amount of footage normally produced for a Hollywood picture, but his models were extremely difficult to animate.[150]

ZigZag the Grand Vizier is possibly the most inventive cartoon villain ever created. Williams hoarded many of the scenes for himself, incorporating Vincent Price's lisping delivery into the acting. ZigZag's brilliant design is further complicated by his extra finger-joints. Each digit sports several rings. Animating such a decorated, graceful hand — and feet with octopus tentacles that uncoil with every step — presented mind-boggling challenges.

The new romantic lead, Tack, is so named because a shoemaker's nail incessantly dangles out of the corner of his mouth. The tack is the symbolic weapon in a climactic battle of David and Goliath proportions. Its position in the mouth changes the natural symmetry of the face making it difficult to animate. The stylistic joke conceived by Williams was later lost on the distributors controlling the film's fate.

Despite his deep talent pool, Williams continually redrew and reworked the film. *Nasruddin/The Thief and the Cobbler/Arabian Knight* was in a permanent state of revision for 30 years. The master of the shorthand film appeared unable to translate his vision to feature length.

Williams was intent on minimizing language and narrative — as he did in his previous shorts — but he was not disciplined enough to nail down a proper outline. Part of the problem stemmed from his inability to abandon the drawing board and focus on the big picture. Directing a team of animators was not merely a burden, it meant sacrificing his first love. Williams was a compulsive drawer. He often abandoned his supervisory post to sit in a corner and do in-betweens or clean up another animator's drawings. For Williams, the work was not beneath him; it was uplifting. A slice of pure heaven was to go over Ken Harris' work — studying, refining, perfecting.[151]

Rather than work from a script treatment or Leica reel, Williams preferred to send in master animators like Art Babbit to "try out" a scene. Subsequently, he would pull the bits he liked and rework them. This approach resulted in fabulous sequences, but they never quite fit into a continuous story. Williams seemed incapable of sacrificing his perfect jewels for the good of a coherent story, at least a story that appealed to a wide audience. Williams' modus operandi proved to be his Achilles heel.

The Thief and the Cobbler was a money pit. In addition to digging deep into his own pockets, Williams sought private investors. At one time, independent distributor British Lion and producer Gary Kurtz were involved. A Saudi Arabian prince claimed to have a financial stake in the film. Its primary financial pipeline was Williams' commercial operation in London. Campaigns such as Cresta bear, Brobat Bloo, Pushkin Vodka and Tic-Tac brought in awards and a steady stream of clients. But for Williams it was simply a means to an end. "Anything good that came out of commercials in terms of technical expertise was folded into *The Thief,*" says Simon

Wells, former animator for Richard Williams studio.[152] The commercials were merely fodder for the masterpiece that forever had to be fed.

After spurning production deals for almost 25 years, Williams finally turned to Hollywood for help. British producer Jake Eberts met Williams in 1986 at the British Academy Awards, and came away impressed by his passion and commitment. He structured a $24-million deal involving his British company, Allied Filmmakers, and Warner Bros. in the United States. He even invested his own money in the picture. The deal stipulated that Williams deliver a 92-minute animated feature, containing four songs, and a love story between the cobbler and the Princess Yum Yum. After a quarter century, it appeared as though Williams' quixotic quest would finally be realized.

But Williams failed to meet the contract's two-year deadline and story revision. US distributor Warner Bros. gave the completion bond company one extension for a few months, but quickly pulled the plug after watching a preview screening. Williams had completed almost 90 minutes of animation but the footage covered only 60 percent of the script. The critical love-interest scenes were still missing, and not one song had been recorded.

Warner's weren't thrilled with what they saw, not necessarily because they didn't like the animation, but the story wasn't there, and they had waited a very long time to get that.

Warner's swift decision to pull out of the distribution deal surprised the bond company's lawyer, Steve Fayne: "We've had other situations where films have been delivered late ... and if the studio is enthusiastic about the film, you can go and negotiate considerable extensions if you need them." [153]

No one in the executive suite agonized over losing this deal. Apart from Richard Williams, there was no big-name star or director attached to the picture, and no heavyweight producer or creative agency to alienate. If a studio was ever going to walk away from a film, this was the time to do it.

Richard Williams designed and animated the Thurber-like Cresta bear.

Warner's defection might not have been so devastating had the bond company been given a few weeks to find another distributor to pick up the contract. Unfortunately, when Warner's sent the bond company their notice, they alerted the bank. The bank showed up at the bond company's doorstep the next day demanding a cheque for $24-million. Forced to instantly pay up, the Completion Bond Co. became the back-end producer of the film. In the eyes of the industry, a film owned by a guarantor is damaged goods. The insurance house either had to cut its losses and absorb the $24-million, or finish the film on its own. Warner's refused to extend its deadline, but Jake Eberts agreed to wait. His $8-million offer for foreign rights was a big enough carrot for the bond company to forge ahead.

Richard Williams' son, Alex, speculates that the film's freewheeling structure — quite unlike anything ever before attempted — made Warner Bros. nervous. They happily ducked out of the contract. But the real villain of this story is the guarantor, according to Alex, who worked on the film for two years as an animator. The bond company fired Williams and his English production crew, and shipped 12 tons of artwork back to Los Angeles. "I think there was some personal animosity there about my father, and they decided to take the film back to America, and fire the English crew who had spent two years learning how to do this stuff," says Alex Williams. "We were working ridiculous hours — 60 hours each, 20 hours for free — and yet they closed down the London studio and shipped the reels to any freelancer who wanted it." [154]

According to Alex, the film was only five months away from delivery. He believes the bond company should have stuck it out. Fayne and his consultants disagree: "Their weekly footage output was not consistent with what they had to do to meet their schedules. They were churning out 46 seconds a week or whatever it was — unfortunately they weren't covering enough pages in the script. At some point in that process it became apparent to us that this was going to take a rather long time to finish." [155]

The final version released by Miramax Films under the title *Arabian Knight* was nothing less than a brutal rape of Williams' vision. Silly songs were annexed to the existing storyline, and the pantomime leads voiced over. Particularly galling was the bastardization of the thief by Jonathan Winters' interpolative shtick. In a casting calamity, Winters' ribald cracks were transposed over Harris' balletic character. It was as if W.C. Fields were given free rein to ad lib Charlie Chaplin's performances. Envisioned as a film told through movement and with an economy of language, *The Thief and the Cobbler* was suddenly a cacophony of noise — narrative, jokes and babble.

Missing from Miramax's version was the original ninja nursemaid, Grim Natwick's Mad Holy Old Witch, and whole sections of the epic battle at the end of the film. One of the most artful pieces to end up on the cutting-room floor was Russell Hall's thief on stilts, including a hilarious scene showing the thief escaping the guillotine by sticking wooden props onto the chopping block rather than his own hands.

Richard Williams emerged with one small consolation. the Completion Bond Company went out of business, shut down by its parent company after bungling *The Thief*, and other problematic films such as Spike Lee's *Malcolm X*, and Danny DeVito's *Hoffa*.

If the 57-minute unfinished reel of *The Thief and the Cobbler* is any indication, Williams was reconfiguring the entertainment compass. He created intriguing characters without having them mouth a single sentence or break into song. And he pushed the limits of the camera. *The Thief and the Cobbler* might have been the greatest animated film ever produced, but we will never know for sure. Williams gave up animating for a long time, and retreated to Pender Island, British Columbia, after his film was seized.

The Richard Williams story has grown to mythical proportions in Hollywood. Like a character in his own films, Williams is viewed as a man whose obsession became the albatross that eventually destroyed him. It has all the makings of an Oscar-winning script — a flawed hero, a dream and a villain.

Some industry sources believe Williams may have unconsciously sabotaged the film himself. Having announced that he was directing the *War and Peace* of animation, he was haunted by a fear of failure. Williams has refused to comment on the project, but his son Alex calls the gossip "a crock of shit."

"How could anyone spend their whole working life on one film and not want to finish it? He was desperate to finish the film, and it destroyed him that he didn't," says Alex.

How indeed? In a revealing comment to writer Charles Solomon, Williams admits the film was once intended to be his tour-de-force exit from the industry: "For so many years, I figured I'd just finish *The Thief* and quit."[156] If *The Thief* was to be his final cathartic act, it's little wonder he remodelled it over and over. It was to embody everything he stood for — a last will and testament to his art.

At root, Williams' downfall can be traced to his inability to structure story. He always improvised. Colleagues joke that Williams solved story problems by simply drawing around them. "He is a superb animator, a tremendous artist, and has a really gifted vision of visuals, but does he want to tell a story, does he want to tell a story about people, and about emotions?" asks Simon Wells, co-director of DreamWorks SKG feature, *The Prince of Egypt*.

❧ ❧ ❧ ❧ ❧

Despite the loss of his own film, Williams' legacy endures. He worked as animation director on the smash hit *Who Framed Roger Rabbit* (1986), and directed *Raggedy Ann and Andy* (1977). On both films, Williams was the hired gun, but his stamp is indelibly imprinted on both.

Raggedy Ann and Andy was conceived as a musical by two Broadway producers. Williams turned down their offer to supervise the film. After one terrible creative session with a team of former Disney animators, composer Joe Raposo flew to England and begged Williams to reconsider. He did.

Intended as a fun-filled musical adventure involving the rescue of a French doll named Babette from an evil pirate, Williams' strategy was to assemble an all-star cast and give them the freedom to do what they did best. Emery Hawkins was given free rein to draw a ravenous, cancerous candy creature who captures and engulfs the film's poor heroes, Raggedy Ann and Andy. Art Babbitt drew a delusional saggy camel who is the dolls' haphazard guide, and Tissa David created the charming Raggedy Ann. Williams himself animated key scenes including Raggedy Andy's dance number, No Girl's Toy.

Raggedy Ann and Andy was anarchistic: a drawer's delight, a producer's nightmare. "I let everyone run free, in segments. I figured if you have eight terrific animators and you give them eight minutes each, at worst you have 10 shots that don't fit together," explained Williams.[157] Even the colour schemes changed throughout the film. Babbitt animated a scene entirely in blue, and Hawkins chose to colour his scenes in orange and black.

Studies of Raggedy Ann.

The hairpin creative turns almost work in this film. With a stronger script it might have held together. One of the film's major weaknesses was its overuse of cloying musical numbers that bog down the narrative. Williams fought with the producers over this issue and lost. "The producers were a man from the telephone company, a guy from a publishing company, and someone who couldn't stop writing songs!" he reported to the press.[158]

The finished product was a virtual anijam of strong animation sequences, but an unsatisfactory film as a whole. Director Gerry Potterton was eventually called in to oversee the remainder of the film after it went well over budget. By the time Potterton was called in, Williams had fallen back to his familiar habit of redoing animation scenes rather than concentrating

The model sheet for Art Babbitt's camel in Raggedy Ann and Andy.

on directing. Potterton's and Williams' clash over the film cost them a dear friendship.

With *Who Framed Roger Rabbit*, Williams was not given the latitude to repeat his mistakes on *Raggedy Ann and Andy*. Strict parameters, particularly production schedules, were set by director Robert Zemeckis and executive producer Steven Spielberg. With a nailed-down storyboard and creative heavyweights who made final decisions, Williams experimented with character development and articulation.

Who Framed Roger Rabbit was a benchmark for two reasons: it was the first major mix of traditional 2-D cels, digital 3-D animation and live-action footage; it was also the first time in many years that an animated film for adults was a box office hit. The film's success opened a Pandora's box of scripts calling for weird special effects and multimedia mixes. The meteor shower of films that followed include *The Mask*, *Jumanji*, *Casper* and *Space Jam*.

The film, produced by Disney's Touchstone Pictures and Amblin Entertainment Inc., is a gumshoe thriller set in postwar Hollywood. It features a famous toon star named Roger Rabbit who is framed for the murder of Marvin Acme, the man responsible for wacky cartoon inventions. He is also the owner of the real estate upon which Toon Town sits. Roger

enlists the help of private eye Eddie Valiant (Bob Hoskins), a soused sleuth who uncovers a secret plot to kill Marvin and dispose of his will, leaving all his property to the toons. While Eddie tries to hide Roger from the dastardly weasel police and Judge Doom, he searches for the missing will. Meanwhile Roger's voluptuous wife Jessica becomes entwined in the sinister events taking place.

Williams was certainly not trolling for work in Hollywood, nor schmoozing hot young directors. Robert Zemeckis and executive producer Steven Spielberg came to him. His unexpected calling card was the rushes of his incomplete film *The Thief and the Cobbler*. A film projectionist for George Lucas' Industrial Light and Magic (ILM) turned producers onto Williams after screening a portion of the film for his friend and old-time animator Milt Kahl. *Star Wars* heavyweight Robert Watts followed up on the lead and Zemeckis, Spielberg and Williams were introduced.

After the *Raggedy Ann* experience, Williams was not eager to launch into another feature film. Chuck Jones convinced him that if he took the job, the sky would be the limit. For Williams this meant possible backing for *The Thief*.

Who Framed Roger Rabbit was Zemeckis' homage to the forties Warner's toons. It did not reflect Williams' personal style nor his sense of humour, but he accepted the project, and created some of the most explosive personalities to hit

Raggedy Ann and Andy *was anarchistic: a drawer's delight, a producer's nightmare.*

Richard Williams was a compulsive drawer who found it difficult to abandon the animation disc and focus on directing an entire picture.

the big screen in decades. Williams was successful because he could take any design, move it beautifully, and make it work. He was a superb draftsman and the fastest draw in the Western hemisphere.

Williams' challenge was to integrate his rabbit with live-action objects. In earlier films such as Disney's *Mary Poppins* (1964) and *Song of the South* (1946), the live-action camera was frozen, so the animators could easily match their drawings to the action. Interaction between actors and cartoons was minimal. Richard Williams threw all the old mixed media rules out the window.

Based on his experience shooting a couple of Fanta soft drink commercials, Williams believed it was possible to insert characters in a live-action scene shot with a moving camera. So did Zemeckis. Together, they shot a test sequence with Roger tumbling down a staircase and crashing into a bunch of real cardboard boxes. The test scene was so authentic it proved beyond any reasonable doubt that the two film forms could be wed in a new way. According to Williams, Spielberg said the *Roger Rabbit* test was only the second time in his life that he'd seen a historic technical breakthrough. The first time was when he saw Lucas' early tests for *Star Wars*.[160]

Unlike Disney Feature Animation, in which supervising animators would oversee key animators and a team of assistant animators and in-betweeners, there was no standardized clean-up department in Williams' UK studio. Simon Wells cleaned up his own scenes with just two other assistants. Others did the same. Williams didn't insist on conformity. As a result, Roger Rabbit has six different looks.

While Williams' British company was to form the backbone of the animation unit, Disney supplied producer Don Hahn and animation leads Andreas Deja and Phil Nibbelink. The studio was quite unlike Disney's usual set up, and much more anarchic. "Even though the [*Roger Rabbit*] studio was called 'Disney U.K.' it was very much Dick's studio. He ran it much like he did his commercial house. Dick was like a wild stallion pulling the Disney wagon with Disney's associate producer Don Hahn at the reins," says Nik Ranieri, another *Roger Rabbit* alumnus.[161]

On occasion, Williams fell into his old routine — anchoring himself to the drawing table and leaving the storyboard

nent sex characteristics such as eyelashes or breasts. "It's hard to get just a person," says Tilby, who animated elderly women in her previous films.

The women in earlier designs looked miserable. Tilby and Forbis found it difficult to shape a whole personality. So instead they turned their character into a pig to give it a little "joie de vivre." They wanted her to start the day comfortable and happy, but after her encounter to return a little bruised. The film won the Palme d'Or for the best short film at the 1999 Cannes International Film Festival.

Many other female artists have chosen to express themselves through paper cutouts and collages — Bettina Maylone, Lynn Smith and Veronika Soul. Smith and Soul are both American citizens who worked extensively in Canada. The common denominator between them appears to be their desire to work independently using low-tech methods. Their characters also tend to be less representational than ones created by their cartoon-loving brothers. "I'm inspired by garbage, leftovers ... I like it when it gets stranger ... I guess that's what I can't stand about cartooning. It attempts to be real in drawing and it falls flat. There's no finesse, intellect, passion, mystery,"

Richard Williams was called upon to fuse the cartoon and human world in the feature film, Who Framed Roger Rabbit. *Roger Rabbit is a famous toon star who is framed for the murder of Marvin Acme, the man responsible for wacky cartoon inventions. Roger enlists the help of private eye Eddie Valiant (Bob Hoskins), a soused sleuth who uncovers a secret plot.*

same animator might make a slight mistake and be cut down. Joe Haidar experienced Williams' volatile temperament while working on *Who Framed Roger Rabbit*. One day he was blasted for adding a "B" for Baby on the Baby Herman exposure sheets. Days later, he was praised to the hilt for adding a simple shrugging gesture to a background weasel.

Learning at Williams' studio was a double-edged sword for most. Greg Duffell was a 17-year-old Toronto kid fresh off the boat in the summer of 1973. Earlier that year, Williams wrote to Duffell suggesting that he leave school and join his studio in England where they were conducting training courses: "This may be completely against your wishes and your parents' desires but as my own academic background was practically nil and it has never harmed me in any way; perhaps you would like to come in on the ground floor here."[162]

Duffell was a wunderkind back home. Even before completing high school he was snapped up by a commercial studio, and won a young filmmakers competition for his short *And the Slobs Shall Inherit the Arts*. But three weeks after his arrival in London, Duffell was ready to turn around and go home. Williams had a way of throwing his new protégés off the deep end. He put Duffell to work inbetweening for Ken Harris. Duffell was in over his head, and he knew it: "I was severely shocked into reality. I felt embarrassed to even be there in the upper echelon of the animation business. I shouldn't have been put there really, but Dick is an impulsive individual and he likes to see people promoted above their abilities. I think he liked to put people there to sink or to swim." Duffell stood his ground and soaked up as much information as he could. He took Babbitt's one-month course, in-betweened Harris' *Thief* drawings, and under the tutelage of Grim Natwick made a two-minute short and screened it for the entire studio.

After the screening, Duffell caught a glimpse into Williams' heart of darkness. When the lights came back up and the small crowd gave its warm applause, Duffell saw Williams' reaction. "Dick had this funny look on his face," says Duffell.[163] "It was like: 'Somebody else is getting applause in my theatre.' He likes talent but was jealous of it." Duffell later learned that

At the age of 15, Duffell directed the film And the Slobs Shall Inherit the Arts. *At the age of 17, Duffell was recruited by Richard Williams to work in his London studio.*

Williams couldn't wait for the screening and had forced the editor to screen the film for him privately. Williams had an eye for talent, worshipped great work, yet wrestled daily with a terrible dread that one day one of his students might surpass him.

After that screening, Duffell and Williams often clashed. Eighteen months after joining the studio, Duffell quit. The final affront came in the form of a sarcastic letter Williams penned to Chuck Jones. Williams probably never intended to send the letter but wrote it in a fit of pique after Duffell repeatedly refused to take an animation job, and continued to plaster his cubicle with Warner Bros. paraphernalia. The latter probably antagonized Williams the most. Animators could only worship one God. And his monotheistic version wasn't to include Chuck Jones.

Despite his busy schedule — directing a feature film and running a commercial house — Williams found time to formally rebuke a junior employee. The letter and attached note reveal an unexpected bitterness: "I can see you becoming increasingly unhappy as we continue to produce work which is opposed to your conception of what cartoons and animation are all about; and as I don't wish to superimpose my own ideas or even our client's on your own brain, why not go and work with the master himself?"[164]

Over the years, Williams' schizophrenic management style and tendency to launch into a rage exhausted employees. Eventually, they moved on. London's commercial scene is

The Who Framed Roger Rabbit *crew from California including director Robert Zemeckis (third from left) and Richard Williams (third from right).*

literally a Who's Who of former Williams employees who set up their own shops: Dick Purdom, Tony White, Oscar Grillo of Klacto, Alan Dewhurst of Passion Pictures and Pam Dennis of Pizazz Pictures. In Los Angeles, animators such as Eric Goldberg, supervising animator of *Aladdin's* Genie, and Simon Wells, director at DreamWorks SKG, passed through his doors. Canadians Greg Duffell, Chuck Gammage, Nik Ranieri, Joe Haidar and Roger Chaisson are also former employees.

Williams used to say that in order to be a great animator, you have to have worked with a great animator.[165] He made that transfer of knowledge possible by hiring and training new artists at a time when no one else in the world did. Williams, in fact, launched a thousand careers. This was perhaps his greatest legacy.

"For many years I saw Disney as a giant tree that bore no fruit," says Haidar, now a senior animator at Disney. "There was barren landscape around it. One thing you could say about Williams' studio is that wherever apples fell off his tree, other studios sprouted. There's a whole cottage industry in London because of Dick."[166]

chapter 13

The Diaspora: Canadians Abroad

d isney, the powerhouse of American culture, is inundated by Canadians who have headed south for the work and the weather. It's the same story at Warner Bros., DreamWorks SKG, MGM, Pixar and Industrial Light and Magic. It takes a special combination of Canuck and chameleon to infiltrate these animation empires from their perches in the Great White North.

"We are the guys upstairs who aren't invited to the party downstairs, so we sneak in through the heat ducts. And because we look like them and talk like them, we get away with it," says Disney animator Jamie Oliff.[167]

Oliff is sitting in a California eatery with his Canadian comrades: Duncan Majoribanks, Nik Ranieri, Roger Chaisson and Joe Haidar. Across the table they debate the relationship between birthright and art. They can agree on only one thing — Canadians tend to have passive-aggressive personalities, and they are more likely to work harder at their craft. Their theory was illustrated by honorary Canadian Tom Sito (an American who worked for years at Nelvana), who drew a cartoon comparing Canadian, American and British animators on a job search. While the American and British animators were happy to wait around for something to happen at home, the Canadians spread out a map of the world and were considering jobs in Oman and Uganda.

For all these peripatetic souls, the nesting grounds where they learned how to fly were centred around the National Film Board, Sheridan College and Richard Williams' Studio in London. While the NFB was instrumental in the development of homegrown auteurs of animation, the primary source of diaspora animators is Sheridan College, located in Oakville, Ontario.

It was providence that Sheridan even incorporated an animation program into its visual arts department in 1967. Although the amalgam of art and commerce fit the college canon, the animation industry was not faring well. Commercial animation studios took a beating in the late sixties. The largest company, run by Al Guest, collapsed due to fights with its American co-producer, and Crawley Films in Ottawa suspended animation production after completing *The Wizard of Oz* series. Nevertheless, the Dean of Visual Arts, William Firth,

WHAT WILL **YOU** Do when the film's **OVER?!**

oh Dear I'm sure The Company shall Provide .... elsewise Something will Turn up.

BRITISH ANIMATORS

Ah have faith in WALT DIZZEY that they won't let me down!

AMERICAN ANIMATORS

OKay Rej, There's a STUDIO IN UGANDA where you KNOW the DIRector, ARRANGE the VISAS. Glen, you Go To Oman and check out The T.V. scene there.

CANADIAN ANIMATORS

Tom Sito illustrates the differences between animators from various nations.

convinced Sheridan President Jack Porter that an animation program could generate jobs and stimulate economic growth in the region. It was a bold gamble, but they had one major advantage. The closure of Guest's studio meant the college could purchase the necessities for a song. Even Guest's cameraman, Karl Hagan, defected to the college to handle technical operations.

Rather than employ NFB veterans, Firth hired two commercial animators working in the United States: George Martsegis, an animator of training films at the UCLA Health Science Center, and Bill Matthews, an animator at Cal Tech's Jet Propulsion Laboratory. Neither was a master animator, but each hammered home the classical animation approach propagated by Disney — bouncing ball exercises, flag waving, walk cycles, 3-D animation on paper, lip sync, layout, soundtrack breakdown and timing. In the first few years, the animation unit was housed in a condemned brick high school in Brampton. In March 1971 the studio moved to the new campus in Oakville. As student interest increased, so did faculty additions. Tom Halley (director of The Jackson-5 series and co-director of *Yellow Submarine*), Jim Macaulay (Halas and Batchelor), Dick Friesen (Disney), Zlatko Grgic (Zagreb Film), and Kaj Pindal (National Film Board) were the core instructors at the school.

Sheridan teachers embraced the axiom, If you train the workers, the industry will come. It was a self-fulfilling prophecy. "The philosophy was not that we were teaching a professional level of competence, but to encourage our kids to go out in the world to find the backing — somehow either get established in the existing studios, or try to set up studios of their own and try to get an industry started [in Canada]," says Matthews.[168] It worked to some extent. Sheridan grads were fodder for new companies like Nelvana and Atkinson Film-Arts. But the opportunities to mature professionally were limited. Feature films *Rock and Rule*, and *Heavy Metal* offered limited possibilities. The really ambitious graduates fanned out across

Chuck Jones visits Sheridan College: (left to right) Bill Matthews, Chuck Jones, Tom Halley, Dick Friesen and Jim Macaulay.

Europe and the United States. British studios run by Richard Williams, Oscar Grillo, Eric Goldberg, Tony White and Dick Purdum were top destination spots, as well as Don Bluth's studio in Dublin and Idéfix in Paris. These companies served as de facto post-graduate training centres.

It was an open secret that the Canadian gypsies traversed back and forth across borders in order to work in their chosen field. Top commercial houses in the US and Britain bent immigration laws and hired Canadian émigrés, and were increasingly sending animation work abroad. Striking artists working at studios such as Hanna-Barbera were protesting the flow of work out of the country. American animators also kept a watchful eye on the notorious band of green card seekers. One of the aggrieved workers forced onto the picket line was none other than Bill Matthews, the former Sheridan instructor. Having helped generate a viable export commodity, Matthews now stood on US soil with his finger in the dike hoping to stem the work flow out of the US.

Sheridan College was a source of raw talent, and it was Richard Williams who nurtured it. His London-based studio was vigorous and creative at a time when Disney's feature filmmaking operation was flailing. Despite his mercurial nature, Williams trained scores of young animators. By contrast, veterans Frank Thomas, Milt Kahl and Ollie Johnston were

Sheryl Sardinia's Sheridan student film, Eternity.

Sheridan College student Jon Minnis hit the jackpot when his short, Charade, *won an Oscar in 1984.*

unable to lead a fresh cavalry of young stars at Disney Studios. During the production of *The Fox and the Hound* (1977), the company's most promising artists — Don Bluth and John Pomeroy — quit Disney and set up their own operation. *The Fox and the Hound* should have marked the symbolic passing of the torch from the remaining Nine Old Men to the new generation. Instead it signalled a revolt.

Richard Williams did not always engender loyalty either. Nevertheless, he took it upon himself to recruit the masters and hold seminars for his young employees. His influence culminated with the production of *Who Framed Roger Rabbit*. For one year, Williams conducted a sizable group of gifted animators who gave their all to the seminal film. Rumours circulated that Disney would capitalize on the local talent by keeping its UK office open after *Roger Rabbit* was completed. Those hopes were dashed after the film wrapped. Disney shut its UK operation and Williams kept only a skeleton staff to continue work on his own feature, *The Thief and the Cobbler*.

Who Framed Roger Rabbit made Disney honchos stand up and take notice of the sizable pool of artists across the ocean. Over the next few years, Disney systematically hired Williams-trained animators, including former employee Eric Goldberg (the Genie of *Aladdin* and Philoctetes of *Hercules*) and the Canadian migrants, Nik Ranieri, Joe Haidar, Roger Chaisson and Ken Duncan. Disney's revival in the late eighties can be attributed in part to the Canadian artists who brought the characters to life. Canadians brought "new blood" into Disney.[169]

Classical animators are offered characters in much the same way actors are cast in feature films. Top Canadian animator/designers are often assigned the "quirky" sidekicks and nasty villains. Few are assigned to animate the all-American, square-jawed heroes or the perky heroines.

A Who's Who of Canadian-crafted caricature includes: Sebastian the crab, Abu the monkey, Timon the meerkat, Lumiere the candlestick, Meeko the raccoon, Panic the underworld henchman and villains, Ratcliffe, Hades and the Queen of Egypt.

The supervising animators behind the characters were Duncan Majoribanks, Nik Ranieri, Brian Ferguson, Mike Surrey and Dave Brewster. They are the animation equivalents of Dan Akroyd and Mike Meyers, the stars of Canadian comedy.

As the lead animator, the artist gives a little piece of himself to every character. He must interpret conceptual designs, craft the postures and attitude, and ensure that each drawing absorbs the personality he envisions. There is more to animation than raw drafting talent. An animator must pare down the basic elements of his character and codify the behaviours. He must find a shorthand to describe the soul.

Many artists place Duncan Majoribanks on the top rung of animators in the world. Majoribanks led teams that produced some of Disney's most memorable characters before DreamWorks lured him away. Majoribanks was part of the early wave of Canadians hired by Disney to kickstart their feature animation department in the mid-eighties. He supervised animation on: Sebastian the crab in *The Little Mermaid* (1989); the rambunctious tease, Abu the monkey in *Aladdin* (1992); McLeach in *The Rescuers Down Under* (1990); and the villain Ratcliffe in *Pocahontas* (1995).

Tall, dark and pensive, Duncan Majoribanks is the thinking man's animator, who writes extensive bios to develop his characters. His style has been described by contemporaries as "elegant." Whereas other artists use a heavy pencil to render and shade volume and form, Majoribanks can shape with a single stroke of a pen. "There is an economy of line that you can spot in his roughs," says animator Roger Chaisson, a former Sheridan classmate who also animates Disney sidekicks.

Sebastian and Abu are not simply supporting characters, they are scene stealers. Agility and spunk are their common traits. But Majoribanks is as comfortable drawing the verbose Sebastian as he is tackling pantomime critters such as Abu, the monkey who deftly mocks the infatuated Aladdin by pretending to be Princess Jasmine.

Classical animators are offered characters in much the same way actors are cast in feature films. Canadian animators such as Duncan Majoribanks were often recruited to draw the comic sidekicks. Majoribanks' sure lines instill life into The Little Mermaid's *Sebastian the crab.*

A defining moment in Majoribanks' career was a scene in *The Rescuers Down Under*, in which the evil animal poacher, McLeach, is celebrating his capture of the bald eagle. Standing on the edge of the cliff, McLeach leaps into the air and shouts: "Did ya see that, I got her, perfect shot, per-fect shot!" As he jumps, his long coat wraps around his legs. The movement shows a natural body language that assimilates nicely with the vocal performance. The director also asked Majoribanks to change the perspective mid-scene — to make it look as though the camera moves from its position below the cliff and is swept up 180 degrees to a spot above the character. Such requests from a director demand intense drafting and absolute authority over perspective.

Nik Ranieri has a unique style described by colleagues as all angles and accents. The long face and heavy eyelids of former Canadian finance minister, Marc Lalonde, caricatured in his student film, Common Problems *(1984), bears an unmistakable resemblance to the anthropomorphized candlestick he animated in Disney's* Beauty and the Beast *(below).*

"I was very anti-Disney in my school days," says Majoribanks, who left Sheridan College prematurely to form his own company, Animage, with Roger Chaisson and Mark Simon. [170] "I didn't like the look of the rounded, streamlined characters. After I worked in animation for a while, I realized that this was a really sound, industrial design that worked."

He was offered many jobs in the eighties, but stuck it out in the classical studios. A fan of Majoribanks' pre-Disney work, *Ren & Stimpy* creator John Kricfalusi once offered him a job on the CBS remake of *Mighty Mouse: The New Adventures.*

But Majoribanks wasn't buying into Kricfalusi's evangelical mission to liberate cartoonists from the children's ghetto: "John has always had conviction of his genius," Majoribanks observed drily. His own approach is more pragmatic. He views animation as more of a trade than an art form. "The thing that makes animation a business is that it's a collaborative medium," says Majoribanks, unapologetically. "This suits my own personality; the whole becoming greater than the sum of its parts."

Nevertheless, Majoribanks is impressed with the boundaries Kricfalusi is pushing: "You can't fully appreciate John's work unless you've done Saturday morning and you know what you are up against." And Majoribanks should know; he's been there.

He once worked 110 hours without sleep on a jobber in Canada before moving to the United States, where he survived by working on Hanna-Barbera's *Captain Caveman.*

Five years after moving to Los Angeles, Majoribanks was handling the artwork and development on a slate of projects that producer Ruby Spears pitched to the networks. It was the time of deregulation and everyone was pushing toy concepts. *Turbo Team*, a series about a boy who turns into a car, was one of his designs, as well as the *Rambo* and Chuck Norris cartoon shows.

After a stint on director Brad Bird's pilot, *Family Dog*, Disney offered Majoribanks a job on *The Little Mermaid*. "I sort of lucked into Sebastian, the crab. I came to Disney when everyone else was hauled off to work on *Roger Rabbit*. I walked in off the street and wound up with the lead character," says Majoribanks modestly. More accurately, he drew some experimental production scenes that caught the eye of Jeffrey Katzenberg, former chairman of Walt Disney Pictures.

❅❅❅❅❅

Nik Ranieri has a unique style described by colleagues as all angles and accents. The long face and heavy eyelids of former Canadian finance minister, Marc Lalonde, caricatured in his student film *Common Problems* (1984), bear an unmistakable resemblance to the anthropomorphized candlestick he animated in Disney's *Beauty and the Beast*. At times, Ranieri's characters resemble himself — a lanky, meticulous man who always aspired to be a cartoonist. Acetate runs through his veins.

Ranieri's characters resemble himself — a lanky, meticulous man who always aspired to be a cartoonist — as visualized by Jamie Oliff's caricature.

Ranieri has carved a niche for himself as a great animator of villains and wise-cracking sidekicks. He has climbed the pegboard of Disney's evil ones, starting with Ursula the Sea Witch, who attempts to thwart the dreams of the little mermaid, and Jafar, power-hungry vizier in *Aladdin*. Promoted to supervising animator, Ranieri landed responsibility for the coveted role of arch-villain in *Hercules* (1997). It was easy for Nik to animate the character, says animator Jamie Oliff: "Nik is Hades."

Ranieri's start in the art world was inauspicious. He flunked Art Fundamentals during his first year at Sheridan College, but reapplied one year later to the animation program after animating 12 creative bumpers for a Toronto late-night, low-budget, variety show. After graduating from

Sheridan College in 1984, Ranieri spent several years working in Canadian animation studios, first for Atkinson Film-Arts in Ottawa, followed by stints at Montreal's commercial house, Pascal Blais, and Toronto's Lightbox Productions.

As a junior animator at Atkinson Film-Arts, Ranieri had chutzpah. He gained notoriety after he personally rated studio animators from one to ten and pinned his results on the bulletin boards. At Atkinson-Crawley, Ranieri worked on *The Raccoons* specials, and the infamous Rush rock video.

Following a friend's career trajectory into commercials, Ranieri moved to Montreal to work for director Pascal Blais. Ranieri's proclivity for Tex Avery takes was not shared by clients. He pitched a wacky storyboard for a local Montreal Honda dealer but it was nixed and replaced by a "milque toast" version. Soon after, he quit Pascal Blais to work for a fellow Warner Bros. fan, Greg Duffell, of Lightbox Productions.

Ranieri was in sync creatively with Duffell, but Duffell's pursuit of perfection made him a difficult taskmaster. Ranieri's active desire to improvise commercial boards cheesed off Duffell, who fired him. Despite their differences, Ranieri remains impressed with the quality of Duffell's work: "When everyone else was Xeroxing, Duffell was hand-inking cels." He worked alongside Duffell on the Sugar-Crisp and Rice Krispies accounts. "I would say my style evolved while working in Canada. Greg taught me so much about straight ahead animation. It was torture, but the time I spent there was invaluable."

When Ranieri applied to Walt Disney in 1987, he was virtually unknown. Despite a reel of solid animation, Disney UK hired him to do basic clean-up and assistant work on *Who Framed Roger Rabbit*. When animator Dave Brown showed Ranieri's reel to Williams, he promptly promoted him.

Ranieri animated two great scenes starring Roger Rabbit. One features Roger tripping down a set of stairs and shouting: "Hey, Eddie let's get outta here!" Rather than tripping down the steps, Ranieri animated Roger hopping down them like a bunny. When Williams came back from a trip to Los Angeles, he "flipped" over Ranieri's extemporiza-

Rough animation of Hercules' Hades by Nik Ranieri. Villains are a Ranieri specialty. Few Canadians are assigned the all-American square-jawed heroes in Walt Disney films.

tion. Although others loved Ranieri's version, Williams forced him to redo it to his specifications. And so began Ranieri's love-hate relationship with Williams. "It is black or white with Dick, there is no inbetween. He either curses you or he praises you." The outburst meant he was now one of the boys. Ranieri went on to animate Roger in the climactic scene in which Roger bursts

through the manhole cover in the Acme factory where the evil Judge Doom is holding Jessica Rabbit and Eddie hostage.

Mike Surrey sketches an imagined meeting between Nik Ranieri and Al Hirschfeld, the line king of Broadway caricatures.

Williams' studio was Ranieri's springboard to Disney proper in Los Angeles. His first gig was animating Wilbur the albatross in *The Rescuers Down Under*. "[Working at Disney] can be quite intimidating at first, but I tried not to compare myself to anyone there. Instead, I tried to figure out what approach I could give to a scene that was uniquely me." Ranieri perfected the evil élan of Disney villains, but his signature style is the elongated, sarcastic Lumiere in *Beauty and the Beast* — a self-styled caricature.

A master of lip sync, Ranieri staged a personal coup when he animated *Pocahontas'* mute raccoon Meeko. He brilliantly mimed a playful bathtub scene in which Percy and Meeko devour a bowl of cherries. "My goal was to convey Meeko's thought process to the audience without use of dialogue," says Ranieri. For example: "Hi there, ... oh, you want a cherry? ...okay, one for you ... and these for me ... is everybody happy ... you don't look happy, I better get out of here ... and if you're not gonna eat that cherry I guess I will.' Meeko's innocence conflicts with Percy's cynicism."

Voice and visuals merge expertly in Ranieri's Hades, Lord of the Underworld. The character borders on impersonation. Actor James Woods is transformed into a sleazy and caustic cartoon. In preparation for the role, Ranieri studied Woods' mannerisms during the recording sessions, and even took snapshots capturing Woods' basic expressions for anger, joy, sadness, etc.

Nik Ranieri was a hard act to follow. As he portrays in these drawings, Surrey felt overshadowed by Ranieri...

As supervising animator, Mike Surrey exercised his comic chops on Timon the meerkat in the Disney feature The Lion King.

Ranieri views his task as part creation, part translation. He took production designer Gerald Scarfe's original design, but brought it to life by assiduously studying the timing and expressions of the actor. It was a delicate balance between imitation and illustration. "When working with a voice that is somewhat recognizable, I like to add a little visual similarity to the design. I feel it helps the voice appear as though it's coming from that character. When that's not possible, you tend to rely on facial expressions, gestures and body language of the actors as an inspiration for your characters' performances."

All the physical humour Woods employed in the studio found its way into an early scene in which Zeus invites Hades to join in festivities celebrating the birth of Hercules. With a great deal of shoulder shrugging, hand gesticulation and chin thrusts, Hades replies: "Love to babe, but unlike you Gods lounging about up here, I regrettably have a full-time gig that you by the way so charitably bestowed upon me, Zeus. So, can't, love to but can't."

Among the tribe of Canadian expatriates vying for animation's top jobs, there is both collaboration and competition. They alert one another about job prospects, but also joust in friendly rivalry.

Ranieri convinced Jamie Oliff, animator on Mushu the dragon in *Mulan* (1998), to apply at Disney. He also urged art director Ric Sluiter and lead animator Mike Surrey to try.[171]

Surrey rose through the ranks almost as quickly as Ranieri. But before he was promoted to supervising animator himself, he sketched a comic panel showing Ranieri entertaining excited journalists. At the time Surrey drew the picture, he felt rather overshadowed by his former Sheridan classmate and supervising animator on *Beauty and the Beast*. They were both assigned to work on *The Lion King* (1994), but Ranieri was clearly viewed as the rising star. It was a tough act to follow.

"When Nik left [*Lion King*] to work on *Pocahontas*, it allowed me to step out of his mighty shadow, hence the second drawing of me stepping out of the dark," says Surrey.[172] His internal wrestling match with the little green monster was short-lived. Surrey's own rise at Disney features has been rapid. The solid sense of space, volume and weight he imbues in his characters is recognizable.

In four years, Surrey climbed from animation apprentice on *Prince and the Pauper* (1990) to lead animator on *The Lion King*. Although he was one of the animators working on the princely Aladdin, he is clearly in his element with the jesting meerkat in *The Lion King*. "I don't know what it is about Canadians. We seem to hang on to the silly elements of animation as opposed to dreaming of drawing serious characters," says Surrey.

By the time Surrey completed Sheridan College in 1987, business was picking up in the animation industry. Rather than undertaking the customary tour of duty in Canadian commercial houses, he headed straight to New York with classmate Brian Ferguson to work on the feature film *Strawberry Fields* produced by the New York Institute of Technology (NYIT). In lieu of a regular paycheque, the graduates were awarded "scholarships" to work on the project. The scholarship system was actually an ingenious way of circumventing the US visa requirements, according to Surrey. "It was a shady way of getting us into the country as art students to work on the film," he says. The production studio was annexed to a mental hospital and green buses with blacked out windows would arrive daily. Strange screams and cackles could be heard across the courtyard. "It was the kind of place that scared you during the day," says Surrey.

Strawberry Fields was NYIT's attempt to marry computer-generated images with 2-D animation. The film was never released. The gig lasted for one year, by which time Surrey was hired by Universal to work on the sequel to Don Bluth's *American Tail*. In 1990, Walt Disney Studio hired Surrey to work on *The Prince and the Pauper* (1990), and later assigned him to assist Ranieri in *Beauty and the Beast*. Promoted on

...until he was promoted to lead animator on The Lion King.

Brian Ferguson's confident line drawings of Hades' henchman Panic.

Aladdin, Surrey animated the sequence of Jasmine meeting Aladdin, who is promoting himself as Prince Ali.

After *Aladdin*, Surrey was bumped up a notch again — this time as key animator of Timon in *The Lion King*. His favourite scene in the film is the Timon and Pumbaa duet, "The Lion Sleeps Tonight." Normally such a scene would take seven weeks of hard labour. Timon's entire 30-second romp (calculated to be 45 feet of drawings) was animated by Surrey in only one week. Worried that production was falling behind schedule, the producers were preparing to hand the scene over to another animator. Surrey fought hard to keep the scene for himself. The producers gave in, but only on the condition that it be completed in one week. The odds were against him, particularly when problems arose syncing the music to the animation. In the end he delivered. Surrey captured an amateur performer who belts out his favourite tune.

If Timon is a little Warner, Surrey's most recent character, Tarzan's primate pal, Terk, is pure Disney indignant and cute. Voiced by Rosie O'Donnell, Terk's roughhouse tumbling and sassy attitude complement the terse ape man, *Tarzan* (1999).

Brian Ferguson learned the Disney ropes by working as backup animation for his fellow pilgrims from Canada. He was right-hand man for Nik Ranieri with Meeko the raccoon, and for Mike Surrey on Timon in *The Lion King*. Like these two, he's described as a guy "with a latent sense of humour." In *Hercules*, he finally stepped out from their shadows.

Panic, one of Hades' henchmen in *Hercules*, was Ferguson's first supervising animation job: "Panic is completely up my alley. He fidgets and moves a lot and can transform himself into other characters. He's never boring to work on."[173] Panic's metamorphosis from benign-looking bunny to comic miscreant is one of Ferguson's favourite scenes: "It has it all: humour, cuteness and the chance to see the characters' personalities shine through. And it's on model."

Other animators cite their favourite Panic scene as the one in which Panic sheepishly offers Hades a drink of his Hercules logo cup: "Slurp! Slurp! Heh, heh.... Thirsty?"

From nimble sidekicks, Ferguson graduated to the corpulent matchmaker in *Mulan*.

He proved he could successfully move around weighty characters, and still deliver a decisive comic punch. The character does a little slapstick when she is accidentally set on fire as she tries to extract a cricket from her kimono.

Dave Brewster was handed the plum "bad girl" part in the DreamWorks feature The Prince of Egypt.

Walt Disney wasn't the only magnet for Canadians hell-bent on classical animation. DreamWorks and Warner Bros. (feature animation unit) were also destinations they dreamed of.

Dave Brewster was handed the plum "bad girl" part in the DreamWorks feature *The Prince of Egypt,* based on the epic biblical story of Moses and Ramses. He was also brought on to do lead work on Ramses, the heir to the mighty Pharaoh and the brother of Moses. Another Canadian, another villain. Well, almost.

DreamWorks is attempting to develop more realistic characters that depart from the usual caricatures, according to Brewster: "At Disney, most villains want to rule the world for no reason. My favourite question is: 'Do villains think they are bad?' At Disney the answer is yes. At DreamWorks (the villains) think they are the good guys."[174]

With Ramses, Brewster set out to draw a character that resembles a person the audience might have as a relative. He did not set out to illustrate pure evil. His goal was to create a character that is more grey than black and white.

"I hope people like (Ramses) as a person. I hope they understand the forces that caused him to make the choices he made. I hope you look at him and see your brother or sister. Moses is in pain at the end of this film. I want the audience to understand why."

Brewster also accepted the villain role in DreamWorks' second feature, *The Road to El Dorado,* set during the times of the Inca Empire.

Warner Bros. is home to Alex Williams, who exchanged his law career for one in animation. It wasn't a whim. He learned the art of drawing at the feet of the master himself, his father Richard Williams. After the debacle of *The Thief and the Cobbler,* Williams threw in the towel and headed for law school. But animation was in his blood and he couldn't stay away.

In 1996, Williams joined Warner Bros.' new feature animation department, and was assigned to lead the animation team for the villain, Lord Ruber, in *Quest for Camelot. Quest for Camelot* is the story of a teenaged girl named Kaley who embarks on a quest to recover King Arthur's sword, which was stolen by Ruber (Gary Oldman).

Ruber, who wants to conquer the kingdom of Camelot, is a character who appears sane one minute and quite mad the next. To capture the almost schizophrenic mood shifts, Williams created the "Ruber nervous twitch," which occurs at times of emotional intensity.

Williams also gave his character a "wrestler's strut" and head wobble, just the way cocky wrestlers enter the ring. Williams also gave each body movement a slightly different time, which makes it uncomfortable to watch.

There was one final touch. "I gave him big hands with broken nails that look creepy on close-ups," says Williams. "At the end of the film his hand becomes welded to the sword Excalibur, and his arm becomes a turning, rotating mechanical sword."[175]

Most Canadians have specialized in the offbeat or the merely evil. But a handful have defected to the side of good. Ken Duncan and Joe Haidar both got their feet wet at Disney Feature Animation on villainous characters, but have now become the exceptions to the maple leaf rule by drawing heroes.

Former animator on McLeach in *The Rescuers Down Under*, and Jafar in *Aladdin*, Duncan is the supervising animator for the romantic female leads in both *Hercules* and *Tarzan*.

In defence of his defection from comedic sidekicks, Duncan says he tried "to capture the screwball comedy approach" with Meg in *Hercules*. "This film has a lot more fluidity, stretch, squash and hitting a pose — the stuff that I liked working with Oscar [Grillo] and Richard Williams [in England]," says Duncan.[176]

Duncan inherited Meg after Majoribanks left for DreamWorks. Prior to that, Duncan animated the small supporting character, Thomas, in *Pocahontas*. Thomas is a naive swashbuckler who arrives in the New World on captain John Smith's ship. As a supportive straight man, "he was kind of a bore," says Duncan. However, he gamely captures Thomas' split-second hesitation as he aims his gun at Indian warrior Kocum. As he presses the trigger, a flash of internal conflict crosses his face. The scene is pivotal to the story because it sets in motion the war machine between the Natives and the Europeans.

Unlike some of Disney's other famous heroines, Meg is not an innocent wearing rose-coloured glasses. This time, the sexy lead is collaborating with the bad guy — at least at the start. Meg is a siren used by Hades to bewitch the naïve Hercules.

Duncan describes her as a betrayed woman — tough but wary. She is Mae West to Belle's (*Beauty and the Beast*) Sandra Dee. In her first encounter with Hercules, Meg gives a sexy salute as she bids good-bye to her young hero: "Thanks for everything, Herc! It's been a real slice." Production designer Gerald Scarfe could never have imagined that his "swoop" line would be so well interpreted by sashaying hips and alluring lip curls.

Directors Ron Clements and John Musker wanted more sex appeal for their love interest; a little more leg, or in this case, a little shoulder. The storyboard called for Meg to pull down the strap of her dress and tempt Hercules with a little flesh. Duncan's interpretation proved too provocative for management. And so began the talks over cutting the whole bit. Duncan balked and management compromised. She was allowed to keep the strap dangling, just as long as she was not seen as a provocateur. Duncan assumed the supervisory reins on the female lead Jane in Disney's movie *Tarzan* and was joined by fellow Canadian Doug Bennett.

Typical of the wandering Canadians, Joe Haidar went from Sheridan to a cheap TV series in Ottawa — *Hiawatha* — before flying to London to join Richard Williams' studio. He got a break from Phil Nibbelink, a Disney animator sent over to London to work on *Who Framed Roger Rabbit*. Richard Williams sought new talent, but would not promote Haidar from his job as assistant. "Phil took pity, and decided to give me small pieces of animation from his scenes without Dick knowing," recalls Haidar. After Williams approved a number of the scenes, Nibbelink finally informed him that the background characters were being done by Haidar. Rather than getting angry, Williams just said: "Okay, great, let's keep that up."

Haidar was hired by Disney to work on the Roger Rabbit short, *Tummy Trouble* (1989), and later, *The Rescuers Down Under*. Although he's done his fair share of off-beat roles, he recently animated more straightman roles such as John Smith in *Pocahontas* (under John Pomeroy), and Shang in *Mulan*.

In the mid-nineties, Haidar accepted a standing offer from the head honchos to pitch a feature. At the time, the Disney execs, Jeffrey Katzenberg, Michael Eisner and Roy Disney Jr., would hear ideas from any animator who had the guts to try. The animators dubbed the sessions "The Gong Show." Luckily for Haidar, the gong did not sound, and the execs liked his twist for a feature based on Hercules so much they assigned directors to it.

A Canadian had penetrated the inner sanctum, a half-century after Disney's characters had marched on Parliament Hill.

Ric Sluiter

Sluiter headed the art direction department of *Mulan*, a film based on a Chinese fable. A young girl disguises herself as a man to help fight an invasion by the Hun army, and Sluiter's primary job was to soften production designer Hans Bacher's bold poster style.

"My rendering style is less graphic than Hans Bacher's. I bring atmosphere and sensitivity to the film," says Sluiter. "The look of *Mulan* can be summed up in two words: poetic simplicity."

The Tang Dynasty (600 AD) became the reference for the Disney film because of its simple shapes and minimal detail compared to the Ming and Ching dynasties. The goal was to keep the backdrops clear and full of negative space to give the characters room to manoeuvre. "We wanted to keep it lyrical, pure, spacious and atmospheric; a lot of Chinese calligraphy."

Sluiter also looked to the original artwork of the Disney feature *Bambi*, which employed unique brushwork and simple, elegant lines. Sluiter's mantra was, less is more.

Sluiter's career trajectory was unusual. He worked for years as a mechanic until his mother-in-law talked him into going back to art school. "She was from Schrieber (Ontario) and she always wanted to be a writer," he recalls. She sat me down and said: 'I grew up in a small town where everyone grew up, got married and got pregnant, and never lived out their dreams. You have a chance to live out your dream. Go back to art school. Just do it!'"

So at age 24, Sluiter enrolled in Sheridan's animation program. He quickly hooked up with another serious animation student — Nik Ranieri, with whom he made the parliamentary parody, *Common Problems*.

He almost left animation and went into illustration, but dreamed of working for Disney. When Nik Ranieri called him from Los Angeles to tell him that Disney was opening a studio in Florida, Sluiter applied and was hired. The rest is history.

Paul Sabella

Vice-president of MGM's animation unit, Paul Sabella was given his first break by Montreal's Gerald Potterton in 1968. For two years, Sabella, a graphic artist trained in Egypt, worked as an animator on the feature *Tiki-Tiki* and Potterton's *Reader's Digest* series. Sabella and partner Julian Szuchopa formed Boxcar Films in the early eighties, and subsisted on animated spots for *Sesame Street*, and animating the Captain Sternn sequence of *Heavy Metal*. Sabella move to Los Angeles in 1989 where he worked as senior vice-president of production at Hanna-Barbera for three years. When Turner Broadcasting bought out H-B, Sabella left to produce the new Pink Panther cartoons for MGM. As vice-president of animation, Sabella is responsible for numerous Saturday-morning cartoons, and the feature *All Dogs Go to Heaven II*.

chapter 14

Shock Troops of Animation

First we have to blow up the Disney studio, get all the animators out of there, detox them. Then we have to kill Saturday morning and come up with a new word for cartoon. They consider it as children's entertainment, and that's a horrible handicap.

— John Kricfalusi on mainstream animation

nimation has emerged from the Dark Ages. Long considered an entertainment medium for children, animation experienced a renaissance in the early nineties. Generation Xers embraced it as a vehicle for satire and gross humour. Reclaimed by young adults, the genre elbowed its way onto prime-time television, and back into the movie theaters. It became a cultural stimulant for grown-ups.

The leader of the revolution was John Kricfalusi, the Canadian creator of *The Ren & Stimpy Show* (1990–95). Kricfalusi brought a self-deprecating edge to television. Not only did he inject offbeat adolescent humour, he pushed to restore art to the craft of animation. It was his goal to reinstate full-blown animation with fantastic gags.

Animation evolved because a new television forum emerged: cable. In the late eighties, networks such as Nickelodeon, Fox and MTV were mere weblets in search of a larger audience.

Cable executives looked to independent animators to supply them with irreverent fare that would separate them from the big three networks. Cable's invitation to independent animators was akin to a moose call. Artists went into hormonal overdrive. According to Kricfalusi, "It's as if, for 40 years, you taped everyone's groin shut and no one could have sex anymore, then all of a sudden you take all the tape off and everyone's all crusty and smelly, but they start fucking again and say: 'Wow, isn't this fun.' "[177]

The new broadcasters opened a Pandora's box. Animators who had been coiled in the square studios pumping out Saturday-morning schlock sprang into action. They had studied the Max Fleischer and Warner Bros. shorts and rued being born in the wrong era. Suddenly, there was a glimmer of hope. Two Canadians — Kricfalusi, followed later by Danny Antonucci, the creator of *The Brothers Grunt* (1994–95) — leaped out of the starting box. With their design arsenal and passion for animation, they took on traditional kids' TV, and reinforced scatological humour on the tube.

Nickelodeon executives Geraldine Laybourne and Vanessa Coffey gave the impetus to the new wave of animation. They wanted to break away from the traditional fare on compet-

John Kricfalusi as a kid in Canada. One of the last times John wore a suit.

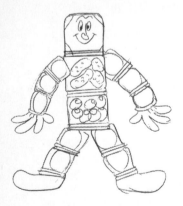

Jarzan, drawn from memory by John Kricfalusi years later.

ing networks. Kricfalusi was exactly the crusader they were seeking — a frustrated renegade with a mountain of ideas and a feverish pitching style.

Nickelodeon negotiated all rights for one of his creations — *Ren & Stimpy*. The cartoon quickly became a number one hit on Nickelodeon and MTV. At its peak, it attracted 2.2 million viewers, almost half of whom were adults over 18. It spawned a huge merchandising campaign, and was the progenitor of the profane toon popular on today's airwaves. Nearly half a century after the decline of the American cartoon, Kricfalusi reawakened audiences to the unadulterated joy of great design, and stretch and squash characters.

Kricfalusi was a typical nerdy preteen, obsessed with decoding the secret of animation. By age seven, he was rushing home to watch American cartoons: "*Huckleberry Hound* was on one channel and *Quick Draw McGraw* on another, and I'd go nuts wondering which one I would watch."

By dissecting comic book characters into grids, he learned how to draw. "Once I got the hang of drawing the characters, I started writing stories about them. I was drawing storyboards with Hanna-Barbera characters without knowing what a storyboard was. Then I got really nerdy and wrote up illustrated biographies of each character. Eventually, I started inventing my own characters and writing stories with them. Jarzan was a guy made up of jars. He had a best friend, Nosy Hotface. I actually wrote a letter to Walt Disney suggesting that his next feature be Nosy Hotface in Africa."

Like many young animators, Kricfalusi learned through experimentation, and by drawing unflattering caricatures of his sister. Kricfalusi's mother, Mary-Lou, claims they could never find a piece of paper around the house.[178] The family always knew "Johnny" had the ability to be a fine artist, they just didn't know if he would apply himself.

Despite his obvious talent, Kricfalusi failed art in high school in Ottawa. He was popular, the girls liked him, but he lacked discipline and motivation. Exasperated by his son's lack of initiative, Michael Kricfalusi decreed: "Go back to school, get a job or leave the house." Kricfalusi moved out at age 17. His father thought he'd end up in the gutter, but after kicking around Ottawa for two years, Kricfalusi applied to Sheridan College.

His defiant approach to teachers continued in college. Kricfalusi soon decided he could learn more about animation by attending animation screenings organized by Toronto eccentric Reg Hartt. He also became a regular patron of Bob Jaques' cartoon parties. Jaques had rescued a batch of old black and white cartoon film prints from a distribution company before they were melted down for silver. The wannabe animators watched them over and over and over.

Kricfalusi quit Sheri-dan before completing half the course. He viewed his instructors as mere proselytizers of the Disney religion and left in search of work.

Nelvana passed him over, so he headed straight for Los Angeles, where he paid his dues working in the animation trenches of Filmation and Hanna-Barbera. It was there that Kricfalusi came to the conclusion that writers were the root of all evil in cartoon land. He argued that in order to be a good animation writer, a person must be able to cartoon. "It goes without saying that you have to be able to write, but imagine trying to write a symphony if you've never played an instrument. Good grammar is not going to help you."[179]

In Kricfalusi's utopian world, animators would write and render their own stories and gags, and the ink and paint departments would be repatriated from the Orient. Banishing writers from production was Kricfalusi's first act of defiance as senior director on the CBS remake *Mighty Mouse: The New Adventures* (1987). Series producer Ralph Bakshi (director of *Fritz the Cat*) backed him up.

Bakshi and Kricfalusi were already collaborating on ideas before they pitched *Mighty Mouse* to CBS. In the summer of 1983, the duo developed a handful of original cartoon characters and story concepts to sell to broadcasters. Kricfalusi's favourite was *Brik Blastoff of the Outback*, a saucy sciencefiction series developed with the Playboy Channel in mind. The proposal was replete with sexual innuendoes such as: "Maybe if I cover the monster's eyes with my bra, we can escape!"

John Kricfalusi with animation legend Bill Hanna at Hanna-Barbera.

Brik was a character designed with the Playboy channel in mind.

Brik's youthful sidekick Jimmi is the cartoon precursor to Jimmy the Idiot Boy.

Perhaps wary of racism charges levelled at Bakshi for his previous feature *Heavy Traffic*, Playboy did not bite. No doubt their black character Sturtevant Stuyvesant — described in their notes as a "stereotype's stereotype" — made potential backers draw a deep breath. Their sidekick looked like Sidney Poitier when drawn in a frontal view, but when seen in profile sported lips that hung to his knees.

Brik never made it to air — in fact none of the original proposals from Bakshi and Kricfalusi were picked up — but the ghost of *Brik* past resurfaced in the *The Ren & Stimpy Show,* and much later in Kricfalusi's "Spumco Comic Book." Brik's teenage sidekick Jimmi is the cartoon precursor to Jimmy the Idiot Boy, and Nit Hoatzin, Brik's psycho female recruit bears a strong resemblance to Jimmy's girlfriend Sody Pop. The summer of 1983 was a fruitful one; but it would take six more years before he managed to harvest the ideas.

Despite his uneven track record as an animation feature film director in Hollywood, Ralph Bakshi still carried clout. By the mid-eighties, he attempted a TV comeback. With Kricfalusi overseeing the animated segments, he produced and directed the Rolling Stones' Harlem Shuffle music video (1986). After years of beating down the doors of TV executives, Bakshi talked CBS executive Judy Price into buying *Mighty Mouse: The New Adventures* (1987–88).

CBS argued for something tried and true — a property with marquee value. So Bakshi called their bluff. He blurted out an offer to remake the old Terrytoons character and Price agreed to buy it. Four years after their original brainstorming sessions, Bakshi and Kricfalusi were in production.

Despite protests from CBS honchos, the animators wrote and directed the stories themselves. Kricfalusi announced that it was the first cartoonist-made show in 25 years.

Liberated from boring scripts, the animation team comprised of Kricfalusi, Tom Mitten and Jim Reardon literally exploded.

"After you have been oppressed, your first impulse is to be completely anarchic. Any kind of weird drawing or idea we came up with, we did." The result was a multitude of expressions, interesting non-perspective backgrounds and surreal stories. Kricfalusi wrote and directed eight of 26, 11-minute cartoons, and oversaw the rest.

The learning curve was steep. The choreography and timing of the shows were off. Since nobody had been animating there, no one knew how to time. "Probably 80 percent of [the experiments] failed, but at least I got them out of my system," says Kricfalusi.

Mighty Mouse was a harbinger of things to come. It gave animators the taste of the possible. But as Kricfalusi was soon to discover, artistic freedom brought many headaches, mostly of the censorship kind. Bakshi was forced to cut three and a half seconds from "The Littlest Tramp" episode of *Mighty Mouse* when a Kentucky family complained that the steroid-bulked rodent appeared to be sniffing cocaine. The complaint reached the pages of *The New York Times* and *Time* magazine.[180]

Despite its flaws, the series got rave reviews everywhere — from *Parenting* magazine to *Spin. Time* magazine placed it in the year's top ten shows, alongside the televised Iran Contra hearings.

Kricfalusi and Bakshi fought continuously. Firing and rehiring became a ritual performance. Bakshi refused his demand for a big chunk of the show's profits and merchandising rights, and Kricfalusi finally quit for good. "John is very, very emotional," says Bakshi. "He goes with his gut, and he doesn't know how to back down."[181]

Kricfalusi was offered a stint at DIC Enterprises remaking Bob Clampett's *Beany and Cecil* for ABC (1988). Once again he clashed with DIC management when it demanded scripted and storyboarded cartoons. Unapproved scenes kept sneaking into shows. Weeks after its debut, *Beany and Cecil* was yanked off the air.

Instead of throwing in the towel, Kricfalusi formed Spumco in 1989 with former *Mighty Mouse* colleagues Bob Camp, Jim Smith and Lynne Naylor. Together, they refined the style, colours and ideas they had pioneered on *Mighty Mouse*. With a pile of cartoon ideas, Kricfalusi began systematically pitching the networks again.

John Kricfalusi created this Christmas card for the Clampett family.

Kricfalusi kept sneaking unapproved scenes into the remake of the Beany and Cecil TV series. Weeks after its debut, ABC yanked it off the air.

The original "Your Gang" concept sketches for Ren Hoek and Stimpson J. Cat.

The Spumco team was running out of possible markets for their outrageous material when Nickelodeon announced it wanted animator-driven cartoons. It also stressed that it would cater to kids' tastes, that parents' ideas should not reign supreme.

Vanessa Coffey, Nickelodeon's vice-president of animation, was camped out in a hotel suite in Los Angeles listening to cartoonist pitches when Kricfalusi delivered one of his famous rapid-fire pitches. It was mid-summer and the air conditioner in her hotel room was broken. Kricfalusi not only worked himself into a lather, but he also sprayed sweat all over her.

Of the five concepts offered, Coffey expressed interest in two characters from his "Your Gang" presentation: a puffy cat and a rabid-looking Chihuahua. Flown to New York, Kricfalusi made another apoplectic pitch, and Nickelodeon offered to fund not just one, but two pilots. But when he learned that the cable network wanted all rights, Kricfalusi balked. Nickelodeon's goal was to follow in the footsteps of Disney and Warner Bros. and establish a permanent library of evergreen cartoons. That meant ownership. Kricfalusi agreed to relinquish rights on *The Ren & Stimpy Show*, but held on to his — and Nickelodeon's — favourite character, Jimmy. He viewed *Ren & Stimpy* as an offering.

"The creator-driven thing is a press invention to make people think how noble they are," says Kricfalusi. "What [cable networks] really wanted was hungry studios [like his] dying to break out of the mainstream who would knock themselves out to make great shows and hand over the merchandising rights." Previously, most of the shows were spun off of existing licensed properties. In the nineties, the penny-pinching cable nets started waking up to the possibilities of ancillary markets and moneys.

It took Spumco eight months to finish the pilot, *Big House Blues* (1990), in which the two heroes are carted off to a dog pound to be gassed for the "big sleep." There was much experimenting with characters, backgrounds and techniques. During the making of the first episode, Stimpy went from being mere "furniture" to an imbecile with flashes of brilliance. Coffey suggested Ren's character be "softened" to make him less insectlike and more likeable.

Ren and Stimpy are also appealing because they play such fabulous foils. Ren is a manic, skeletal Chihuahua who delights in tormenting his mentally deficient feline buddy, Stimpy. When Ren vents himself on the world, it's frightening. He is a living, breathing, teenaged super-ego. If he had the strength he'd rip everything to shreds, but he doesn't. Instead, Ren inflicts his neuroses on his dumpy pal. Stimpy is an idiot savant, a cat unnaturally obsessed with his litter box. On occasion, he rises above his abysmally low IQ and experiences an epiphany. Whereas one has an endless supply of love and trust, the other is basically an asshole. They are the nineties hard-core version of Abbott and Costello or Laurel and Hardy.

Nickelodeon honchos had reservations from the start. Coffey was torn between passion for Kricfalusi's vision and the cold corporate calculation that the show had to work for kids. They originally nixed the pilot plot to have one of the characters dying and asked that the more overt homosexual scenes — a flirtatious dog-catcher and Ren's dream fantasy — be clipped. The series order wasn't confirmed until a theatrical screening and plenty of thumbs-up test-marketing took place. Even then, the order was conservative: only six episodes.

Kricfalusi didn't know what the fuss was all about; after all, Nickelodeon had built its reputation as a network of boogers and farts. According to Kricfalusi, the only difference was that "our boogers weren't just little green things, we had magnificent renaissance paintings of boogers, beautifully rendered with special effects highlights. They could talk and sing. We went to town on boogers."

Spumco went through the roller-coaster of approvals. Keeping to a proper schedule became a serious problem. Storyboards travelled back and forth, and gags slipped in without network approval. In "Stimpy's Big Day," Spumco inserted a reference to the Pope in a poem penned by Stimpy: "I may not be the president/I may not be the Pope./But as long as I have Gritty Kitty,/I shall never mope." Subsequent story ideas such as a papal hockey team were quickly banished.[182] On occasion, Coffey sided with Spumco, but more often Nickelodeon execs were scissors-happy.

The fanzine *Wild Cartoon Kingdom* published a number of the network changes, termed broadcast "boners." They included underwear sniffing, armpit scum, butt picking and burning fart gags. A leech posing as a doctor who sucks Ren

The pilot for Ren & Stimpy, *Big House Blues, in which the two heroes are carted off to a dog pound to be gassed for the Big Sleep.*

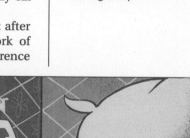

Spumco went through the roller coaster of approvals. A leech posing as a doctor who sucks Ren dry was excised from the episode "Nurse Stimpy."

Stimpy happily
volunteers to donate
his butt fat so his
friend Ren can have
pectoral implants.

dry was excised from "Nurse Stimpy."

Each episode was replete with "in-jokes." A sample of *The Ren & Stimpy Show* take-offs includes: *Wild Kingdom*, starring Marlon Perkins; Disney's *101 Dalmatians*; *Captain Video* space operas; and children's classics such as *Robin Hood*.

As if parodying old TV reruns wasn't enough, there were plenty of pokes at commercials that target kids. A commercial that resurfaces on *The Ren & Stimpy Show*'s television set is a sales pitch for Log — a chunk of inert wood that can be accessorized with such items as wigs and gowns. Kricfalusi's more ingenious toy take-off is My Little Brother (read My Little Pony), a toy that girls can blame when they get into trouble. Ren and Stimpy also spend hours playing "Don't Whiz on the Electric Fence" game, and there is a mock spot for Sugar Frosted Milk.

Powdered Toast Man
was a parody of the
orchestrated cereal
product tie-in that was
popular in the fifties.

Powdered Toast Man is a super-hero that flies into Ren and Stimpy's house one morning to deliver a new breakfast cereal, "Powdered Toast." This kind of orchestrated product tie-in was popular in the fifties with such characters as Snap! Crackle! and Pop! (Rice Krispies), Toucan Sam (Fruit Loops), and Tony the Tiger (Frosted Flakes). Powdered Toast Man, however, does not have the moral fibre of Superman or Batman. As a guest star on an episode, this faux defender of good over evil assumes the reins of power when the President's fly gets stuck. His first act is to heat up the chilly Oval Office by burning a couple of cumbersome documents — the Bill of Rights and the Constitution. It is an outrageous act of civil disobedience by an anti-hero.

In the memorable episode "Stimpy's Invention," Stimpy creates the Happy Helmet, which he forces wretched Ren to wear to cheer him up. The helmet is essentially a diabolical thought control device, which forces Ren to behave in a blissfully vacant manner. Ren no longer bursts into fits when mishaps occur, he just tunelessly sings, "Happy, Happy, Joy, Joy." Meanwhile, his convulsing body telegraphs just how tortuous it is to suppress his anger and frustration. The happy helmet is the cartoon version of soma, the drug in Aldous Huxley's *Brave New World*, which keeps the masses too apathetic to rebel.

In reaching the 18-plus crowd, some of the shows go beyond satirical jokes, and inject genuine pathos into the storylines. "Son of Stimpy," originally called Stimpy's First Fart, opens with Stimpy wandering the streets insisting "He's real, he's real." The object of his passionate search and rescue is Stinky the Fart, a little gaseous emission that slipped out of Stimpy's bum one day and escaped. Stimpy's search becomes an existential search of self. The fart is Stimpy's alter ego.

Although he wouldn't like the analogy, Kricfalusi's more complex cartoons read as postmodern fables, not unlike some of the work by National Film Board animators Richard Condie, who made *The Big Snit* — a parable of nuclear holocaust — and Paul Driessen, who animated *An Old Box*, a bittersweet tale of Christmas spirit and generosity. Although these animators make films with messages they still stuff their cartoons with physical gags, non sequiturs and strange behavioural idiosyncrasies.

Ren sings: "Happy, Happy, Joy, Joy," but his convulsing body telegraphs just how tortuous it is to suppress all anger and frustration. The happy helmet is the cartoon version of soma, a drug described in Aldous Huxley's book, Brave New World.

Kricfalusi laid the graphic ground-work, but Bob Jaques and his wife Kelly Armstrong of Carbunkle Cartoons in Vancouver executed the best shows. Even Kricfalusi thought it impossible, but Carbunkle multiplied the dramatic expressions and poses in the layouts. Kricfalusi describes their style as "beautiful-ugly."[183] From far-out epileptic contortions in "Stimpy's Invention," to the famously contentious scene of "Man's Best Friend" (in which Ren viciously pummels George Liquor), Carbunkle became Spumco's animation house of choice. In later years, it became the house of emulation.

John Kricfalusi retained copyright of George Liquor and Jimmy the Idiot Boy. Their exploits are now available on Spumco's Internet site.

After only six episodes, *The Ren & Stimpy Show* became a bona fide hit. Because of repeated delays, the same shows were recycled. Familiarity bred cult followers. Over 100 fan clubs sprouted up, home video sales soared, and a compilation album of songs featured in the show was produced. Even Jay Leno and Arsenio Hall included the duo in their talk show monologues, and Sunday-morning viewing parties became a trend on college campuses.

Nickelodeon sank big money into the early episodes, more than any other Saturday-morning series. Now they were eager to capitalize on their investment. They ordered 26 episodes, but the number was quickly scaled back to 13 half-hours. Everyone prayed the second season would be easier. It wasn't. Spumco couldn't keep up. The battles over storyboards ate up precious days of pre-production and exhausted Kricfalusi. Tension within the studio also mounted.

As the show grabbed national headlines, Spumco artists made credit grabs. Insiders jokingly referred to creative fist-fights, but heads began to roll. Kricfalusi fired storyboard artist Jim Gomez and designer Lynne Naylor stepped down. Nickelodeon played off partners Bob Camp and Kricfalusi by offering Camp a crack at directing a feature film and other goodies. "I warned John to cover his back," says Jaques.[184]

By all accounts, Kricfalusi was a tough taskmaster — a perfectionist for line quality and strong layouts. "John would tear off pieces of the drawings (on a layout) where he didn't like the lines and paste another piece of paper over it and redraw it," says Mark Kausler, a freelance animator who worked on "Stimpy's Invention."[185] "He knew that everything degrades overseas." At first, artists viewed his dictatorial approach as one of "artistic integrity." Revisionist accounts cast him as an obsessive tyrant prepared to exact blood from his loyal crew to get perfection.

Meanwhile, story ideas and gags continued to be trashed. A phallic-looking tailbone shown in a close-up of George Liquor's butt was recoloured, and a version of "Out West" that has the dynamic duo gutted and filleted was vetoed. But it was "Man's Best Friend," an episode starring George Liquor, all-American redneck, that led to Kricfalusi's dismissal. *The Ren & Stimpy Show*'s adoption by a sadistic owner — George Liquor — ends with Ren turning on his foster parent and beating him unconscious with an oar. One journalist termed it "an abused child's revenge fantasy." But Nickelodeon was not amused, and on September 21, 1992, it issued a statement that Spumco was no longer in charge of production. Former Spumco partner Bob Camp took over the show and produced it at Nickelodeon's in-house studio, Game Productions. Half of Spumco's employees went along.

The showdown was inevitable. Kricfalusi had been co-opted by a broadcaster that wanted to capitalize on the popularity of counterculture cartoons and comics. But having mounted that horse, Nickelodeon was unable to rein it in. As animation historian Mark Langer points out, Kricfalusi was part of an "animatophilia" group that defines itself simply as being outside the norm of mainstream society, and any absorption on the part of dominant culture threatens its very existence.[186] The harder Nickelodeon pushed, the more Kricfalusi sought to define his show by loading it with references that only diehard animation fans or consumers of junk TV would know and appreciate. The envelope of good taste for youngsters was constantly challenged.

"*The Ren & Stimpy Show* is an enigma. I knew it would be a hit, but I didn't know why," says Coffey. In the end, she gave up trying to understand the creator: "I was trying to put a square peg into a round hole." Nickelodeon would not make the same mistake twice. Future "creative-driven" shows were produced at Nickelodeon's Game Productions studio.

Kricfalusi was the underdog, and many rushed to his defense. Journalists such as Richard Gehr of the *Village Voice* said it was like "taking Twin Peaks away from David Lynch."[187] Matt Groening, creator of *The Simpsons*, joined in the chorus stating: "It's like taking Dr. Frankenstein away from his monster."[188]

A typical Kricfalusi bodacious babe.

After Nickelodeon removed him off The Ren & Stimpy Show, *Kricfalusi started "Spumco Comic Book" (above) and launched an Internet cartoon series.*

There were those with much more to lose who still stuck by him. Art director Jim Smith remained at Spumco when he could have continued to work on the show with Camp. Carbunkle Cartoons, Kricfalusi's favourite service house, did not seek a contract renewal after it finished the second season, and gave up big money. At Kricfalusi's Spumco headquarters, those that moved with Camp were considered traitors. Layout artist Eddie Fitzgerald was knighted in a magazine when he refused to shake Camp's hand.

With the support of Chris Gore, editor of the new *Wild Cartoon Kingdom*, Kricfalusi attempted a grassroots revolt. The magazine printed hate mail to Nickelodeon executives. A typical missive, signed by Judy Bartlett and Tony Cruz, read: "We are very disappointed in your actions, and would have Nickelodeon removed from our cable selection if it were possible. As it is, we will no longer watch your channel, nor will other members of our family (ranging in age from six to sixty-five) as we cannot condone your selling out in such a cowardly manner." [189]

Gore advised Kricfalusi on merchandising opportunities and even promoted his new endeavours, which included Jimmy the Idiot Boy and George Liquor dolls and cel-painting kits. Kricfalusi signed a deal with Marvel for Comic Book, starring Jimmy, George and Sody Pop. Unfortunately, sales of his products were not as successful as he had hoped, and after one issue, Marvel Comics decided not to pursue a continuing series.

Kricfalusi fought back. He released "Spumco Comic Book" through Dark Horse Comics, and launched an Internet cartoon series. He even went backstage after a Bjork concert and convinced the singer to hire him to do a music video. In her "I Miss You" single, Bjork hams it up with cartoon Jimmy.

Kricfalusi's personal crusade for quality animation has made him a hero with cartoon fans and a pariah to broadcasters. Initially, rival broadcasters welcomed Kricfalusi — the new prince of animation — with open arms. Kricfalusi responded by pitching outrageous and politically incorrect characters. He pitched Jeffrey Katzenberg, former chairman of Walt Disney, a scene in which Jimmy the Idiot Box takes a crap in an outhouse. He developed the TV pilot, *A Real Goddamn Christmas*, for Fox Television starring Jimmy and George. But in addition to script changes, Fox requested a new character for the series. After spending 10 years refining these, Kricfalusi was unwilling to part with them. He did score one success. Cartoon Network's Linda Simensky hired him to produce and direct a handful of *Ranger Smith* cartoons.

Kricfalusi proved to the animation community that he was a martyr tied to the stake of commercials. He has not yet been able to convert his cultural capital into another cartoon series. His scorched earth policy has left him with few safe harbours. His unshackled creativity has had an enormous impact on the animation community. But like Richard Williams, his obsession is exacting a price on his career. One by one, his partisans have burned out and moved on. Unable to beat the establishment at its own game, Kricfalusi laments that he has been "blackballed." His erstwhile patron — and latter-day nemesis — Vanessa Coffey, has a different take: "I don't think the networks are as eager to massage his ego as we were."[190]

Once indefatigable, Kricfalusi is showing signs of battle fatigue. He is weary from watching his design style mimicked by other studios, tired of pitching his shows to broadcasters who want unlimited merchandising rights, and exhausted by the prospect of the long haul ahead.

Every studio and broadcaster has latched onto the retro graphic style and buddy roles. Fruity colours have invaded many cartoons, from *Rocko's Modern Life* to *Cow and Chicken*. Broadcasters may not be buying Kricfalusi's new shows, but they are imitating his old one. Spumco alumni have frequently been called upon to do *Ren & Stimpy* knock-offs. Lynne Naylor, known for her "cheesecake" female designs similar to Kricfalusi's own voluptuous babes, went on to art direct *Snookums and Meat* for Walt Disney Television.

Years after its debut, broadcasters are still trying to replicate *The Ren & Stimpy Show*'s magic formula. It continues to be the artistic measuring stick. Its success showed to the cable networks that kids' television does not have to be homogeneous.

"John turned everyone onto style, colour and timing," says Jaques. "Cartoons are better made now." The retro fifties backdrops Kricfalusi adopted made a big comeback in animated TV shows, not to mention the expansive emotional range

Ren & Stimpy *paved the way for shows like* Cow and Chicken.

and extreme "off-model" physical distortions of his cartoons. Jaques' own snappy animation style has also been imitated and mutated by overseas studios such as Korea's Rough Draft. More pragmatic than his old friend, Jaques worked on remakes such as the *Woody Woodpecker* series for Universal Studios.

The Ren & Stimpy Show was successful because it stayed small and intimate. The stories revolved around two characters and their relationship to the world. This went against the grain of contemporary animation, which is to cut faster and create complicated plots with multiple, interacting characters. Ren and Stimpy never needed anyone else; they were compelling enough in themselves. They were true stars. So is their maker.

In a restaurant near his former Melrose Place office, Kricfalusi orders up a cheeseburger smothered in bacon and a glass of iced tea. He stops drawing cartoons on the paper tablecloth long enough to reach into his glass and pull out ice cubes to crunch on. Time-morph this image, and he's a young boy diving into a box of Sugar Corn Pops, digging around to find the prize hidden inside.

A station ID for MTV was the basis for Danny Antonucci's TV series The Brothers Grunt.

Despite his disappointments, Kricfalusi still retains childhood atavisms. He embodies the spirit of today's animation fans, whose collective memories are a pastiche of commercial jingles, sitcom stereotypes, cartoon characters and breakfast cereal box tops. In both *The Ren & Stimpy Show* and his later merchandising endeavours, Kricfalusi explores the postmodern reflex to sift through the cultural detritus in the wasteland of television in search of familiar touchstones.

With its ironic use of music videoclips, mock bumpers and fake commercials, *The Ren & Stimpy Show* — as well as later cable TV shows such as MTV's and *The Brothers Grunt* — reaffirms the collective experience of growing up in a TV culture while simultaneously parodying it.

The cartoons mirror the dialectical dilemma of teens torn between fascination with anti-establishment pop culture icons, and cynicism towards the inevitable commercialism their heroes fall into.

This satirical approach has also been successfully used in the past by *Mad Magazine, Saturday Night Live,* and Canadian shows such as *SCTV* and *Codco,* which also regurgitate old TV serials and spit them out as camp or parody. The difference between formats is simply that animation can push the envelope faster and farther; to go where no man has ever gone before into galaxies of bad taste.

The slicker, frenetic pace of *Ren & Stimpy*, and Danny Antonucci's *The Brothers Grunt*, captures the schizophrenic mood of the nation's youth — the first generation of college educated non-achievers. Judging by the demographics, Kricfalusi and Antonucci have uncorked the anxieties of young graduates frustrated by their limited opportunities to get a real job — as opposed to a McJob, flipping hamburgers or waitressing.

The Brothers Grunt doesn't quite reach the pathological proportions of John Kricfalusi's *Ren*. By comparison, Antonucci's characters are more sedate. The hypertension manifested in straining muscles, engorged arteries and dilated eyes leads to an implosion in the brothers Grunt, rather than the explosion of rage and frustration that typifies Ren. Whereas the havoc wreaked by the brothers Grunt is almost accidental, Kricfalusi purposefully unleashes his characters on the world.

Vancouver-based Antonucci and Kricfalusi are alumni of Canada's Sheridan College, and share an affinity for bursting capillaries painted in candy colours. But they diverge on geographic matters and the importance of being Canadian. Whereas Antonucci makes his home in Canada and has been mentored by Marv Newland of Vancouver's International Rocketship, Kricfalusi attaches little importance to his Canadian roots or his Sheridan education.

When business slowed down at Rocketship, Antonucci started pitching some of his sick and twisted concepts to MTV for station IDs. One S & M spot that eventually aired shows a tongue sliding out of a zipper and spanking an MTV logo. A second interstitial featured five cancerous characters, each grunting painfully as eyes bulge and veins pop. The scene cut to an MTV logo plopping into a toilet bowl. Scatological humour reigns supreme on cable and retains pride of place on Antonucci's drawing board. The spot impressed MTV executive producer of animation Abby Terkuhle. He asked Antonucci to make a pilot based on the gelatinous Grunt brethren.

In the spirit of animation's brotherhood, Antonucci promptly made a series that also has fun at the expense of pop-culture icons. In *Viva Vegas* — a take on the old Elvis movie of the same title — Antonucci's brothers Grunt travel to casino country. At the slot machines, one brother pulls off the arm of a Ronald Reagan look-alike gambler — à la Lupo the Butcher — and throws the appendage to a decrepit Elvis, who is busking on the street, in order to pay for his bottle of brightly coloured pills. The scene ends with nasty gangsters flinging their undies at a sexy Tom Jones.

Edd

They're friends because they have the same name

Ed, Edd n Eddy

Puberty is unforgiving

a d a n n y a n t o n u c c i c a r t u n a

Danny Antonucci sent this one page pitch to Cartoon Network's Linda Simenski.

Like Kricfalusi, Antonucci had no intention of catering to the Saturday-morning crowd. In fact, he wasn't even catering to the MTV crowd, which was annoyed when *The Brothers Grunt* took over the time slot originally held by *Beavis and Butt-head*. The MTV audience seemed to find *The Grunt Brothers* more offensive than its precursor. "There was instant hatred for the show by the fans," says Antonucci.

Antonucci is happy about making people uncomfortable, even if it just means disrupting their schedule and blowing away their expectations. "I think we succeeded in putting a bug up America's ass."[192]

Antonucci's second TV series, *Ed, Edd n Eddy* (1999), has been dubbed "Lupo's babies," after Antonucci's cult cartoon, *Lupo the Butcher*. Despite comparisons to his original short, *Ed, Edd 'n Eddy* is a mellow kids' version for the Cartoon Network.

The Eds live on the same cul-de-sac in the suburbs. But similarities between the trio end there. Tough guy Ed, and brainy, polite Edd find themselves caught up in Eddy's wacky schemes to raise money for candy and other goodies. The Eds are pubescent boys with an entrepreneurial streak.

Canadian animators like John Kricfalusi and Danny Antonucci pushed animation as a forum for disaffected youths. The animated shows they directed are less a social commentary than a cultural mirror that acknowledges the ingrained stupidity of the tube, by making smart comedy out of North America's dumbing-down. They are testing the limits of television raunchiness.[181]

John Kricfalusi is the leader of the pack. His influence in the growing field of animation is exceeded only by a group of computer geeks responsible for the special effects revolution. Kricfalusi ignited a slumbering passion for traditional adult cartoons, while Canadian software programmers and digital artists invented a whole new cinematic lingo. Hollywood will never be the same.

chapter 15

Digital Genesis

---

he earliest depictions of man on computer are akin to Neanderthal cave paintings. Top flight academics from the University of Waterloo laboured over complex mathematical formulas just to compose simple line drawings on a computer screen. That was the seventies. By the mid-eighties, an aging computer graphics crooner crafted by a group of Montreal researchers boasted metallic-skin and could display stock expressions.

Within two decades, the unthinkable had become reality. Dinosaurs were brought back from extinction, the cyborgs of science fiction novels given forms, and the Titanic resunk. But the most impressive technological advance was the evolution of an inorganic character that can convey human emotion — the cybertoon. Since 1995, animators have crafted characters capable of jealousy, anger and fear — creatures that project soul.

These are heady times for these former nerds of the NURBS. With such power at their fingertips, it's no wonder computer graphic imagery (CGI) artists such as Dave Andrews and Steve Williams jokingly compare themselves to the Almighty.

"Animation is the fulfillment of the romantic dream as embodied in Victor Frankenstein," says Dave Andrews, an animator at Industrial Light and Magic, who supervised the construction of the Martians from outer space for Tim Burton's film, *Mars Attacks*. "I'm going to be God. I'm going to create. It's my big chance to populate the world."[193]

Andrews and fellow Canadians Jenn Emberly and Linda Bel populated Burton's film with a delegation of brain-bulky aliens inspired by 1960's bubblegum cards.

Williams was the animation muscle behind ILM's state-of-the-art features, *The Abyss, Terminator 2: Judgment Day, Jurassic Park*, and *The Mask*. Among his animation credits are the pseudopod that reaches out and connects with Mary Elizabeth Mastrantonio, the shape-changing T-1000 that battles Arnold Schwarzenegger, Spielberg's flesh-gouging raptors and the Tex Avery–styled face on actor Jim Carrey. Only time constraints affect his omnipotence: "God was given unlimited time to create new life. The animator is given about a year."[194] The swelling ranks of CGI artists have become the superheroes of cinema. Back in the eighties,

The joy of animation as told by ILM supervising animator Dave Andrews: "I'm going to be God. I'm going to create. It's my big chance to populate the world."

they called themselves the "raster blasters." Rasters were the guys who eschewed vector graphics and wrote their own rendering programs. If they had bothered with a team uniform, it would most probably have sported the maple leaf. That's because the first top guns of the morph and the make-believe were Canadian. The term *raster blaster* has gone the way of the Tyrannosaurus Rex because good rendering programs can now be bought off the shelf. But the new animation kingpins working in the top service and production houses still carry Canadian passports.

At Industrial Light and Magic alone, the company's Canadian team photograph in the mid-nineties shows no less than 40 players. Pixar Animation Studios, DreamWorks SKG, Sony Imageworks, Pacific Data Images, and Disney have also witnessed a quiet invasion of Canucks.

From the very start, Canadians have played a major role in the evolution of digital imaging. Their dominance in the land of 3-D graphics is due to several factors: software, software and more software. To be precise, Alias, Softimage, Side Effects Software and Vertigo: four 3-D software packages developed in Canada that are in wide use today; plus a booty of 2-D paint and compositing systems developed by companies such as Discreet Logic, ToonBoom and Taarna.

The relationship between software developers and production houses was symbiotic. As post-production companies purchased off-the-shelf 3-D packages, they needed to hire talent to operate it. With the import of technology came the influx of animators and programmers familiar with the software. US firms soaked up many of the talented spline-meisters and polygon mappers in the eighties and early nineties. Every major production house employs animators, modellers or technical directors who started on early versions of Canadian software.

Steve Williams and Eric Armstrong sparked the CGI revolution by building the T-Rex leg for Jurassic Park.

Williams, a successful demo artist for Alias and later Side Effects Productions (the precursor to Side Effects Software), was snapped up by ILM — where he helped to perfect the T-2 morph from man to molten metal.

Williams, in turn, helped to recruit a number of Canadians — Eric Armstrong, Geoff Campbell, Wade Howie, Philip Alexy, Les Major, Robert Coleman and Dave Andrews, to name a few — who were either familiar with Canadian turnkey systems or trained at his alma mater, Sheridan College. A talent pipeline was constructed. Because the Canadians deployed in large production houses explored the outer limits of the packages, they remained in constant touch with the software programmers back home. With such a strong feedback loop, the dominance of the Canadian technology has been assured.

Alias, Softimage and Side Effects — today's big three high-end computer animation packages — built their temples on foundations laid by the University of Waterloo, and on the ruins of Omnibus Computer Graphics, a high-tech development company that collapsed in 1986. Omnibus, founded in 1982 by John Pennie, was one of the first companies in the world to grab digital technology by the horns and wrestle with it. Pennie, a Toronto native, was originally a partner in Image West, a California-based company that used analog computers to distort video images. It was an early form of computer animation that relied on matte techniques, and was used successfully to create a "force field" in the feature film *Logan's Run* (1976).

Omnibus was one of the first companies to bring computer animation out of the academic closet and onto the commercial production stage.

In 1976, Image West held 25 percent of the computer animation market, which at the time was worth $10 million worldwide. Pennie knew it was a dead end: "Most of the film industry and television producers did not take computer animation seriously at the time because of the limitations in analog technology."[195]

Pennie looked into his crystal ball and predicted that digital animation would be the wave of the future. Developed in university labs in North America, digital technology was a ripe product for industry plucking. Pennie wanted Image West to harvest the new fruit, but his partner Cliff Brown wanted no part of it. So in 1980, Image West was split, and Pennie formed Omnibus Computer Graphics with $2 million and a deal to become the first licensee of software developed by the New York Institute of Technology Computer Graphics Laboratory (NYIT).

Omnibus was one of the first companies to bring a computer animation program out of the academic closet and onto the commercial production stage. But there was a hefty price tag attached to it, both in monetary terms and staff workload. By the time Pennie bought NYIT software, its original developers had left the university to try their luck on the West Coast. As Omnibus' first animators soon discovered, technical support was nil. In addition, there were huge chunks of information missing from the software.

Green employees such as Will Anielewicz and Doug MacMillan were pushed into the programming deep end. Not only did they have to master every piece of equipment, run the VTRs and mix effects, but they also had to translate the so-called package.

"To learn how to run something, we would get some obscure manual page that was written as a thesis, in a language that no one else could understand," says MacMillan, who tried calling the NYIT graduate students who had written the code, only to be told to bug off.[196] There were a lot of late nights trying to decode the code for simple 'tween and paint programs.

"My job was to connect the technology and the product," says Anielewicz.[197] The connection was tenuous at the best of times. "John (Pennie) was the master of the facade; pretending to have something that he didn't have," he says. Nevertheless, clients were prepared to pay $50,000 for a computer-generated spot that today looks like it was rendered by a low-end Macintosh.

Eventually, Omnibus managers recruited Greg Hermanovic, who worked at Spar Aerospace designing the Canadarm robotic arm for the space shuttle, to head up a proper in-house programming team to co-ordinate efforts between the company's offices in Toronto, Los Angeles and New York. Hermanovic's fellow code writer, Kim Davidson, a University of Waterloo alumnus, was also brought aboard to develop much of Omnibus' proprietary source code — including its PRISMS software program — and as a render writer. Other programmers, such as Paul Breslin, worked on simple geometric 3-D programs. The team built polygon sorting algorithms, frame buffer code and texture mapping algorithms.

For several exciting years in the mid-eighties, Toronto's Omnibus Video was one of the hottest computer animation firms in North America. It was research and development created on the fly, driven by clients who needed tailor-made programs to create unique special effects. Because the software was so rudimentary, animators spent more time writing themselves out of production jams than actually animating. When the software team couldn't help, crews had to improvise by finding video shortcuts. "We'd shoot anything under camera and out of focus and try to fit it into textures," says Anielewicz. Sometimes they pointed a camera at a television screen, and blurred the image to achieve a glowing effect that they could then composite onto a computer-generated object.

Chrome was a particularly popular look for logos and hockey pucks. The chrome-to-matte ratio was called the "crow-factor," because the in-house crew used to joke that "birds and clients are attracted to bright shiny objects."[198]

One of their more bizarre improvisations to simulate liquid chrome for logos was dubbed the "toilet paper effect." It was created by pointing a camera at a rotating cylinder wrapped in toilet paper. A playback of this videotape was rewound over and over under a graphic hold-out matte of the logo. The blurred image of the toilet paper gave the logo a special metallic sheen. "From then on, I was always proud to see, attached to artwork that was waiting to be prepared for edit, the letters 'TP' for toilet paper," says MacMillan.

The company's big break came when Alvin Toffler awarded it the contract to do the special effects for the television series based on his book *The Third Wave*. Appropriately, it was a futurist who hired this fledgling CGI company. Omnibus' new special effects equipment burst into flames shortly after production began. The crew was once again forced to improvise. Despite production gaffes, Omnibus raised $4.5 million on the Toronto Stock Exchange following the series' success. It would later produce some reflecting spaceship effects for *Flight of the Navigator* (1986).

Like many top computerized production houses, Omnibus' bread and butter came from designing logo tags. Broadcasters were big clients, and Omnibus juggled the three biggies in Canada — CBC, CTV and Global. It also created the long-running *Hockey Night in Canada* tag, memorable primarily because the sports event is a national institution. One of the better commercials produced in-house was a Kodak spot involving a live long-jump athlete who morphs into a sapling and grows into a mature tree. It is considered one of the earliest attempts at morphing.

Chrome was a popular texture for logos. Omnibus employees referred to the chrome-to-matte ratio as the crow factor because they joked that "birds and clients are attracted to bright shiny objects."

*Omnibus' test sequence
for the feature film
Flight of the Navigator.*

*Marilyn Monrobot is a
precursor to the
Terminator 2 cyborg.*

Before ray tracing technology was available, CGI artist Les Major constructed a virtual office building and even simulated a reflection in a marble lobby floor by inverting data. In-house animator Mark Mayerson created Marilyn Monrobot, an articulated human figure. Virtual Marilyn had yellow hair, light skin tones and tight fitting top and shorts. She was a precursor to *Terminator 2: Judgment Day* (1991).

In the summer of 1986, Omnibus gobbled up two of its US rivals: Digital Productions (*The Last Starfighter* and *2010*), the only production company with a Cray X-MP supercomputer, and Robert Abel & Associates, at the time considered one of the most creative commercial houses in the world.

For a fleeting moment, Pennie was poised to compete with Lucasfilm's Industrial Light and Magic. But months after its fateful purchase of Robert Abel & Associates, Omnibus itself came tumbling down — a house of cards that collapsed under a mountain of debt.

Pennie made the fatal mistake of closing his deal with Abel, a company with a $12-million debt, before assuring that his company's additional share offering proceeded as planned. A series of behind-the-scene machinations delayed the offering and spooked investors. Despite the fact that Omnibus stood to make over $50 million in sales and had fully one-quarter of the international market, the banks decided to foreclose in April 1987.

Insiders still speculate about how the field would look today if the mighty Omnibus had not struck out. Some say Pennie was a true visionary who was simply stabbed in the back by auditors and investors. After all, this was a man who foresaw a time when digital backlots and props would be leased out: a practice that is now a reality. Others say Omnibus collapsed because Pennie's attempts to consolidate proved too costly and the cheaper minicomputers and turnkey systems entering the market would have edged them out anyway. But Pennie points to the success of code developed by his former employees, and to the current consolidation in the market — the marriage of the US hardware giants Microsoft and Silicon Graphics to Canadian software entrepreneurs Softimage and Alias.

The result was both the death of a giant, and the birth of a phoenix. The company's roster of 30 software and creative people spun out into new ventures, taking with them a wealth of experience.

An early computerized bird produced by Omnibus programmers.

Omnibus' former creative director, Dan Philips, works as a special effects supervisor in Los Angeles. He was instrumental in building the computerized 3-D ballroom sequence in *Beauty and the Beast*, and is now part of the special effects unit working at DreamWorks SKG.

While working at Disney, Linda Bel designed many of the camera moves used in the famous ballroom scene. She moved to ILM in 1995 to work on Draco, the friendly dragon voiced by Sean Connery in the film *Dragonheart*. Will Anielewicz, Doug MacMillan and Robert Marinic eventually joined ILM's commercial division.

The demise of Omnibus left the field open to other budding software companies. Omnibus head programmers Greg Hermanovic and Kim Davidson acquired exclusive rights and title for the PRISMS code, and within a year of Omnibus' demise set up their own development shop, Side Effects Software. Several other firms rose to the challenge: Vertigo, Alias and Softimage.

The oldest remaining software company still around today is Vertigo. Founded in 1982, Vertigo expanded with the intention of building a vertically integrated system complete with hardware and software. Its first marketable version in 1986 combined the SGI Iris 2400 and Sun 3/160 workstations.

Cubicomp, the software firm platforming on Compact PCs, snapped up Vertigo in late 1987 and renamed it Cubicomp Canada. To better promote its capabilities, artist Sharon Calahan directed *Night Café* (1988), a 3-D short featuring dancing salt and pepper shakers. But less than three years after purchasing Vertigo, Cubicomp itself collapsed. Vertigo was once again in technological deep water without a financing lifeboat.

Linda Fawcus, a former employee, believed that the northern arm of Cubicomp still had enormous potential. She convinced her then-boyfriend, James Stewart, to buy it. Stewart and three financial partners purchased the company from the bank in August 1990.

Alias/Wavefront demo artist Chris Landreth pushed the envelope of the software program by creating the end *(above).*

Landreth's latest film Bingo *(1998) takes human form to the next level.*

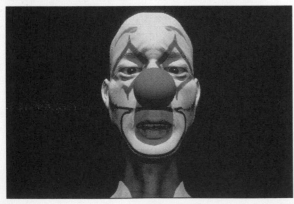

"The idea was that I would buy the rights for the technology, finish the current release, sell the updated 9.3 version to existing clients, make a lot of money, and shut it down," says Stewart.[199] The short-term deal turned into an eight-year adventure for the former Vancouver lawyer. Resuscitated once again, Vertigo's object modelling and animation powered such films as *Congo*, *Escape from LA* and *Ace Ventura*.

Vertigo repositioned itself in the marketplace to become platform-independent. In 1995, the company announced it would port its software to the Macintosh. The new target market was no longer high-end users, but graphic artists doing desktop publishing — creative folks who were intimidated by 3-D applications.

Vertigo lived up to its name. The corporate shake-ups over the past 20 years are indeed dizzying. It survived, but the original employees were absorbed by their competitors. Calahan worked as a lighting technical director on Pixar's *Toy Story* and *A Bug's Life*. Whereas Omnibus burst apart, sending its former employees to all the ends of the earth, most of Vertigo's talent slowly leached back into the Canadian software industry.

Nigel McGrath is not a computer programmer, but in the mid-eighties, he provided the corporate infrastructure for two new Toronto-based companies that also arose from the ashes of Omnibus. McGrath supplied programmer Kim Davidson with a day job and office space until his Side Effects software was saleable. He also fronted Alias co-founders, Stephen Bingham and Susan McKenna.

McKenna and Bingham approached McGrath in 1984 because they wanted to produce a computer-animated TV show, but couldn't afford Omnibus' price tag. At the time, McGrath and Associates were using a rudimentary 2-D graphic system to produce cheap 2-D graphics for corporate clients. The Alias pair couldn't understand why a 3-D system based on the same principles of McGrath's 2-D Dekenic system was not available on the market. Their goal was to make a simpler 3-D software system.

McGrath lent McKenna and Bingham his company's name in order to raise money through Canadian grants and tax credits. Dave Springer, a 21-year-old whiz-kid from Sheridan College was their first employee.

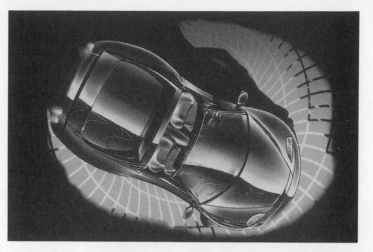

Springer went to work writing Alias' code. "He was the classic early hacker, and I think it was some of his energy that led us down interesting paths," says McGrath.[200] Other programmers such as Mike Sweeney, Rob Kreiger, Will Anielewicz and Tom Burns joined the R & D team. Whereas Anielewicz and Kreiger focused on user interface and modelling, Mike Sweeney turned his attention to rendering. Sweeney is the original raster blaster. He developed his University of Waterloo ray-tracing thesis into a full-fledged production system, and applied it to Alias' earliest version.

It was nothing short of a marketing miracle that Alias survived its first pass on the floor of the 1985 trade show, Siggraph. "Every day and night we were back at the hotel coding to make sure that the thing did not crash on the showroom floor," says Kreiger.

An unexpected turn led the entrepreneurs to the world of industrial design. Bingham and McGrath, both car enthusiasts, paid a visit to Ron Hill, director of General Motors' aerodynamics design team in Detroit. Alias had made a splash at Siggraph in 1985, but they were running on demo software. Alias desperately needed a major client to prove its technology was marketable. The package also had to run without a life support system of programmers.

Alias' first industry patron was General Motors' aerodynamics design team in Detroit. The company's engineers were impressed with Alias' demo package because the quality of the images it generated surpassed anything else on the market.

Alias' demo package had one advantage over its competitors. Sweeney's rendering system may have been slow, but the quality of the images it generated far surpassed anything else on the market. Hill and his aerodynamics team at General Motors were so excited by Alias' fluid, realistic graphics, they literally pressed their noses to the computer screens when

A Team Canada photo taken at Industrial Light and Magic's back lot.

The computer generated pseudpod in The Abyss.

shown early Alias graphics. The GM employees were so convinced by Alias' product, that they produced their own video on Alias software and pitched three prototype units to their own board of directors.

"All we had to do was to tag along, and Ron Hill sold the system internally," says McGrath. Industrial design was reborn. With Alias software and Silicon Graphics platforms, GM scrapped hand-drawn sketches and clay models.

The General Motors deal was a twofold blessing. Blue chip clients such as Honda, Motorola, Goodyear, Kraft, the National Aeronautics and Space Administration and Mitsubishi jumped on the bandwagon. Collectively, they gave Alias the clout to make an initial public offering on NASDAQ in mid-1990. The demand of these early clients also forced Alias programmers to work out modelling bugs quickly, design better interfaces and speed up its rendering time. The GM legacy remains; Alias is still considered the number one modeller on the market.

When director James Cameron contracted ILM to do the effects for his ambitious project *The Abyss* (1989), the post-house purchased Alias software and conscripted Alias' brash demo artist, Steve Williams. *The Abyss* is a suspense thriller about a crew stationed in an underwater oil-drilling rig; the crew encounter a life-force at the bottom of the sea — one that can transform itself into a watery serpent and actually pene-trate the rig. Cameron kept telling the special effects team that if the pseudopod didn't work out he could always cut out the sequence.[201] Fortunately, he didn't have to. With CG artists Mark Dippé and Jay Riddle, Williams constructed a rippling, reflective creature that gracefully and elegantly connects with Deepcore crew members Lindsey and Bud Brigman (Mary Elizabeth Mastrantonio and Ed Harris). It was a CG magic moment.

It was not long before Cameron was back, this time bran-dishing a script that would wholly depend upon the CG skills of ILM. *Terminator 2: The Judgment Day* (1991) is a film about a metal-cyborg Terminator (Arnold Schwarzenegger) who returns from the future to protect John Connor, the 10-year-old boy destined to be a rebel leader in the year 2029. Schwarzenegger-as-machine must face off with a new cyborg prototype, a T-1000 capable of controlled liquefaction. The updated version of the Terminator can change shape into objects of equal density and mend injuries such as bullet holes or fiery blasts.

Cameron's script called for ultimate morphing — a seamless blend of live-action and CG elements. The cyborg had to blend smoothly from a human form to molten mate-rial even while walking or running. Alias once again played a key role in designing the T-1000 digital skeleton, and more Canadians joined ILM.

Steve Williams and Eric Armstrong constructed the leg bones and generated a walk cycle of a Tyrannosaurus Rex dinosaur as a test for the film Jurassic Park. *When director Steven Spielberg saw their results, he pulled the plug on the stop-motion studio and threw his resources into the computer graphics studio at ILM.*

Geoff Campbell, a young Montreal animator who directed the admirable short *The Treadmill,* faced a baptism under fire when he joined ILM in 1990. Like every animator, Campbell had to present his takes at a daily screening of rushes. For days, he worked on the scene in which the T-1000 bursts through the walls of the psychiatric hospital and bolts across a parking garage. When the clip was screened, Campbell was embarrassed because his cyborg was suddenly running in a very odd manner: "I remember my first take at dailies because I had made a change at the last minute and it caused all the parts of the program to be recalculated. One little change snowballed into something horrible ... I wanted to get on the first plane and go home."[202] Campbell soon left over this creative hump. Most recently he worked as a model supervisor on the blockbuster, *Men in Black.*

Praised for his work on T-2, Steve Williams was already becoming tired of producing graphic eye candy. Williams no longer wanted to make just the special effects icing for films; he wanted to create the star. He finally got his chance with *Jurassic Park* (1993). When producers Kathleen Kennedy and Frank Marshall originally approached ILM, all they requested was a shot of a stampeding herd of gallimimus. The rest of the dinosaurs were to be models shot using stop-motion or puppeteered by 16 or more animators. "I wanted the protagonist — the Tyrannosaurus Rex," says Williams.[203] Filmmakers shied away from CG characters and still preferred to work with the creatures shops.

To prove his point, Williams graphically constructed the leg bones of a T-Rex using the Alias modelling package. It was an unsanctioned move, but it paid off. The producers were so impressed that they advanced ILM money for Williams and fellow Canadian Eric Armstrong to construct the skin and generate a walk cycle. Spielberg pulled the plug on the stop-motion studio when he saw ILM's results, and threw his lot in with the computer team. The announcement revolutionized creature animation. Phil Tippett's puppet stop-motion shop was swept into the digital era. The natural movement created with new Canadian software, and realistic skin textures, made the dinosaurs appear photorealistic. With one remarkable film, Williams had transformed ILM from a special effects post-production house to an animation birthing unit.

The program that moved the dinosaur muscle mass with frightening authenticity was Softimage, an animation software package developed by French-Canadian Daniel

The program that moved the Jurassic Park *dinosaur muscle mass with frightening authenticity was Softimage, an animation software package developed by French-Canadian Daniel Langlois.*

Langlois. Trained in graphic design, Langlois was fascinated with the possibility of creating within a computer environment when he joined the National Film Board of Canada's French animation unit in 1979. René Jodoin and later Robert Forget, executive producers of French animation, poured energy and money into early computer animation. They relied on the expertise of the National Research Council (NRC) and the University of Waterloo.

In 1975, Peter Foldès of the NRC produced *La Faim* (*Hunger*) at the NFB using an early analog system to draw line characters. There could be no rendering or texture, but the film was noteworthy for its smooth transitions and form. Langlois was assigned to apply the 3-D system to the NFB's first stereographic 3-D Imax computer-animated films, *Transitions* and *Emergency*.

While employed at the NFB, Langlois was hired to design and co-direct a film initiated by Pierre Lachapelle, Philippe Bergeron and Pierre Robidoux of Université de Montréal. The film, *Tony De Peltrie* (1985), was conceived as a realistic, human-like character. Built using Taarna software developed by Lachapelle, *Tony De Peltrie* made waves at industry events because, for the first time, an animated character was able to convey the subtle emotions of an aging crooner — complete with flickering eyelids and wistful sighs. Tony fell far short of an organic man. On top of the fact that he looked like a strange hybrid between singer Tony Bennett and former Canadian Prime Minister Brian Mulroney, the character retained the metallic hard look of computer graphics. Despite international accolades, the software was still cumbersome. It took four programmers more than three years to produce $6\frac{1}{2}$ minutes of film. Still, the number crunchers did more than just plug in digits. For the first time, real acting was involved.

Peter Foldès of the National Research Council in Ottawa used an early analog system to draw line characters for the NFB film, La Faim (Hunger).

Tony De Peltrie was the first believable human character generated by a computer. Tony was able to convey the subtle emotions of an aging singer — complete with flickering eyelids and wistful sighs.

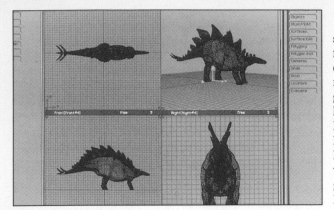

Wire-frame renderings of dinosaurs produced by computer.

Convinced he could develop software that was more artist-friendly, Langlois founded his own company, Softimage, in the summer of 1986. After months of plugging away on his own, Langlois hired former Alias programmer Mike Sweeney, as well as Laurent Lauzon, Kavey Kardan, Richard Mercile and Eric Lebel. In 1988, with a $350,000 investment by a group of Toronto investors, Langlois launched his software package Creative Environment.

The package became an instant hit with high-end users. Although it was launched after Alias, it was easier to use and better suited to moving models around. According to Williams, the "inverse kinematics" feature that Softimage added to its 1991 package, *Actor*, put it four years ahead of Alias.

Developed by Dominique Boisvert, Softimage's latest tool provided built-in knowledge of physiology and muscular movement. So if an animator commanded his character to raise its arm, the shoulder and hand would move naturally in response. The new program forced the competition to go back to the drawing board. Even though accolades were slow in coming (the Academy of Motion Pictures waited until 1998 to recognize Softimage's contribution), the industry pounced on the new technology.

Alias offered a good design package for the fantasy creature from the deep in *The Abyss* and the chromatic cyborg of T-2. But ILM used Softimage's package to animate Madeline Ashton's (Meryl Streep's) bizarre neck-twisting scene in *Death Becomes Her* (1992), a gory film about two fading actresses who find immortality in a bottle.

"*Death Becomes Her* was a test for *Jurassic Park*," says Eric Lebel, former Softimage programmer who spent months going back and forth from Montreal to Marin County in California to perfect the "draw-over" feature requested by ILM.[204] The goal was to ensure that the CGI elements would match the live-action shots. Before Lebel perfected this tool, rendered images would often come out larger than the positioned wire-frame models because the techniques used to remove the jagged lines common to computer graphic drawings enlarged the picture. The feature was later renamed "Rotoscope," an homage to the Max Fleischer invention. Not only does it match CG with the live-action, but an animator can also now trace live-action images to create 2-D or 3-D elements.

The inverse-kinematics feature gave the dinosaurs of *Jurassic Park* smooth and natural movement. On the heels of media hoopla over the CGI dinosaurs, Softimage floated its initial public offering at US$9 and raised US$10 million. Its star was rising.

The next step would be to integrate 3-D and 2-D effects, but a full-range digital studio would require a large injection of money. Langlois met with America's Number One corporate behemoth, Microsoft, which was eager to ensure that 3-D software for the low-end market would be compatible with PC platforms.

The wire-frame construction built with Alias software, transforms Stanley Ipkiss (Jim Carrey) into a real life cartoon.

Microsoft took the plunge and in 1994 acquired all of Softimage's stock. The buyout caused a shockwave through the industry. In response to the Microsoft-Softimage merger, Silicon Graphics bought out Alias and Wavefront Technology (a competing American software company) one year later to secure its place in the CG world. Both Canadian companies were absorbed into US conglomerates.

No longer a small industry of entrepreneurs and struggling hackers, CG had hit the big leagues, and everyone in Hollywood was taking notice. "A lot of directors, in the effects industry ... shelved their ideas ten years ago because there was no way to realize them," says Williams. Suddenly, ILM and other special effects houses were inundated with scripts that had been gathering dust.

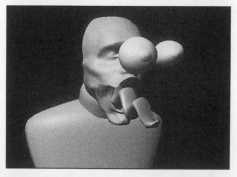

Steve Williams was assigned a supervisory position on *The Mask* (1994), and Eric Armstrong was put in charge of *Casper* (1995). One film would successfully mimic the exaggerated squash and stretch of classical animation; the other would push the envelope of character animation.

ILM needed more animators. Both Williams and Armstrong pushed to hire animators over programmers. "When I first got here, the people who traditionally called themselves animators, were people who understood computers, not how to draw," says Williams, who recruited Sheridan graduates Philip Alexy and David Andrews. Of the 14 animators hired for *Casper*, not one had ever touched a computer in their lives. "The idea was that we needed people who were trained in the art of acting," says Armstrong.[205] In the CG animation department, ILM suddenly became top heavy with Canadians.

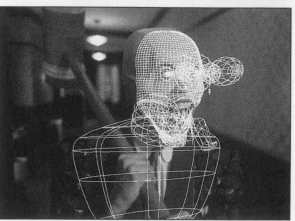

Canadian technical director Habib Zargarpour animated the green swamp gas emitted by the mask when actor Jim Carrey placed it over his face. Steve Williams dubbed the greenish vapour "Habib gas," a term that is still used by computer animators. It was a joke at the time, but according to Zargarpour some of the other technical directors were miffed because their names are not attached to their inventions. Wes Takahashi told Zargarpour: "I do lasers and they call it lasers. I do plasma and they call it plasma ... and you come and make gas and they call it Habib gas. I don't get it."

Robert Coleman, a graduate of Concordia University, was told: "We will teach you Softimage, but you have to show us that you know the fundamentals of animation, because that's hard to teach people. You've either got it in your bones or you don't. It's a sense of weight, timing, character and performance."[206]

Chris Armstrong, an animator who worked on a number of traditional spots for Toronto's The Animation House, was part of ILM's second hiring wave. Although his specialty was cutout puppets and pastels, he did not find the transition difficult: "I was really doing exactly the same thing as I was doing before but without a lot of the headaches. I didn't have to stand under the camera for hours moving little things around. I could sit at a desk and do a better job at it."[207]

The Mask was a transitional film for ILM. New Line Cinema's plan was to take the black humour of a *Dark Horse Comics* character and turn it into a zany romantic comedy adventure. Williams and his special effects crew were charged with animating the extreme facial and bodily contortions of Stanley Ipkiss (Jim Carrey) whenever he donned the diabolical mask. A Warner Bros. fan, Williams was eager to go beyond the "stereotypical gags" that director Charles Russell initially requested.

"We battled a little bit here and there because I thought we should have pushed it a little further in many areas like bulging eyes and shit like that," says Williams. "As it went on, [Russell] got a little more used to it, and started saying, 'Oh let's really exaggerate it more.' So all the dog stuff we went crazy on." The end result is pure Tex Avery mania. ILM was still advancing its technical wizardry, but now people were having a little fun.

Casper (1995) took ILM through the next hoop, but not without a lot of pain. The animators achieved better facial expression and movement than a claymation character, but they were sometimes forced to try 40 takes until animation directors Eric Armstrong and Phil Nibbelink gave it the thumbs up. The team of 30 animators also had to work on 400 shots involving its cast of virtual ghosts. It was an enormous leap. The same year Casper was released, ILM introduced realistic CG hairy animals in the film *Jumanji* (1995).

Geoff Campbell, a digital model supervisor, worked on "Caricature" software that could deliver better facial expressions. "We would work with our software department on a daily basis, both for working out bugs and to discuss requests for improving the software," says Campbell. He adds: "No one else was writing this kind of program at the time, and it pushed the envelope of facial animation."

These experiments were later incorporated into *Dragonheart* (1996), *101 Dalmations* (1997) and the blockbuster film *Men in Black* (1997).

Animators achieved better facial expressions and movement during the production of Casper.

Linda Bel moved from Disney to ILM because of breakthroughs that would let her explore CG character animation. The task of creating conversation scenes with the dragon Draco (voiced by Sean Connery) tested her skills as an animator. The mythological creature of *Dragonheart* is perhaps the first photorealistic CG star of the movies. Using the Caricature program, Bel tackled scenes that required Draco to emote tenderness, pain and even love. These were the first CGI close-ups.

The evolution of fully lip-synced characters took off after *Dragonheart*. "More and more we've seen camera's coming in for the close-up and holding on to the character in broad daylight without the camera shaking or rain falling which would help cover up any computer graphic limitation," says Campbell. Virtual characters have to hold their own on screen today.

Visual effects supervisors Jim Mitchell and Mark Miller approached David Andrews to animate a Martian test for Tim Burton's upcoming faux sci-fi feature *Mars Attacks!* (1996). Just as Steve Williams and Eric Armstrong made Spielberg a 3-D believer, Andrews' three-minute test convinced Burton to scrap the 60 puppets already constructed for his film and throw everything into making CGI Martians.

It was a creative coup to get a traditional animation director to embrace the 3-D computerized world. Andrews relished his supervisory role, and the chance to make "photo-realistic characters that make fun of photorealism." *Mars Attacks!* was pure camp; a film featuring skeletal, bug-eyed, candy-coloured creatures who vocalize the way a turkey garbles. Andrews led an all-star Canadian line-up including sequence supervisors Linda Bel, Jenn Emberly and Chris Armstrong.

Draco, the star of Dragonheart, was the first photorealistic creature produced by ILM. It was an evolutionary leap from the T-Rex of Jurassic Park.

Small Soldiers marked a small victory by computer animators in the battle to gain some creative control over the films they service.

Mars Attacks! was a litmus test. As a puppet animator, Burton has an enormous advantage over other live-action directors; he understands composing for three-dimensional space, says Andrews. Thanks to new program advances, the animators would quick-render 20 Martians at a time. "Tim guided us along the path to finding out how the Martians moved and behaved," says Andrews.[208] "From the start, his idea was that they should be birdlike and reptilian, with darting eyes and sharp movements. Tim also let us get a little cartoony with them even through they had to be 'real.' Once we found timings that interpreted the characters we were off."

Director Joe Dante's film *Small Soldiers* (1998) marks a small victory by ILM animators in the battle to gain some creative control in the films they service. According to Andrews, the animators were given much more input in the film than in previous films. Director Joe Dante directs animators like actors, says Andrews. He adds that Dante motivates them "and then the animators produce a take-one performance and he looks at it and responds to it."[209]

Small Soldiers is a darker, meaner *Toy Story*. Commando Elite action figures outfitted with defective military computer chips escape from their boxes to do battle with their programmed enemy, the Gorgonites.

Even though the CGI toys are plastic-looking and exhibit a limited set of behaviours, they interact well with real-life characters Alan (Gregory Smith) and Christy (Kirsten Dunst). The correct eyelines and subtle performances prove beyond a reasonable doubt that CGI characters are believable.

The credits in *Small Soldiers* also reveal a shift in the post-production hierarchy. No longer buried at the tail end of the credits, Andrews' title as animation supervisor appears in the film opener. *Small Soldiers* represents the increasing clout of supervising animators in feature filmmaking today.

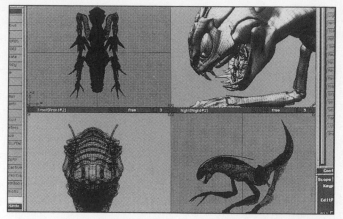

With the aid of the computer, computer generated monstors have become more realistic.

Rob Coleman also moved up the creative ladder, accepting an animation supervisory role in *Men in Black*, a film about secret immigration agents who police the hidden space alien community on Earth. Coleman has established a good reputation for his graphic recombinant work. Part of the huge box office success of *Men in Black* is the credible exchanges between the hideous-looking aliens and the secret agents played by Will Smith and Tommy Lee Jones.

Coleman's creatures look like they belong in a natural world. Achieving this kind of realism is no easy feat. It has meant pushing for more elaborate background plates and insisting that directors provide better feedback at an earlier stage of production.

The easiest transition for Coleman was on the film set of George Lucas' *Star Wars: Episode I The Phantom Menace* (1999). As the owner of ILM, Lucas understands animation even in its roughest form. The pinnacle of Coleman's career was working alongside his boss to create the rubbery amphibian, Jar Jar Binks. The awkward ally of Obi-Wan Kenobi is clearly the CGI progeny of the maladroit creatures he supervised in *Men in Black*.[210]

The demand for better caricature animation has forced high-end effects houses like ILM to mix and match packages and in some cases write supplementary code. As a result, animators demand packages that allow them to rewrite standardized code to custom fit their projects. Having moved into the mainstream, Softimage and Alias' off-the-shelf packages offered limited flexibility. But a third Canadian software company, run by former Omnibus employees, endeared itself to high-end users by allowing them easy access to the software itself.

In 1997, Kim Davidson, Greg Hermanovic, Paul Breslin and Mark Elendt of Side Effects Software won a Scientific and Technical achievement award from the Academy of Motion Picture Arts and Sciences for the development of the PRISMS software. Side Effects software has been used in the TV series Monster by Mistake! Davidson is the executive producer of the series.

Side Effects, formed by Greg Hermanovic and Kim Davidson, stayed afloat in the late eighties by upgrading the old PRISMS code and selling it to Omnibus' former clients — CFX in London, and Omnibus Japan. While Hermanovic spent two years developing new software, Davidson shouldered the company's financial responsibilities by animating and directing commercials for Side Effects Corporation, a production company owned by Nigel McGrath and Jim Muir. McGrath hoped Alias would hire the programming duo, but Davidson and Hermanovic remained independent. "I just wanted to continue doing what I loved doing — coding and animating. I saw no one else doing that in Toronto. So I became an entrepreneur by default," says Davidson.

Unlike its competitors, Side Effects has no intention of selling out to a southern giant. Its software — PRISMS and its latest entry, Houdini — is loved by animators for its flexibility and easy plug-in architecture. PRISMS' tools were difficult for artists to learn, but Houdini's interface has been described in *Computer Graphics World* as user-friendly. The reviewer summed up the company's new package as more like a fine champagne in a beer-and-soda world.

While considered a second-tier software supplier, Side Effects has first-tier clients including Digital Domain, the effects house that handled *Apollo 13* and *Titanic* (1998). Side Effects' software allowed *Titanic's* CGI crew to integrate the graphic elements of each individual shot, as well as to generate the foam and spray of water along the bow of the ship and the bits of debris and ice floes that litter the water as the *Titanic* goes under.

Despite rapid developments on the technological frontier, animators are still kept on a short leash. Many are chomping at the bit, demanding greater editorial control. Hollywood let the technological genie out of the bottle and now the genie wants to call the shots. At ILM, the tension is palpable. Many top-notch animators such as Les Major left in search of "real acting scenes."[211]

Everyone is hoping that someone will come up with an exciting and different use for their talents.

The most famous 3-D artist is also the industry's most vocal critic. Steve Williams is not afraid to bite the hand that feeds him. Steven Spielberg supported Williams' vision of *Jurassic Park*, but when rumours circulated that Spielberg's company, Amblin Entertainment, was considering a Bugs Bunny remake, Williams went ballistic: "They should be executed for this," says Williams. "They are bastardizing this piece of art. [The software] was not really intended to be [developed] so greasy producers could come in here and slime it by just using it to generate capital and marketing campaigns."

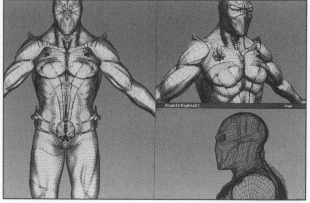

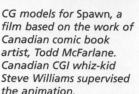

CG models for Spawn, *a film based on the work of Canadian comic book artist, Todd McFarlane. Canadian CGI whiz-kid Steve Williams supervised the animation.*

On more than one occasion, he has panned ILM projects such as *The Flintstones*, *Casper* and *101 Dalmatians*. In 1996, Williams threw in his hat as "top monkey" at ILM to become a headline act. Signed as a second-unit director and visual effects supervisor director on New Line Cinema's feature *Spawn* (1997), Williams rocketed into the Hollywood stratosphere.

Spawn is a dark adaptation of Calgary-born Todd McFarlane's comic book depicting an assassin brought back to life to do the devil's work. Spawned by evil forces, the

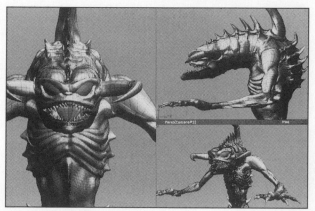

creature clings to the shreds of humanity that remain in his soul and chooses justice over destruction. McFarlane, the artist behind Spiderman's remake, quit Marvel Comics in 1992 following disputes over creative control and royalties. When New Line Cinema offered McFarlane a film deal, he insisted upon his own creative team, which included Steve Williams as visual effects co-ordinator and Mark Dippé as director.

Steve Williams is the CGI counterpart to McFarlane; he is the pseudo-rebel who believes the industry has remained formulaic, and has not fully grasped the potential of the new computer technology. The two made an effective tag team during promotional tours of the film.[212]

Despite lofty hype, *Spawn* is not a cinematic revelation. It's a muscle-flexing retrospective of everything that Williams and director Mark Dippé have innovated over the years — molten metal morphs, Habib gas and Tex Avery touches. The fresh eye candy comes from the debut of a flowing red digital cape. Fabric is still a final frontier waiting to be conquered by programmers. Williams pushed the bar up a notch with *Spawn's* suit.

Spawn is interesting, not because of its use of the special effects, but because the artists involved in the evolution of CG graphics got their chance behind the steering wheel. Graphic artists are finally getting their due. Where they take feature filmmaking is still a mystery.

On the one hand Williams is hoping for a *Ren & Stimpy* revolution in the CGI world. On the other, he warns that the industry is relying too heavily on special effects thrills. He refers to the crasser features as "tornado porn" and predicts that people will eventually get sick of effects films.

It is anyone's guess where the technology and people will take the industry. Cloning actors is not a futuristic fantasy. Many companies are already using motion capture systems that can record body movements using attached sensors. The data from the sensors is transferred to a computer, which in turn breaks the information into co-ordinates that can be further manipulated on a screen.

"Soon, Indiana Jones–like characters will only exist in a digital world. We won't have to pay an actor, there will be no drug addictions, and actors will be on the set every day," Williams says tongue in cheek. "And when Arnold gets fat, we'll just cut off his head and replace his body."

Objections have been raised about the ethics of cloning actors. Another fear is simply that computer animators will eventually outwit themselves out of a job. When it first hit the market, the motion capture technology was dubbed "Satan's Rotoscope."

The spectre of job redundancy seems unfounded. It is easy enough to create a human form using motion capture systems, but it takes talent to instill humanity into CGI creatures. The animator still provides the art and soul. Even today.

As for Canadians, these resilient artists keep reinventing the form, and recycling themselves in strange ways. From propagandists to commercial vendors to 3-D creature creators. The small community rebounds time and time again to assert itself in a cultural landscape once dominated by Disney.

A CGI Giant

The man who became a major innovator of entertainment technology for the purpose of entertainment started his career by developing a computer application used as a diagnostic tool for cardiologists.

Bill Reeves, Pixar Animation Studio's technical director received his doctorate at the University of Toronto in 1980 by extracting essential motion from imagery derived from angiograms. It was an early wire frame showing heart rate and blood flow.

"What I wanted to do was represent very simple shapes that move through time," says Reeves of his early research. "That is the very basis of animation."[213]

After graduation, Reeves was hired by Ed Catmull at Lucasfilm where he contributed to the special effects in *Star Trek II: The Wrath of Khan* (1982) and *Young Sherlock Holmes* (1985). While working on a life-generating "Genesis" sequence in *Star Trek II*, Reeves developed a new image-synthesis technique called particle systems. The program generated complex and detailed images such as fire, fireworks, trees, grass and flowers. With that one innovation, Reeves has become a titled CGI Lord — the Father of Particle Systems.

Had he stayed at Lucasfilm, Reeves would no doubt have been immersed in photorealistic special effects. Instead, he left Lucasfilm along with Catmull and Lasseter when Steve Jobs bought Lucasfilm's computer division and set up Pixar in 1986.

Under Jobs, Pixar began an intense research and development period. For years, Reeves focused on refining Pixar's software to improve the look of computer graphic characters. There were many hurdles to overcome, such as motion-blur, depth of field, lip-sync, flesh, fur and fabric.

Pixar's first years were dominated by a six-month cycle of coding followed by the production of a new short film. After each film,

Luxo Jr.

the team discussed the next hurdle to be overcome and turned their minds to the new code that would get them there.

Lasseter focused on story and character; Catmull and Reeves led programming R & D on their modelling programs — Marionette, MenV and RenderMan. Accolades piled up fast and furious.

The first film they produced was *André and Wally B* (1985), which proved that computers, in the right hands, could reproduce squash and stretch.

The Pixar short, *Luxo Jr.* (1986), is an endearing film about a parental unit lamp and its offspring. The animation team brought inanimate objects to life using the MenV system, which was built by Reeves and Eben Ostby for the film. Nominated for an Oscar award, *Luxo Jr.* demonstrated the potential of computer animation. Much to Reeves' surprise, MenV held up for more than a decade.

Tin Toy.

By the time Pixar produced its next short, *Tin Toy* (1988), Reeves and Lasseter hit gold — an Oscar statue. *Tin Toy* is the amusing tale of a tin soldier who is unceremoniously slobbered upon by a baby. The film was also the vehicle to test the company's newest software package, RenderMan. The system, which was developed with a team that included Canadian Darwyn Peachey, created high-quality photo-realistic image synthesis.

But all this R & D was just a prelude to the big bang, *Toy Story* (1995) — a 3-D feature film about a group of toys that come to life. The film portrays a cast of familiar toys whose egos and rivalries revolve around the amount of time each spends with their young owner, Andy.

Rivalry between the two central characters evolves into a big-hearted buddy picture intended to stimulate the tear ducts of adults and children alike — a Disney-feel flick. In fact, in order to get the project off the ground, Pixar signed a three-picture marketing deal with Disney Studios in 1991.

John Lasseter (left) and Bill Reeves pick up an Oscar for Tin Toy.

By casting toys as the main characters, Pixar principals skirted the realm of realism: the characters could look mechanical or plastic; but they still had to project personality. They had to act.

News that Pixar was going to fully animate a film from an original script was manna from heaven for creativity-starved animators. It sparked another exodus from Canada.

Jimmy Hayward, a senior animator on the 3-D TV series *ReBoot* quickly applied for a job. Pixar recruiters were not overly impressed with the crude animation, but they were agog over the amount of footage Hayward generated each month on the show. "(Supervising animator) Pete Docter told me: 'If we could just slow you down, we might be able to turn you into a half decent animator," recalls Hayward.[214]

Hayward was handed a number of action scenes involving the film's two heroes, Buzz Lightyear and Woody. He is responsible for their escape from the evil neighbour Sid, and for the dramatic rocket scene in which Woody and Buzz are catapulted into a moving van.

Sheridan graduate Glenn McQueen jumped from Pacific Data Imaging to Pixar to work on *Toy Story*. Like his Disney counterparts, McQueen was quickly singled out for the satirical scenes. "I get the sardonic, sarcastic smug assholes," he says.[215] Although McQueen describes his talent as a "spastic flair," it was his poignant scene of Buzz dressed in an apron and forced into tea service by young Hanna that stands out. McQueen effectively telegraphs Buzz's humiliation. Scenes like this one proved to critics and audiences alike that digital characters could emote.

When Pixar started developing its second and third pictures, the Canadian quick drawers were promoted. Hayward moved on to *Toy Story 2*. McQueen accepted a supervisory role on *A Bug's Life*, Pixar's second feature.

A Bug's Life is a delightful film that challenges community conformity. The film stars a creative ant named Flik who marches to his own beat. But the individualist ant gets into trouble when one of his inventions destroys the stockpile of food his colony has collected to pay off the grasshopper militia. Ostracized by his colony, Flik turns his skills to saving his friends who face starvation or a nasty grasshopper offensive.

"The most difficult part was the number, variety and complexity of characters," says McQueen. "*Toy Story* was a buddy movie, but (*A Bug's Life*) had a big ensemble cast so that each character was way more complex."

Reeves was handed the task of overseeing the film's 430 crowd scenes that involved as many as 800 CGI ants at any given time. "It was important to try and get the ants to respond as if they were individually animated," says Reeves.

What's left for this technological whiz? According to Reeves, most of the CGI films made in this century feature insects and toys — figures with hard smooth surfaces and static environments. Truly organic subjects will only emerge in the 21st century.

The Wizard of Antz

Where there's CGI creatures, there's Canadians. Rex Grignon and Eric Armstrong are two key Canadians who have influenced emerging studios such as Pacific Data Images (PDI) and Sony Imageworks.

In 1990, Rex Grignon formed PDI's character animation group with Tim Johnson (co-director of *Antz*). "It had largely a creative mandate that drove the development of tools," he says. In 1992, the team won an Emmy award for best visual effects for the TV show, *The Last Halloween*, and created the first computer-generated Pillsbury Doughboy™. After five years of experimentation, the group was ready to tackle a feature film; unfortunately, PDI was not.

The company was unsettled, and the prospect of making a CGI character film was dim. Grignon moved to Pixar to work on *Toy Story*. There he animated the nasty scene in which Sid is viciously amputating dolls, and he animated some of the inventive contraptions seen in *Toy Story*'s Pizza Planet scene.

But the pull back to his alma mater was too much. Grignon left Pixar after *Toy Story* and returned to PDI to work as a supervising animator on the DreamWorks SKG film *Antz* (1998).

Even though Grignon was busy overseeing a colony of animators for the film, he did animate several of General Mandible's speeches (voiced by Gene Hackman) — the conniving commander who threatens to dethrone the queen and drown the entire colony in order to engineer his own super race.

Eric Armstrong has been instrumental in Sony Pictures Imageworks' transition from small service house to a full-blown CGI studio.

When Armstrong was recruited by Sony three years ago, he had just completed an arduous stint as animation

Rex Grignon

General Mandible from Antz.

supervisor on *Casper*. Starting at Sony meant building a department from scratch. Special effects heavyweight Ken Ralston was also brought on board, and the company did some work on the feature films, *Contact* and *Starship Troopers*. After getting their feet wet as a service house, Armstrong led the search for the best software to tackle character development.

Sony Imageworks' unreleased short film *Backstage Magic* was the testing ground for future films such as *Stuart Little*, a CGI/live-action feature based on E.B. White's story about a mouse. *Stuart Little* is a departure from the kind of projects Armstrong worked on at ILM. *Casper* was largely cartoony, while *Stuart Little* is more photorealistic.

The ratio of animation to live-action has hit an industry high. "I remember when we did *Jurassic Park*, there were 50 [animation] shots; in *Casper* there were 300 and with *Stuart Little* there are even more," says Armstrong.[216] By steering Sony's CGI character development, Armstrong has upped the ante.

Booting Up TV Production

Software is the jewel in the Canadian crown. But the country has another CG feather in its cap: it is the first country to produce 3-D animation for television.

The first 3-D toon on the tube was by ARCCA Animation in Toronto, which produced the short-lived series, *Captain Power and Soldiers of the Future* (1987). The series wasn't entirely CG; it could only boast quick 3-D computer inserts. The first completely computer-animated series was *ReBoot* (1994), produced by Mainframe Entertainment in Vancouver.

ReBoot was a concept that was floated in London, England, for years before its partners teamed up with producer Chris Brough, and moved to Vancouver to take advantage of talent and tax breaks. Ian Pearson and Gavin Blair developed the idea for a computer animation series after producing computer images for Dire Straits' music video, "Money for Nothing," in the mid-eighties. With Phil Mitchell and

writer John Grace, the team developed a promo clip. It was not overly impressive.

"Honest to God, it looked like animated billiard balls," says Brough. "It had no warmth, the geometric shapes were very inorganic. But there was a strength to the concept that I liked a lot." With his British co-producer, Brough brought the project to Canada in 1993. Canada had a low dollar, a wealth of animator talent, indigenous software companies, and generous research and development tax credits. The new venture needed all the help it could get.

The producers knew they had to reinvent the wheel to make *ReBoot*. The company, renamed Mainframe Entertainment, pre-sold the series to ABC in the United States. There was one major hitch; it took them 18 months to produce the pilot and money quickly ran out on the remaining episodes. The company was running "on a wing and a prayer," says Brough.

The early version of Softimage often crashed three times a day. The software was not designed to handle so much information. Mainframe became a de facto test laboratory for Softimage. If there was a bug, the *ReBoot* team found it and tried to hack their way through it.

The first year *ReBoot* animators encountered 15,000 bugs. Sometimes they'd lose entire profiles or erase three weeks worth of rendering.

When Brough's British partner went belly-up, Alliance Equipcap became *ReBoot*'s saviour. Alliance stepped up to the plate and interim-financed the series.

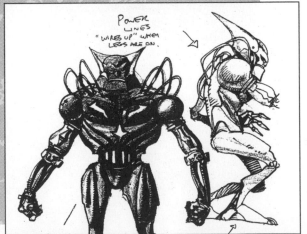

The evolution of Megabyte from Brendan McCarthy's drawing board to finished computer rendering.

Canada's largest production company, Alliance, made its first foray into the multimedia arena.

ReBoot literally takes place inside a mainframe computer, which is populated by humanoid data sprites, android biomes and evil viruses. The main hero, Bob, is an emissary sent by Super Computer to do battle with the evil viruses Megabyte and Hexadecimal.

ReBoot's storyline is confusing, but young viewers tuned in to see its virtual city and characters. Trying to translate the "computerese" sprinkled throughout became a strong selling point. The writers playfully use technical jargon such as "cut and paste the truth," "toggle your microprocessor" and "quit file." To know and to love *ReBoot* requires some net-surfing knowledge.

ReBoot works because it's a marriage between concept and technology. By creating characters out of computer innards, the series' creators correctly assessed that cyberliterate children are willing to

Reboot

believe in an intelligent galaxy that lies beyond the circuitry of a mainframe computer. Kids also accepted the limitations of computer graphic characters.

For several years in the mid-nineties, Mainframe had little competition. Only Fantome in France produced a CGI TV show. For its work, Mainframe Entertainment was inducted into the Smithsonian Institution's 1998 Innovation Collection for its groundbreaking creation of the world's first 100-percent computer-generated weekly television series. Its proprietary lip-syncing program and rendering program were celebrated.

Despite the accolades, Mainframe couldn't afford to relax in the competitive world of computer animation. In an attempt to outmanoeuvre its rivals, Mainframe signed a deal with Imax Corporation in March 1999. The deal was to produce 3-D feature films for the big, big screen.

By the end of the decade, companies such as C.O.R.E. Digital Pictures, Dan Kretch Productions, Side Effects and Nelvana had broken into the 3-D computerized production field.

The debut work of Toronto's C.O.R.E. Digital Pictures featured a

visual cascade of electronic images that make up the data uploading sequence of 320 gigabytes of information dumped into the brain of *Johnny* (Keanu Reeves) *Mnemonic.* C.O.R.E. founders Kyle Menzies and Bob Munroe are themselves grounded in Canadian sci-fi series such as *TekWar* and *LEXX: The Dark Zone Stories* (1996). In fact, William Shatner, executive producer

LEXX: The Dark Zone Stories

*C.O.R.E. and
the Canadian Goose.*

of *TekWar*, is a hands-off chief executive officer and minority partner in the company.

The company made its mark in Hollywood with the Columbia Pictures feature, *Fly Away Home*. "If you want dinosaurs, you go to ILM; if you want geese, you come to C.O.R.E.," quips co-founder Bob Munroe, referring to the film's scenes of CGI flying Canadian geese. Walt Disney hired the company for "goose-work" on its remake of *Flubber*, as did the Imax Corporation.

For the Dimension Films/Miramax feature *Mimic* (1997) starring Mira Sorvino, Munroe developed a simplified lighting package. In *Dr. Dolittle* (1998) starring Eddie Murphy, Munroe developed a fur management program for the rats. "Fur Plug-In," as it is aptly named, simplifies the hair geometry found in Side Effects' Houdini package. Essentially, C.O.R.E. had to make three-dimensional rat upper bodies and track them to the lower bodies of the real rats.

C.O.R.E. is the quintessential mid-sized Canadian company, trying to decide whether or not to stay small and independent or to expand by pushing its proprietary software.

Nelvana is one of the few traditional cel animation houses to undertake 3-D animation. The company hit paydirt when it signed kids writer/ artist William Joyce to develop a TV show for preschool-

Rolie Polie Olie

ers. Recruited to submit designs for the pre-production of *Toy Story*, Joyce's style lends itself to 3-D animation.

His happy spherical family *Rolie Polie Olie* (1998) won kids over when it premiered on the Disney Channel. *Rolie Polie Olie* does not look like an obvious extension of a video game. Computer animation has found its TV groove with this show.

Prior to *Rolie Polie Olie*, Nelvana's 3-D experience was limited to its minority partnership in *Donkey Kong Country*, a show based on the Nintendo video game. Scott Dyer, former president of Windlight Studios of Minneapolis, led Nelvana into uncharted territory. As Nelvana's vice-president for information technology, he credits *Rolie's* success to Nelvana's classical touch: "Our production set-up is a more 2-D style ... we use traditional storyboards and Leica reel cuts."[217]

Rolie Polie Olie signals a breakthough in CGI television. Critics judged the show on design and creative elements rather than technological advances. Thanks to Nelvana, the medium is no longer the message.

Is That All Folks?

It was not supposed to be like this. An animation studio within the National Film Board of Canada was an afterthought — a whim of founder John Grierson when he lured Norman McLaren to his wartime unit. Documentaries were the bread and butter of the Canadian film community. Canadians excelled at this craft, and their work was recognized around the world. But something changed.

The Canadian documentary is no longer the apple of the international eye; animation is. This role reversal did not happen overnight. It was an unconscious takeover. McLaren hired a handful of talented drawers and shaped them into animation artists.

Their numbers and influence grew at the NFB, and before long many pursued their ambitions and dreams beyond the confines of the studio.

Canadian animation is like a Darwinian social experiment. The medium has morphed and evolved over time. Regional isolation gave rise to wonky new creatures and styles. Propagandists reinvented themselves as commercial vendors. The advent of animation schools brought exponential growth.

Many of the most talented drawers found work outside Canada. But in the late eighties, a core community of Canucks reclaimed a chunk of the cultural landscape dominated by the American studios. Companies like Nelvana, Cinar and Ciné-Groupe have fought to keep production local, while exporting their ideas around the world.

After all these years of struggle and survival, the great Canadian cartoon caper continues.

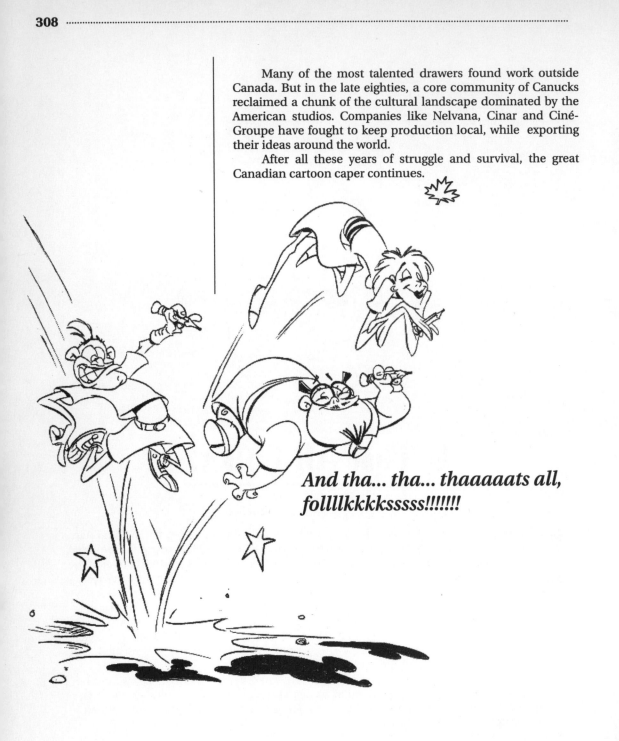

And tha... tha... thaaaaats all, follllkkkksssss!!!!!!!

Source Material

1   Gene Walz, "Charlie Thorson and the Temporary Disneyfication of Warner Brothers Cartoons," in *Reading the Rabbit: Explorations in Warner Bros. Animation,* ed. Kevin Sandler (New Brunswick, NJ: Rutgers, 1998): pp 49-66.
2   Charlie Thorson, letter to brother Joseph Thorson, 11 June 1935, Mg. 31E 38, vol. 29, file 12. National Archives of Canada (hereafter NAC). In the letter, Thorson writes that he was promoted from the story to design department at Disney. In a subsequent letter dated 29 April 1937, Charlie claims that he designed all the characters for *Little Hiawatha*.
3   Charlie Thorson, letter to Joseph Thorson, 11 June 1935.
4   Gene Walz, *Cartoon Charlie: The Life and Art of Animation Pioneer Charles Thorson* (Winnipeg: Great Plains Publications, 1998).
5   Bob Givens, interview with author.
6   Sigrunn Magnason, interview with author.
7   *Canadian Motion Picture Digest* (5 January 1922): 6.
8   Peter Morris, *Embattled Shadows: A History of Canadian Cinema, 1895-1939* (Montreal: McGill-Queen's University Press, 1978).
9   M.O. Mitchell, "The Silhouette Films of Bryant Fryer," *Motion*, vol. 5, no. 3: 16-19
10 Peter Morris et al.
11 Andre Martin, "In Search of Raoul Barré," *Cinematheque Quebecoise*, 1976.
12 *ibid*.
13 Forsyth Hardy, *Grierson on Documentary* (London: Faber & Faber, 1966).
14 Joyce Nelson, *The Colonized Eye Rethinking the Grierson Legend* (Toronto: Between the Lines, 1988).
15 Marjorie McKay, "History of the National Film Board." McKay Papers, 31E97, NAC. In her unpublished manuscript McKay quotes a letter written by Julian Roffman.
16 John Grierson, "Interview with John Grierson," McGill University Archives, vol. C12, AC2527 (1972): 116.
17 *ibid*.
18 Grant Munro, interview with author.
19 *ibid*.
20 Guy Glover, "Dreamland II," transcript from National Film Board film directed by John Kramer, Production 25272, McGill University Archives (15 December 1977).
21 Stephen Bosustow, letter to Jim MacKay, personal collection.
22 Rick Salutin, "The NFB Red Scare," *Weekend Magazine*, September 1978, p.17.
23 Arthur Irwin papers, NAC.
24 Robert Verrall, letter to author, 28 April 1997.
25 Marjorie McKay et al.
26 Arthur Irwin papers, NAC.
27 *ibid*.
28 Wolf Koenig, interview with author.
29 Colin Low, "Organization of a Cell Cartoon Film Report." Unpublished manuscript in National Film Board Archives (hereafter NFBA), 1951.
30 Don Mulholland, memo to Arthur Irwin, 2 October 1950, NFBA, No. 08-209.
31 C.R. James, "The NFB of Canada: Its Task of Communication." PhD diss., Ohio State University, Ann Arbor, Michigan, 1964.
32 Eve Lambart, interview with author.
33 Frank Mosley, memo to Don Moffat, 8 January 1957, NFBA.
34 Michael Spencer, memo to Pierre de Bellefeuille, 21 August 1956, NFBA.
35 Gerry Potterton, interview with author.
36 Don Mulholland, letter to Tom Daly, 16 October 1956, NFBA.
37 Derek Lamb, interview with author.
38 Grant McLean, memo to Tom Daly, 11 March 1963, NFBA.

39 Kaj Pindal, interview with author.
40 Marc Glassman, "Drawings on Both Sides of Their Brains."
   Ottawa 96 Animation Festival Magazine (October 1996), p.84.
41 Colin Low, interview with author.
42 Wally Gentleman, *Take One* (May-June 1968).
43 Robert Verrall, interview with author.
44 Don Arioli, *Cinema Canada* (Summer 1976).
45 *ibid.*
46 Don Arioli, interview with author.
47 Michael Mills, interview with author.
48 John Weldon, *Bravo*, interview directed by Don McWilliams, NFB, 1996. Videocassette.
49 John Weldon, interview with author.
50 Ishu Patel, interview with author.
51 Guy Cote, *Figuring It Out: Twenty-Five Years of Filmmaking at the National Film Board* (Montreal: SGCT/ONF, August, 1985). In 1977, a judiciary panel ruled that 99 percent of all freelance employees to the NFB whose contracts had been renewed periodically over the years, were de facto employees. Two years later, over 100 employees were added to the NFB's roster which meant even more dollars were being spent on salaries and overhead costs, and fewer real dollars made available to hire outside people. This converged with a 10 percent budget cut between 1979 and 1981.
52 Sid Adilman, "Oscar Winner Out of a Job," *Toronto Star*, 26 April 1980.
53 Gary Evans, *In the National Interest: A Chronicle of the National Film Board of Canada from 1949-1989* (Toronto: University of Toronto Press, 1991). Notes on sponsorship allocations: In 1975, approximately one-third of government film production went out to tender (Minutes of the NFB, 13-14 June 1975). After 1978, over 70 percent of sponsored films were farmed out to the private sector (see also, Minutes of the NFB, 15-16 June 1979). All sponsorship filmmaking ended in 1983.
54 Robert Verrall, telephone interview with author, March 1997.
55 Doug MacDonald, interview with author.
56 Gayle Thomas, interview with author.
58 David Verrall, interview with author.
59 Barrie Angus McLean, interview with author.
60 Robert Everett-Green, "High Profile, Low Return," *Globe and Mail*, 31 August 1996, p. C3.
61 Brian Johnston and Mark Clark, "Screen Shadows," *Maclean's*, 17 July 1989, p. 41.
62 Norman McLaren, "On René Jodoin," *ASIFA newsletter*.
63 Yves Leduc, "Chronicle of a Special Orientation: The Animation Studio of NFB's French Program," *Perforations*, vol. 10, no. 2 (1991): 4.
64 Jacques Drouin, *Perforations*, vol. 10, no. 2 (1991): 11.
65 Co Hoedeman, interview with author.
66 Pierre Hebert, interview with Marcel Jean.
67 Normand Roger, interview with author.
68 Robert Forget, interview with Marcel Jean.
69 Barrie Helmer, letter to author, 18 April 1997.
70 Chris Delaney, interview with author.
71 Carl Macek, *The Art of Heavy Metal: The Movie* (New York: Zoetrope, 1981), p. 30.
72 Michael Hirsh, interview with author.
73 Charlie Bonifacio, interview with author.
74 Ann Johnston, *Maclean's*, 28 April 1980, p. 54.
75 Robin Budd, interview with author.
76 John Collins, interview with author.
77 David Fine, interview with author.
78 Vic Atkinson, interview with author
79 Bill Stevens, interview with author.

80   Mark Rubenstein, interview with author.

81   Jamie Oliff, interview with author.

82   Sheldon Wiseman, interview with author.

83   Lee Williams, interview with author.

84   Greg Bailey, interview with author.

85   Jacques Pettigrew, interview with author.

86   Barrie Helmer, letter to author.

87   Jim MacKay, interview with author.

88   Al Guest, interview with author.

89   Frank Nissen, interview with author.

90   Jaan Pill, "Becoming Animated," *Cinema Canada* (August 1976), p. 28.

91   Vladimir Goetzelman, interview with author.

92   Bob Fortier, interview with author.

93   Adam Shaheen, interview with author.

94   *Ad News Insight*, December 1994.

95   Pascal Blais, interview with author.

96   Barrie Helmer, interview with author.

97   Joanne Morgan, *Playback* (25 October 1993): p. 25.

98   Marv Newland, interview with Mary Maddever.

99   Helena Jenson, letter to Dairy Bureau of Canada, 25 May 1990.

100 Mike Scott, interview with author.

101 Chris Hinton, interview with author.

102 Al Sens, interview with author.

103 Giannalberto Bendazzi, *Cartoons: One Hundred Years of Cinema Animation* (Indiana: Indiana University Press, 1994).

104 Marv Newland, interview with author.

105 Mike Grimshaw, interview with author.

106 J. Falconer, interview with author.

107 Dan Collins, interview with author.

108 Amanda Forbis, interview with author.

109 Wendy Perdue, e-mail to author, 9 November 1997.

110 Evelyn Lambart, interview with author.

111 Norman McLaren, letter to Evelyn Lambart dated 18 February 1956, in Lambart files at NAC.

112 Norman McLaren, letter to Evelyn Lambart dated 6 July 1963, in Lambart files at NAC.

113 Evelyn Lambart, personal diaries, in Lambart files at NAC.

114 Caroline Leaf, interview with author.

115 Derek Lamb, interview with author.

116 Wendy Tilby, interview with author.

117 Grant Munro, "Sand Beads & Plasticine," Wide Angle Magazine, vol. 3, no. 2 (1979): 63.

118 Joyce Borenstein, interview with author.

119 Gayle Thomas, interview with author.

120 Norman McLaren, "The Definition of Animation: A Letter from Norman McLaren with an Introduction by Georges Sifianos," *Animation Journal*, vol. 3, no. 2 (Spring 1995): 66.

121 Gretchen Weinberg, "MC et Moi (A Spiritual Portrait of Norman McLaren)," *Film Culture*, no. 25 (1962): 47.

122 Don McWilliams, interview with author.

123 Grant Munro, interview with author.

124 Norman McLaren, *Creative Process: Norman McLaren*. Directed by Donald McWilliams. Produced by David Verrall. NFBC, 1990. Videocassette.

125 May Ebbitt Cutler, "The Unique Genius of Norman McLaren," *Canadian Art*, no. 97 (May-June 1965).

126 William Jordan, "Norman McLaren: His Career and Techniques," *Quarterly of Film, Radio and Television*, vol. 8 (University of California Press, Berkeley, CA 1953-54): 7.

127 Alfio Bastiancich, "The Art of Norman McLaren," *The Work of Norman McLaren* (Turin: Giappichelli Editore, 1981), p. 77.

128 John Grierson, *Creative Process: Norman McLaren*. Directed by Donald McWilliams. Produced by David Verrall. NFBC, 1990. Videocassette.

129 Pierre Vinet "Multi-McLaren," *Take One*, vol. 1, no. 1, (September, 1966): 19.

130 May Ebbit Cutler, *ibid*.

131 *Has Anybody Here Seen Canada*, transcript, p. 6.

132 *Toronto Telegram*, 20 March

133 John Canemaker, "George Dunning," *George Dunning Exhibition, Annecy Festival Catalogue*, June 1983.

134 John Coates, interview with author.

135 *Film Digest Review,* no. 64, January 1948. National Film Board of Canada. Found in the film files of Cadet Rouselle.

136 Colin Low, interview with author.

137 Jimmy Murakami, "I Met George Dunning," *George Dunning Exhibition, Annecy Festival Catalogue*, June 1983.

138 Dusty Vineberg, "Waste-basket to Potential Oscar," *Montreal Star*, 24 February 1962.

139 *ibid*.

140 Frédéric Back, interview with author.

141 Charles Solomon, "The Passion of Frédéric Back," *Animation Magazine* (Spring 1988): 13.

142 Joan Irving Herman, "Back's 'Crac' Shot," *Cinema Canada* (June 1982): 15.

143 *ibid*.

144 Paul Driessen, interview with author.

145 Harvey Deneroff, *Animation World Magazine.*

146 Gerry Potterton, interview with author.

147 David Robinson, *Sight and Sound* (Summer 1973): 151–54.

148 Brian Davis, "Animated Conversations," *Film Report*, 1975.

149 Leonard Maltin, *Print* (March/April, 1977): 72.

150 Russell Hall, interview with author.

151 John Lewell, "Richard Williams: Making His Own Legend," *Films and Filmmaking* (April 1992): 17.

152 Simon Wells, interview with author.

153 Stephen Fayne, interview with author.

154 Alex Williams, interview with author.

155 *ibid*

156 Charles Solomon, "Top Draw," *Animation Magazine*, (Summer 1988): 14.

157 Leonard Maltin, *ibid*. as fn 149.

158 Jerry Beck, "Behind Roger Rabbit," *Animation Magazine*, (Summer 1988): 22-27.

159 Chuck Gammage, interview with author.

160 Jeremy Clark, "Rabbit Talk," *Films and Filming* (August 1988): 24

161 Nik Ranieri, letter to author, 21 October 1996.

162 Richard Williams, letter to Greg Duffell, nd.

163 Greg Duffell, interview with author.

164 Richard Williams, letter to Chuck Jones, 27 September 1974.

165 John Canemaker, "Behind the Scenes With Raggedy Ann and Andy," *Millimeter* (February 1976): 42

166 Joe Haidar, interview with author.

167 Jamie Oliff, interview with author.

168 Bill Matthews, interview with author.

169 Réjean Bourdages, interview with author.

170 Duncan Majoribanks, interview with author.

171 Ric Sluiter, interview with author.

172 Mike Surrey, interview with author.
173 Brian Ferguson, interview with author.
174 Dave Brewster, interview with author.
175 Alex Williams, e-mail to author, 18 August 1998.
176 Ken Duncan, interview with author.
177 John Kricfalusi, interview with author.
178 Mary-Lou and Michael Kricfalusi, interview with author.
179 Jerry Beck, "Who's The Greatest Hero Rodents of Mouseville Ever Had?" *Animation Magazine*, (Summer 1988): 23.
180 "The Mighty Mouse Affair," *Animation Magazine*, (Summer 1988): 5.
181 Daniel Cerone, *Los Angeles Times*, 9 August 1992: 6.
182 *ibid.*, p. 41.
183 Dan Persons, *Cinefantastique* (June 1993): 49.
184 Chris Reccardi, interview with author.
185 Mark Kausler, interview with author.
186 Mark Langer, "Animatophilia, Cultural Production and Corporate Interests: The Case of 'Ren & Stimpy,'" *Film History*, vol. 5 (1993): 125–41.
187 Richard Gehr, "You Filthy Worms! The Ren & Stimpy Show's Creator Gives Hell to Nickelodeon," *Village Voice,* 17 November 1992.
188 Jennifer Pendleton, "Groening Sides with Ren Artist," *Daily Variety*, 25 September 1992.
189 Judy Bartlett and Tony Cruz, *Wild Cartoon Kingdom*, vol. 7, no. 13 (1993): 5.
190 Vanessa Coffey, interview with author.
191 Danny Antonucci, interview with author.
192 John Leland, "Battle For Your Brain," *Newsweek*, 11 October 1993, p. 50. In this article, Leland touches on the new "dumbing down" phenomenon on television.
193 David Andrews, interview with author.
194 Deidre Kelly, "The Animated Steve Williams," *Globe and Mail*, 14 April 1995, p. C1.
195 John Pennie, interview with author.
196 Doug MacMillan, interview with author.
197 Will Anielewicz, interview with author.
198 Doug MacMillan, e-mail, 15 March 1998. In the e-mail, he quotes animator Paul Griffin.
199 Jim Stewart, interview with author.
200 Nigel McGrath, interview with author.
201 Mark Cotta Vaz, *Industrial Light and Magic Into the Digital Realm* (New York: Ballantine Books, 1996), p. 200.
202 Geoff Campbell, interview with author.
203 Steve Williams, interview with author.
204 Eric Lebel, e-mail, 10 March 1998.
205 Eric Armstrong, interview with author.
206 Robert Coleman, interview with author.
207 Chris Armstrong, interview with author.
208 Mark Cotta Vaz, "Martial Art," *Cinefex*, no. 68, (December 1996): 78.
209 Jenny Peter, "Small Soldiers Lined Up to Do CGI Battle," *Animation Magazine* (July 1998): 9.
210 Robert Coleman, e-mail to author, December 1998.
211 Les Major, e-mail to author, March 1998.
212 Alexandra Gill, "Comic Spawns Movie Offspring," *Globe and Mail*, 9 August 1997, p. C4.
213 Bill Reeves, interview with author.
214 Jimmy Hayward, interview with author.
215 Glen McQueen, interview with author.
216 Eric Armstrong, *ibid*.
217 Scott Dyer, interview with author.

Index

Titles appear in italics. Illustrations are indicated by page numbers in italics. A page number followed by the word "caption" refers to information appearing within the caption of an illustration on that page.

3-D computer animation 51, 89, 126, 136, 138, 147, 236, 275-306 *see also* computer animation

Photo Credits